FIX-IT and ENJOY-IT!

5-INGREDIENT RECIPES

FIX-IT and ENJOY-IT!

5-INGREDIENT RECIPES

Quick and Easy – For Stove-Top and Oven!

By *The New York Times* bestselling author

PHYLLIS PELLMAN GOOD

Intercourse, PA 17534
800/762-7171
www.GoodBooks.com

Cover illustration and illustrations throughout the book by Cheryl Benner
Design by Cliff Snyder

FIX-IT AND ENJOY-IT!® 5-INGREDIENT RECIPES
Copyright © 2008 by Good Books, Intercourse, PA 17534

International Standard Book Number: 978-1-56148-627-4 (paperback edition)
International Standard Book Number: 978-1-56148-629-8 (hardcover gift edition)
International Standard Book Number: 978-1-56148-628-1 (comb-bound paperback edition)
Library of Congress Catalog Card Number: 2008023273

Library of Congress Cataloging-in-Publication Data
Good, Phyllis Pellman, 1948-
  Fix-it and enjoy-it 5-ingredient recipes : quick and easy - for stove-top and oven! / Phyllis Pellman Good.
    p. cm.
  Includes index.
  ISBN 978-1-56148-627-4 (pbk. : alk. paper) -- ISBN 978-1-56148-628-1 (comb. : alk. paper) --
  ISBN 978-1-56148-629-8 (hardcover : alk. paper) 1. Quick and easy cookery. 2. Cookery, American.
  I. Title.
  TX833.5.G674 2008
  641.5'55--dc22   2008023273

Table of Contents

About
Fix-It and Enjoy-It 5-Ingredient Recipes

You need a good supply of gumption, dogged persistence, and stubborn intentions if you want to cook and eat at home these days.

Most of us live crowded lives. Most of us find it nearly impossible to sit down to a meal with our family or friends, especially during the week.

Yet we believe in the benefits of shared mealtimes at home. Kids develop a greater sense of well-being and perform better at school. A table spread with tasty food can give all of us relief from the many electronic screens that are hungry for our attention. The kitchen table can be a tempting meeting place.

BUT HOW DOES THE FOOD GET THERE?!

You're holding one solution—*Fix-It and Enjoy-It 5-Ingredient Recipes*!

The more than 780 recipes in this handy, lip-smacking collection offer you a way to prepare quick, "make-it-again" meals.

And you don't need to be a cooking genius to be successful with these recipes.

Remember!
- Each recipe has only 5 ingredients or fewer.
- All of the recipes come from home cooks from across the country.

What qualifies as a 5-ingredient recipe?
1. Any recipe with 5—or fewer—ingredients.
2. Water does *not* count.
3. Salt and pepper count as *one* ingredient.
4. Ingredients listed as *optional* do *not* count.
5. Non-stick cooking spray does *not* count.
6. The "base" over which the recipe is to be served (for example, crackers or chips, rice, pasta, or potatoes) does *not* count.

The pass-it-on tradition

Good cooks love to share their recipes. They don't possess them; they pass them on.

This collection holds favorite recipes from many home cooks. These recipes work—and they are loved. They have been tested around countless tables—and they've been begged for!

Thank you, home cooks and recipe-testers, for sharing your gems and your know-how. We all benefit from your generosity. Because of you, we all have a greater chance of eating well and of being richly sustained in body and spirit.

So choose a recipe and start cooking—even if you're short on time or confidence in the kitchen. Remember, whenever you use *Fix-It and Enjoy-It 5-Ingredient Recipes*, you're in the company of fine home cooks, and they are cheering you on!

Phyllis Pellman Good

Appetizers

Fruit Dip

Linda Eberly Miller
Harrisonburg, VA
Stacy Stoltzfus, Grantham, PA
Diane Eby, Holtwood, PA
Janet L. Roggie, Lowville, NY

Makes 1½–2 cups

Prep Time: 5–10 minutes

7 ozs. marshmallow cream
8-oz. pkg. cream cheese,
  softened
2 Tbsp. orange juice
  concentrate, not
  reconstituted
1½ tsp. grated orange zest

1. Beat the ingredients together with an electric beater. Chill.
2. Serve with an assortment of fresh fruit (apples, oranges, kiwi, bananas, grapes, strawberries, and more) cut into bite-size pieces.

Tips:
1. You can change the flavor of this dip by substituting other fruit juices for the orange juice: strawberry, lime, blueberry, peach, cherry, and so on.
Or add herbs and/or spices to complement your selection of fruit: ground ginger, ground cinnamon, chopped mint and/or lemon verbena, and others.
2. If you cut the fruit in advance of serving, dip apples (and any other fruit that may turn brown) in lemon juice.
3. Keeps 1 week+ in refrigerator.

Marshmallow Fruit Dip

Joyce Shackelford
Green Bay, WI

Makes 3½ cups

Prep. Time: 15 minutes

8-oz. pkg. cream cheese,
  softened
6-oz. container cherry
  yogurt
8-oz. container frozen
  whipped topping,
  thawed
7 ozs. marshmallow cream
assorted fresh fruit, cut up

1. In a medium-sized bowl, beat cream cheese and yogurt together, either by hand or with a mixer, until blended.
2. Fold in whipped topping and marshmallow cream.
3. Serve with cut-up fresh fruit.

Strawberry Fruit Dip

Diann Dunham, State College, PA

Makes 1½–2 cups

Prep Time: 5 minutes

7 ozs. marshmallow cream
8-oz. pkg. strawberry cream
  cheese spread, softened
1–2 Tbsp. milk, *optional*

1. Mix marshmallow cream and cream cheese spread together and chill. If too thick, stir in a little milk.
2. Serve as a dip for cut-up fresh fruit or as a topping for pound cake.

Note from tester: We spread our leftover dip on graham crackers. Yum!

Sweet Fruit Dip

Sharon Swartz Lambert
Harrisonburg, VA

Makes 2½ cups

Prep Time: 10 minutes

4 ozs. (or half an 8-oz. pkg.)
  cream cheese, softened
1 cup whole berry
  cranberry sauce
1 cup thawed whipped
  topping

1. Beat cream cheese and cranberry sauce with electric mixer on medium speed until well blended.
2. Gently fold in whipped topping.
3. Cover and refrigerate at least one hour, or until ready to serve.

Note: Serve with strawberries, red and green peppers, pineapple, or kiwi cut into bite-sized pieces for dipping.

Dairy Maple Fruit Dip

Eileen Eash
Carlsbad, NM

Makes 1½ cups

Prep Time: 10 minutes

8-oz. pkg. cream cheese,
  softened
½ cup sour cream
¼ cup sugar
¼ cup brown sugar
2 Tbsp. maple syrup

1. Beat all ingredients in mixing bowl, either by hand or with a mixer, until smooth.
2. Chill. Serve with cut-up fresh fruit.

Pumpkin Dip

Irene J. Dewar
Pickering, ON

Makes 1½–2 cups

Prep Time: 15 minutes

8-oz. pkg. cream cheese,
  softened
½ cup brown sugar
½ cup canned pumpkin
2 tsp. maple syrup
½ tsp. cinnamon

1. Place first 3 ingredients in a medium-sized bowl. Beat with a mixer at medium speed until well blended.
2. Add syrup and cinnamon and beat until smooth.
3. Cover and chill 30 minutes.
4. Serve with apple slices, pound cake, banana or zucchini bread, or gingersnap cookies.

A Tip —

  Beginner cooks should always measure carefully. With more experience you learn to adjust recipes.

Thanksgiving Dip

Janice Yoskovich
Carmichaels, PA

Makes about 2 cups

Prep Time: 5 minutes
Cooking/Baking Time: 10 minutes

1 can whole berry
  cranberry sauce
⅓ cup brown sugar
1 Tbsp. prepared mustard
3 Tbsp. prepared
  horseradish
2 8-oz. pkgs. cream cheese

1. Warm sauce and sugar in a saucepan over low heat until melted and well blended. Stir to make sure sugar is dissolved.
2. Add mustard and horse-radish, continuing to warm over low heat, just until the mixture is well blended.
3. Place each cream cheese block on a serving plate. Spoon spicy cranberry sauce over top of cheese.
4. Serve with crackers.

Tip: The sauce keeps well, so you can use half the sauce and 1 block of cheese and refrigerate the remaining half of the sauce for another occasion.

Cranberry Cream Cheese Appetizer

Christie Detamore-Hunsberger
Harrisonburg, VA

Makes 12 servings

Prep. Time: 20–25 minutes
Cooling Time: 45–60 minutes

1 cup water
1 cup sugar
12-oz. fresh, *or* frozen,
  cranberries
½ cup apricot preserves
2 Tbsp. lemon juice,
  optional
⅓ cup slivered almonds,
  toasted
8-oz. pkg. cream cheese

1. In pan over medium heat, bring water and sugar to a boil without stirring. Boil for 5 minutes.
2. Add cranberries and cook until berries pop and sauce is thickened, about 10 minutes. Remove from heat.
3. Cut apricots in the preserves into small pieces. Add to cranberry mixture.
4. Stir in lemon juice if you wish.
5. Cool cranberry-apricot mixture to room temperature.
6. Stir in almonds.
7. Spoon over cream cheese block. Serve with crackers.

Pina Colada Fruit Dip

Joan Brown
Warriors Mark, PA

Makes 2½ cups

Prep Time: 10 minutes
Cooling Time: 2–4 hours

8-oz. can crushed
  pineapple, undrained
¾ cup milk
½ cup sour cream
4-oz. box coconut instant
  pudding

1. Mix all ingredients in a medium-sized mixing bowl.
2. Place in fridge and chill several hours before serving.
3. Serve with cut-up fruit and pieces of pound cake.

Taffy Apple Dip

Arlene Snyder
Millerstown, PA
Deborah Heatwole
Waynesboro, GA
Shirley Unternahrer Hinh
Wayland, IA

Makes 1½ cups

Prep. Time: 10 minutes

8-oz. pkg. cream cheese,
softened
½ cup brown sugar
1 tsp. vanilla
6 apples, cut into wedges

1. In a small bowl, beat cream cheese, brown sugar, and vanilla until smooth and creamy.
2. Serve with apple wedges.

Variation: Stir in 1 bag of toffee chips just before serving.
— **Shirley Unternahrer Hinh**
Wayland, IA

Creamy Peanut Ginger Dip

Melanie Mohler
Ephrata, PA

Makes 1¾–2 cups

Prep Time: 10 minute

1 cup creamy peanut
butter
¼ cup soy sauce
6 Tbsp. apple cider
vinegar, *or less* (see Note below)
1" cube peeled ginger,
chopped
½ cup fresh cilantro,
chopped
¼ cup hot water

1. Combine everything but the water in a blender.
2. Pulse until smooth, about 20 seconds, while gradually adding the hot water.
3. Serve with fresh veggies, bread, or crackers.

Note: If you prefer a milder and less "vinegary" taste, reduce the vinegar to 2 Tbsp., or to taste.

Apple Dip with Peanut Butter

Janet L. Roggie
Lowville, NY

Makes 2⅔–3 cups

Prep. Time: 10 minutes

8-oz. pkg. cream cheese,
softened
1 cup peanut butter
1 cup brown sugar
¼ cup milk
4 apples, cut into wedges

1. In mixing bowl, combine first 4 ingredients until well blended.
2. Serve with apples.

Tip from the tester: This is also a real treat as a spread on bagels or toast. And it would be great as a filling for whoopie pies, too.

Black Bean Dip

Jean Turner
Williams Lake, BC

Makes 1¾ cups

Prep. Time: 10 minutes

14-oz. can black beans,
   drained and rinsed
½ cup sugar-free salsa, hot
   or mild
2 Tbsp. lime juice
¼ tsp. cumin
salt and pepper to taste

1. In a food processor,
combine black beans, salsa,
lime juice, and cumin.
Process until smooth. Season
with salt and pepper.
2. Transfer to small bowl
to serve.
3. Garnish with cilantro,
sliced green onions, and
chopped sweet peppers,
if you wish. Serve with
triangles of pita bread.

*Tip from the Tester: Turn
this into a sandwich filling by
adding 1 cup shredded cheddar
cheese and ½ cup sour cream.
Fold together gently and stuff
into a pita pocket. Eat as is, or
warm in the microwave first.*

Bean Dip

Karla Baer
North Lima, OH

Makes 3½ cups

Prep. Time: 5 minutes
Chilling Time: 1–2 hours

¼ of a small can of
   jalapeno peppers
15-oz. can refried beans
1 pint sour cream

1. Chop peppers. Place
in mixing bowl, along with
beans. Blend thoroughly.
2. Fold in sour cream.
3. Cover and then chill to
allow flavors to blend.
4. Serve with tortilla chips,
pita chips, or veggie sticks.

*Tip: Adjust the amount of
hot peppers to meet your taste
preferences.*

Chili with Beans Dip

Carol Sherwood
Batavia, NY

Makes 4 cups

Prep Time: 10 minutes
Cooking/Baking Time: 20 minutes

8-oz. pkg. cream cheese,
   softened
16-oz. can chili with beans
1–1½ cups shredded
   cheddar cheese

1. Spread softened cream
cheese in the bottom of a 10"
pie plate or baking dish.
2. Top with chili and
beans.
3. Sprinkle cheese over
chili.
4. Bake at 350° for about 20
minutes, or until cheese melts
and dip is warmed through.
5. Serve with tortilla chips.

*Variations: After Dip is
warmed, garnish with ¼ cup
chopped green onion and ½
cup diced fresh tomatoes, before
serving.*

—Colleen Heatwole
Burton, MI

A Tip —

   Keep it simple! Use prepared foods if you need to.
Grandma had more time at home to cook even though she
was busy with housework.

Taco Dip
Esther Burkholder
Millerstown, PA

Makes 10 servings

Prep. Time: 5 minute
Cooking/Baking Time: 15 minutes

16-oz. can refried beans
1 cup sour cream
1 cup salsa
1 cup shredded mozzarella,
   or cheddar, cheese
bag of taco chips

1. Layer first 4 ingredients
in 9" pie pan or casserole dish
in the order listed.
2. Bake at 350° until cheese
is melted and heated through,
about 15 minutes.
3. Serve with taco chips.

*Tip: Make this dish low-fat
by using fat-free refried beans,
light sour cream, and low-fat
cheese.*

Hot Pot Bean Dip
John D. Allen
Rye, CO

Makes 3½ cups

Prep. Time: 10 minutes
Cooking/Baking Time: 20 minutes

1 can bean and bacon soup
1 tub garlic cheese spread
8 ozs. sour cream
1 green onion, chopped
   fine

1. Place soup and cheese
into a saucepan. Stir until
mixed thoroughly.
2. Heat over low heat until
cheese melts. Stir frequently
to prevent sticking.
3. Meanwhile, fold onion
into sour cream in a small
bowl. Stir gently into bean-
cheese mixture.
4. When warmed through,
ladle into a serving bowl.
Or place in a slow cooker,
turned to Low. (The dip
can stay in the cooker for
serving for several hours. Stir
occasionally.)
5. Serve with corn or taco
chips.

Party-Starter Bean Dip
Leona Yoder
Hartville, OH

Fills a 9" pie plate, about 15 servings

Prep. Time: 15 minutes
Cooking/Baking Time: 20 minutes

16-oz. can refried beans
8-oz. pkg. cream cheese,
   softened
12-oz. jar salsa, *divided*
slices of jalapeno peppers,
   optional

1. Preheat oven to 350°.
Spread beans into bottom of a
greased 9" pie pan or oven-
safe dish.
2. Beat cream cheese until
creamy in a medium-sized
mixing bowl. Add ⅔ cup
salsa and beat until smooth.
3. Spread creamy cheese
over beans. Bake 20 minutes.
4. Let cool 5 minutes.
5. Spread remaining salsa
over hot dip and garnish with
jalapeno slices, if you wish.
6. Serve with tortilla, pita,
or other sturdy chips.

Chili Cheese Dip

Colleen Heatwole
Burton, MI

Makes 3½ cups

Prep. Time: 10 minutes
Cooking/Baking Time: 20–25 minutes

8-oz. pkg. cream cheese, unflavored, softened
15-oz. can chili without beans
4 ozs. shredded sharp cheddar cheese

Garnishes:
chopped green onion
diced tomato

1. Heat oven to 350°.
2. Spread cream cheese on bottom of 9" pie plate.
3. Spread with chili.
4. Sprinkle with cheddar cheese.
5. Bake 20–25 minutes, or until cheese is melted.
6. Garnish with chopped green onion and tomato.
7. Serve with tortilla chips.

Nacho Dip

Ranita Reitz
Remington, VA

Makes about 5 cups

Prep. Time: 5 minutes
Cooking/Baking Time: 3–10 minutes

1 lb. Velveeta, *or* American, cheese, cut into small cubes
15-oz. can no-beans chili
1 cup salsa
tortilla chips

1. Mix cut-up cheese, chili, and salsa in a microwave-safe bowl.
2. Microwave, covered, on High until heated through, stirring every minute or two.
3. Serve warm with tortilla chips.

No Bean Dip

Jennifer Crouse
Mt. Crawford, VA

Makes 6 cups

Prep. Time: 10 minutes
Cooking/Baking Time: 25 minutes

8-oz. pkg. cream cheese, softened
1 large can no bean chili
2 cups salsa, any flavor
1½ cups shredded cheddar cheese

1. Spread cream cheese in bottom of 9 × 13 baking pan.
2. Pour chili over cream cheese. Pour salsa over chili. Top with cheddar cheese.
3. Bake at 350° for 25 minutes.
4. Serve with tortilla chips.

Chili Cheese Dip

Doyle Rounds
Bridgewater, VA

Makes 4 cups

Prep. Time: 5 minutes
Cooking/Baking Time: 10–12 minutes

15-oz. can chili con carne without beans
1 lb. American cheese, cubed
4-oz. can chopped green chilies

1. Combine chili, cheese, and chilies in a saucepan or fondue pot.
2. Heat over medium-low heat, stirring frequently until the cheese melts.
3. Serve warm with tortilla chips.

Variation: If you prefer the chili and chilies to be more dominant, cut the cheese back to ½–¾ lb.

Cheese Dip

Lena Hoover
Ephrata, PA

Makes 3 cups

Prep Time: 15 minutes

8-oz. pkg. cream cheese,
softened
8-oz. tub cheddar cheese
spread
½ cup (scant) mayonnaise
⅓ cup chopped walnuts

1. Mix first 3 ingredients together in a medium-sized bowl.
2. Spoon dip into serving dish and cover with chopped walnuts.
3. Cover and chill. Serve with fresh vegetable sticks, your favorite chips, triangles of pita bread, or thinly sliced baguettes.

Dill, Feta, and Garlic Cream Cheese Spread

Kathleen Rogge
Alexandria, IN

Makes about 3 cups

Prep Time: 15 minutes
Chilling Time: 4 or more hours

2 8-oz. pkgs. cream cheese,
softened
8-oz. pkg. feta cheese,
crumbled
3 cloves garlic, peeled and
minced
2 Tbsp. chopped fresh dill,
or 2 tsp. dried dill

1. In a medium bowl, thoroughly blend ingredients with electric mixer.
2. Cover and chill for at least 4 hours.
3. Serve in a dish alongside firm, raw veggies or crackers.

Tips:
1. Cut back the garlic if you prefer.
2. After mixing the ingredients together, chill them thoroughly, and then shape into a cheese ball before serving.

Southwest Cheese Dip

Eileen Eash
Carlsbad, NM

Makes 4+ cups

Prep. Time: 25–30 minutes
Cooking/Baking Time: 6–8 minutes

1 lb. cubed American
cheese, plain *or*
Mexican-flavored
8-oz. jar cheese spread
6 green onions, sliced,
including tops
1 lb. bacon, cooked and
crumbled
4-oz. can chopped green
chilies

1. Place cheeses and onions in a medium-sized micro-wave-safe bowl. Microwave on High for 4–8 minutes, stirring every 2 minutes, until cheese is melted.
2. Remove from oven. Gently stir in bacon and chilies until well mixed.
3. Serve with chips or fresh vegetables.

Tip: Serve in a slow cooker, turned to Low, if you want to keep the dip warm and spreadable. Stir occasionally to prevent sticking.

Cheesy Pizza Dip

Janeen L. Zimmerman
Denver, PA
Anna Musser
Manheim, PA
Rhonda Freed
Croghan, NY

Makes 6 cups

Prep Time: 10 minutes
Cooking/Baking Time: 18–20 minutes

2 8-oz. pkgs. cream cheese, softened
2 tsp. dried Italian seasoning
2 cups shredded mozzarella cheese
1½ cups shredded Parmesan cheese
12-oz. jar salsa

1. Preheat oven to 350°.
2. In a medium-sized mixing bowl, combine cream cheese and seasoning. Spread into bottom of a greased 9" pie plate.
3. In the mixing bowl, combine mozzarella and Parmesan cheeses. Sprinkle half over cream cheese mixture.
4. Spread salsa over shredded cheeses.
5. Top with remaining shredded cheese.
6. Bake 18–20 minutes, or until bubbly.
7. Serve with raw vegetables, chips, pita bread pieces, or baguette slices.

Variations:
1. *Instead of baking the Dip, place it into a microwave-safe pie plate or dish, and then microwave on High for 3 minutes, or until cheese melts.*
2. *Substitute 1½ cups of pizza sauce for the salsa.*

—Rhonda Freed
Croghan, NY

Salsa Dip

Beverly High
Bradford, PA

Makes 3½ cups

Prep. Time: 10 minutes

8-oz. pkg. cream cheese, softened
½ cup sour cream
1 cup salsa
¾ cup grated mozzarella cheese

1. In a medium-sized mixing bowl, beat cream cheese until soft and creamy. Fold in sour cream.
2. Spread mixture in a 9" pie plate.
3. Spoon salsa over top.
4. Sprinkle with mozzarella cheese.
5. Cover and refrigerate until serving.
6. Serve with tortilla chips, crackers, and/or crusty bread.

Tip from Tester: *Garnish with sliced black olives or jalapeno peppers.*

Hot Cheesy Mexican Dip

Jean Turner
Williams Lake, BC

Makes 2½ cups

Prep. Time: 5–10 minutes
Cooking/Baking Time: 4 minutes

1 cup cheese whiz
1 cup salsa
7-oz. can black olives, chopped
2 Tbsp. cream cheese, softened
3 Tbsp. chopped fresh cilantro, *divided*

1. Beat cheese, salsa, olives, cream cheese, and 2 Tbsp. cilantro in a microwave-safe bowl with an electric mixer on medium speed until well blended.
2. Microwave at Power 5 for up to 4 minutes or until warm, stirring after 2 minutes.
3. Garnish with remaining 1 Tbsp. cilantro. Serve with your favorite crackers.

Sour Cream Dip

Esther S. Martin
Ephrata, PA

Makes 2 cups

Prep Time: 5 minutes

16-oz. container sour
   cream
2 tsp. sweet pepper relish
2 tsp. sugar, *optional*
2 tsp. dry Ranch dressing
   mix

1. Mix all ingredients
together in a medium-sized
mixing bowl.
2. Serve with fresh
vegetables, chips, pretzels, or
crackers.

Veggie Dip

Mary Ann Bowman
East Earl, PA
Arlene Snyder
Millerstown, PA

Makes 2 cups

Prep. Time: 5 minutes
Chilling Time: 1+ hours

1 cup sour cream
1 cup mayonnaise
1 tsp. seasoned salt
1 tsp. minced onions
1 tsp. chives

1. Mix all ingredients
together until well blended.

2. Cover and chill for an
hour or more to allow flavors
to blend.
2. Serve with fresh veg-
etables, crackers, or pretzels.

*Tip: This is a flexible recipe!
Before serving, taste. Then stir
in additional herbs, such as
fresh or dried parsley or dill,
if you wish. Or add freshly
ground pepper or chopped
garlic.*

Veggie Dip

Janelle Nolt
Richland, PA

Makes about 2 cups

Prep Time: 10 minutes

2 8-oz. pkgs. cream cheese,
   softened
½ cup mayonnaise, light *or*
   regular
⅓ cup Parmesan cheese
10 slices bacon, fried and
   crumbled, *or* 3 Tbsp.
   bacon bits
minced onion to taste

1. In a large mixing bowl,
blend cream cheese and
mayonnaise together until
smooth.
2. Stir in remaining
ingredients.
3. Serve with veggie sticks
or crackers.

Vegetable Dip

Beth Shank
Wellman, IA

Makes 3 cups

Prep. Time: 10 minutes
Chilling Time: 8 hours

2 cups mayonnaise (not
   salad dressing)
1 Tbsp. dill weed
3 Tbsp. dried parsley
1 cup sour cream
3 Tbsp. dried onion
dash of salt, *optional*

1. Place all ingredients in
a medium-sized mixing bowl
and stir together well.
2. Cover and refrigerate for
8 hours, or overnight to allow
flavors to blend.
3. Serve with cut-up fresh
vegetables.

Hot Artichoke and Spinach Dip

Jennifer Archer
Kalona, IA

Makes 2½ cups

Prep Time: 10–15 minutes
Cooking/Baking Time: 20–25 minutes

6-oz. jar marinated artichoke hearts, drained
9–11-oz. pkg. frozen creamed spinach, thawed
¼ cup mayonnaise
¼ cup sour cream
½ cup grated Parmesan cheese
1 garlic clove, minced, *optional*

1. Chop artichoke hearts and place in small bowl. Stir in spinach.
2. Fold in mayonnaise and sour cream.
3. Mix in Parmesan cheese and garlic if you wish.
4. Spoon into a small baking dish. Bake at 350° for 20–25 minutes, or until bubbly.
5. Serve warm with tortilla or pita chips.

Artichoke Dip

Janie Steele
Moore, OK

Makes 3½ cups

Prep. Time: 10–15 minutes
Cooking/Baking Time: 30–40 minutes

2 13¼-oz. cans artichoke hearts, drained
½ cup mayonnaise
½ cup sour cream
1½ cups grated Parmesan cheese
salt and pepper to taste

1. Mash the artichoke hearts with a fork in a medium-sized mixing bowl or in a food processor.
2. Place all ingredients into mixing bowl and blend together thoroughly.
3. Spoon into a greased baking casserole.
4. Bake at 350° for 30–40 minutes.
5. Serve with your favorite snack crackers.

Hint from Tester: *We used this recipe for a bridal shower and got many compliments!*

Artichoke-Chilies Dip

Irene J. Dewar
Pickering, Ontario

Makes 2½ cups

Prep. Time: 5 minutes
Cooking/Baking Time: 3–4 minutes

8-oz. jar of artichoke hearts, drained and chopped
4-oz. can chopped green chilies, drained
½ cup mayonnaise
½ cup grated Parmesan cheese

1. Combine all ingredients in a medium-size mixing bowl. Place in microwave-safe dish.
2. Microwave for 3–4 minutes on High, until hot and bubbly.
3. Serve with corn chips, cut-up fresh vegetables, or breadsticks for dipping.

A Tip —

Don't be afraid to try new or unusual ingredients.

Buffalo Wing Dip

Barbara Kuhns, Millersburg, OH
Ann Bender, Ft. Defiance, VA

Makes 8 cups

Prep. Time: 20 minutes
Cooking/Baking Time: 45 minutes

3 uncooked boneless,
skinless chicken breast
halves
2 8-oz. pkgs. cream cheese,
softened
1 cup bottled Ranch
dressing
2 cups shredded cheddar
cheese
12-oz. container buffalo
wing sauce

1. Cut up chicken into 1"
cubes. Place half the cubes in
a microwave-safe dish. Cover
with waxed paper and microwave on High for 3 minutes.
Stir. Cover and microwave
another 2 minutes, or until
chicken is cooked through,
but not dried out.
2. Remove cooked chicken
from dish and set aside. Repeat
with remaining chicken breasts.
3. While chicken is cook-
ing, mix cream cheese and
Ranch dressing together in a
large mixing bowl.
4. When thoroughly
blended, stir in shredded
cheese and buffalo wing
sauce.
5. When chicken is cooked,
cut it more finely. Then fold
into the rest of the sauce.
6. Place in a baking dish.
Bake at 350° for 45 minutes.

7. Serve warm with celery
sticks and tortilla chips.

Variations:
*1. Use grilled chicken in
place of the uncooked chicken
breasts. Skip Steps 1 and 2.*
*2. Use 2 10-oz. cans of
chunk chicken, drained, instead
of the 3 uncooked chicken
breast halves. Skip Steps 1 and
2 above. And use your favorite
hot sauce in place of the buffalo
wing sauce.*

—Ann Bender
Ft. Defiance, VA

Slow Cooker Reuben Dip

Jenny R. Unternahrer
Wayland, IA

Makes 6 cups

Prep. Time: 25 minutes
Cooking/Baking Time: 1½ hours

12-oz. block Swiss cheese,
grated
1 lb. deli corned beef,
chipped *or* sliced thin
12–15-oz. can sauerkraut,
drained
half a 16-oz. bottle
Thousand Island
dressing

1. Gently mix all ingredients together in slow cooker.
Heat on Low until cheese is
melted, about 1½ hours.
2. Add more dressing as
needed to keep the consistency you want.

3. Serve with sliced rye
or marbled cocktail bread or
with rye, or your favorite,
crackers.

Taco Dip with Fresh Tomatoes

Linda Hartzler
Minonk, IL
Kathryn Yoder
Minot, ND

Makes 4 cups

Prep. Time: 15–20 minutes

2 8-oz. pkgs. cream cheese,
softened
16 ozs. sour cream
1 envelope dry taco
seasoning mix
1 cup shredded sharp
cheddar cheese
1½ cups chopped tomatoes

1. Mix cream cheese, sour
cream, and taco seasoning
together.
2. Spread into a 9" pie plate
or dish.
3. Top with shredded
cheese and then with tomatoes just before eating.
4. Serve with tortilla chips.

*Variations: You can add
shredded lettuce, chopped red
and green peppers and cucumbers, plus any other favorite
salad ingredients to the dip just
before serving.*

—**Kathryn Yoder**
Minot, ND

Black Bean Salsa

Kathy Hertzler
Lancaster, PA

Makes 5 cups

Prep. Time: 15 minutes
Chilling Time: 8 hours

2 15-oz. cans black beans,
  rinsed
1 cup corn (if canned, drain)
1 large tomato, diced
8 stems cilantro, chopped
4 Tbsp. lime juice
salt and pepper to taste,
  optional
chopped garlic *and/or*
  sliced scallions, *optional*

1. Gently toss all ingredients together in a large mixing bowl.
2. Cover and let marinate in the refrigerator overnight.
3. Serve with lime or plain-flavored tortilla chips.

Fruit Salsa

Dorothy Lingerfelt
Stonyford, CA

Makes 3–4 cups

Prep Time: 15 minutes
Standing Time: 4 hours–1 day

3 pieces of whole fresh
  fruit (peaches, pears,
  apples, apricots, kiwi,
  strawberries, mangoes,
  papaya, pineapple, *or a
  combination of fruits),*
  chopped
1 Vidalia onion, chopped
2 4-oz. cans chopped
  chilies, *or your choice
  of fresh chilies, seeds
  removed and
  chopped*

1. Stir ingredients together gently until well mixed.
2. Let stand for at least four hours and up to 1 day to develop the flavors.
3. Serve as a topping or a side to grilled or roasted meats, or as a dip for tacos or other sturdy crackers.

Taco Dip

Janice Muller
Derwood, MD

Makes about 8 cups

Prep Time: 25 minutes
Cooking/Baking Time: 10 minutes

16-oz. pkg. cheese spread
2 8-oz. pkgs. cream cheese,
  softened
16-oz. jar chunky salsa
1 envelope dry taco
  seasoning mix
1 lb. ground beef, browned
  and drained of drippings

1. Place cheeses in a large saucepan. Stir over low heat until melted.
2. Combine salsa, taco seasoning, and browned beef in a bowl. Stir into cheese mixture.
3. Heat on low 10 minutes, stirring frequently.
4. Serve with tortilla chips.

Tip from Tester: This would be good as filling in a wrap and eaten as a burrito.

Hamburger Cheese Dip

Robin Schrock
Millersburg, OH

Makes 8 cups

Prep. Time: 10–15 minutes
Cooking/Baking Time: 30–35 minutes

1 lb. hamburger
small onion, chopped, about ¼ cup
8 ozs. hot taco sauce, *or* salsa
1 tsp. Worcestershire sauce
1 lb. Velveeta cheese, cubed
dash garlic powder, *optional*

1. Brown hamburger with chopped onion in a skillet. Drain off drippings.
2. Add remaining ingredients and heat until cheese is melted.
3. Serve warm with tortilla chips for dipping.

Tip from Tester: *We made this for a 25th wedding anniversary party, and, of the three dips served, this one was the big hit. The guests loved it!*

Spicy Sausage Dip

Bob Hunsberger
Harrisonburg, VA

Makes 6–7 cups

Prep. Time 15 minutes
Cooking/Baking Time: 25 minutes

1 lb. sage sausage
15-oz. can Rotel tomatoes with chilies
2 8-oz. pkgs. cream cheese, softened

1. Brown sausage in large pan. Drain off drippings. Chop sausage fine.
2. Place sausage back in pan. Add tomatoes and cream cheese. Simmer until cream cheese is melted, stirring frequently.
3. Serve warm with tortilla chips. To keep warm for an extended period, place dip in slow cooker turned on Low.

Tip: *Serve any leftovers the next morning, either warm or cold, as a bagel spread for breakfast.*

Guacamole

Kara Maddox
Lincoln, NE
Judy Houser
Hershey, PA

Makes about 1¼–2 cups

Prep. Time: 10 minutes

2 avocados
½ cup chopped red onion
½ cup cubed tomatoes
salt and pepper to taste
1 tsp. lime juice

1. Cut the avocados in half, remove the stone, and peel. Then mash the avocados in a medium-sized mixing bowl with a fork.
2. Stir in remaining ingredients gently.
3. Serve with cut-up fresh vegetables and corn chips.

Turbo Guacamole

Cliff Snyder
Waterloo, ON

Makes ¾ cup

Prep Time: 5 minutes

1 avocado
1 Tbsp. sour cream
1 Tbsp. mayonnaise
¼ tsp. salt
¼ tsp. pepper (I always use freshly ground)
¼ tsp. lemon juice

¼ tsp. balsamic vinegar,
optional
dash of Tabasco sauce,
optional
dash of Worcestershire
sauce, *optional*

1. Cut avocado in half
Remove pit. Peel off the skin.
2. Place peeled avocado in
a mixing bowl. Add all other
ingredients. Mix, using a fork
to squish the avocado. Don't
try to puree the guacamole—
ideally some small chunks of
avocado should remain intact.
3. Serve on a dipping tray
along with salsa and lightly
seasoned taco chips.

*Tip: This guacamole can also
be used as a delicious spread
on toasted bagels, or try it on
a sandwich instead of butter or
mayonnaise.*

Mexican Layered Dip
Karla Baer, North Lima, OH

Makes 6 cups

Prep. Time: 10–15 minutes
Chilling Time: 1–2 hours

1 container frozen avocado
dip, thawed (if you can't
find frozen, prepared
guacamole will work)
½ pint sour cream
8 ozs. taco sauce
8 ozs. Monterey Jack
cheese, shredded

1. Spread avocado dip in
bottom of 8" nonmetallic dish.
2. Spread sour cream over
top.
3. Pour taco sauce over
sour cream.
4. Sprinkle cheese over
taco sauce.
5. Cover and chill 1–2
hours.
6. Serve with tortilla chips.

Smoked Salmon Dip
Lois Ostrander
Lebanon, PA

Makes 2 cups

Prep Time: 10 minutes
Chilling Time: 2–3 hours

2 6-oz. cans smoked
salmon
8-oz. pkg. cream cheese,
softened
⅓ cup ground walnuts *or*
parsley, *optional*

1. Mix salmon and cream
cheese, in a medium-sized
mixing bowl, using a fork.
2. Chill for an hour or so
until mixture becomes stiff
enough to handle.
3. Shape into a ball. Return
to mixing bowl and fridge.
Let stand for another hour or
so to blend flavors.
4. Just before serving,
roll in ground nuts or finely
chopped parsley, if you wish.
5. Serve with crackers.

*Tip from Tester: In addition
to spreading this on crackers, I
used it for breakfast on a bagel,
and then topped it off with
sliced tomato and onion. I will
definitely serve this to guests!*

Crab Dip
Susan J. Heil
Strasburg, PA

Makes about 2 cups

Prep Time: 10 minutes
*Cooking/Baking Time: 15–20
minutes*

8-oz. pkg. cream cheese,
softened
2 Tbsp. milk
¼ cup minced onion
1 Tbsp. Worcestershire
sauce
14-oz. can crabmeat,
drained and picked
through for shells

1. Beat cream cheese and
milk together in a medium-
sized mixing bowl until
smooth.
2. Stir in onion and
Worcestershire sauce until
well blended.
3. Fold in crabmeat.
4. Place Dip in an oven-
proof serving dish.
5. Bake at 350° for 15–20
minutes, or until bubbly.
6. Serve warm with
crackers for dipping.

*Variation: Add salt and
pepper to taste.*

Creamy Shrimp Appetizer

Kathleen A. Rogge
Alexandria, IN
Annabelle Unternahrer
Shipshewana, IN
June S. Grafl
Denver, PA

Makes about 3 cups

Prep Time: 20 minutes

8-oz. pkg. cream cheese
¾ cup ketchup, *divided*
2 7-oz. cans tiny shrimp, rinsed and drained well

1. Cut block of cream cheese in half lengthwise, so that you have two slabs, each of the original length and width, but with only half the thickness. Place slabs side-by-side on a large plate or platter.
2. Pour ⅔ of the ketchup over the cream cheese blocks, allowing it to run down over the sides a bit.
3. Spoon shrimp over the ketchup.
4. Spoon the remainder of the ketchup over the shrimp.
5. Serve with crackers of your choice or crisp rye rounds.

Variation: Use cocktail sauce instead of ketchup.

—**Annabelle Unternahrer**
Shipshewana, IN

—**June S. Grafl**
Denver, PA

Shrimp Dip

Donna Treloar
Hartford City, IN

Makes 2⅔ cups

Prep Time: 3–5 minutes
Chilling Time: 1–2 hours

10¾-oz. can cream of shrimp soup, undiluted
8-oz. pkg. cream cheese, regular *or* reduced fat, softened
1 tsp. cocktail sauce, *optional*
1 can tiny whole shrimp

1. Beat condensed soup and softened cream cheese with electric mixer until smooth.
2. Add cocktail sauce, if desired, and blend.
3. Rinse shrimp and drain. Fold in to keep shrimp whole, or beat in with mixer.
4. Chill. Serve with chips or crackers.

Cheese Bread Dunkers

Carol Lenz, Little Chute, WI

Makes 8 servings

Prep. Time: 5–10 minutes
Cooking/Baking Time: 10–12 minutes

8-count pkg. hot dog buns
2 cups shredded cheddar cheese
garlic salt to taste
jar of favorite spaghetti sauce

1. Preheat oven to 350°.
2. Open, split, and place buns on cookie sheet. Sprinkle with cheese. Shake garlic salt to taste over cheese.
3. Heat in oven for 10–12 minutes.
4. Heat spaghetti sauce in microwave and divide among individual-serving-size cups.
5. Dunk warm cheese bread into spaghetti dipping sauce.

Tips:
1. You can use any bread for this recipe, including slightly stale or forgotten-in-the-freezer bread, because it crisps up in the oven. Hot dog buns are simply good dunkers.
2. Try different kinds of cheeses, or mix two or more to add variety. We like mozzarella and Parmesan together.
3. Bake breadsticks according to their package instructions. Use as dunkers.

—**Kendra Dreps**, Liberty, PA

Rose's Bread Dip

Rose Hankins, Stevensville, MD

Makes 1+ cups,
enough for 6–8 servings

Prep Time: 3 minutes

1 cup extra-virgin olive oil
3 Tbsp. freshly snipped
Italian herbs (for
example, oregano, basil,
thyme, *or* rosemary), *or* 1
Tbsp. dried Italian herbs
2 cloves garlic, minced
1 Tbsp. red wine vinegar

1. Mix all ingredients together and pour into small dipping bowls, 1 for each person.
2. Serve with crusty French, Italian, or artisan breads, sliced or cut into chunks for dipping.

Stuffed Mushrooms

Doris Herr, Manheim, PA

Makes 18 mushrooms, or 9 servings

Prep Time: 30 minutes
Cooking/Baking Time: 25 minutes

18 medium-sized
mushrooms
1 stick (¼ lb.) butter, melted
¼ cup chopped onions
¼ cup chopped celery
1 cup dry cornbread
stuffing
¼ cup water

1. Wash mushrooms. Carefully remove stems. Set stems aside.
2. Lightly grease a shallow 7 × 11 baking dish.
3. Melt butter in a small skillet. Dip mushroom caps into melted butter in skillet. Place upside down in prepared baking dish.
4. Chop ½ cup mushroom stems. Place in butter in skillet, along with chopped celery and onion. Saute in butter.
5. Mix stuffing crumbs with water in a small bowl. Add to vegetables in skillet and stir.
6. Spoon mixture into mushroom caps.
7. Bake at 350° for 25 minutes.

Variations:
1. Use flavored stuffing instead of the cornbread stuffing.
2. Replace celery with crumbled blue cheese.
— Lena Stauffer
Port Matilda, PA

A Tip —
Glass dishes tend to bake faster than aluminum ones.

Stuffed Mushrooms

Carolyn Snader
Ephrata, PA

Makes 8–12 servings

Prep Time: 30 minutes
Cooking/Baking Time: 30 minutes

12 large mushrooms, about
2–2½" in diameter
6-oz. can crabmeat, picked
over to remove shell and
cartilage
2 slices bread, toasted and
chopped fine
1 egg
minced onion, *optional*
1 cup grated cheese

1. Take stems off mushroom tops. Chop stems, either by hand or in a food processor.
2. In a medium-sized bowl, mix crabmeat, bread (chopped either by hand or in a food processor with the mushroom stems), egg, and onion if you wish, together with the chopped mushroom stems.
3. Stuff tops with mixture. Place on one layer, stuffed-side up in a greased baking dish.
4. Bake at 375° for 20 minutes.
5. Top with grated cheese. Bake an additional 10 minutes, or until cheese is browned.

Stuffed Jalapenos

Barbara Walker
Sturgis, SD

Makes 12 servings

Prep. Time: 20 minutes
Cooking/Baking Time: 45 minutes

12 fresh jalapeno peppers,
   halved lengthwise and
   seeded
8-oz. pkg. cream cheese,
   softened
12 slices bacon

1. Preheat oven to 400°.
2. Use rubber gloves to
seed and slice peppers. Keep
hands away from your face;
the liquid and seeds from the
peppers can burn your eyes.
3. Stuff each pepper half
with cream cheese.
4. Wrap half a slice of
bacon around each stuffed
pepper.
5. Place in single layer on
baking sheet.
6. Bake for 45 minutes, or
until bacon is done.

Bacon-Wrapped Water Chestnuts

John D. Allen
Rye, CO

Makes 10–12 servings

Marinating Time: 1 hour
Prep. Time: 45 minutes
Cooking/Baking Time: 30 minutes

1 can water chestnuts,
   drained
¼ cup soy sauce
1 lb. bacon
½ cup brown sugar

1. Soak the water chestnuts
in soy sauce for 1 hour.
2. Cut the bacon in half
crosswise. Fry until limp but
not crisp.
3. Roll the chestnuts in
brown sugar.
4. Wrap bacon around the
chestnuts and secure with
toothpicks. Place on a baking
sheet.
5. Bake at 350° for 30
minutes.

Prosciutto and Pear Canapes

J. B. Miller
Indianapolis, IN

Makes 24 canapes

Prep. Time: 15 minutes

3 Tbsp. butter
1 Tbsp. fresh sage leaves,
   or 1 tsp. crumbled dried
   sage
24 thin slices of narrow
   French bread cut about
   ⅜" thick
2–3 ripe pears
12 thin slices of prosciutto

1. Bring butter to room
temperature and add sage,
stirring until well blended.
Spread the sage butter over
each slice of bread.
2. Cut the pears in half
and remove the cores. Cut
each half into 6 thin wedges.
Cut each slice of prosciutto
crosswise in half.
3. Mound a piece of
prosciutto on top of each slice
of bread and top with wedge
of pear.
4. Place on a platter and
serve.

A Tip —
   I fry several pounds of bacon and then freeze it for quick
access when I need it for a recipe.

Shrimp Mousse on Cucumber

J. B. Miller
Indianapolis, IN

Makes 36 slices

Prep. Time: 10 minutes

3 green onions
3-oz. pkg. cream cheese, at room temperature
1 lb. cooked baby shrimp
3 Tbsp. fresh lemon juice
10"-long seedless cucumber, *or* 2 smaller cucumbers

1. Trim the green onions and cut into small pieces. Place them in a food processor and pulse several times to chop.
2. Add the cream cheese and mix. Add the shrimp and lemon juice and puree until creamy and smooth.
3. Slice the cucumber about ¼" thick and place on serving platter.
4. Spoon 1 Tbsp. mousse on top of each cucumber slice, or place mousse in pastry bag and pipe onto cucumbers.

Cheese-Wrapped Olives

Darla Sathre
Baxter, MN

Makes 36 servings

Prep. Time: 30 minutes
Chilling Time: 1 hour
Cooking/Baking Time: 15–20 minutes

8 ozs. shredded cheddar cheese
1¼ cups flour
1 stick (½ cup) unsalted butter, melted
jar of green olives (about 36 or so), drained

1. In a medium-sized bowl, mix cheese and flour. Add melted butter and mix thoroughly.
2. Mold a little dough around each olive, shaping it into a ball.
3. Place wrapped olives 2" apart on ungreased cookie sheet.
4. Cover and chill at least one hour.
5. Bake uncovered for 15–20 minutes at 400°, until wrapping is golden brown.

Cheese Puffs

Darla Sathre
Baxter, MN

Makes 36 servings

Prep. Time: 15–20 minutes
Cooking/Baking Time: 12–15 minutes

1 stick (½ cup) butter, softened
1 cup flour
½ tsp. garlic salt
2 cups shredded cheese, any flavor

1. In a medium-sized bowl, mix all ingredients together. Form into balls 1" in diameter.
2. Place balls on an ungreased cookie sheet, leaving space around each one.
3. Bake at 425° for 12-15 minutes. Serve hot.

Tip: You can form the balls early in the day, place on the cookie sheet, and store in the refrigerator until ready to bake and serve.

Puffy Cheese Squares

Kathy Hertzler
Lancaster, PA

Makes 10–12 servings

Prep. Time: 45–60 minutes
Chilling Time: 8 hours or
*   overnight*
Cooking/Baking Time: 12–15
*   minutes*

1 lb. loaf unsliced white
   bread
3-oz. pkg. cream cheese
¼ lb. sharp cheddar
   cheese, grated
1 stick (½ cup) butter
2 egg whites, stiffly beaten

  1. Trim crusts from bread
and discard crusts.
  2. Cut bread into 1" squares.
  3. Melt cheeses and butter
together. Use either your
microwave, or place in the
top of your double boiler.
  4. Remove from heat and
fold in stiffly beaten whites.
  5. Spear a bread cube with
a fork and dip into cheese
mixture until well coated.
  6. Place coated squares on
lightly greased cookie sheet
and refrigerate overnight,
covered.
  7. Bake at 400° for 12–15
minutes, or until puffy and
brown. Serve warm.

*Note: You'll probably have
some bread left over.*

Cheddar Cheese Puffs

Becky Frey
Lebanon, PA

Makes 10–15 puffs

Prep. Time: 10 minutes
Cooking/Baking Time: 12–15
*   minutes*

1 cup cheddar cheese,
   shredded
½ cup flour
half a stick (¼ cup) butter,
   softened
½ tsp. dry mustard

  1. In a medium-sized bowl,
mix all ingredients together
well. Using your hands
ensures that the mixture is
thoroughly mixed.
  2. Roll into 1" balls. Place
1" apart on ungreased baking
sheet.
  3. Bake at 400° for 12–15
minutes, or until lightly
browned.
  4. Serve warm.

Shrimp/Cheese for Muffins

Ruth Ann Bender
Cochranville, PA

Makes 8–10 servings

Prep Time: 10 minutes
Cooking/Baking Time: 15 minutes

4-oz. jar Old English
   cheese spread
1 stick (½ cup) butter
3 Tbsp. mayonnaise
4½-oz. can shrimp,
   drained
6 whole English muffins

  1. Melt butter and cheese
in heavy saucepan, stirring
occasionally.
  2. While butter and cheese
are melting, split muffins.
  3. When butter and cheese
are melted together, turn off
heat and stir in mayonnaise.
Continue stirring until
slightly thickened.
  4. Fold in shrimp. Immediately spread on muffin
halves.
  5. Place muffin halves on a
baking sheet. Bake at 350° for
10 minutes. Serve warm.

Mini Pizzas

SuAnne Burkholder
Millersburg, OH

Makes 10 servings

Prep. Time: 10 minutes
Cooking/Baking Time: 10–15 minutes

12-oz. tube refrigerated
   buttermilk biscuits
15-oz. can pizza sauce
10 slices pepperoni
¾ cup shredded
   mozzarella cheese

1. Flatten each biscuit into a 3" circle and press into a greased muffin cup.
2. Spoon 1 Tbsp. pizza sauce over each biscuit. Top with a slice of pepperoni and 1 Tbsp. cheese.
3. Bake at 425° for 10–15 minutes, or until golden brown.

Tips:
   1. You'll have about half the pizza sauce left, so you may want to double the other ingredients and have twice the number of pizzas!
   2. Kids love to help make this recipe.

Onion Toasties

Marie Skelly
Babylon, NY

Makes 12 small slices

Prep. Time: 15 minutes
Cooking/Baking Time: 5–7 minutes

½ cup mayonnaise
¼ cup finely chopped
   onion
½ cup grated Parmesan *or*
   Romano cheese
12-oz. loaf sliced party rye
   bread

1. Stir together first 3 ingredients in a small mixing bowl.
2. Spread 1½ Tbsp. mixture on each bread slice. Place slices on baking sheet.
3. Bake at 450° 5–7 minutes, or until browned. Serve immediately.

A Tip —

   Freeze extra onions and celery rather than letting them spoil in the refrigerator. You can use them later in chili, soups, or barbecue.

Cheesy Shrimp Melts

Mary Seielstad
Sparks, NV

Makes 8–32 servings

Prep. Time: 10–15 minutes
Cooking/Baking Time: 15 minutes

1 lb. cooked and peeled
   small shrimp
1 cup shredded sharp
   cheddar cheese
6 Tbsp. chopped celery
   and onion mixed, or one
   or the other alone
¼ cup mayonnaise
4 English muffins

1. Mix first 4 ingredients together.
2. Heat oven to 350°.
3. Split English muffins. (To serve as a smaller appetizer, cut each half into halves or quarters.) Place on cookie sheet. Heat or toast 5 minutes, just until lightly browned.
4. Remove from oven and spread with shrimp mixture. Return to oven for 12 to 15 minutes, or until mixture is bubbly.

Hints from tester:
   1. Sprinkle with a dash of freshly ground pepper in Step 4, just before placing in oven.
   2. For the non-seafood eaters, substitute cooked chicken for the shrimp.
   3. Top with a few cubes of fresh tomato just before serving.

Baked Crab Rangoon

Diane Eby
Holtwood, PA

Makes 12 servings

Prep Time: 20 minutes
Cooking/Baking Time: 20 minutes

6-oz. can white crabmeat,
  drained and flaked
4 ozs. (half an 8-oz. pkg.)
  cream cheese, softened
¼ cup thinly sliced green
  onions, plus 2 Tbsp.,
  divided
¼ cup mayonnaise
12 won-ton wrappers

1. Mix crabmeat, cream cheese, ¼ cup onions, and mayonnaise in a small mixing bowl.
2. Spray 12 medium-sized muffin cups with cooking spray. Gently place one won ton wrapper in each cup, allowing edges of wrappers to extend above sides of cups. Fill evenly with crabmeat mixture.
3. Bake at 350° for 18–20 minutes, or until edges are golden brown and filling is heated through. Serve warm.
4. Garnish with 2 Tbsp. chopped green onions before serving, if you wish.

Sausage and Turkey Cheese Balls

Jan Rankin
Millersville, PA
Della Yoder, Kalona, IA
Sarah Miller, Harrisonburg, VA
Rebecca Meyerkorth
Wamego, KS
Vera H. Campbell
Dayton, VA
Charlotte Shaffer
East Earl, PA

Makes 60+ balls

Prep. Time: 20–25 minutes
Cooking/Baking Time: 15–20 minutes

1 lb. regular loose sausage
1 lb. ground turkey
4 cups shredded sharp
  cheese
6–8 minced green onions,
  optional
1½ cups buttermilk baking
  mix

1. Preheat oven to 375°.
2. Mix all ingredients. Form into 1" balls.
3. Place on lightly greased baking sheet, making sure that the balls are not touching each other.
4. Bake 15–20 minutes, or until golden brown.

Tip: You can mix the ingredients for the balls in advance and freeze them on a baking sheet to be baked later. When ready to serve, thaw, preheat oven to 375°, and follow directions in Step 4.

Variation: You can use only sausage, if you wish.
  —**Della Yoder**
    Kalona, IA
  —**Sarah Miller**
    Harrisonburg, VA
  —**Rebecca Meyerkorth**
    Wamego, KS
  —**Vera H. Campbell**
    Dayton, VA
  —**Charlotte Shaffer**
    East Earl, PA

Cream Cheese Balls

Anne Townsend
Albuquerque, NM

Makes 10–12 servings

Prep. Time: 15–20 minutes
Chilling Time: 2½–3½ hours

8-oz. pkg. cream cheese,
  softened
2–2½-oz. pkg. corned beef,
  chopped fine
1 tsp. prepared horseradish
¼ cup grated Parmesan
  cheese
pretzel sticks

1. Place cream cheese in a medium-sized bowl. Stir in corned beef and horseradish.
2. When well mixed, refrigerate for 2–3 hours, or until thoroughly chilled and stiff.
3. Shape into small walnut-size balls.
4. Put Parmesan cheese in a small bowl. Roll each

ball in the cheese. Place on serving plate.

5. Chill in fridge 30 minutes or longer.

6. When ready to serve, pick up each ball and push a pretzel stick in each one (like a toothpick). You may garnish with cherry or grape tomatoes and parsley for a colorful appetizer.

Tips:

1. Garnish each ball with half a cherry or grape tomato and a dusting of parsley flakes for a colorful appetizer.

2. The balls are equally tasty if you use chipped beef instead of corned beef.

Smoky Bacon Wraps

Janice Crist, Quinter, KS
Marie Raber, Millersburg, OH
Martha Mullet, Sugarcreek, OH
Mary Ann Bowman
East Earl, PA

Makes 3½ dozen wraps

Prep Time: 15–30 minutes
Cooking/Baking Time: 30–40 minutes

1 lb. sliced bacon
16-oz. pkg. miniature smoked sausage links
1 cup packed brown sugar

1. Cut each bacon strip in half lengthwise.

2. Wrap 1 piece of bacon around each sausage. Secure each one with a toothpick. Place on foil-lined 10 × 15 baking pan.

3. Sprinkle with brown sugar.

4. Bake uncovered at 400° for 15–20 minutes. Turn each piece over and continue baking for another 15–20 minutes, or until bacon is crisp and sausage is heated through.

Tips:

1. Serve these as an appetizer, or for breakfast.

—**Janice Crist**
Quinter, KS

2. Use brown-and-serve sausages, cut in half, instead of the miniature smoked links.

—**Martha Mullet**
Sugarcreek, OH

—**Mary Ann Bowman**
East Earl, PA

Hint from the Tester: Instead of the brown sugar, spoon ½ cup of your favorite barbecue sauce over the bacon-wrapped sausages.

Apricot Wraps

Doyle Rounds
Bridgewater, VA

Makes about 4½ dozen wraps

Prep. Time: 10 minutes
Cooking/Baking Time: 25 minutes

14-oz. pkg. dried apricot halves
½ cup whole almonds
1 lb. sliced bacon
¼ cup plum, *or* apple, jelly
2 Tbsp. soy sauce

1. Fold each apricot around an almond.

2. Cut bacon strips into thirds vertically. Wrap a strip around each apricot and secure with a toothpick.

3. Spread out over two ungreased 10 × 15 baking pans.

4. Bake uncovered at 375° for 15 minutes. Turn each wrap over. Continue baking 10 more minutes, or until bacon is crisp.

5. While wraps are baking, combine jelly and soy sauce in a small saucepan. Cook and stir over low heat for 5 minutes, or until warm and smooth.

6. Remove apricots to paper towels and drain. Serve with sauce for dipping.

Ham Pinwheels
Arlene Snyder
Millerstown, PA

Makes 80 pinwheels

Prep. Time: 20 minutes
Chilling Time: 2 hours or more

8-oz. pkg. spreadable cream cheese with chives
8 thinly sliced slices of deli boiled ham
box of snack crackers

1. Spread cream cheese to edges of each ham slice.
2. Beginning at short end, roll up tightly. Cut each roll crosswise into 10 slices.
3. Refrigerate on covered trays or platters for 2 hours or more, until ready to serve.
4. Just before serving, place 1 pinwheel on each snack cracker.

Variations:
1. Blend 2 Tbsp. dry Ranch dressing mix into cream cheese before spreading on ham slices.
2. Serve pinwheels without a cracker base.
—**Mary Lynn Miller**
Reinholds, PA

Ham Roll-Ups
Kristine Martin
Newmanstown, PA

Makes 20 roll-ups

Prep. Time: 5–10 minutes
Cooking/Baking Time: 15 minutes

1 tube crescent rolls
4 slices deli boiled ham
4 ozs. sliced Swiss cheese, *or your favorite variety of cheese*
4 tsp. prepared mustard

1. Separate crescent rolls, making 1 rectangle out of 2 triangle-shaped pieces, for a total of 4 rectangles. Press out perforated lines.
2. Spread ham, cheese, and mustard over rectangles. Roll up.
3. Cut each roll into 5 pieces. Lay on greased cookie sheet. Bake at 350° for 15 minutes.
4. Serve warm.

Ham & Cheese Crescent Roll-Ups
Sue Pennington, Bridgewater, VA

Makes 8 servings

Prep Time: 5–10 minutes
Cooking/Baking Time: 15–19 minutes

8-oz. can refrigerated crescent dinner rolls

8 thin slices deli boiled ham
4 thin slices cheddar cheese, each cut into 4 strips

1. Separate dough into 8 triangles.
2. Place 1 piece of ham on each triangle. Place 2 strips of cheese down center of ham. Fold in edges of ham to match shape of dough triangle.
3. Roll up crescent, ending at tip of triangle. Place with tips down on ungreased baking sheet.
4. Bake at 350° for 15–19 minutes, or until golden brown. Immediately remove from cookie sheet. Serve warm.

Tiny Cheese Quiche
Carolyn Snader
Ephrata, PA

Makes 15–18 mini-quiches

Prep Time: 20–30 minutes
Cooking/Baking Time: 12–15 minutes

2 ready-made pie crusts
1 cup grated cheddar cheese
1 large egg
½ cup milk
2 tsp. chives
paprika, *optional*

1. Roll out unbaked pastry and cut into 2½" circles. Press into mini-muffin pan cups.

2. Combine cheese, egg, milk, and chives in blender or mixer. Blend until smooth.

3. Using measuring cup with pouring spout, fill each pastry-lined muffin cup ¾ full. Sprinkle with paprika if you wish.

4. Bake at 375° for 12–15 minutes, or until browned and set.

5. Allow to rest for 5 minutes before serving.

Hint from Tester: Instead of blending the chives into the quiche filling, sprinkle them over the tops of the mini-quiches before baking. The lovely green flecks will be more visible.

— **Linda Miller**
Harrisonburg, VA

Dried Beef Cheese Log
Ida H. Goering
Dayton, VA

Makes about 12–15 servings

Prep. Time: 20 minutes
Chilling Time: 3–4 hours

8-oz. pkg. cream cheese, softened
¼ cup Parmesan cheese
2 tsp. prepared horseradish
1½ cups chipped dried beef, *divided*

1. Combine cream cheese, Parmesan cheese, horseradish, and ½ cup dried beef in a large mixing bowl. Mix well.

2. Chill for 2–3 hours.

3. With your hands and/or a spoon, form into a log. Roll in remaining 1 cup dried beef, patting it on to make it adhere.

4. Chill. Serve with crackers.

Variation from Tester:
Reduce dried beef to either ½ or 1 cup. Stir all of the dried beef into the log. Roll log in ½–¾ cup chopped walnuts (instead of additional dried beef).

Dried Beef Cheese Ball
Janet Oberholtzer
Ephrata, PA

Makes 24 servings

Prep Time: 10 minutes
Chilling Time: 4–8 hours, or overnight

2 8-oz. pkgs. cream cheese, softened
1 cup dried beef, chopped fine
¾ tsp. celery salt
½ tsp. onion powder
¾ cup parsley flakes, *or* **chopped nuts of your choice**

1. With a mixer, cream the cream cheese.

2. Stir in dried beef, celery salt, and onion powder. Mix well.

3. Form into a ball with your hands.

4. Wrap well, or cover, and refrigerate for 4–8 hours.

5. Just before serving, roll in parsley flakes or nuts. Serve with assorted crackers.

Tips:
1. A food processor or mini chopper works well for chopping the dried beef.
2. If you wish, divide the cheese mixture (after Step 2) in half and form 2 smaller balls. When chilled, roll 1 in parsley flakes and the other in nuts.

Cream Cheese Onion Wraps
Teddy Decker
Albuquerque, NM

Makes 10–12 servings

Prep. Time: 15–30 minutes

2 bundles green onions
2½-oz. jar dried beef
8-oz. pkg. cream cheese, softened

1. Clean green onions and cut off root ends.

2. Spread cream cheese thickly on a slice of dried beef.

3. Lay an onion at the short end of a slice of dried beef with the cream cheese spread on top. Wrap the onion up with the dried beef. Repeat with the remaining onions and slices of dried beef.

4. Serve.

Tuna Snacks

Rose Hankins
Stevensville, MD

Makes 10–12 servings

Prep Time: 10 minutes
Standing Time: 5 minutes

¼ cup mayonnaise
3 Tbsp. pickle relish
6-oz. can albacore white
    tuna
1 hard-boiled egg, cut up
¼ cup diced celery

1. Mix mayonnaise and relish in small bowl. Let stand for 5 minutes.
2. Mix tuna, egg, and celery in large bowl. Add mayonnaise mixture.
3. Serve over crackers, pita chips, or with pretzels.

Chicken Salad Roll-Ups

F. Elaine Asper, Norton, OH

Makes 8 roll-ups

Prep. Time: 20 minutes
Cooking/Baking Time: 30 minutes

2 5-oz. cans boned chicken,
    or 1¼ cups leftover
    cooked chicken
1 medium green pepper,
    finely chopped
2 Tbsp. mayonnaise
½ tsp. salt
8-oz. tube refrigerated
    crescent rolls
¼ chopped pimento,
    optional

1. In a medium-sized bowl, mix chicken, green pepper, mayonnaise, and salt together. Set aside.
2. Grease baking sheet.
3. Separate crescents into 4 rectangles, using 2 triangles to make 1 rectangle. Press out the perforations.
4. Place 2 dough rectangles on a lightly floured surface, overlapping short sides slightly. With floured rolling pin, roll to 15 × 4 inches.
5. With spoon, spread half the chicken mix on dough, ½" from the edges on all sides.
6. Start at short side and roll up jelly-roll fashion. Cut into 4 equal slices. Place on cookie sheet.
7. Repeat Steps 5–7 with remaining 2 dough rectangles.
8. Bake at 375° for 30 minutes, or until golden brown.

Quesadillas

Melanie Mohler
Ephrata, PA

Makes 8 servings

Prep Time: 5 minutes
Cooking/Baking Time: 5 minutes

2 10" flour tortillas
2 ozs. cheddar cheese,
    shredded
2 ozs. mozzarella cheese,
    shredded

Optional ingredients:
1 small tomato, diced
¼ cup green pepper, finely
    chopped
¼ cup fresh mushrooms,
    sliced
picante sauce
sour cream

1. Sprinkle half the cheddar cheese, mozzarella cheese, and your choice of the optional ingredients (tomatoes, green pepper, fresh mushrooms) on half of each tortilla. Fold over and press edges to seal lightly.
2. Coat skillet with nonstick cooking spray. Turn burner to medium heat. Place tortillas in heated skillet.
3. Grill until browned and crisp. Turn over carefully with a spatula and continue to brown until cheese is melted.
4. Remove from skillet and cut into quarters.
5. Serve with picante sauce or sour cream for dipping, if you wish.

Cheesy Spinach Swirls

Rebecca Meyerkorth
Wamego, KS

Makes 6–8 slices

Prep. Time: 15 minutes
Cooking/Baking Time: 25–30 minutes
Standing Time: 10 minutes

10-oz. pkg. frozen chopped spinach, thawed and drained
2 cups shredded mozzarella
1 cup finely chopped onion
1 garlic clove, minced
10-oz. tube refrigerated pizza crust

1. Combine first four ingredients in a bowl and mix well.
2. Roll pizza dough into a 10 × 14 rectangle, sealing holes.
3. Place filling on crust, spreading to approximately 1 inch from edge.
4. Roll up like a jelly roll, starting with a long side. Pinch the ends shut.
5. Place seam-side down on a greased baking sheet.
6. Bake at 400° for approximately 25–30 minutes, or until golden brown.
7. Allow to stand for 10 minutes. Cut into 6–8 slices.

Feta Festive Pinwheels

Valerie Drobel
Carlisle, PA

Makes 50 1" pinwheels

Prep. Time: 15 minutes
Chilling Time: 2 hours

4-oz. pkg. crumbled feta
¼ cup dried cranberries, chopped
1 tub soft green onion cream cheese
6 10" flour tortillas

1. Combine feta cheese, chopped cranberries, and cream cheese in a medium-sized bowl. Spread evenly on each of 6 tortillas.
2. Roll tortillas up tightly and wrap each in plastic wrap. Refrigerate for at least 2 hours.
3. Slice each tortilla into 1" thick slices.

Tip: Use spinach tortillas for a Christmas appetizer, or for any special occasion.

Delicious Seasoned Pretzels

Esther S. Martin
Ephrata, PA

Makes 15 servings

Prep. Time: 10 minutes
Cooking/Baking Time: 45 minutes

2 bags small pretzels, each 1 lb. 2-oz. size
½ cup vegetable *or* canola oil
1-oz. pkg. dry Ranch dressing mix
1 tsp. dill weed

1. Mix oil, dry dressing mix, and dill weed well in a small bowl.
2. Place pretzels in large roaster pan. Pour oil over top. Stir.
3. Bake at 250° for 45 minutes. Stir once or twice while baking.

Tip: These are best served hot right out of the oven.

A Tip —

   Always have ingredients for simple recipes on hand.

Cheese Pastry Sticks

Sandra Haverstraw
Hummelstown, PA

Makes about 30 straws

Prep. Time: 15 minutes
Cooking/Baking Time: 10–12
minutes

half a stick (¼ lb.) butter,
    softened
¼ lb. grated sharp cheddar
1 tsp. salt
¼ tsp. cayenne pepper
1 cup regular flour

1. In a large mixing bowl,
grate cheese into butter. Mix
with hands or wooden spoon.
2. Add salt and cayenne.
Work in flour until all
ingredients are thoroughly
blended.
3. Roll out dough in
⅛"-thick sheet. Cut into strips
about ½" wide and 5"–6" long.
4. Pick up each strip at
ends and twist slightly as you
place onto baking sheet. Place
the strips about 1" apart.
5. Bake at 350° for 10–12
minutes, or until golden.

*Tip: Good with cold drinks
before dinner. Also excellent as
a go-along with salads or soups.*

Thanksgiving Turkey Favors

Esther J. Mast
Lancaster, PA

*Prep. Time: about 1 minute per
favor*

Oreo cookies
candy corn
chocolate-covered raisins

1. Separate a cookie and
lay cream side up.
2. Press a whole cookie on
end into cream.
3. Press six candy corns
into cream center of whole
cookie to make a fan tail.
4. Press a chocolate
covered raisin in front for
head.
5. Make as many as needed
for favors at your Thanksgiving meal.

*I made these with my grand-
children last Thanksgiving, and
it's sure to become a tradition!*

Sharp Cheese Ball

Margaret Jarrett
Anderson, IN

Makes about 3 cups

Prep Time: 10–15 minutes
Chilling Time: 2–3 hours

8-oz. pkg. cream cheese,
    softened
1 jar Old English cheese,
    softened
4 ozs. Roquefort, *or* blue,
    cheese, softened
⅛ tsp. garlic salt
chopped pecans

1. Mix all cheeses and
garlic salt thoroughly in a
large mixing bowl. Push
together in the bowl into
a ball shape. Cover and
refrigerate.
2. Chill for 2–3 hours to
make the cheese easier to
handle. Form into a ball with
your hands.
3. Roll in chopped pecans.
4. Place on foil or plastic
wrap and wrap securely.
Refrigerate until ready to use.

*Tip: Serve the cheese on a
platter surrounded by crackers,
sturdy chips, and/or celery
sticks.*

Herby Cheese Ball
Jenelle Miller
Marion, SD

Makes 2½–3 cups

Prep. Time: 10 minutes
Chilling Time: 2–3 hours

2 8-oz. pkgs. reduced-fat
  cream cheese, softened
3½ cups shredded sharp
  cheddar cheese, softened
1-oz. pkg. dry Ranch
  dressing mix
1 cup finely chopped
  pecans

1. Using a heavy duty
mixer and a large bowl, beat
together first 3 ingredients
until thoroughly blended.
Push mixture together in
bowl, cover, and refrigerate.
2. After chilling for 2–3
hours to firm up the cheese,
form into 2 balls with your
hands.
3. Roll balls in pecans to
coat all surfaces.
4. Wrap in plastic wrap.
Refrigerate until ready to use.
5. Serve with crackers.

Zesty Cheese Ball
Mary Ann Bowman
East Earl, PA

Makes 3½ cups

Prep. Time: 10 minutes
Chilling Time: 2–3 hours

4 ozs. sharp cheese, grated
  and softened
3 8-oz. pkgs. cream cheese,
  softened
2 tsp. Worcestershire sauce
¼ tsp. onion salt
¾–1 cup finely chopped
  pecans

1. Mix first 4 ingredients
together in a large mixing
bowl. When thoroughly
blended, push ingredients
together, cover, and refrigerate.
2. After mixture has
firmed up, about 2–3 hours,
shape into one or two balls
with your hands.
3. Roll ball(s) in pecans.
Wrap well and refrigerate
until ready to use.
4. Serve with crackers.

Beefy-Onion Cheese Ball
Ruth Ann Horst
Dayton, VA

Makes 2½ cups

Prep. Time: 10–15 minutes
Chilling Time: 2–3 hours

2¼-oz. jar dried beef (low-
  sodium, if you can find
  it)
3 scallions
2 8-oz. pkgs. cream cheese,
  at room temperature

1. Chop dried beef and
onion into small pieces.
2. Mix with cream cheese
in a good-sized mixing bowl.
3. When thoroughly
blended, push ingredients
together, cover, and refrigerate until firm, about 2–3
hours.
4. When firm, shape into a
ball with your hands. Wrap
and refrigerate until ready to
use.
5. Serve with crackers.

*Variation: Add 2 Tbsp.
Worcestershire sauce to Step #2.*

—**Linda Hartzler**, Minonk, IL

Zippy Cheese Ball

Kathleen A. Rogge
Alexandria, IN

Makes 3½ cups

Prep Time: 20–30 minutes
Chilling Time: 2–3 hours

2 8-oz. pkgs. cream cheese, softened
½ cup Parmesan cheese, grated
½ cup prepared horseradish, drained
4.25-oz. can (⅔ cup) chopped black olives
5-oz. dried beef (low-sodium, if you can find it), chopped fine

1. Blend all ingredients well in a large mixing bowl.
2. Push everything together in a ball-like shape, cover, and refrigerate until firm, about 2–3 hours.
3. When thoroughly chilled, form into 1 or 2 balls with your hands.
4. Wrap and refrigerate until ready to use.

Tips from tester:
1. Roll ball in chopped pecans before serving.
2. Place prepared ball on a serving platter and surround with fresh parsley sprigs.
3. Serve with celery sticks.

Ranch Cheese Balls

Arlene Snyder
Millerstown, PA

Makes 3½ cups

Prep. Time: 10 minutes
Chilling Time: 2–3 hours

2 8-oz. pkgs. cream cheese, softened
8 ozs. marbled cheddar cheese, grated and softened
2 tsp. Worcestershire sauce
1 tsp. lemon juice
1 Tbsp. dry Ranch dressing mix
¾–1 cup chopped smoked almonds, *optional*

1. Mix all ingredients, except the almonds, together thoroughly in a large bowl. Push ingredients together into a ball shape.
2. Chill 2–3 hours, or until firm. Then shape into a ball with your hands.
3. Wrap well and refrigerate, or if you wish, first roll in chopped nuts.
4. Serve with crackers.

Pineapple Cheese Ball

Mary Lynn Miller
Reinholds, PA

Makes 4–4½ cups

Prep. Time: 15 minutes
Chilling Time: 2–3 hours

2 8-oz. pkgs. cream cheese, softened
1 small onion, grated *or* chopped fine
2 cups chopped pecans, *divided*
8-oz. can crushed pineapple, drained
1 tsp. Season-All

1. In a large mixing bowl, mix together all ingredients, except 1 cup nuts. Push into ball shape, cover bowl, and refrigerate.
2. Chill 2–3 hours, or until firm.
3. Form into 1 or 2 balls with your hands and roll in remaining nuts.
4. Wrap and refrigerate until ready to serve.

34

Warm Broccoli Cheese Spread

Mary Ann Bowman
East Earl, PA

Makes 3½ cups

Prep. Time: 10 minutes
Cooking/Baking Time: 25 minutes

8-oz. pkg. light cream cheese, cubed, at room temperature
8 ozs. light sour cream
1 envelope dry Italian salad dressing mix
10-oz. pkg. frozen chopped broccoli, thawed, drained, and patted dry
2 cups shredded reduced fat cheddar cheese, *divided*

1. In a large mixing bowl, stir together cream cheese, sour cream, and salad dressing mix until blended.
2. Fold in broccoli and 1½ cups cheese.
3. Spoon into shallow 1-quart baking dish coated with non-stick cooking spray.
4. Bake uncovered for 20 minutes at 350°. Remove from oven and sprinkle with remaining cheese.
5. Bake 5 minutes longer, or until cheese is melted.

Tip: Serve with wheat crackers.

Cheese Spread for Bread

Jean Binns Smith
Bellefonte, PA

Makes 3+ cups

Prep. Time: 15 minutes
Cooking/Baking Time: 20 minutes

4 ozs. grated mozzarella cheese
4 ozs. grated cheddar cheese
8 ozs. grated Monterey Jack cheese
1 Tbsp. garlic powder
1 cup mayonnaise

1. In a large bowl, mix cheeses and garlic powder until well blended.
2. Add mayonnaise. Mix well.
3. Split 2 loaves of French bread horizontally.
4. Spread cheese mixture on cut sides of both loaves.
5. Spray 2 baking sheets with non-sticking cooking spray.
6. Place bread on baking sheets. Bake 20 minutes at 350°, or until cheese melts and browns.

Tomato Cheese Spread

Clara Yoder Byler
Nartville, OH

Makes 1 cup

Prep. Time: 5–7 minutes
Cooking/Baking Time: 5 minutes
Chilling Time: 1 hour

half a can tomato soup (⅔ cup)
½ cup shredded cheese of your choice
½ tsp. dry mustard
¼ tsp. instant minced onion

1. Cook ingredients in a small saucepan over moderate heat, stirring constantly until cheese is melted.
2. Chill until somewhat stiffened.
3. Serve as a cracker dip or sandwich filling.

A Tip —
You can freeze cheese and use it later in cooking or baking.

Olive Spread

Susan Kasting, Jenks, OK

Makes 3 cups

Prep. Time: 10–15 minutes

2 8-oz. pkgs. cream cheese,
  softened
16-oz. can black olives,
  finely chopped
½ cup green olives, finely
  chopped
1–2 cloves garlic, minced
2 Tbsp. lemon juice
¾ cup chopped parsley,
  optional

1. In a large mixing bowl,
blend all ingredients together.
Push into ball shape in the
bowl, cover, and refrigerate.
2. When firm, shape with
your hands into two balls.
3. If you wish, roll in
chopped parsley.
4. Wrap and refrigerate
until ready to use.
5. Serve with crackers or
cut-up fresh vegetables.

Pineapple
Cheese Spread

Mary Puskar, Forest Hill, MD

Makes 3 cups

Prep Time: 15 minutes

8–10-oz. jar pineapple
  preserves

2 10-oz. jars apple jelly
5-oz. jar prepared
  horseradish
1½ Tbsp. dry mustard
8-oz. pkg. cream cheese

1. In a medium-sized mixing
bowl, stir all ingredients
together until well blended.
2. To serve, spread over a
block of cream cheese.

Tips:
  *1. Use a good cracker like
Carr's Wafers.*
  *2. This recipe makes a lot.
Keep any leftovers in a jar in the
refrigerator and use as needed.*

Chicken Spread

Makes 2⅓ cups

Prep. Time: 20 minutes
Chilling Time: 2–3 hours

2 cups ground cooked
  chicken
1 Tbsp. onion, ground *or*
  minced fine
8-oz. pkg. cream cheese,
  softened
1–2 Tbsp. mayonnaise
½ tsp. Salad Supreme
  seasoning

1. Mix chicken and onion
together.
2. Blend in softened cream
cheese.
3. Add mayonnaise and
Salad Supreme seasoning.
4. Refrigerate to blend
flavors for 2–3 hours.
5. Serve on crackers.

Shrimp Spread

Marie Raber, Millersburg, OH

Makes about 5 cups

Prep. Time: 15 minutes

2 8-oz. pkgs. cream cheese,
  softened
1 cup sour cream
8–10-oz. jar cocktail sauce
¼ cup shredded Mexican
  blend cheese
2 4-oz. cans tiny shrimp

1. In a large mixing bowl,
mix cream cheese and sour
cream well. Spread in a long
baking or serving dish.
2. Top with cocktail sauce.
3. Sprinkle with cheese.
4. Rinse and drain shrimp.
Sprinkle over all.
5. Serve with crackers.

*When I was growing up,
our family of 7—3 girls and 2
boys plus parents—sometimes
would make half a batch of
this shrimp dish when we were
together for the evening. It
would all be gone before we
went to bed!*

Breakfast and Brunch Dishes

Breakfast Casserole

Eunice Fisher
Clarksville, MI
Donna Barnitz
Rio Rancho, NM
Linda Eberly Miller
Harrisonburg, VA
Shari Ladd, Hudson, MI

Makes 6 servings

Prep Time: 15 minutes
Cooking/Baking Time: 1 hour

half a pkg. frozen hash
browns, thawed
6 eggs
½ lb. cooked sausage,
bacon, *or* ham
4 ozs. shredded cheddar
cheese
½ cup milk

1. Mix all ingredients
together and pour into a
greased baking dish. (You
may mix the night before to
relieve the stress in the morning. Refrigerate it overnight.)

2. Bake at 350° approxi-
mately 1 hour, or until set.
If the Breakfast Casserole
begins to get too brown, cover
with foil.

Tips:
*1. Use hash browns with
onions and peppers for
enhanced flavor.*
—Donna Barnitz
Rio Rancho, NM

*2. Add salt and pepper to
taste, if you wish.*

Variations:
*1. You can cut back the
amount of meat to ½ cup, if
you wish.*
—Shari Ladd
Hudson, MI

*2. You can easily double this
recipe.*
*3. I like to add cooked
vegetables to Step 1 for extra
flavor and nutrition.*
—Linda Eberly Miller
Harrisonburg, VA
—Shari Ladd
Hudson, MI

Breakfast Casserole (egg-less)

Jean Butzer, Batavia, NY

Makes 4–6 servings

Prep Time: 20 minutes
Cooking Time: 1 hour

1 lb. bulk sausage
30-oz. pkg. frozen shredded
hash browns, thawed
16-oz. container French
onion dip
2 cups sour cream
2 cups shredded cheddar
cheese, *divided*

1. Brown the sausage in a
skillet. Drain.
2. In a large mixing
bowl, combine the browned
sausage, hash browns, French
onion dip, sour cream, and 1
cup shredded cheese.
3. Spread mixture in a greased
9 × 13 baking pan. Bake at
350° for 45 minutes.
4. Sprinkle with remaining
cheese and bake an additional
15 minutes.

Breakfast Scramble

Carlene Horne
Bedford, NH

Makes 4–6 servings

Prep Time: 20 minutes
Cooking/Baking Time: 10 minutes

½ cup onions, chopped
1 cup green *or* red bell
  peppers, chopped
1-lb. pkg. link sausage
3 cooked potatoes, cubed
4 eggs, broken into bowl

1. Put onion and peppers into skillet.
2. Mix in link sausage cut into chunks. Cook until sausage browns.
3. Stir in potatoes and heat through.
4. Stir in eggs. Continue cooking until eggs are just set.
5. Cut into wedges and serve.

Tip from Tester: I served with salsa as a side dish.

Sausage, Eggs, and Bread Dish

Betty B. Dennison
Grove City, PA
Jan Pembleton, Arlington, TX

Makes 6 servings

Prep. Time: 10–15 minutes
Chilling Time: 1 hour
Cooking/Baking Time: 1 hour

1 lb. bulk sausage
6 eggs
1½ cups milk
4 cups stale bread, cubed
4 ozs. shredded cheddar
  cheese

1. Brown sausage in a skillet and drain. Set aside.
2. In a large mixing bowl, beat eggs and then add milk.
3. Fold in cubes of stale bread, cheese, and sausage.
4. Pour into an 8 × 8 greased baking dish.
5. Refrigerate for 1 hour.
6. Bake at 325° for 1 hour. Cut into squares to serve.

Breakfast Sausage Ring

Joanne E. Martin
Stevens, PA

Makes 8 servings

Prep Time: 15 minutes
Cooking Time: 40–45 minutes
Standing Time: 10 minutes

2 lbs. bulk pork sausage
2 eggs, beaten
1½ cups fine dry bread
  crumbs
¼ cup chopped parsley,
  optional
salt and pepper to taste,
  optional

1. Lightly grease a 9" oven-safe ring mold.
2. In a large mixing bowl, mix all ingredients well. Then pack into the mold.
3. Bake at 350° for 20 minutes.
4. Remove from the oven and pour off any accumulated fat. Return to oven to bake for 20 minutes more.
5. Remove from oven and allow to stand for 10 minutes. Turn onto a platter and fill the center with scrambled eggs.

A Tip —

Get all your ingredients together before starting a recipe. Place them on the left side of your work area. Move them to the right side as you finish with them.

Easy Breakfast Casserole

Barbara Walker, Sturgis, SD

Makes 8 servings

Prep Time: 20 minutes
Chilling Time: overnight
Cooking Time: 1 hour

stale *or* sturdy bread slices
   to cover bottom of 9 × 13
   baking pan
1½–2 lbs. bacon, fried until
   crispy and broken up
2 cups shredded cheese,
   your choice of flavors
12 eggs
1 cup milk

1. Cover the bottom of a greased 9 × 13 baking pan with slices of bread cut to fit.
2. Sprinkle the bacon and cheese over bread.
3. Use a blender and blend the eggs and milk. Pour over the top.
4. Refrigerate overnight.
5. Bake 1 hour at 350°.

Variations from Tester:
   1. If you wish, add 1 tsp. salt and ½ tsp. black pepper to Step 3.
   2. To add more flavor, sauté 1 thinly sliced onion and 1 thinly sliced green pepper in 1 Tbsp. butter. Scatter over bacon in Step 2, before adding shredded cheese.
   3. Serve with salsa as a topping for those who enjoy some kick with their eggs!
   — Leann Brown, Lancaster, PA

Sausage and Grits Casserole

Orpha Herr, Andover, NY

Makes 6–8 servings

Prep Time: 20 minutes
Cooking/Baking Time: 1 hour

1 lb. bulk pork sausage
3 cups hot cooked grits
2½ cups shredded cheddar
   cheese
3 Tbsp. butter, *optional*
3 eggs, beaten
1½ cups milk
pimento strips and parsley,
   optional

1. Cook sausage until browned. Drain well. Spoon into lightly greased 9 × 13 baking dish.
2. In a large mixing bowl, combine hot cooked grits, cheese, and butter if you wish. Stir until cheese and butter are melted.
3. In a separate bowl, combine eggs and milk. Then stir into the grits mixture. Pour over sausage in pan.
4. Bake at 350° for 1 hour, or until set in the middle.

Tip: You can use instant or quick grits. And you can cook the grits while the sausage is browning.

Note: I was given this recipe by a co-worker in Alabama while we were both working on a clean-up project with Mennonite Disaster Service. I've come to love grits!

Breakfast in a Bag

Donna Lantgen, Golden, CO

Makes 1 serving

Prep Time: 1–2 minutes
Cooking Time: 12 minutes

2 eggs
Optional ingredients:
   ¼ cup cooked sausage
   1 slice cooked bacon,
      crumbled
   ¼ cup cooked and
      cubed ham
   thin onion slices
   several Tbsp. chopped
      red *or* green bell pepper
   several Tbsp. sliced
      black olives
   ¼ cup sliced mushrooms
   ¼ cup grated cheese of
      your choice
   ¼ cup chopped fresh
      tomato

1. Place a 4-qt. saucepan, ⅔ full of water over high heat. Bring to a boil.
2. Meanwhile, place 2 raw eggs in a sturdy plastic bag. Holding it shut, mash the eggs a bit.
3. Add optional ingredients of your choice. Press the air out of the bag. Zip close, or tie shut with a twisty.
4. Place bag in boiling water and cook for 12 minutes.
5. Remove from water and slide egg right out of the bag.

Tips:
   1. If you want, top with sour cream and salsa.
   2. Serve this to guests! If your kitchen allows, have a "make-your-own-omelet" meal.

Elegant Scrambled Eggs

John D. Allen
Rye, CO

Makes 6–8 servings

Prep. Time: 15 minutes
Cooking/Baking Time: 10 minutes

12 eggs
½ tsp. salt
⅛ tsp. pepper
2 Tbsp. butter
2 Tbsp. whipping cream

1. Combine the first three ingredients in a large bowl. Beat until well mixed.
2. Melt butter in a skillet making sure the bottom is covered. Add eggs. Have the heat set at medium.
3. Stir constantly until eggs firm up but are not dry. Remove from heat.
4. Stir in the cream. Serve immediately.

Creamed Eggs

Deborah Heatwole
Waynesboro, GA
Janice Crist, Quinter, KS
Jolyn Nolt, Lititz, PA

Makes 4 servings

Prep. Time: 10 minutes (to hard-boil the eggs)
Cooking/Baking Time: 20 minutes

2 Tbsp. butter
¼ cup flour
2 cups milk
¼–½ tsp. salt
pepper to taste
4 hard-boiled eggs, sliced

1. Melt butter in a saucepan. Add flour and stir until smooth and bubbly and lightly browned.
2. Slowly whisk in milk. Cook until thick and bubbly, stirring continuously.
3. When sauce thickens, stir in salt and pepper. Fold in hard-boiled eggs. Heat through.
4. Serve hot over toast points.

Variation: For a little more zest, add 2 tsp. Worcestershire sauce and 2 tsp. prepared mustard to Step 3 when you stir in the salt and pepper.

—**Janice Crist**, Quinter, KS

Tip from Tester: This makes a substantial breakfast, but also a light lunch or supper served with a salad.

—**Gloria Frey**, Lebanon, PA

Cheddar-Ham Oven Omelet

Jolene Schrock
Millersburg, OH

Makes 9–12 servings

Prep Time: 10 minutes
Cooking/Baking Time: 40–45 minutes
Standing Time: 10 minutes

16 eggs
2 cups milk
8 ozs. shredded cheddar cheese
¾ cup cubed fully cooked ham
6 green onions, chopped
sliced mushrooms and green peppers, *optional*

1. In a large bowl, beat eggs and milk until well blended. Stir in cheese, ham, and onions. Add optional ingredients if you wish.
2. Pour the egg mixture into a greased 9 × 13 baking dish.
3. Bake, uncovered, at 350° for 40–45 minutes, or until a knife inserted near the center comes out clean. Let stand 10 minutes before cutting and serving.

Variation: Add ½ tsp. salt and ¼ tsp. pepper, if you wish, to Step 1.

Breakfast Delight

Agnes Dick
Vanderhoof, BC

Makes 4 servings

Prep Time: 20–25 minutes
Cooking/Baking Time: 15 minutes

¼–½ lb. bacon, sliced
   sausage, *or* cubed, sliced,
   or chipped cooked ham
4 eggs
salt and pepper to taste
¼ lb. sliced *or* grated
   cheese of your choice

1. Fry bacon or brown sausage or ham in a non-stick skillet. Remove and keep warm.
2. Break eggs into a mixing bowl. Stir in seasonings. Beat with a fork; then pour into hot skillet.
3. Lay meat on top of eggs. Lay cheese on top of meat.
4. Fold one-third of egg/meat/cheese mixture into the center of the pan. Fold the opposite side over into the center of the pan to form a "blanket." Roll or flip the whole "blanket" over and cook until done.

Omelet Roll

Anita Troyer, Fairview, MI

Makes 6 servings

Prep Time: 15–20 minutes
Cooking/Baking Time: 20 minutes

---

6 eggs
1 cup milk
½ cup flour
1 cup shredded cheddar
   cheese
1 cup browned sausage

Optional **filling ingredients:**
   sliced mushrooms
   sliced onions
   cubed cooked ham
   crispy bacon pieces

1. Blend eggs, milk, and flour in a blender until frothy. Pour into a *well greased* 9 × 13 baking pan. Bake at 450° approximately 20 minutes until fully cooked in the center.
2. As soon as you remove pan from oven, gently turn the pan upside down on a baking sheet. The eggs should drop onto the baking sheet in one piece.
3. Sprinkle cheese and sausage onto eggs. Add any optional filling ingredients that you wish. Starting at the narrow end of the omelet, roll it up jelly-roll fashion.
4. You can serve the eggs immediately, or refrigerate and reheat when you are ready to serve the omelet.
5. Slice and serve with salt and pepper, prepared mustard, and/or salsa, if you wish.

Baked Eggs

Carolyn Lehman Henry
Clinton, NY

Makes 6 servings

Prep. Time: 20–30 minutes
*Cooking/Baking Time: 30–45
   minutes*

½ lb. bacon
12 eggs
1 cup cheddar cheese,
   shredded
1 can cream of chicken
   soup

1. Saute bacon in a large skillet unto crisp.
2. Meanwhile, break eggs into a large mixing bowl and beat just until mixed.
3. Remove cooked bacon and place on paper towels to drain. Reserve 2 Tbsp. drippings in skillet, and drain off the rest.
4. Pour eggs into skillet and scramble just until cooked in reserved bacon drippings.
5. While eggs are cooking, place shredded cheese and soup in mixing bowl. Stir until blended.
6. When eggs are lightly cooked, add to cheese-soup mixture in bowl. Fold together gently. Crumble in bacon.
7. Spoon into a greased 7 × 11 baking dish. Bake at 350° for 30–45 minutes.

Shirred Eggs on Spinach

Scarlett von Bernuth
Canon City, CO

Makes 5–6 servings

Prep Time: 15 minutes
Cooking/Baking Time: 20 minutes

1 lb. fresh spinach,
   chopped fine
1½ cups dry bread crumbs,
   divided
½ tsp. salt
dash of pepper
6 eggs
¼ cup grated cheese of
   your choice

1. Wash spinach. Shake off water and place spinach in a large saucepan. Cover and wilt over medium heat for 1–2 minutes.
2. Remove from heat and stir in 1 cup bread crumbs, salt, and pepper.
3. Spoon spinach mixture into a flat, shallow, greased baking dish.
4. Break eggs into a bowl, being careful not to break the eggs. Pour over spinach mixture.
5. Cover with the remaining ½ cup bread crumbs. Sprinkle the cheese over all.
6. Bake at 375° for 15 minutes, or until the eggs are well set and the bread crumbs are browned.

Eggs Florentine

Mary Ann Wasick
West Allis, WI

Makes 2 servings

Prep. Time: 10 minutes
Cooking/Baking Time: 5–7 minutes

1 Tbsp. butter
2 cups fresh spinach,
   torn, with heavy stems
   removed
3 large eggs
½ cup milk
sliced cheese of your
   choice

1. Melt butter in a nonstick skillet.
2. Maintaining a low heat, add spinach and cover for 2–3 minutes. Stir once or twice.
3. Meanwhile, whisk eggs and milk together in a small bowl.
4. Pour over spinach in skillet.
5. Cook over low heat until eggs are almost set. Then add slices of cheese to cover eggs.
6. Turn off heat, and cover skillet for a minute, or until cheese melts into eggs.
7. Serve, offering salt, pepper, and cubed fresh tomatoes, if you wish.

Mexican Egg Casserole

Jan McDowell
New Holland, PA

Makes 3–4 servings

Prep Time: 10 minutes
Cooking Time: 45 minutes
Standing Time: 20 minutes

1 small can chopped green
   chilies, drained
¼ cup chopped onion
1 cup your choice of
   shredded cheese
1 cup Monterey Jack
   cheese, shredded
4 eggs, beaten frothy

1. Spray an 8 × 8 baking dish with non-stick cooking spray.
2. Spread chilies and onion in bottom of dish.
3. Cover with cheeses.
4. Pour eggs over top.
5. Bake for 45 minutes at 325°.
6. Let stand 20 minutes before cutting into squares.

Mexican Omelet

Irma H. Schoen
Windsor, CT

Makes 1 serving

Prep. Time: 3 minutes
Cooking/Baking Time: 2–3 minutes

2 large eggs
2 Tbsp. water
1 Tbsp. butter
¼ cup salsa, room temperature

1. Beat eggs with a fork in a small mixing bowl.
2. Stir in water.
3. Heat butter in a non-stick (or regular) frying pan.
4. Add eggs and cook to desired doneness.
5. Drain salsa a bit to remove some of the liquid. Then spoon over one-half of the egg.
6. Fold egg over salsa and slide onto dinner plate.

Santa Fe Quiche

Jeanne Allen
Rye, CO

Makes 6 servings

Prep. Time: 15 minutes
Cooking/Baking Time: 45 minutes
Standing Time: 10 minutes

9" prepared* pie shell
3 cups grated Mexican cheese
4 eggs
½ cup milk
4-oz. can chopped green chilies, drained

1. *With the sharp tines of a fork, prick the pie shell bottom and sides. Bake in a 400 degree oven for 10–12 minutes until it begins to brown. Check halfway through the baking time to see if the crust is bubbling. If it is, prick the bubbles and continue baking. This pre-baking helps keep the bottom crust from getting soggy.
2. Remove pre-baked shell from oven. Spread the cheese over the bottom.
3. In a medium-sized mixing bowl, beat the eggs and milk together.
4. Stir the chilies into the egg and milk mixture.
5. Pour into the pie shell and bake at 400° for 45 minutes.
6. Allow to stand for 10 minutes before cutting.

Tip from Tester: *Add 1 cup or so of diced fresh tomato to Step 4.*

Bacon & Cheese Crustless Quiche

Deb Herr
Mountaintop, PA

Makes 6–8 servings

Prep Time: 15 minutes
Cooking/Baking Time: 40–45 minutes
Standing Time: 10 minutes

8 slices bacon, cut into squares
½ lb. cheddar, *or* Monterey Jack, cheese, cut into strips
2 Tbsp. flour
4 large eggs
1½ cups milk

1. Place bacon squares in skillet and fry until crisp. Remove from drippings and place on paper towels to drain.
2. Meanwhile, in a medium-sized mixing bowl, toss cheese with flour.
3. In another large mixing bowl, beat eggs slightly. Add milk, bacon, and floured cheese. Mix well.
4. Spray a 9" pie pan with non-stick cooking spray. Pour egg mixture into pan.
5. Place filled pan in the middle of the oven. Bake at 350° for 40–45 minutes, or until a toothpick inserted in center comes out clean.
6. Cool 10 minutes before cutting into wedges and serving.

Breakfast Pizza with Eggs

Judy Ann Govotsos
Frederick, MD
Norma Grieser, Clarksville, MI

Makes 8–12 servings

Prep Time: 30 minutes
Cooking/Baking Time: 25–30
minutes
Standing Time: 5 minutes

1 lb. bulk sausage
1 large onion, chopped,
  optional
8 eggs
salt and pepper to taste
¾–1 lb. cheddar cheese
2 tubes refrigerated
  crescent rolls

1. Brown sausage in a saucepan. Drain off drippings.
2. Unroll crescent rolls and roll out to cover greased cookie sheet, pinching up edge of dough to form edge of crust.
3. Sprinkle sausage, and onion if you wish, over crust.
4. In a large mixing bowl, beat eggs. Stir in salt and pepper. Pour over crust in cookie sheet.
5. Sprinkle with cheese.
6. Bake at 325° for 25–30 minutes.
7. Allow to stand for 5 minutes. Then cut into wedges and serve.

Tip: You can make this ahead of time and then freeze it until needed. Before serving, defrost and reheat in the oven for 10–15 minutes at 350°.

Tip from Tester: Add 1 Tbsp. chopped fresh basil or thyme to the eggs and seasonings in Step 4. Or if you don't have fresh herbs, use 1 tsp. dried basil or thyme.

Breakfast Pizza with Mushrooms

Dennie Hagner
Montague, MI

Makes 8–10 servings

Prep Time: 10 minutes
Cooking Time: 30 minutes
Standing Time: 5 minutes

8-oz. tube refrigerated
  crescent rolls
1 lb. bulk sausage
4-oz. can mushrooms,
  drained
1 cup shredded mozzarella
  cheese
1 cup shredded cheddar
  cheese

1. Separate crescent roll dough into eight triangles. Place on pizza pan with points toward center. Press over bottom and up sides to form crust. (If your pizza pan is bigger than the crust, pinch up the outside edge of dough to hold the ingredients within the crust.)
2. Bake at 350° for 10 minutes.
3. Meanwhile, brown sausage in skillet. Drain sausage of drippings. Spoon over crust.

4. Sprinkle mushrooms and cheeses over sausage.
5. Bake at 350° for 15 minutes, or until cheese melts.
6. Allow to stand for 5 minutes. Then cut into wedges and serve.

Tips from Tester:
1. This is a generous amount of meat. You could cut it back to ½ or ¾ lb.
2. You could fit the crust into a 10" pie pan instead of using a pizza pan.

Sausage Cheese Biscuits

Mary Lynn Miller, Reinholds, PA

Makes 10 servings

Prep Time: 20 minutes
Cooking/Baking Time: 10–15
minutes

10-oz. tube refrigerated
  buttermilk biscuits
8-oz. pkg. brown and serve
  sausage links
2 eggs
½ cup shredded cheddar
  cheese
3 Tbsp. chopped green
  onions

1. Roll out each biscuit into a 5" circle. Place each in an ungreased muffin cup.
2. Cut sausages into fourths. Brown in a skillet. Drain off drippings.
3. Divide sausages among biscuit-lined cups.

4. In a small bowl, combine eggs, cheese, and onions. Spoon 1 Tbsp into each cup.

5. Bake at 400° for 10–15 minutes, or until browned.

Maple Toast and Eggs
Lori Newswanger
Lancaster, PA

Makes 12 servings

Prep Time: 15–20 minutes
Cooking/Baking Time: 18–20 minutes

12 bacon strips, diced
½ cup maple syrup
half a stick (¼ cup) butter
12 slices firm-textured white *or* whole wheat bread
12 eggs

1. Cook bacon until crisp. Remove from skillet and drain on paper towels.

2. In the microwave, or in a small saucepan, heat syrup and butter until butter is melted. Set aside.

3. Trim crusts from bread if you wish. Flatten slices with a rolling pin. Brush one side generously with warm butter-syrup mixture.

4. Press each slice into an ungreased muffin cup with syrup side down.

5. Divide bacon among muffin cups. Break one egg into each cup. Cover with foil.

6. Bake at 400° for 18–20 minutes, or until eggs are done to your preference. Serve immediately.

Stuffin' Egg Muffin
Judi Robb
Manhattan, KS

Makes 6 servings

Prep Time: 15–20 minutes
Cooking Time: 20–25 minutes
Standing Time: 5 minutes

6-oz. pkg. stuffing mix for chicken
12 eggs
3 Tbsp. real bacon bits
½ cup shredded Colby and Monterey Jack cheese, mixed

1. Preheat oven to 400°.

2. Prepare stuffing mix as directed on package, omitting standing time.

3. Spray 12 muffin cups with cooking spray.

4. Press ¼ cup stuffing firmly onto bottom and up sides of muffin cups. Form a ¼" rim of stuffing around top of each cup.

5. Crack 1 egg into each stuffing cup. Sprinkle with bacon bits and cheese.

6. Bake 12–18 minutes, or until yolks are set.

7. Let stand 5 minutes before serving.

Baked Pancakes
Shelia Heil
Lancaster, PA

Makes 5–6 servings

Prep Time: 5 minutes
Cooking Time: 15 minutes

your favorite packaged pancake mix for 10–12 pancakes
water, according to instructions on box
butter, *optional*
maple syrup, *optional*

1. In a good-sized mixing bowl, stir water into your favorite packaged pancake mix. Make enough batter for 10–12 pancakes.

2. Pour mixture into greased 9 × 13 baking pan. Bake at 400° for 15 minutes, or until cake is golden brown.

3. Cut into 10 or 12 squares and serve with butter and maple syrup if you wish.

Tip: *This is a great recipe when you don't have time to stand at the stove and make piles of pancakes. They taste just as delicious, but allow you time to do whatever else you need to do.*

Fluffy "Homemade" from the Box Pancakes

Valerie Drobel
Carlisle, PA

Makes 4 servings

Prep. Time: 5 minutes
Cooking/Baking Time: 4–6 minutes

2 cups buttermilk baking mix
2 eggs
1½ cups milk
1 cup ricotta cheese
1 Tbsp. lemon juice

1. Combine all ingredients in a large mixing bowl. Mix until smooth.
2. Lightly oil surface of griddle and heat to approximately 350°. Or warm your skillet.
3. Pour batter onto griddle or into skillet in 5" circles. Cook until bubbly (about 2–3 minutes).
4. Flip, and cook 2 minutes more.

Tip from Tester: Add ¾ cup fresh blueberries to Step 1, if you wish.

Potato Pancakes (with flour)

Doris M. Zipp
Germantown, NY
Clara Yoder Byler
Hartville, OH

Makes 3–4 servings

Prep Time: 10–15 minutes
Cooking/Baking Time: 10–15 minutes

1 egg
1 small onion, peeled and cut in chunks
2 Tbsp. flour
3 cubed raw potatoes, peeled *or* unpeeled
3 Tbsp. olive *or* vegetable oil

1. Blend egg, onion, and flour in mini-food processor until onion is chopped.
2. Place mixture in mixing bowl and stir in potatoes.
3. In a skillet, heat oil until very hot. Drop scant ⅓ cupfuls of potato mix several inches apart. Gently flatten each into a 4" circle.
4. Fry until dark golden brown, turning once. Drain on paper towels and keep warm in a 200 degree oven while frying the remainder.
5. Butter, sour cream, or applesauce make good toppings.

Tip from Tester: For toppings, substitute plain yogurt for the sour cream, or use sour cream with chives.

Potato Pancakes (with pancake mix)

Jan Carroll
Sugar Grove, IL

Makes 6 servings

Prep Time: 9–10 minutes
Cooking/Baking Time: 6–10 minutes

olive, *or* vegetable, oil
3 cups shredded raw potatoes, peeled *or* unpeeled
½ cup chopped onion
½ cup pancake mix
2 Tbsp. water
½ tsp. salt

1. Heat olive or other vegetable oil in pan. The oil should cover the bottom of the skillet ⅛" deep.
2. Mix all remaining ingredients together. Drop by ¼-cup measures into hot oil. Flatten little cakes with the back of a spoon. Fry 2–3 minutes or until golden brown. Flip over to brown other side.
3. Drain pancakes on paper towels.

Tips:
1. You can use thawed hash browns in place of fresh potatoes.
2. Not only are these great for breakfast, you can also use them as a side dish with roast beef or baked or grilled ham.

Crepes

Norma Grieser
Clarksville, MI

Makes 4–6 servings

Prep Time: 5 minutes
Cooking/Baking Time: 15 minutes

3 eggs
½ cup milk
¼ cup flour
pinch of salt
2 Tbsp. butter, melted,
    plus some for greasing
    skillet

1. Mix all ingredients together in a mixing bowl with a wire whisk.
2. Grease skillet with butter. Heat over medium high heat.
3. Put 2½ Tbsp. (or just a bit over half of a ¼ cup measure) of mixture in hot skillet. Immediately pick up skillet and let batter roll around bottom of pan to form a thin layer in skillet. Cook until lightly browned.
4. Flip and cook other side. You may need to use your fingers to flip the crepes.
5. Remove from skillet when lightly browned. Spread with maple syrup or your favorite jam. Roll up and enjoy.

Tip from Tester: *Top the rolled-up crepes with sliced fresh peaches, sprinkled with confectioners sugar!*

Banana Fritters

Naomi Cunningham
Arlington, KS

Makes 1 serving

Prep. Time: 10 minutes
Cooking/Baking Time: 10 minutes

1 large ripe banana,
    mashed
3 Tbsp. flour
1 Tbsp. sugar
1 egg, beaten
½ tsp. baking powder

1. Combine mashed banana, flour, and sugar in a small bowl, mixing until smooth.
2. Add beaten egg and baking powder. Stir until smooth.
3. Spray skillet with cooking spray. Heat until hot.
4. Drop about 1–2 Tbsp. batter into skillet. Heat until browned on one side.
5. Flip and continue heating until browned.
6. Cool completely. Roll in sugar and serve.
7. You can multiply the ingredients to serve more! Cook in batches in skillet.

Old-Timey French Toast

Jennifer Kellogg
Whately, MA

Makes 4–6 servings

Prep Time: 5 minutes
Cooking Time: 5–8 minutes

1 cup milk
2 whole eggs
¼ cup sugar
1 tsp. grated nutmeg,
    divided
16-oz. loaf of sliced bread,
    white *or* wheat

1. In a large mixing bowl, whisk together the milk, eggs, sugar, and half of the nutmeg.
2. Spray bottom of skillet with cooking spray.
3. Dip individual slices of bread into milk mixture and place in hot skillet. Cook until golden brown.
4. Sprinkle each slice with remaining nutmeg. Flip over to brown the other side.
5. Serve immediately.

Note: *This has been a favorite of mine since I was a child. My French-Canadian grandmother used to make this French toast as a special treat.*

Oven French Toast

Rhoda Nissley
Parkesburg, PA

Makes 6–8 servings

Prep Time: 10 minutes
Cooking Time: 15 minutes

1 cup orange juice
6 beaten eggs
¼ tsp. ground cardamom, *optional*
1 stick (½ cup) butter
12 slices sturdy white bread
½–1 cup maple syrup, warmed

1. In a shallow bowl, combine orange juice and eggs. Blend well.
3. Add cardamom if you wish.
4. Divide butter between 2 10 × 15 jelly roll pans.
5. Turn oven to 450°. Place pans in oven to melt butter. Remove from oven when butter is melted.
6. One by one, dip bread slices in egg mixture to coat both sides. Place 6 slices on each pan.
7. Bake at 450° for 5 minutes. Turn each slice over and bake 5 more minutes.
8. Drizzle with syrup before serving.

French Toast Casserole

Stacy Stoltzfus, Grantham, PA
Kaye Taylor, Florissant, MO

Makes 12 servings

Prep. Time: 10–15 minutes
Chilling Time: overnight
Cooking/Baking Time: 45 minutes

10 slices bread, cubed
2 8-oz. pkgs. cream cheese
12 eggs, beaten well
2 cups milk
½ cup pancake syrup
cinnamon, *optional*

1. Place half of bread cubes in a greased 9 × 13 pan.
2. Cube the cream cheese and scatter on top of bread.
3. Put the rest of the bread cubes on top.
4. In a large bowl, beat eggs, milk, and pancake syrup with an electric mixer. Pour over top of bread and cream cheese.
5. Sprinkle top with cinnamon, if you wish.
6. Refrigerate overnight. In the morning, bake at 375° for 45 minutes. Cut into squares or dish out with a spoon.
7. Serve hot with syrup. (Fruit syrups are especially good.)

Tip: We love this with fruit scattered with the cream cheese cubes: berries, diced, apples, peaches, etc.

Breakfast Bread Pudding

Jean H. Robinson
Cinnaminson, NJ

Makes 6–8 servings

Prep Time: 10 minutes
Standing Time: 30 minutes– 8 hours
Cooking/Baking Time: 1 hour

½ loaf French bread, cut into 16 slices 1" thick
6 large eggs
2½ cups milk, *or* half and half
½ cup honey
2 Tbsp. orange zest
maple syrup, *optional*

1. Spray a 9 × 12 baking pan with non-stick cooking spray.
2. Lay bread slices flat in the baking pan.
3. In a large mixing bowl, beat together eggs, milk, honey, and orange zest. Pour over bread slices and allow bread to absorb liquid for 20 minutes, or overnight if that's more convenient for you. (Cover the bread and refrigerate it if it will be standing overnight.)
4. Bake for 60 minutes at 350°.
5. Allow to stand for 10 minutes before serving. Serve with maple syrup as a topping, if you wish.

Scrapple
Sara Kinsinger
Stuarts Draft, VA

Makes 8 servings

Prep Time: 15 minutes
Cooking/Baking Time: 30 minutes
Chilling Time: 4–8 hours

1½ cup yellow cornmeal
3 cups water, *divided*
1 lb. ground pork sausage
½ tsp. salt
10¾-oz. can chicken broth
butter

1. Blend together cornmeal and 1 cup water.
2. In a large saucepan, combine pork sausage with salt and chicken broth. Gradually add 2 more cups water being careful to separate sausage into fine pieces. Bring to a boil.
3. Slowly add cornmeal to the mixture, stirring constantly with a wire whisk. Reduce heat and simmer uncovered 15 minutes. Turn into a 9 × 5 × 3 pan. Refrigerate covered.
4. To serve, cut into slices ¼" thick. Saute in hot buttered skillet until golden brown. Serve with pancake syrup or fried cornmeal mush.

Old-Fashioned Cornmeal Mush
Sara Kinsinger
Stuarts Draft, VA
Jolene Schrock
Millersburg, OH

Makes 15–18 servings

Prep Time: 15 minutes
Cooking/Baking Time: 35–45 minutes
Chilling Time: 4–8 hours

2 cups cornmeal
2–3 tsp. salt
2 cups cold water
6 cups boiling water

1. In a large mixing bowl, combine cornmeal, salt, and cold water.
2. When well mixed, stir in boiling water.
3. Pour mixture into a large heavy saucepan. Bring to a boil, stirring it well and frequently until it boils.
4. After mixture is boiling, cover the pan. Turn heat lower, but so that the mush simmers for 45 minutes.
5. Pour cooked cornmeal mush into a loaf pan. Chill until set.
6. Cut into ½" slices. Fry in butter or vegetable shortening until crispy around the edges. When browned on one side, turn to brown the other side.
7. Serve hot with honey or syrup.

Variation: For a heartier breakfast (or lunch or supper), serve with sausage gravy as a topping.
—**Jolene Schrock**
Millersburg, OH

Tip from Tester: For crispier fried mush, make the slices thinner in Step 6.

Grits Au Gratin
Patricia Howard, Green Valley, AZ
Lizzie Ann Yoder, Hartville, OH
Janie Steele, Moore, OK

Makes 6 servings

Prep Time: 20–25 minutes
Cooking/Baking Time: 60 minutes

½ cup raw grits, *or* 2 cups cooked grits
1 stick (½ cup) butter
2 eggs, beaten
milk
8 ozs. cheddar cheese, grated, *divided*

1. Cook grits according to package directions.
2. Cut butter into bite-size pieces. Grate cheese. Reserve ½ cup grated cheese for topping.
3. Mix butter pieces and remaining cheese into hot grits.
4. Beat eggs in a 1-cup measure. Fill remaining space in cup with milk. Mix egg-milk mixture into grits.
5. Spoon into a buttered 1½-quart casserole. Bake uncovered for 45 minutes at 350°. Top with reserved cheese and bake 15 minutes longer.

Peanut Butter Granola

Mary Kathryn Yoder
Harrisonville, MO

Makes 9–12 servings

Prep. Time: 10–15 minutes
Cooking/Baking Time: 20 minutes

---

1 cup crunchy peanut butter
6 Tbsp. oil
1½ cups brown sugar
7½ cups dry quick oats

1. In a microwave-safe bowl, mix the peanut butter and oil together. Microwave on High for 45 seconds. Stir. Continue heating for 30-second intervals, followed by stirring, until mixture melts but doesn't scorch. Or heat in a saucepan over low heat, stirring frequently until peanut butter melts into oil.

2. Stir in the brown sugar. Mix well.

3. In a large mixing bowl, pour over the oats and stir together thoroughly.

4. Pour granola into a greased shallow pan. Bake at 300° for 15–20 minutes, stirring after 10 minutes.

Peanut Butter Granola Surprise

Julette Rush
Harrisonburg, VA

Makes 9 servings

Prep Time: 20 minutes
Cooking Time: 25 minutes

---

1 stick (½ cup) butter
½ cup apple juice concentrate, thawed
1 cup peanut butter
¾ cup brown sugar
6 cups dry oats, quick *or* rolled

1. Melt butter, apple juice concentrate, peanut butter, and brown sugar in a saucepan over low heat. Stir occasionally to keep it from sticking or scorching. Or put the ingredients in a microwave-safe bowl. Microwave on High for 45 seconds. Stir. Continue cooking for 30-second intervals, stirring in between, until mixture melts together.

2. Put oats in large, greased roast pan or baking dish and pour mix over. Stir together well.

3. Bake at 350° for 25 minutes, stirring occasionally.

Tip from Tester: Stir ½ cup raisins and ½ cup sunflower seeds into the baked granola.

Blueberry Breakfast Sauce

Doyle Rounds
Bridgewater, VA

Makes 1¾ cups

Prep Time: 5 minutes
Cooking/Baking Time: 7 minutes

½ cup sugar
1 Tbsp. cornstarch
⅓ cup water
2 cups fresh *or* frozen blueberries

1. In a 2-quart saucepan, combine sugar and cornstarch. Gradually stir in water. Add blueberries.

2. Bring to a boil over medium heat, stirring constantly. Boil for 1 minute, stirring occasionally.

3. Serve warm or cold over pancakes, French toast, or waffles. Or allow to cool and serve over ice cream.

Strawberry Breakfast Syrup

Stacy Stolzfus
Grantham, PA

Makes 2 cups

Prep. Time: 5 minutes
Cooking/Baking Time: 20–25 minutes

2 cups frozen strawberries in juice, thawed
¼ cup maple syrup, more or less to your taste
orange zest from one orange

1. Put everything into a saucepan and stir well. Bring to a boil and reduce heat to a simmer. Keep pan uncovered while cooking.
2. Cook until the liquid is reduced to a syrupy-consistency, about 20 minutes.
3. Serve hot over French toast, pancakes, or waffles.

Tip: You can change the fruit and flavoring of this recipe to whatever you prefer: blueberries with lemon zest, peaches with cinnamon, red raspberries with lemon, etc.

Breakfast Smoothie

Jeanette B. Oberholtzer
Manheim, PA

Makes 5 servings

Prep Time: 5 minutes
Cooking Time: 5 minutes

1 banana, sliced
1–1½ cups cut-up fruit, fresh *or* frozen
½–1 cup vanilla yogurt
orange juice
more cut-up fresh fruit for garnish

1. Put banana, fruit, and yogurt in blender.
2. Add enough orange juice to reach 4½-cup line in a 5-cup blender.
3. Blend on high until smooth.
4. Garnish with fruit and/or fresh mint. Serve immediately.

Tips:
1. If you use unsweetened fruit, you may want to add a little honey or sugar to Step 1.
2. If you use frozen fruit, the smoothie will have more of a milk-shake consistency.

Breakfast Fruit

Mary B. Sensenig
New Holland, PA

Makes 6 servings

Prep. Time: 2–3 minutes

1 cup sliced strawberries
1 cup blueberries
1 cup sliced banana
½ cup pineapple tidbits
½ pint strawberry yogurt

1. In a medium-sized mixing bowl, mix fruit together gently.
2. Put in serving bowl. Top with yogurt.

Tip: Fresh, frozen, or canned fruit works well in this dish.

A Tip —

Buy fruits and vegetables when they are in season. They will be cheaper, and their quality will be greater than those that are out of season and have been shipped long distances.

Old-Fashioned Crumb Cake

Mary Jane Musser
Manheim, PA
Sharon L. Anders
Alburtis, PA

Makes 12 servings

Prep Time: 5–10 minutes
Baking Time: 35–40 minutes

3 cups flour
2 cups sugar
½ cup shortening
1 tsp. baking soda
1 cup milk

1. In a large mixing bowl, mix flour and sugar together.
2. Cut shortening into flour-sugar mixture with a pastry cutter until crumbly.
3. Reserve 1 cup crumbs for topping. Set aside.
4. In a small bowl, dissolve baking soda in milk. Stir into dry mixture until thoroughly mixed.
5. Put batter in two greased 8" pans. Top with reserved crumbs.
6. Bake at 350° for 35 minutes, or until tester inserted in center of pans comes out clean.

Variation: *Use 1½ cups brown sugar instead of 2 cups sugar.*
— **Sharon L. Anders**
Alburtis, PA

Tip from the Tester: *To add flavor, add ½ tsp. cinnamon to Step 1.*

Brunch Cake

Lauren Eberhard
Seneca, IL

Makes 12 servings

Prep. Time: 15 minutes
Cooking/Baking Time: 35–45 minutes

2 eggs
1 Tbsp. oil
18¼-oz. box yellow cake mix
21-oz. can apple pie filling
¼ cup sugar / 2 Tbsp. cinnamon mix

1. In a large bowl beat the eggs and oil until frothy.
2. Stir in dry cake mix.
3. When well blended, stir in pie filling. Mix until everything is moistened.
4. Put batter in a lightly greased 9 × 13 baking pan.
5. Sprinkle cinnamon sugar over top.
6. Bake at 350° for 35–45 minutes, or until a toothpick inserted in the center comes out clean.
7. Serve warm. Add a dollop of vanilla whipped topping to each serving, if you wish.

Tip from the Tester: *For added flavor use cherry pie filling instead of apple pie filling.*

Cinnamon Flop

Grace Mumaw
Harrisonburg, VA

Makes 6 servings

Prep. Time: 10 minutes
Cooking/Baking Time: 15–20 minutes

1 cup sugar
3 Tbsp. butter, softened, and *divided*
1 cup milk
2 tsp. baking powder
1¾ cup flour, plus additional for dusting

1. Cream sugar and 1 Tbsp. butter together, stirring vigorously.
2. In a small bowl, mix milk and baking powder together. Then stir into sugar/butter mixture.
3. Blend in flour.
4. Spoon dough into a lightly greased 8 × 8 baking pan.
5. Dust top of batter with flour. Then sprinkle brown sugar (about ¼ cup) and cinnamon (about ¼ tsp.) over top. Dot with little cubes of remaining butter. (The butter will sink into cake and make yummy caves.)
6. Bake at 375° for 15–20 minutes, or until toothpick inserted in center comes out clean.

Breakfast Buns

Arlene Snyder
Millerstown, PA
Jean M. Butzer
Batavia, NY
Mary Ann Bowman
East Earl, PA

Makes 12 servings

Prep Time: 15–30 minutes
Standing Time: 8 hours or
* overnight*
Cooking/Baking Time: 30–35
* minutes*

3.5-oz. pkg. dry
** butterscotch cook-and-**
** serve pudding mix**
¾ cup brown sugar
1 stick (½ cup) melted
** butter**
½–¾ cup broken nuts of
** your choice**, *optional*
frozen dough for 18–24
** dinner rolls, walnut-size**

1. In a medium-sized bowl, mix dry butterscotch pudding mix and brown sugar together.
2. Place melted butter in another bowl.
3. Put nuts in bottom of bundt cake pan, or one-piece angel-food cake pan.
4. Roll frozen dinner rolls, one at a time, in melted butter, and then in brown sugar mixture.
5. Stack coated rolls evenly in prepared cake pan.
6. Sprinkle with remaining sugar and pudding mix. Pour remaining butter on top. Let stand overnight at room temperature.

7. In the morning, bake at 350° for 30–35 minutes. Then invert onto serving tray.

An alternative preparation method:

1. Stack frozen rolls in a greased bundt pan. Sprinkle with dry pudding mix.
2. In a small mixing bowl, combine melted butter and brown sugar. Stir in 1 tsp. cinnamon. Pour over rolls.
3. Cover tightly with greased foil. Let rise on countertop over night.
4. Uncover in the morning and continue with Step 7 above.

—**Jean M. Butzer**
Batavia, NY

Tip: You can assemble these ahead and freeze them in the baking pan. Get them out of the freezer the evening before you want to serve them for breakfast. In the morning, proceed with Step 7.

Tip from Tester: Use grated coconut instead of broken nuts.

Cinnamon Bubble Bread

Erma Martin, East Earl, PA
Arleta Petersheim, Haven, KS
Lori Lehman, Ephrata, PA

Makes 12 servings

Prep Time: 20 minutes
Cooking Time: 30 minutes

4 7½-oz. tubes refrigerated
** biscuits**

1 cup sugar
2 tsp. cinnamon
1 Tbsp. vanilla, *optional*
½–1 cup granulated *or*
** brown sugar, according**
** to your taste preference**
2 sticks (1 cup) butter

1. Quarter biscuits.
2. In a small bowl, mix 1 cup sugar and cinnamon together. Roll each biscuit piece in mixture.
3. Drop pieces into a greased 9 × 13 cake pan, or into a 10" bundt or tube pan.
4. Sprinkle any remaining sugar-cinnamon mixture over biscuit pieces in pan.
5. Melt butter and ½ cup sugar (or more), and vanilla if you wish, together. Pour over biscuits.
6. Bake at 350° for 30–40 minutes, or until baked through and lightly browned.
7. When done, turn 9 × 13 pan upside down on a baking sheet, or a bundt pan upside down onto a serving plate. Serve warm with coffee or tea!

Variation: Add ½ cup chopped nuts to Step 5, if you wish.

—**Lori Lehman**
Ephrata, PA

Easy Doughnuts

Monica Yoder, Millersburg, OH

Makes 8 servings

Prep Time: 10 minutes
Cooking/Baking Time: 6 minutes

¾ cup vegetable oil, *divided*
tube of 8 large refrigerated
   biscuits
½ cup sugar
¼ tsp. ground cinnamon

1. Heat ½ cup of the oil in
a medium-sized skillet over
medium-low heat.
2. Use a 1" round cookie
cutter to cut a hole in the
center of each biscuit; reserve
the extra dough for "holes."
3. Test the heat of the
oil by dipping the edge of
a doughnut in the pan. The
edge will bubble if the oil is
hot enough.
4. Place 4 doughnuts and
holes in skillet and cook
until golden brown, about
1–1½ minutes on each side.
Transfer to a wire rack or
paper-towel lined plate to
drain.
5. Add remaining oil to the
skillet and cook remaining
doughnuts and holes.
6. In a large bowl, combine
sugar and cinnamon. Gently
toss the warm doughnuts
in the mixture, a few at a
time. Serve warm or at room
temperature.

*Tip: You can also toss the
doughnuts in confectioners sugar.*

Apple Cinnamon Pan Biscuits

Gretchen Maust
Keezletown, VA

Makes 20 servings

Prep Time: 10 minutes
Cooking Time: 15–20 minutes

3½ cups self-rising flour
½ tsp. cinnamon
⅔ cup shortening
1 large grated apple
1¼ cups milk

1. Measure flour and cin-
namon into mixing bowl and
stir together. Cut in shortening with a pastry cutter until
thoroughly mixed.
2. Grate apple and stir
gently into mixture.
3. Add milk and mix
lightly. Too much stirring will
cause biscuits to be tough.
4. Pat dough into a greased
jelly-roll pan. Bake at 400°
just until lightly browned.
5. Add Topping if you
wish. Cut into squares and
serve warm.

Optional **Topping:**
When biscuits finish
baking, drizzle with a glaze
made by mixing 2 Tbsp.
melted butter, 3 Tbsp. milk,
1½ cups confectioners
sugar, and ½ tsp. cinnamon
together. Or sprinkle with
confectioners sugar.

Jam Pockets

Jennifer Archer
Kalona, IA

Makes 4 servings

Prep Time: 15 minutes
*Cooking/Baking Time: 18–20
   minutes*

8-count tube refrigerated
   crescent rolls
flour for work surface
4 Tbsp. cream cheese
4 Tbsp. fruit jam, flavor of
   your choice

1. Carefully unroll the rolls
on lightly floured surface.
Divide along dots to form 4
equal rectangles.
2. Gently pinch and
smooth dough to eliminate
the diagonal dotted lines.
3. Place one tablespoon
cream cheese and one
tablespoon jam in center of
each rectangle. Bring corners
to the center and pinch
together to seal.
4. Transfer to baking sheet
and bake at 400° for 18–20
minutes.

*Tip from Tester: Double
the pleasure by placing 1
tablespoon of cream cheese
and 1 tablespoon of jam on
each single triangle (rather
than on each rectangle, formed
by 2 triangles). Or place 2
tablespoons of cream cheese
and 2 tablespoons of jam on
each rectangle.*

Breads

No Knead Bread

Alica Denlinger
Lancaster, PA

Makes 4 loaves

Prep Time: 4–5 hours
Baking Time: 35 minutes

1 cup sugar
4 tsp. salt
4½ cups lukewarm water
5 Tbsp. oil
3 Tbsp. yeast
scant 12 cups flour

1. In a very large mixing bowl, stir together sugar and salt.
2. Add water, oil, and yeast. Mix well.
3. Gradually add flour. Batter will be thick, but too sticky to knead.
4. Cover with a tea towel and set in a warm place. Let rise 1½ hours.
5. Punch down. Cover with a tea towel, set in a warm place, and let rise again.

6. Lightly grease 4 loaf pans. Cut dough into 4 equal pieces. Shape into 4 loaves. Place each into a loaf pan. Cover each with a tea towel, set in a warm place, and let rise until double.
7. Bake at 325–350° for 35 minutes.
8. Rub crust with butter if you wish, when finished baking.

A Tip —

To test for the right water temperature when making bread, run the water over your upturned wrist. If it's not too hot and not too cold, you've got the right "lukewarm" water temperature for dissolving yeast.

Fast and Easy Pizza Crust

Rosalie D. Miller,
Mifflintown, PA

Makes 5 servings

Prep Time: 15 minutes
Cooking/Baking Time: 15 minutes

1 Tbsp. yeast
1 cup warm water
1 tsp. sugar
1 tsp. salt
2 Tbsp. vegetable oil
2½ cups flour

1. Preheat oven to 425°.
2. In a large mixing bowl, stir yeast and warm water together until yeast dissolves.
3. Stir in rest of ingredients. Add more flour if still sticky.
4. Let rest 5-10 minutes.
5. Lightly flour pizza pan. Then roll out dough on pizza pan.
6. Top with your favorite pizza ingredients. Bake for 15 minutes.

Herbed Beer Bread

Joan Brown, Warriors Mark, PA

Makes 1 loaf

Prep Time: 5 minutes
Cooking/Baking Time: 65 minutes

3 cups self-rising flour
3 Tbsp. sugar
1 Tbsp. Italian herbs
½ cup Parmesan cheese, grated
12-oz. can of beer at room temperature
cornmeal, *optional*

1. In a large mixing bowl, combine dry ingredients. Mix well to combine.
2. Stir in beer.
3. Turn batter into greased bread pan. Sprinkle with cornmeal if you wish.
4. Bake at 325° for 65 minutes.
5. Brush top with softened butter if desired. Turn out to cool on rack.

A Tip —

Roll out homemade pizza dough on a surface dusted with cornmeal. It improves the texture, workability and taste.

Cheddar Garlic Biscuits

Mary Jane Hoober
Shipshewana, IN
Jolene Schrock
Millersburg, OH
Darla Sathre, Baxter, MN
Ruth Shank, Monroe, GA
Elaine Patton
West Middletown, PA
Joyce L. Moser
Copenhagen, NY
Shari Ladd, Hudson, MI
Amber Swarey, Honea Path, SC
Denae Villines, Whitewater, KS
Marsha Sabus, Fallbrook, CA

Makes 12 servings

Prep. Time: 5–10 minutes
Cooking/Baking Time: 8–10 minutes

2 cups buttermilk baking mix
⅔ cup milk
½–1 cup cheddar cheese, shredded, according to how much you like cheese
2 Tbsp. melted butter
⅛–¼ tsp. garlic powder, according to your taste preference
1 Tbsp. parsley flakes, *optional*

1. Heat oven to 450°.
2. In a medium-sized mixing bowl, mix the buttermilk baking mix, milk, and shredded cheddar to form a soft dough.
3. Drop by spoonfuls onto ungreased cookie sheet.
4. Bake 8–10 minutes.

5. Mix butter, garlic powder, and parsley flakes if you wish, in a small bowl. Brush over warm biscuits.

Tip from Tester: There are always variations that could be added or exchanged with the ingredients listed above: bacon bits added for breakfast muffins; minced onion, finely chopped garlic cloves, crisp-cooked carrot bits, and/or cooked chopped ham for any time!

Seasoned Biscuits

Elaine Patton
West Middletown, PA

Makes 10–15 servings

Prep Time: 15 minutes
Cooking/Baking Time: 14–16 minutes

5⅓ Tbsp. (⅓ cup) butter, melted
1–2 tsp. dried minced onion
1 tsp. poppy seeds
½–1 tsp. dried minced garlic
2 12-oz. tubes refrigerated buttermilk biscuits

1. In a bowl combine butter, onion, poppy seeds, and garlic.
2. Separate each tube of biscuits into 10 biscuits. Dip each biscuit in butter mixture. Stand up on end in a lightly greased 10" fluted tube pan or bundt pan. Stack them as needed.

3. Bake at 400° for 14–16 minutes, or until golden brown.

4. Immediately invert onto a serving plate. Serve warm.

Mini Sour Cream Biscuits

Kendra Dreps
Liberty, PA

Makes 12 servings

Prep Time: 5 minutes
Cooking/Baking Time: 13–15 minutes

1 cup buttermilk baking mix
½ cup sour cream
half a stick (¼ cup) butter, melted

1. Combine all ingredients in a medium-sized mixing bowl.

2. Drop by rounded tablespoonfuls into miniature muffin pan cups.

3. Bake at 425° for 13–15 minutes, or until golden brown.

Tip from Tester: *These are good topped with sausage gravy or served with chili.*

Herb Biscuits

Sharon Timpe
Jackson, WI

Makes 7 2½" biscuits

Prep Time: 10 minutes
Cooking/Baking Time: 14–15 minutes

2 cups self-rising flour*
½ tsp. dried oregano, crushed
½ tsp. dried basil, crushed
5⅓ Tbsp. (⅓ cup) butter, plus 2 Tbsp. butter, at room temperature
¾ cup buttermilk

1. Preheat oven to 450°.

2. Combine flour, oregano, and basil in a medium-sized mixing bowl.

3. Cut ⅓ cup butter into flour mixture with pastry blender until crumbly.

4. Add buttermilk, stirring just until moistened.

5. Turn dough onto a lightly floured surface and knead 3 or 4 times.

6. Place 2 Tbsp. butter in a 10" cast-iron skillet. Place skillet in the oven for 5 minutes to melt butter.

7. Meanwhile, pat or roll dough out until ½" thick. Cut out biscuits with a 2½" round biscuit cutter. (Gather the scraps together and re-roll if needed.)

8. Remove skillet from oven and place dough rounds in skillet.

9. Bake for 14–15 minutes, until lightly brown.

Tips from Tester:
*1. * If you don't have self-rising flour, substitute the following for each cup of flour:*
⅞ cup regular flour
1½ tsp. baking powder
½ tsp. salt
2. These biscuits are light and fluffy, but with crusty bottoms! Delicious!

French-Onion Drop Biscuits

Vicki J. Hill
Memphis, TN

Makes about 16 biscuits

Prep Time: 5 minutes
Cooking/Baking Time: 10–15 minutes

2 cups buttermilk baking mix
8-oz. carton French onion dip
¼ cup milk

1. Combine baking mix and onion dip in a medium-sized mixing bowl.

2. Stir in milk just until moistened.

3. Drop by rounded tablespoonfuls onto greased baking sheet. Keep the biscuits about an inch apart.

4. Bake at 450° for 10–14 minutes, or until golden. Serve warm.

Tip: *This recipe also works well with other flavored dips.*

Maple Biscuits

Jean M. Butzer
Batavia, NY

Makes 10 servings

Prep Time: 10 minutes
Cooking/Baking Time: 15–20 minutes

½ cup maple syrup
2 Tbsp. butter
8-oz. tube refrigerated buttermilk biscuits
2 Tbsp. orange juice
½ cup finely chopped nuts

1. Pour syrup into an ungreased 8 × 8 baking pan. Top with pieces of butter.
2. Place pan in a 400° oven until butter melts. Remove from oven and stir to blend.
3. Separate biscuit dough into individual biscuits.
4. Place orange juice in a small bowl. Place nuts in another small bowl.
5. Dip each biscuit in orange juice. Then roll each in nuts.
6. Lay coated biscuits in pan over syrup and butter mixture.
7. Bake at 400° for 15–20 minutes.

Tip from Tester: *If you don't have maple syrup, substitute 3 Tbsp. brown sugar and 2 Tbsp. corn syrup, mixed together well.*

Herbed Pull-Apart Bread

Maryann Markano
Wilmington, DE

Makes 8 servings

Prep Time: 10 minutes
Cooking/Baking Time: 15–20 minutes

1 tube refrigerated breadstick dough
2 Tbsp. butter, melted
¼ tsp. dried basil
¼ tsp. dried thyme
¼ tsp. dried oregano

1. Preheat oven to 350°.
2. Remove dough from can and slice into 8 rounds. Do not unroll the twists.
3. Place rounds on an ungreased baking sheet, slightly overlapping dough. Arrange in 2 rows of 4.
4. Combine the other ingredients in a small bowl. Mix well.
5. Brush herb butter over tops of rolls, using all the mixture.
6. Bake for 15–20 minutes, or until golden brown.

A Tip —

To preserve garlic longer separate garlic cloves from the bud. Place in plastic containers and freeze. Take out what you need when you need it.

Parmesan Pull-Apart Bread

Jennifer Archer
Kalona, IA

Makes 4 servings

Prep Time: 15 minutes
Cooking/Baking Time: 25–30 minutes

5⅓ Tbsp. (⅓ cup) butter, melted
4 ozs. freshly grated Parmesan cheese
2 tsp. Italian seasoning
2 cloves minced garlic
11-oz. pkg. refrigerator dinner rolls, *or* bread dough

1. Combine butter, cheese, seasoning, and garlic in a small mixing bowl.
2. Separate rolls and cut into pieces.
3. Dip pieces into butter mixture. Arrange coated pieces in a greased 8 × 8 baking pan.
4. Bake at 375° for 25–30 minutes.

Cheesy Garlic Bread

Erma Martin, East Earl, PA
Janet Oberholtzer, Ephrata, PA
Diane Eby, Holtwood, PA
Laura R. Showalter, Dayton, VA
Betty Moore, Plano, IL

Makes 12 servings

Prep. Time: 5–10 minutes
Cooking/Baking Time: 3–5 minutes

1-lb. loaf French *or* Italian bread
1 stick (½ cup) butter, softened
4 garlic cloves, minced, *or* ½ tsp. garlic powder
¼ tsp. dried oregano
3–4 Tbsp. grated Parmesan cheese

1. Cut French bread in half lengthwise.
2. In a small bowl, combine butter, garlic, and oregano.
3. Spread on cut sides of bread. Sprinkle with Parmesan cheese.
4. Place bread halves on baking sheet. Broil 3 minutes, or until golden brown. (Watch closely to prevent burning.)
5. Slice and serve hot.

Variations:
1. Instead of, or in addition to, the oregano, add 1 tsp. dried parsley to Step 2.
—**Diane Eby**, Holtwood, PA

2. Instead of, or in addition to, the oregano, use ¾ tsp. Italian seasoning
—**Laura R. Showalter**
Dayton, VA

3. Instead of broiling the bread, put the cut sides of the bread halves together. Wrap them in aluminum foil. Grill for about 5 minutes, or warm in the oven, preheated at 400°, for 5 minutes.
—**Betty Moore**, Plano, IL

Cheddar Garlic Bread

Natalia Showalter
Mt. Solon, VA
Kristine Martin
Newmanstown, PA

Makes 10–12 servings

Prep. Time: 15 minutes
Cooking/Baking Time: 3–5 minutes

2 cups shredded cheddar cheese
¾ cup mayonnaise
2 Tbsp. minced garlic
2 Tbsp. butter, melted
⅛ cup chopped fresh chives, *optional*
⅛ cup chopped fresh parsley, *optional*
paprika to taste, *optional*
French bread, sliced ½" thick

1. Combine all topping ingredients in a medium-sized mixing bowl.
2. Spread on bread slices. Place on baking sheet.
3. Broil 3–5 minutes, or until golden. (Watch carefully; it can burn quickly!)

Tip from Tester: You can make the topping a day or two ahead of when you want to serve the bread.

Rosemary Romano Bread

Doyle Rounds
Bridgewater, VA

Makes 14–16 servings

Prep Time: 5 minutes
Optional Standing Time: 2–3 hours
Cooking/Baking Time: 15 minutes

1 stick (½ cup) butter, softened
½ cup grated Romano cheese
1 garlic clove, minced
1 tsp. minced fresh rosemary
1-lb. loaf French bread, halved lengthwise

1. In a mixing bowl, stir together the softened butter, cheese, garlic, and rosemary. Allow to stand for 2–3 hours to allow flavors to blend, if you have time.
2. Spread topping over cut sides of bread.
3. Place halves with cut side up on an ungreased baking sheet.
4. Bake at 400° for 15 minutes, or until lightly browned. (Check frequently to be sure the bread isn't getting too dark.)
5. Slice and serve warm.

Garlic Cheese Crescents

Janie Steele
Moore, OK

Makes 8 servings

Prep Time: 10–15 minutes
Cooking/Baking Time: 11 minutes

1 refrigerated pkg. 8
  crescent rolls
¼ cup semi-soft cheese
  with garlic and herbs
2 Tbsp. chopped walnuts
small amount of milk
1 Tbsp. seasoned dry
  bread crumbs

1. Unroll crescent rolls.
Separate into triangles.
2. Mix cheese and walnuts
together in a small mixing
bowl.
3. Place a rounded tea-
spoon of cheese mixture on
wide end of each triangle and
roll up.
4. Place crescents point-
side down on lightly greased
baking sheet.
5. Brush lightly with milk.
Sprinkle with bread crumbs.
6. Bake at 375° for 11
minutes.

Festive Party Bread

Jan Mast
Lancaster, PA
Darla Sathre
Baxter, MN

Makes 6–8 servings

Prep. Time: 15 minutes
Cooking/Baking Time: 25 minutes

1-lb. unsliced loaf
  sourdough bread
1 lb. Monterey jack cheese,
  sliced
1 stick (½ cup) butter,
  melted
½ cup chopped green
  onions
2–3 tsp. poppy seeds

1. Cut bread in grid
pattern, making slices about
every inch, without slicing
completely through the
bottom.
2. Insert cheese between
cuts.
3. In a medium-sized
mixing bowl, combine butter,
onions, and poppy seeds.
Spoon over bread/cheese.
4. Wrap bread in foil.
5. Place on a baking pan.
Bake at 350° for 15 minutes.
6. Uncover. Bake an
additional 10 minutes, or
until cheese melts.

Popovers

Barbara Sparks
Glen Burnie, MD

Makes 12 popovers

Prep. Time: 10 minutes
Cooking/Baking Time: 30 minutes

1 cup sifted flour
2 eggs, beaten
1 cup milk
¼ tsp. salt
1 medium onion, diced,
  optional

1. Combine all ingredients
in a large mixing bowl.
2. Beat at high speed with
a mixer for 3 minutes.
3. Grease 12 muffin tins.
Pour batter into tins, making
each half-full.
4. Bake at 450° for 15
minutes. Then reduce heat
to 350° and bake 15 more
minutes. Do not open oven
door while popovers are
baking, or they will fall.

Tortillas

Christine Weaver
Reinholds, PA

Makes 8–12 servings

Prep Time: 10 minutes
Standing Time: 10 minutes
Cooking/Baking Time:
10 minutes for each tortilla

4 cups flour
2 tsp. salt
2 tsp. baking powder
4 Tbsp. shortening
1½ cups warm water
oil

1. Combine dry ingredients in a large mixing bowl.
2. Cut in shortening with a pastry cutter.
3. Add water until the dough forms a ball.
4. Place dough on a lightly floured surface. Knead 15–20 times. Let rest 10 minutes.
5. Form dough into 12 balls.
6. Roll each ball on flour- or cornmeal-covered board until a bit thinner than pie crust.
7. Fry each tortilla in 2 Tbsp. oil in hot skillet, 5 minutes per side.

Tips:
1. I usually double the recipe and freeze the tortillas that remain.
2. To save time, I use 2 skillets on the stove, rolling out the next tortillas while the pans are cooking.

Kentucky Corn Bread

Colleen Heatwole
Burton, MI

Makes 8–12 servings

Prep Time: 15 minutes
Cooking/Baking Time: 12–18 minutes
Standing Time: 10 minutes

1 cup self-rising flour
1 cup self-rising white corn-bread mix
1½ cups milk
¾ cup buttermilk
¼ cup lukewarm water

1. Preheat oven to 450°.
2. Combine all ingredients in order given in a large mixing bowl.
3. The corn bread is best baked in a 9" or 10" cast-iron skillet, sprayed with non-stick cooking spray, for 12–18 minutes, or until toothpick inserted in center comes out clean.
   It can also be baked in an 8 × 8 baking pan. If the pan is glass, reduce temperature to 425°.
4. Allow to cool for 10 minutes. Then cut into squares and serve warm.

I like to personalize my recipes. In my file, this is "Mattie Ruth's Kentucky Corn Bread." It brings back memories of the many, many good meals she fixed in Kentucky—and still does!

Mattie Ruth prefers the Martha White brand of self-rising flour and cornmeal mix, but I have used other brands with good success. (The recipe tester discovered that Jiffy Corn Muffin mix works well.)

Mattie Ruth, of Turners Creek, Kentucky, still makes this corn bread almost daily. And she takes it to many potlucks!

—Colleen Heatwole
Burton, MI

A Tip —

Substitute whole wheat flour for some of the white flour in bread, rolls, cookies and cakes.

Easy Muffin Surprise

Carolyn A. Baer
Conrath, WI

Makes 12–18 muffins

Prep Time: 10 minutes
Cooking/Baking Time: 15–20 minutes
Standing Time: 10 minutes

18¼-oz. box yellow cake mix
⅔ cup yellow cornmeal
3 eggs
1½ cups jam *or* jelly, any flavor
½ cup warm (tepid) water

1. In a large mixing bowl, combine cake mix and cornmeal. Stir well.
2. In a separate smaller bowl, combine all remaining ingredients well.
3. Gently fold wet ingredients into dry, mixing only until everything is moistened.
4. Grease and then flour 12 muffin tins. Spoon batter in, filling each ⅔ full. If you have batter left over, prepare up to 6 more muffin tins and fill each ⅔ full.
5. Bake in 375 degree oven for 15–20 minutes, or until tester inserted in center of muffins comes out clean. Allow to cool for 10 minutes in tins before removing muffins.

Pecan Muffins

Melissa Sensenig
Newmanstown, PA
Rhoda Atzeff
Lancaster, PA
Rhonda Freed
Croghan, NY

Makes 12 full-size muffins, or 30 mini-muffins

Prep Time: 10 minutes
Cooking/Baking Time: 15–20 minutes

1 cup brown sugar
½ cup flour
1 cup chopped pecans *or* walnuts
10⅔ Tbsp. (⅔ cup) melted butter
2 eggs, beaten

1. Combine first 3 ingredients in a large mixing bowl.
2. In a separate smaller bowl, combine butter and eggs.
3. Stir wet mixture into flour mixture just until moistened.
4. Grease muffin tins. Spoon in batter, filling each tin about ⅔ full.
5. Bake at 350° for 15–20 minutes. Lift out of pans immediately.

Tip: These freeze well and do not take long to thaw.

Flip-Flopped Nut Rolls

Jeannine Janzen
Elbing, KS

Makes 6 rolls

Prep. Time: 5 minutes
Cooking/Baking Time: 20–25 minutes
Standing Time: 10 minutes

½ cup chocolate syrup
2 Tbsp. butter, melted
½ cup chopped pecans
11-oz. can refrigerated breadsticks

1. Preheat oven to 350°.
2. In a 9" round cake pan, combine syrup and butter.
3. Sprinkle nuts over mixture.
4. Separate, but do not uncoil, breadsticks. Arrange dough coils over nuts.
5. Bake for 20–25 minutes, or until golden brown.
6. Remove from oven and immediately flip pan upside down on serving plate.
7. Let stand 10 minutes. Remove pan and serve.

> **A Tip —**
>
> Use a portion of non-fat yogurt in cake mixes instead of all the oil that's called for.

Lemon Parfait Loaf
Dorcas Alpirez
Willards, MD

Makes 2 loaves

Prep Time: 10 minutes
Cooking/Baking Time: 40 minutes

18¼-oz. box white, *or* yellow, cake mix
1 small box instant lemon pudding
½ cup vegetable oil
1 cup lukewarm water
4 eggs

1. In a large mixing bowl, mix all ingredients together.
2. Pour into 2 lightly greased 5 × 9 loaf pans.
3. Bake at 350° for 40 minutes, or until tester inserted in centers of loaves comes out clean.

Rhubarb Jelly
Evelyn Page, Gillette, WY
Lavina Hochstedler
Granc Blanc, MI
Sharon Timpe, Jackson, WI
Sherry Kauffman, Minot, ND

Makes 8 cups

Prep. Time: 5–12 minutes
Cooking/Baking Time: 10–15 minutes

5–7 cups rhubarb, chopped fine
3½–4½ cups sugar, according to your taste preference
21-oz. can pie filling
2 .3-oz. pkgs. raspberry gelatin

1. In a large saucepan, combine rhubarb and sugar. Cook together, stirring constantly until rhubarb is tender.
2. Stir in pie filling.
3. Remove pan from heat. Stir in gelatin and mix until dissolved.
4. Place in 1-cup jars and seal according to directions on jar-lid package. Or place in freezer containers and freeze.

Variation: I add 2 Tbsp. lemon juice to Step 3.

—**Sharon Timpe**, Jackson, WI

Rhubarb Jam
Rhonda Freed
Croghan, NY

Makes 4 cups

Prep. Time: 15 minutes
Cooking/Baking Time: 10 minutes
Standing Time: 8 hours or overnight

---

5 cups rhubarb, cut fine
4 cups sugar
.3-oz. pkg. strawberry gelatin

1. Mix rhubarb and sugar together in a mixing bowl. Cover and let stand in the refrigerator overnight.
2. Next day, in a medium-sized saucepan, boil for 5 minutes, stirring constantly.
3. Immediately, mix in gelatin until dissolved.
4. Boil an additional 3 minutes. Let cool a bit. Then pour into freezer containers.
5. Freeze until ready to use.

Rhubarb Cherry Jam

Naomi Ressler
Harrisonburg, VA
Jean Gray
Beatrice, NE

Makes 4 pints

Prep Time: 25–30 minutes
Standing Time: 8 hours or overnight
Cooking/Baking Time: 20–25 minutes

6 cups chopped rhubarb
4 cups sugar
21-oz. can cherry *or* blueberry pie filling
6-oz. cherry, black cherry, *or* raspberry gelatin

1. Mix sugar and rhubarb in a mixing bowl. Cover and allow to stand overnight.
2. Boil sugar and rhubarb in a medium-sized saucepan for 15 minutes or more, until rhubarb is tender. Stir constantly
3. Stir in pie filling and gelatin. Bring to a boil.
4. Place in jars and seal, following directions on canning-lid package. Or allow to cool, spoon into freezer containers, cover, and freeze.

Variation: You can skip the overnight standing step by cooking the rhubarb in 1 cup water until tender. Then stir in sugar and cook 3–5 more minutes, stirring constantly. Then proceed with Step 3.

—**Jean Gray**, Beatrice, NE

Peach Apricot Jam

Mary Jane Musser
Manheim, PA

Makes 9 cups

Prep Time: 10 minutes
Cooking Time: 30 minutes

4 cups peaches, peeled
20-oz. can pineapple (crushed, chunks, *or* sliced), undrained
6 cups sugar
.6-oz. pkg. apricot gelatin

1. Put half the peaches and half the pineapple together in blender. Process until smooth.
2. Pour into large saucepan.
3. Repeat with remaining peaches and pineapple.
4. Stir sugar into fruit mixture. Bring to boil. Simmer 15 minutes.
5. Remove from heat and add gelatin, stirring to dissolve.
6. Put in freezer containers. Cool, cover, and then freeze.

Honey Butter

Janelle Reitz
Lancaster, PA

Makes ½ cup

Prep Time: 5 minutes
Chilling Time: 1 hour

1 stick (½ cup) butter, softened
2 Tbsp. honey
1 tsp. cinnamon

1. Cream butter with a mixer.
2. Add remaining ingredients and mix until well blended.
3. Chill for at least 1 hour to set.

Tip: Bring to room temperature before serving.

Soups, Stews, and Chilis

Chicken Noodle Soup

Colleen Heatwole
Burton, MI

Makes 8 servings

Prep Time: 15 minutes
Cooking Time: 45–50 minutes

2½ quarts chicken stock
½ cup diced celery
½ cup diced carrots
8-oz. pkg. egg noodles
2 cups cooked, diced
   chicken

1. Bring stock to boil in a medium-sized stockpot.
2. Add celery and carrots. Simmer for about 7 minutes, or until vegetables are tender but not overcooked.
3. Add noodles and chicken. Return soup to boil. Continue to cook another 5–7 minutes, or until noodles are tender but not mushy.
4. Taste for salt, and add only if needed.

Tip: I like to use my own home-made chicken stock, but there are other acceptable substitute soup bases. Experiment until you find one you like. Canned chicken stock works. I do find that when I use stock made only from bouillon, it is very salty and lacks flavor.

This recipe came from Evelyn Ford, one of the best cooks at our church. She was the cook demonstrator at our "Apples of Gold" meetings, where we older women taught cooking skills to the younger women at church.

Chicken Spinach Soup

Carna Reitz, Remington, VA

Makes 4–6 servings

Prep. Time: 5 minutes
Cooking/Baking Time: 20 minutes

6½ cups chicken broth,
   divided
2 cups cooked chicken
1–2 cups frozen chopped
   spinach
salt and pepper to taste
½ cup flour

1. Put 6 cups broth, chicken, spinach, and salt and pepper in a large stock pot. Bring to a boil.
2. Meanwhile, mix flour and remaining ½ cup broth together in a jar. Put on lid and shake until smooth. When soup is boiling, slowly pour into soup to thicken, stirring constantly.
3. Continue stirring and cooking until soup thickens.

Potato-Cheese Soup

Mary Kathryn Yoder
Harrisonville, MO

Makes 5 servings

Prep Time: 20 minutes
Cooking Time: 20 minutes

4 medium-sized potatoes,
   peeled and cut into
   chunks
4 slices bacon
1 small onion, *optional*
4 cups milk
¾ tsp. salt
pepper to taste
¾ cup shredded cheese,
   your choice of flavors

1. Place potato chunks in a saucepan. Add 1" water. Cover and cook over low heat until very tender.
2. Meanwhile, cut bacon into 1" lengths. Place in a large saucepan, along with the onion if you wish. Cook until tender.
3. When potatoes become tender, mash in their cooking water.
4. Add mashed potatoes and milk to bacon, and onion if using.
5. Stir in salt, pepper, and cheese. Cook over low heat, stirring occasionally to distribute cheese as it melts.
6. Soup is ready when cheese is melted and soup is hot.

Tips:
1. When you mash the potatoes, you can let them be a little lumpy. That adds interesting texture to the soup.
2. You can use leftover mashed potatoes if you have them.

Creamy Broccoli Soup

SuAnne Burkholder
Millersburg, OH

Makes 3–4 servings

Prep. Time: 10–15 minutes
Cooking/Baking Time: 15–20 minutes

4 cups milk, *divided*
2 Tbsp. cornstarch
1½ cups cut-up broccoli
1 Tbsp. chicken-flavored
   soup base
salt to taste

1. Heat 3 cups milk and chicken base in a stockpot over low heat until hot.
2. Meanwhile, place cut-up broccoli in a microwave-safe dish. Add 1 Tbsp. water. Cover. Microwave on High for 1½ minutes. Stir. Repeat until broccoli becomes bright green and just-tender. Be careful not to overcook it! Drain broccoli of liquid.
3. In a small bowl, or in a jar with a tight-fitting lid, mix together 1 cup milk and cornstarch until smooth. Slowly add to hot milk mixture.
4. Simmer gently, stirring constantly. When slightly thickened, add broccoli and salt.

Quickie French Onion Soup

Mary Puskar, Forest Hill, MD

Makes 6–8 servings

Prep Time: 5–10 minutes
Cooking Time: 1 hour

half a stick (¼ cup) butter
3–4 good-sized onions
   (enough to make 5 cups
   sliced onions)
¼ cup flour
6 cups beef broth, *or* 3
   14½-oz. cans beef broth,
   or 6 cups water with 6
   beef bouillon cubes
6–8 melba rounds, *optional*
2 cups grated mozzarella
   cheese, *optional*

1. Melt butter in a large saucepan.
2. Meanwhile, slice onions.
3. Saute onions in butter. After they become tender, continue cooking over low heat so that they brown and deepen in flavor, up to 30 minutes.
4. Sprinkle with flour. Cook 2 minutes.
5. Stir in broth, or water and bouillon cubes. Cover.
6. Heat to boiling and simmer 20 minutes.
7. Ladle into individual serving bowls.
8. Top each with melba rounds and/or grated cheese if you wish. For extra beauty and flavor, broil until cheese melts, but first make sure that the soup bowls can withstand the broiler heat. They could crack.

Tip: This recipe doubles very easily.

Chunky Beef Chili

Ruth C. Hancock
Earlsboro, OK

Makes 4 servings

Prep Time: 30 minutes
Cooking Time: 1¾–2¼ hours

2 Tbsp. vegetable oil, *divided*
1 lb. beef stew, cut into 1½" thick pieces
1 medium onion, chopped
1 medium jalapeno pepper with seeds, minced, *optional*
½ tsp. salt
2 14½-oz. cans chili-seasoned diced tomatoes

1. Heat 1 Tbsp. oil in stockpot over medium heat until hot.
2. Brown half of meat in oil. Remove meat from pot and keep warm.
3. Repeat with remaining beef. Remove meat from pot and keep warm.
4. Add remaining 1 Tbsp. oil to stockpot, along with the onion, and the jalapeno pepper if you wish.
5. Cook 5–8 minutes, or until vegetables are tender. Stir occasionally.
6. Return meat and juices to stockpot. Add salt and tomatoes.
7. Bring to a boil. Reduce heat. Cover tightly and simmer 1¾–2¼ hours, or until meat is tender but not dried out.

Sausage Chili

Norma I. Gehman
Ephrata, PA

Makes 4–6 servings

Prep Time: 15 minutes
Cooking Time: 15 minutes

1 lb. loose sausage
¼ cup diced onion
2 Tbsp. flour
15½-oz. can chili beans in chili sauce
14½-oz. can diced tomatoes, undrained

1. Brown sausage in a large stockpot.
2. Add ¼ cup diced onion. Cook over medium heat until tender.
3. When onion is cooked, sprinkle 2 Tbsp. flour over mixture. Stir until flour is absorbed.
4. Add chili beans and diced tomatoes with juice. Mix well.
5. Simmer, covered, for 15 minutes.

Tips:
1. For more zip, use hot Italian sausage.
2. Crumble corn chips into the bottom of each serving bowl. Spoon chili over top of chips. Or crumble corn chips over top of each individual serving.

3. Grate your favorite cheese over top of each individual serving.
4. This recipe taste even better when warmed up a day later.

Quick and Easy Chili

Carolyn Spohn
Shawnee, KS

Makes 3–4 servings

Prep Time: 10 minutes
Cooking Time: 25 minutes

½ lb. ground beef, *or* turkey, browned and drained
1 medium-sized onion, chopped
2 cloves garlic, minced
2 15-oz. cans chili-style beans with liquid
8-oz. can tomato sauce

1. Brown ground beef in a large skillet.
2. Drain, leaving about 1 tsp. drippings in pan. Saute onions and garlic until softened.
3. Add beans, with liquid, and the tomato sauce. Bring to a slow boil.
4. Reduce heat to simmer and cook for 15 minutes.
5. Return meat to skillet. Heat together for 5 minutes.

Tip: Leftovers makes good chili dogs.

Ham and Bean Soup

Diane Eby
Holtwood, PA

Makes 6–8 servings

Prep Time: 5 minutes
Cooking Time: 15–20 minutes

1 qt. water
2 cups fully cooked ham, diced
40½-oz. can great northern beans
½ lb. Velveeta cheese, cubed

1. Place water and ham in a large stockpot. Cook for 5 minutes.
2. Add beans. Heat through.
3. Add cheese. Stir until cheese melts.

Speedy International Stew

Mabel Shirk
Mount Crawford, VA

Makes 4 servings

Prep Time: 5 minutes
Cooking Time: 5–10 minutes

2 14½-oz. cans stewed tomatoes (Italian, Mexican, *or* Cajun)
15-oz. can black beans, drained and rinsed
16-oz. can corn kernels, drained and rinsed

1. Place all ingredients in a medium saucepan.
2. Cover and cook over medium heat for 5–10 minutes, stirring occasionally.

Kielbasa Bean Soup

Sharon Swartz Lambert
Harrisonburg, VA

Makes 5–6 servings

Prep. Time: 20 minutes
Cooking/Baking Time: 30 minutes

3 cups water
1 medium-sized potato, peeled and diced
2 carrots, sliced
⅓ cup celery, chopped
8-oz. pkg. Kielbasa, thinly sliced
10-oz. can bean and bacon soup
¼ cup chopped onion, *optional*

1. In large saucepan, bring water to a boil.
2. Add potatoes, carrots, and celery.
3. Reduce to simmer. Cook 10 minutes, or until vegetables are soft.
4. Add kielbasa, can of soup, and onion, if you wish.
5. Simmer 10 additional minutes, or until heated through.

Hash Brown Soup

Gloria Julien
Gladstone, MI

Makes 6–8 servings

Prep Time: 10 minutes
Cooking Time: 20–30 minutes

½ lb. bacon, diced
1 large onion, chopped
48-oz. container chicken
broth
2 lbs. frozen hash browns
1 lb. Velveeta cheese,
cubed

1. Place bacon and onion in a 6-quart stockpot. Cook until tender.
2. Add chicken broth and frozen hash browns. Heat through.
3. Add Velveeta. Stir until cheese melts, but do not boil.

A Tip —

Brown the onion and bacon in the stockpot that you'll be cooking the soup in.

Italian Pasta Soup

Sharon Timpe
Jackson, WI

Makes 6 servings

Prep Time: 10–15 minutes
Cooking Time: 30 minutes

2 14.5-oz. cans chicken
broth
1 cup water
1 cup uncooked elbow
macaroni
18 frozen Italian-style, *or*
regular, meatballs
2 cups fresh spinach
leaves, finely shredded
8-oz. can pizza sauce

1. In a large stockpot, bring broth and water to a boil.
2. Add pasta and meatballs and return to a boil. Lower heat and continue cooking 8 to 10 minutes, or until pasta is done and meatballs are hot. Stir occasionally. Do not drain.
3. Add spinach and pizza sauce. Simmer 2 minutes, or until heated thoroughly.

Escarole, Pasta, and Garlic Soup

Doris M. Zipp
Germantown, NY

Makes 4–6 servings

Prep Time: 10 minutes
Cooking Time: 15–20 minutes

4 Tbsp. olive oil
6 cloves fresh garlic, peeled
and chopped
1 cup dry ditalini
1 large head escarole,
washed and chopped
salt and pepper to taste

1. Place oil and garlic in a medium-sized stockpot. Cook until garlic is light brown.
2. Meanwhile, cook ditalini in another stockpot according to package directions.
3. Add escarole to pot with garlic, and add enough water to cover vegetables. Cook just until escarole is tender.
4. Stir in cooked and drained pasta just before serving.

Tip: Serve topped with grated Romano cheese. Crusty Italian bread makes a good accompaniment.

Tip from the Tester: For a heartier soup, add ½ lb. cooked and chopped sausage or kielbasa to Step 4, if you wish.

Tortellini Soup

Becky Frey
Lebanon, PA

Makes 8–10 servings

Prep Time: 15 minutes
Cooking Time: 20-25 minutes

1, *or more*, garlic clove(s), crushed
crushed red pepper flakes to taste, *optional*
2 15-oz. cans Italian-style stewed, *or* diced, tomatoes, undrained
4 14½-oz. cans chicken broth
16-oz. pkg. frozen cheese tortellini
salt and pepper, *optional*
10-oz. pkg. frozen chopped spinach, *or* 1 lb. chopped fresh spinach

1. Saute garlic and red pepper in nonstick stockpot for a minute or two.
2. Add tomatoes and broth. Cook until tomatoes are soft enough to mash with a potato masher. Mash slightly.
3. Add tortellini, seasonings if you wish, and frozen spinach (if you're using fresh spinach, don't add it yet). Cook until tortellini is tender but not mushy.
4. If you're using fresh spinach, stir it in now. Allow to steam for 2 minutes before serving.

Tip from Tester: *Top each individual serving with grated Parmesan cheese.*

Meatball Tortellini Soup

Lucille Amos
Greensboro, NC

Makes 4 servings

Prep Time: 5 minutes
Cooking Time: 20–25 minutes

14-oz. can beef broth
12 frozen Italian meatballs
1 cup stewed tomatoes
11-oz. can Mexi-corn, drained
1 cup (20) frozen cheese tortellini

1. Bring broth to boil in a large stockpot
2. Add meatballs. Cover and reduce heat. Simmer 5 minutes.
3. Add tomatoes and corn. Cover and simmer 5 minutes more.
4. Add tortellini. Cover and simmer 5 more minutes, or until tortellini is tender.

Oyster Stew

Clara Yoder Byler
Hartville, OH

Makes 8–10 servings

Prep. Time: 15 minutes
Cooking/Baking Time: 30 minutes

2 Tbsp. butter
1 qt. oysters with oyster liquor
1 qt. milk
2 cups cream
1½ tsp. salt
⅛–¼ tsp. pepper

1. Melt butter in large skillet or saucepan. Drain oysters (reserving liquor). One-by-one, place in butter.
2. Cook over medium heat until edges of oysters begin to curl. Remove immediately from heat.
3. Meanwhile, heat milk in a large stockpot to boiling point.
4. Add oyster liquor to hot milk and bring to boiling point.
5. Immediately, add oysters and seasonings.

Beef Main Dishes

Special Roast Beef

Arianne Hochstetler, Goshen, IN
Glenda Weaver, Manheim, PA
Phyllis Wykes, Plano, IL

Makes 9–10 servings

Prep. Time: 10–15 minutes
Cooking/Baking Time: 3 hours

3- to 4-lb. beef roast
½–1 tsp. seasoned salt
1 envelope dry onion soup
   mix
6–8 cut-up potatoes,
   optional
6 carrots, cut into 1" chunks,
   optional
10¾-oz. can mushroom
   soup
half a soup can water

1. Place beef roast in a
deep roasting pan. Sprinkle
seasoned salt over the roast.
Shake onion soup mix over
top.
2. If you wish, place 6–8
potatoes, cut-up, peeled or not,
and carrots, around the meat.

3. In a small mixing bowl,
blend mushroom soup with
water. Pour around roast.
4. Cover tightly and bake
at 300° for 3 hours.

Variations:
*1. You can add flavor to this
dish by browning the beef roast
in 2 Tbsp. butter in a large
skillet before placing in the
roaster.*
*2. You can mix up to 3 cups
water with the mushroom soup
without diluting its flavor, and
then have more gravy to serve
with the meat and vegetables.*
— **Phyllis Wykes**, Plano, IL

*Tip from Tester: Add a few
slices of onion to the potatoes in
Step 2.*

> **A Tip —**
> Thick roasts continue
> to cook inside after being
> removed from the oven.
> Take that into account so
> you don't overcook your
> roast.

Coke Roast

Janelle Nolt,
Richland, PA

Makes 9–10 servings

Prep. Time: 5 minutes
*Cooking/Baking Time: 4–5
hours*

3- to 4-lb. beef roast
10¾-oz. can cream of
   mushroom soup
12-oz. can cola

1. Place beef roast in
roasting pan.
2. In a medium-sized
mixing bowl, blend soup
and cola together. Pour over
roast.
3. Bake at 300° for 4–5
hours.

Wonderfully Tender Round Steak

Dorothy VanDeest
Memphis, TN

Makes 6–8 servings

Prep. Time: 10 minutes
Cooking/Baking Time: 1½ hours

10¾-oz. can cream of
  mushroom soup
1 Tbsp. Worcestershire
  sauce
1 Tbsp. minced instant
  onion, *or* 2–3 Tbsp.
  chopped onion
3- to 4-lb. boneless round
  steak

1. Mix soup, Worcestershire sauce, and onion together in a small bowl.
2. Pour into large electric frying pan.
3. Place round steak on top of mixture.
4. Cover and cook on low for 45 minutes.
5. Turn meat over and cook on low for 45 minutes more.
6. Cut into serving-size pieces. Top with delicious gravy to serve.

A Tip —

Use a meat thermometer to determine if a meat is done. Avoid over- or under-cooking meat.

Bistro Steak with Mushrooms

Gaylene Harden, Arlington, IL

Makes 4–6 servings

Prep. Time: 10 minutes
Cooking/Baking Time: 20 minutes

¼ tsp. pepper, *optional*
1½- to 2-lb. boneless sirloin
  steak, about 1½" thick
2 Tbsp. oil, *divided*
2 cups sliced fresh
  mushrooms
10¾-oz. can golden
  mushroom soup
½ cup dry red wine *or* beef
  broth
3 Tbsp. Worcestershire
  sauce, *optional*
¼ cup water

1. If you wish, rub sides of steak with ¼ tsp. pepper.
2. Heat 1 Tbsp. oil over medium-high heat in nonstick skillet. Cook steak about 5 minutes per side for medium-rare, or more or less, depending upon how you like your steak. Transfer steak to platter and keep warm.
3. Stir-fry mushrooms in same skillet in 1 Tbsp. oil until browned.
4. Stir in soup, wine, Worcestershire sauce if you wish, and ¼ cup water. Bring to a boil. Simmer for 3 minutes. Stir occasionally.
5. Return steak and juices to skillet. Heat through.
6. The steak is great served with mashed potatoes—and it offers plenty of gravy.

Marinated Flank Steak

Flo Mast
Broadway, VA

Makes 4–6 servings

Prep. Time: 10–15 minutes
Marinating Time: 3 hours
Cooking/Baking Time: 12 minutes
Standing Time: 10 minutes

½ cup bottled teriyaki
  sauce
¼ cup soy sauce
4 cloves garlic, chopped
2 lbs. flank steak
¼ cup spicy brown
  mustard

1. In a shallow baking dish, combine the teriyaki sauce, soy sauce, and garlic.
2. Make ¼"-deep cuts about ½" apart on both sides of the steak, cutting diagonally across the grain.
3. Rub both sides with mustard. Place steak in marinade.
4. Cover and refrigerate for up to 3 hours, turning occasionally.
5. Preheat the broiler and line a shallow pan with foil. Broil for 6 minutes on each side for medium rare, basting once on each side with remaining marinade. Let rest before slicing across grain.

Tip from Tester: Broil 1–2 minutes longer on each side for a medium well-done steak.

Henry's Swiss Steak

Freda Imler, Eldon, MO

Makes 8 servings

Prep. Time: 30 minutes
Cooking/Baking Time: 2½–3 hours

½ cup seasoned flour,*
  divided
3-lb. round steak
2 onions
2 Tbsp. oil, *divided*
2 cups cooked tomatoes

1. Pound half the seasoned flour into both sides of the steak.
2. Cut steak into serving-size pieces.
3. Lightly brown 2 sliced onions in 1 Tbsp. oil in a heavy skillet. Remove onions.
4. Add remaining oil if needed and brown meat well on both sides.
5. Place sautéed onions on top of browned steak. Pour 2 cups cooked tomatoes around meat.
6. Cover. Cook slowly until very tender, 2½ to 3 hours.
7. With a wooden spoon, occasionally stir up browned drippings from bottom of skillet. Add small amount of water, if needed, to prevent the steak and vegetables from getting too dry.

* **Seasoned Flour:**
½ cup flour
1 tsp. salt
¼ tsp. pepper

1. Mix together in a small bowl.
2. Store in an airtight covered container and use as needed.
3. You can multiply the ingredients so you have a good supply on hand.

Betty's Beef Stroganoff

Donna Barnitz
Rio Rancho, NM

Makes 5 servings

Prep. Time: 20–30 minutes
Cooking/Baking Time: 1½–2 hours

2 Tbsp. butter
1 lb. round steak, cut in 1" chunks
1 envelope dry onion soup mix
⅔ cup water
3-oz. can sliced mushrooms, drained
1 cup sour cream

1. Melt butter in large skillet. Brown steak for a few minutes on each side.
2. Stir in dry onion soup mix, water, and mushrooms. Cook all ingredients at low heat until beef is tender, about 1½ hours.
3. Just before serving, stir in 1 cup sour cream. Allow to warm but not boil.
4. Serve over noodles.

Uncle Tim's Ground Beef Stroganoff

Timothy F. Smith
Wynnewood, PA

Makes 4 servings

Prep. Time: 30 minutes
Cooking/Baking Time: 10 minutes

10-oz. pkg. noodles
1 lb. ground sirloin
7-oz. can no-salt-added mushroom stems and pieces
10¼-oz. can beef gravy
8 ozs. non-fat sour cream
freshly crushed black peppercorns to taste, *optional*

1. Cook noodles according to package directions in a 4-qt., or larger, stockpot. Drain. Return noodles to stockpot.
2. Brown ground sirloin in a non-stick skillet. Drain. Add to stockpot with cooked noodles. Stir together gently.
3. Drain mushrooms. Add them and all other ingredients to the stockpot with the meat and noodles.
4. Bring to a slow simmer. Continue simmering for about 10 minutes, or until heated through, stirring constantly. Serve immediately.

Depression Meat Loaf

Moreen Weaver
Bath, NY

Makes 8 servings

Prep. Time: 15 minutes
Cooking/Baking Time: 1 hour

1 can evaporated milk
5 slices bread
¾ cup chopped onion
1½ tsp. salt
½ tsp. pepper
2 lbs. lean ground beef
⅓ cup ketchup, *optional*
3 strips bacon, *optional*

1. In a large bowl, pour milk over bread. Let stand until the milk is absorbed.
2. Add onion, salt, and pepper. Stir with a fork until bread softens and is light and fluffy.
3. Mix in ground beef. Shape meat mixture into a loaf. Place in a lightly greased baking loaf pan.
4. If you wish, spread top with ketchup. And if you wish, lay strips of bacon the length of the loaf. Or do one or the other.
5. Bake at 350° for 1 hour.

Memories-of-Italy Meat Loaf

Charmaine Caesar
Lancaster, PA

Makes 6–8 servings

Prep. Time: 15–20 minutes
Cooking/Baking Time: 1 hour

1½ lbs. ground beef
10¾-oz. can mushroom soup
1 egg, beaten
½ cup Italian bread crumbs
2–3 tsp. Italian seasoning

1. Mix all ingredients together well in a large mixing bowl.
2. Form into a loaf. Place in a baking loaf pan.
3. Bake at 350° for about an hour.

A Tip —

Keep a ziplock bag in the freezer to collect the unused ends of bread loaves. When the bag is full, whirl in food processor. Return to bag and freeze—you'll always have fresh bread crumbs at your fingertips.

Easy Pleasing Meat Loaf

Barb Shirk
Hawkins, WI

Makes 8 servings

Prep. Time: 10 minutes
Cooking/Baking Time: 1 hour

2 eggs, beaten
2 lbs. lean ground beef
6-oz. pkg. stuffing mix for chicken
1 cup water
½ cup barbecue sauce, *divided*

1. In a small bowl, beat eggs slightly with a fork.
2. Place beef, stuffing mix, water, beaten eggs, and ¼ cup barbecue sauce in a large bowl. Mix with a wooden spoon or your hands just until blended.
3. Shape meat into an oval loaf. Place in a 9 × 13 baking pan.
4. Top meat with remaining ¼ cup barbecue sauce.
5. Bake 1 hour, or until cooked through.

Marvelous Mini Meat Loaves

Krista Hershberger
Elverson, PA

Makes 6 servings

Prep. Time: 15 minutes
Cooking/Baking Time: 30 minutes

1 lb. extra-lean ground
   beef
6-oz. pkg. stuffing mix
1 cup water
1 tsp. Italian seasoning
¾ cup spaghetti sauce
¾ cup shredded
   mozzarella cheese

1. Mix meat, stuffing mix, water, and seasoning in a large mixing bowl until well blended.
2. Divide the mixture into 4 equal pieces. Then divide each of those pieces into 3 more pieces so that you have a total of 12. Roll each piece into a ball. Flatten and fit each into one of 12 muffin cups sprayed with cooking spray. Make an indentation in the center of each with a spoon.
3. Spoon spaghetti sauce into center of each mini meat loaf.
4. Bake at 375° for 20 minutes, or until meat loaves are cooked through.
5. Top each with cheese. Continue baking for 5 more minutes, or until cheese is melted.

Hamburgers with Mushroom Gravy

Carol L. Stroh
Akron, NY

Makes 6 servings

Prep. Time: 10 minutes
Cooking/Baking Time: 28 minutes

10¾-oz. can beefy
   mushroom soup, *divided*
1½ lbs. ground chuck
1 large egg, beaten
½ cup fine, dry bread
   crumbs
¼ cup finely chopped
   onion
¼ cup water

1. Combine ¼ cup soup, all of the ground chuck and the next 3 ingredients in a large mixing bowl, mixing well.
2. Divide meat mixture evenly into 6 portions. Shape each portion into a ½" thick patty.
3. Brown patties in a large non-stick skillet over medium heat, 3–4 minutes on each side, or until browned.
4. Combine remaining soup and water, stirring well. Pour over patties, cover, reduce to low heat, and simmer gently for 20 minutes, or until done.
5. Serve immediately over mashed potatoes, rice, or noodles.

Tip: If you wish, add ½ lb. sliced fresh mushrooms and/or 1 chopped onion to the skillet in Step 4.

Barbecue Beef Cups

Jennifer Archer
Kalona, VA

Makes 4–5 servings

Prep. Time: 15–20 minutes
*Cooking/Baking Time: 10–12
   minutes*

1 lb. ground beef *or* pork
½ cup barbecue sauce
1 tube of 8–10 refrigerator
   biscuits
¾ cup cheddar cheese,
   shredded

1. Brown meat and drain.
2. Add barbecue sauce and mix well.
3. Place an unbaked biscuit into each muffin cup, pressing to cover bottom and sides of cup. Spoon meat mixture into the biscuit cups.
4. Sprinkle with cheese.
5. Bake at 400° for 10–12 minutes.

BBQ Meatballs

Colleen Heatwole
Burton, MI

Makes 12–15 servings

Prep. Time: 30 minutes
Cooking/Baking Time: 20–25 minutes

3 lbs. ground beef *or* turkey
1 envelope dry onion soup mix
1 slightly beaten egg
8 ozs. saltine crackers, crushed
½ cup barbecue sauce of your choice, plus additional for topping, if you wish

1. Combine all ingredients thoroughly in a large mixing bowl.
2. Shape into meatballs about 1" in diameter.
3. Place meatballs on greased baking sheets, being careful that they don't touch each other.
4. Bake 20–25 minutes at 350°, or until meatballs are well browned.
5. Serve with additional barbecue sauce as a topping, if you wish.

Tip: I like to place the meatballs on baking racks set on the baking pans, so that any grease drips into the pans beneath.

Variation: Use 2 lbs. ground beef or turkey and 1 lb. bulk sausage.

Sweet and Sour Meatballs

Donna Lantgen
Golden, CO

Makes 4 servings

Prep. Time: 5 minutes
Cooking/Baking Time: 1 hour

1 cup brown sugar
16-oz. can crushed pineapple in juice
2 lbs. frozen meatballs

1. Place sugar and pineapples with juice in a mixing bowl and blend together.
2. Stir in meatballs and make sure they're well covered.
3. Spoon into a lightly greased 9 × 13 baking pan. Bake at 350° for 1 hour, or until meatballs brown and sauce is bubbly.

Taco Meatballs

Jeannine Janzen
Elbing, KS

Makes 6 servings

Prep. Time: 15–20 minutes
Cooking/Baking Time: 10–12 minutes

1 lb. hamburger
1 envelope dry taco seasoning
1 egg, slightly beaten

1-lb. block cheddar cheese, cut into small (¼" square, if you can) cubes

1. In a large mixing bowl, combine hamburger, taco seasoning, and egg.
2. Shape approximately 1 Tbsp. meat mixture around each cube of cheese. Place on a baking sheet with an edge, sprayed with non-stick cooking spray. Keep meatballs from touching each other.
3. Bake at 425° for 10–12 minutes, or until meat is browned.

Porcupine Balls

Carol L. Stroh, Akron, NY

Makes 4 servings

Prep. Time: 25–30 minutes
Cooking/Baking Time: 35–40 minutes

½ cup raw rice
½ lb. ground beef
1 tsp. salt
½ tsp. pepper
1 finely chopped onion
1 quart stewed tomatoes

1. Mix raw rice, ground beef, seasonings, and onion together in a large mixing bowl.
2. Shape into small meatballs, each no bigger than a walnut.
3. Spray skillet with non-stick cooking spray. Brown meatballs over medium heat until browned on all sides.

4. Place browned meatballs in a large stockpot. Stir in tomatoes. Cover and bring to a simmer.

5. Simmer slowly, covered, for 30 minutes, or until rice is tender and balls double in size.

Tips:

1. Keep the meatballs small. The tendency is to make them too large. They swell a lot during cooking.

2. Don't worry if the meatballs fall apart a bit. They still make a tasty Spanish rice.

Yummy Sauerkraut

Mary Jane Musser
Narvon, PA

Makes 6 servings

Prep. Time: 15 minutes
Cooking/Baking Time: 1 hour

1 lb. ground beef
31-oz. can sauerkraut
2 cups tomato juice
½ cup brown sugar

1. Brown ground beef lightly in a non-stick skillet. Place in a lightly greased 7 × 11 baking dish.

2. Cover with drained sauerkraut.

3. In a medium-sized bowl, blend tomato juice with brown sugar. Pour over all.

4. Bake at 350° for 45–60 minutes.

Cabbage-Hamburger Casserole

Esther J. Mast
Lancaster, PA
Vera Martin
East Earl, PA

Makes 8–10 servings

Prep. Time: 15–30 minutes
Cooking/Baking Time: 60–75 minutes

1 lb. ground beef *or* venison
1 cup chopped onion
6 cups cut up cabbage
⅓ cup uncooked long-grain rice, *or* ⅔ cup cooked rice
1 can tomato soup
⅓ soup can water

1. Brown ground beef and chopped onion in a skillet.

2. Meanwhile, put all of the cut-up cabbage in a greased casserole.

3. Sprinkle ⅓ cup raw rice over cabbage. Top with meat mixture.

4. In a small mixing bowl, dilute tomato soup with ⅓ soup can of water. Pour over meat mixture.

5. Cover and bake 1 hour at 350°. At the end of the hour, if you've used uncooked rice, test the rice to see if it's cooked. If it's not, cover and continue baking another 15 minutes, or until rice is tender.

Can't-Get-Easier Casserole

Patricia Andreas
Wausau, WI

Makes 4 servings

Prep. Time: 5–7 minutes
Cooking/Baking Time: 10–15 minutes

1 lb. ground beef
1 small onion, diced
1 can tomato soup
1 can corn, *or* your favorite canned vegetable, drained
8-oz. pkg. your favorite dry pasta
shredded cheese, *optional*

1. In a large skillet, brown ground beef and diced onions. Drain off drippings if necessary.

2. Add tomato soup and drained corn to browned meat.

3. Meanwhile, cook pasta in a saucepan according to package directions until al dente (firm but not hard). Drain.

4. Add pasta to meat mixture. Stir gently and add cheese if you wish.

Tip from tester: Add ½ cup salsa (whatever strength you prefer) and 2 tsp. onion flakes to Step 2, for more flavor.

Pizza Casserole

Shelia Heil, Lancaster, PA
Carolyn A. Baer, Conrath, WI
Susan J. Heil, Strasburg, PA

Makes 8 servings

Prep Time: 20 minutes
Cooking/Baking Time: 45–60 minutes
Standing Time: 10–15 minutes

2 lbs. hamburger
1 onion, chopped, *optional*
1 lb. dry noodles, cooked and drained
1½ 30-oz. jars meatless spaghetti sauce, *or* 6 cups pizza sauce
1 lb. cheddar, mozzarella, *or* American cheese, grated

1. Brown hamburger, and onion if you wish, in a large skillet. Drain off drippings.
2. Meanwhile, cook the noodles in a saucepan according to package directions. Drain.
3. Grease a 9 × 13 casserole dish. Spread the noodles in the bottom of the baking dish.
4. Spoon the spaghetti sauce over the noodles. Spoon the meat over the sauce. Sprinkle with the cheese.
5. Bake at 350° for 50 minutes, or until bubbly.
6. Take casserole out of oven and allow to stand for 10–15 minutes. (During the standing time, the juices re-gather and the cheese firms up. That makes cutting easier and distributes the cooking juices more evenly.)

Comforting Noodle Casserole

Sarah Miller
Harrisonburg, VA

Makes 8–10 servings

Prep. Time: 30 minutes
Cooking/Baking Time: 35–40 minutes

1-lb. pkg. noodles
2 lbs. hamburger
1 lb. sharp cheese, *divided*
1 quart corn
2 10¾-oz. cans mushroom soup

1. In a large saucepan, cook noodles as directed on package. Drain.
2. Brown hamburger in a large skillet.
3. Grate cheese. Reserve ¾ cup as a topping for the casserole.
4. In a sizable mixing bowl, combine noodles, hamburger, cheese (all but the reserved ¾ cup), corn, and undiluted mushroom soup.
5. Turn mixture into a 4-quart greased casserole dish (or use 2 smaller baking dishes).
6. Bake uncovered at 350°, or until bubbly and heated through, about 35–40 minutes. (If you use 2 smaller baking dishes, check after 25 minutes.)
7. Ten minutes before end of baking time, sprinkle reserved cheese on top, and then continue baking.

Yum-e-setti

Sharon E. Miller
Holmesville, OH

Makes 5–6 servings

Prep Time: 10–20 minutes
Cooking/Baking Time: 45–60 minutes

12-oz. pkg. wide noodles
10¾-oz. can cream of chicken soup
1 lb. hamburger
10¾-oz. can tomato soup
8 ozs. Velveeta cheese

1. In a large saucepan, cook noodles al dente, according to package directions. Drain.
2. Return cooked and drained noodles to saucepan. Mix with undiluted cream of chicken soup.
3. While noodles are cooking, brown hamburger in a large skillet. Drain off drippings.
4. Add can of tomato soup to browned hamburger.
5. Grease a 2½-qt. casserole. Place half of creamy noodles in bottom of baking dish. Top with half the tomato-hamburger mixture. Repeat.
6. Cover and bake at 325° for 35 minutes, or until bubbly and heated through.
7. Top with slices of cheese. Return to oven and bake uncovered for 10 more minutes.

Tips from Tester:
1. Add ½ tsp. dried basil and ½ tsp. dried oregano to Step 4.
2. Substitute 15-oz. can pizza sauce for tomato soup.

Spaghetti Altogether

Kendra Dreps
Liberty, PA

Makes 8–10 servings

Prep Time: 15–20 minutes
Cooking/Baking Time: 30 minutes

1-lb. pkg. spaghetti, broken into 1½" lengths
1 lb. ground beef *or* bulk sausage (sweet *or* Italian)
28–30-oz. jar spaghetti sauce
10¾-oz can cream of mushroom soup
1 lb. Velveeta, cubed, *or* mozzarella cheese, grated

1. In a large saucepan, cook spaghetti according to package instructions. Drain.
2. Brown hamburger or sausage in a skillet and drain off drippings.
3. In a large bowl, mix all ingredients together.
4. Place in greased 9 × 13 baking pan. Bake at 350° for 30 minutes, or until bubbly and heated through.

Tater Tot Bake

Carolyn Lehman Henry
Clinton, NY
Joyce Nolt
Richland, PA
Janeen L. Zimmerman
Denver, PA
Dorothy Lingerfelt
Stony Ford, CA
Miriam Nolt
New Holland, PA
Marilyn Mowry
Irving, TX

Makes 15–20 servings

Prep. Time: 20 minutes
Cooking/Baking Time: 30–45 minutes

1½ lbs. ground beef
salt and pepper to taste, *optional*
8½-oz. can peas, drained of most of its liquid, *or*
1-lb. pkg. frozen peas
8-oz. pkg. cheese slices
1 can cream of chicken soup
32-oz. pkg. frozen tater tots
2 cloves fresh garlic, *optional*

1. Brown beef in a large skillet. Drain off drippings.
2. Grease a 9 × 13 baking pan. Place browned beef in bottom. Sprinkle with salt and pepper if you wish.
3. Add peas, cheese, and then soup, in that order.
4. Top with tater tots.
5. Bake at 30–45 minutes at 350°, or until bubbly and heated through.

Variations:

1. For a creamier dish, add 1 can cream of mushroom soup, or use 2 cans of mushroom soup or 2 cans of chicken soup.

—**Janeen L. Zimmerman**
Denver, PA

2. If you want to add some zing, sprinkle tater tots with 2 cloves fresh garlic, chopped.

—**Dorothy Lingerfelt**
Stony Ford, CA

Tater Tots and Green Beans

Jena Hammond
Traverse City, MI
Jeannine A. Sheisel
Carolyn Snader
Ephrata, PA

Makes 12 servings

Prep. Time: 20–25 minutes
Cooking/Baking Time: 1 hour

1–1½ lbs. hamburger
1 quart green beans, *or* other vegetables
10¾-oz. can cream of chicken soup
10¾-oz. can cream of mushroom soup
32-oz. bag tater tots

1. Brown hamburger in a large skillet. Drain off drippings.
2. If using frozen or fresh green beans, steam lightly in a saucepan on the stove-top. Or microwave on High for 6 minutes, stirring after 3 minutes. (If using canned beans, go on to Step 3.)
3 Add beans and soup to browned hamburger. Stir together until well blended.
4. Place mixture in greased 9 × 13 baking dish. Put tater tots on top in rows.
5. Bake at 350° uncovered for 1 hour, or until heated through and bubbly.

Variations:
1. Drop the cream of chicken soup. Instead include ½ lb. sliced Velveeta cheese.

2. Instead of mixing the meat, beans, and soups together, layer them into the baking dish: first the hamburger, followed by the tater tots, topped by the green beans, and finally the cheese.
— **Jeannine A. Sheisel**

3. Instead of mushroom soup, use ½ soup can milk to thin the chicken soup.
— **Carolyn Snader**
Ephrata, PA

Hamburger Casserole

Doris Ranck
Gap, PA

Makes 8 servings

Prep Time: 10–12 minutes
Cooking/Baking Time: 1½ hours

1 lb. hamburger
1 tsp. salt
15-oz. can kidney beans, drained
2 cups raw potatoes, cubed
10½-oz. can tomato soup

1. Brown hamburger in a skillet. Stir in salt and beans.
2. Grease a 2-qt. baking dish. Put half of meat in bottom of dish. Top with half the potatoes. Repeat layers.
3. Pour tomato soup over top.
4. Bake covered at 325° for 1½ hours, or until potatoes are tender.

A Tip —

Buy ground beef in bulk, especially when it's on special, and brown it all. Separate it into 1-lb. packs and freeze. When you need a meal quickly, you've got a jump-start.

Hamburger-Vegetable Bake

Jenny R. Unternahrer
Wayland, IA

Makes 6 servings

Prep. Time: 20–25 minutes
Cooking/Baking Time: 20 minutes

1 lb. hamburger
5–6 medium-sized potatoes
1 can cream of chicken
   soup
¾ cup milk
¼ lb. Velveeta cheese, cut
   into small cubes

1. Brown hamburger in skillet and drain.
2. Slice potatoes into saucepan. Add ½ cup water and steam until tender, about 10–15 minutes.
Or place in a microwave-safe dish and microwave, covered, on High for 3 minutes. Stir. Cook on High for another 3 minutes. Stir. Jag with a fork to see if the potatoes are tender. If not, repeat the process until they are. Drain.
3. Combine soup, milk, and cheese in a separate large saucepan and warm until cheese is melted.
4. Add hamburger to cheese mixture.
5. Grease casserole dish and put in half the potatoes, then half of the hamburger mixture. Repeat layers.
6. Bake 20 minutes at 350°.

Variation: Reduce the number of potatoes to 3. Add a 17-oz. can of whole corn, drained, to Step 4. Put all the potatoes in the bottom of the casserole dish. Top with the remaining ingredients.

Beef and Bean Bake

Gretchen Maust, Keezletown, VA

Makes 6 servings

Prep Time: 20 minutes
Cooking/Baking Time: 30 minutes

1 lb. lean ground beef
1 medium-sized onion,
   chopped
1 can cream of mushroom
   soup
½ soup can water
1½ tsp. garlic salt
1 quart green beans,
   cooked and drained
   (reserve liquid and use
   in place of water above)
2 cups grated cheddar
   cheese, *optional*

1. Brown ground beef and onion in a skillet.
2. When meat is browned, stir in mushroom soup, water, and garlic salt.
3. In greased 2½–3-quart casserole dish, layer half the green beans, half the hamburger mixture, and half the grated cheese, if you're including the cheese. Repeat layers.
4. Bake uncovered at 350° for 30 minutes.

20-Minute Cheeseburger Rice

Peggy Clark, Burrton, KS

Makes 4 servings

Prep. Time: 10 minutes
Cooking/Baking Time: 10 minutes

1 lb. ground beef
1¾ cups water
⅔ cup ketchup
1 Tbsp. prepared mustard
2 cups uncooked minute
   rice
1 cup shredded cheddar
   cheese

1. Brown beef in a large non-stick skillet. Drain off drippings.
2. Add water, ketchup, and mustard. Stir well. Bring to a boil.
3. Stir in rice. Sprinkle with cheese. Cover.
4. Cook on low heat for 5 minutes.

Pizza Rice
Wendy Yoder Nice
Goshen, IN

Makes 4–6 servings

Prep. Time: 15 minutes
Cooking/Baking Time: 25 minutes

2½ cups cooked white rice
1 egg, lightly beaten
2 cups mozzarella cheese,
   divided
1 cup pizza sauce
1 cup cubed cooked ham,
   browned ground beef, *or*
   other favorite pre-cooked
   topping

1. In a small bowl, mix cooked rice, egg, and ¼ cup cheese thoroughly.
2. Spread evenly in greased pie pan or other round greased casserole dish.
3. Bake 15 minutes at 425°, or until lightly browned. (Keep the oven set at 425°.)
4. Spread sauce over crust. Add meat and sprinkle with remaining cheese.
5. Bake 8–10 minutes, or until sauce is bubbly and cheese is melted.

Tip from Tester: Use cooked brown rice instead of the white rice. And reduce the cheese to 1 cup if you're concerned about calories.

Un-Stuffed Peppers
Pat Bechtel
Dillsburg, PA
Sharon Miller
Holmesville, OH

Makes 6 servings

Prep. Time: 10–12 minutes
Cooking/Baking Time: 25 minutes

1 lb. ground beef
1 lb. 10-oz. jar spaghetti
   sauce
2 Tbsp. barbecue sauce,
   optional
2 large green peppers (3–4
   cups), coarsely chopped
1¼ cups water
1 cup instant rice

1. In a 12" nonstick skillet, brown ground beef. Drain off drippings.
2. Stir in all remaining ingredients. Bring to a boil over high heat.
3. Reduce heat to medium-low heat and cook, covered, for 20 minutes, or until liquid is absorbed and rice is tender.

Variation: Instead of spaghetti sauce and water, substitute 4 cups tomato juice or V-8 juice.

—**Sharon Miller**
Holmesville, OH

Easy American Chop Suey
Shelia Heil
Lancaster, PA

Makes 6 servings

Prep Time: 15 minutes
Cooking/Baking Time: 1 hour

1 lb. ground beef
2 cans cream soups (celery
   or mushroom work well)
2 soup cans water
¼ cup soy sauce
¾ cup minute rice,
   uncooked
1 tsp. onion flakes,
   optional

1. Brown ground beef in a skillet. Drain off drippings.
2. Meanwhile, in a large mixing bowl, combine soups and water. When smooth, stir in soy sauce, rice, and onion flakes. Stir in browned ground beef.
3. Spread in greased 9 × 13 baking pan. Bake uncovered at 350° for 1 hour.

Quick and Easy Tacos

Audrey Romonosky
Austin, TX

Makes 4–6 servings

Prep. Time: 5 minutes
Cooking/Baking Time: 20 minutes

1 lb. ground beef
1 cup frozen corn
½–1 cup salsa *or* picante sauce, according to your taste preference
10–12 tortillas
guacamole, *optional*
1½ cups grated cheddar cheese, *optional*

1. Brown ground beef in a skillet. Drain off drippings.
2. Add frozen corn and salsa. Cover and simmer 5–10 minutes.
3. Spoon into tortillas and garnish with guacamole and with cheese, if you wish.

Tip from the Tester: Cook the corn and offer it as a topping, rather than mixing it into the filling. Then those who don't enjoy corn won't have it in their tacos, and those who do enjoy it can add it.

Tortilla Chip Quick Dish

Cheryl Martin
Turin, NY

Makes 6 servings

Prep. Time: 13–15 minutes
Cooking/Baking Time: 8–10 minutes

1 lb. ground beef *or* turkey, browned
1 envelope taco seasoning
16-oz. can refried beans
¾ cup water
7 ozs. tortilla chips
1 cup grated cheese

1. Brown meat in a skillet. Drain off drippings.
2. Add taco seasoning, refried beans, and water to browned meat. Mix together.
3. Place chips in a lightly greased 9 × 13 baking dish. Spoon bean mixture over chips.
4. Sprinkle cheese over all.
5. Bake at 350° for 8–10 minutes, or until cheese is bubbly.

Oven Enchiladas

Melanie Thrower
McPherson, KS

Makes 8 servings

Prep. Time: 15 minutes
Cooking/Baking Time: 30 minutes

1 lb. ground beef
2 medium-sized yellow onions, chopped
16 corn tortillas
2 cups shredded Mexican cheese
2 16-oz. cans green chili *or* red enchilada sauce

1. In a skillet, brown ground beef. Drain off drippings.
2. Heat tortillas in nonstick pan to make them flexible.
3. Fill each tortilla with browned beef, topped with onion. Roll up, tuck in sides, and continue rolling. Place side by side on a baking sheet with sides.
4. Sprinkle cheese over top of filled enchiladas. Pour sauce over top.
5. Cover with aluminum foil. Bake at 375° for 30 minutes.

Tip: Serve with dishes of sour cream, salsa, and guacamole as optional toppings.

Easy Enchiladas
Ruth Shank
Monroe, GA

Makes 10 servings

Prep. Time: 30–40 minutes
Cooking/Baking Time: 15 minutes

1–1½ lbs. ground beef
1 envelope dry taco
    seasoning mix
15-oz. can tomato sauce
15-oz. can water
1 pkg. (10 count) medium-
    sized flour tortillas
2 cups shredded cheese

1. Brown ground beef. Drain off drippings. Return beef to pan.

2. Add seasoning, sauce, and water. Mix well. Simmer, covered, for 20 minutes.

3. Spray 9 × 13 baking pan lightly with non-stick cooking spray.

4. Using slotted spoon, spoon mixture into each tortilla and roll up.

5. Arrange rolled tortillas in baking pan. Pour remaining mixture over tortillas. Sprinkle shredded cheese on top.

6. Bake, uncovered, at 350° for 15 minutes.

Tip: Serve with sour cream and taco sauce, if you wish.

Biscuit Tostadas
Angie Clemens
Dayton, VA

Makes 16 servings

Prep. Time: 15 minutes
Cooking/Baking Time: 15 minutes

1 lb. ground beef
1½ cups salsa
7.3-oz. tube refrigerated
    large biscuits
2 cups shredded lettuce
2 cups shredded cheese,
    your choice of cheddar,
    Colby, *or* Monterey Jack

1. Brown hamburger in a skillet. Drain off drippings.

2. Stir in salsa. Heat through.

3. Meanwhile, split each biscuit in half and flatten into 4" rounds.

4. Place biscuit halves on ungreased cookie sheet. Bake at 350° for 10–12 minutes, or until golden brown.

5. Top with meat-salsa mixture, lettuce, and cheese. Serve immediately.

Mexican Biscuit Bake
Laura Irene Shirk
Womelsdorf, PA

Makes 8 servings

Prep Time: 20 minutes
Cooking Time: 30 minutes

1 lb. hamburger
1 medium-sized onion,
    chopped
1 can refrigerated biscuits
26-oz. jar spaghetti sauce
8 ozs. mozzarella cheese,
    grated

1. Brown hamburger with onion in a skillet. Drain off drippings.

2. Cut each biscuit into 4 pieces.

3. In a large mixing bowl, stir together spaghetti sauce and browned hamburger and onions. Stir in biscuit pieces.

4. Place in a lightly greased 9 × 13 baking dish. Bake uncovered at 350° for 25 minutes.

5. Spread the cheese over the top of the casserole. Return to oven and bake an additional 5 minutes, or until cheese is melted.

$25,000 Mexican Dish

Michelle High
Fredericksburg, PA

Makes 8–10 servings

Prep Time: 20 minutes
Cooking/Baking Time: 30 minutes

2 cups buttermilk baking
  mix
1 cup water
2 15-oz. cans refried beans
1–2 lbs. hamburger
16-oz. jar salsa
3 cups shredded cheddar
  cheese
Optional toppings:
  sour cream
  shredded lettuce
  cut-up tomatoes

1. In a large mixing bowl,
mix baking mix, water, and
refried beans together.
2. Spread in a greased
9 × 13 baking pan.
3. Brown hamburger in a
skillet. Drain off drippings.
4. Spoon browned ham-
burger over bean "crust."
5. Spread with salsa. Cover
with cheese.
6. Bake at 350° for 30
minutes.
7. If you wish, offer dishes
of sour cream, lettuce, and
tomatoes as toppings.

Hamburger Crescent Hot Dish

Barbara Walker
Sturgis, SD

Makes 6–8 servings

Prep. Time: 20 minutes
*Cooking/Baking Time: 20–25
  minutes*
Standing Time: 10 minutes

2 8-oz. pkgs. crescent rolls
1 lb. ground beef
¼ cup chopped onion
¾ cup barbecue sauce
6 slices cheese

1. Roll out one package
crescent rolls on baking sheet
to create a rectangle. Press
seams together. Turn up a ½"
edge of pastry the whole way
around this bottom "crust."
2. Brown ground beef and
onion in a large skillet. Drain
off drippings.
3. Stir barbecue sauce into
meat in skillet.
4. Spread over pastry
rectangle. Lay cheese on top.
5. On a second baking
sheet, roll out second package
of crescent rolls to create a
rectangle. Again, press seams
together.
6. Lift off baking sheet and
lay over top of barbecued beef.
Seal sides with the upturned
edge of the bottom crust.
7. Bake at 375° for 20–25
minutes, until lightly browned.
8. Allow to rest for 10
minutes before slicing and
serving.

Bubble Pizza

Jeannine Janzen
Elbing, KS

Makes 4–6 servings

Prep. Time: 20 minutes
Cooking/Baking Time: 30 minutes

½ lb. hamburger
3 cans refrigerated biscuits
1½ cups pizza sauce
½ cup sliced pepperoni
1½ cups shredded
  mozzarella cheese
Optional toppings: green
  pepper, mushrooms,
  ham, bacon, onion, etc.

1. Brown hamburger in a
skillet. Drain off drippings.
2. Meanwhile, cut each
biscuit into fourths. Separate
pieces and toss into a greased
9 × 13 pan, covering the
bottom.
3. Spoon pizza sauce over
biscuits.
4. Spoon hamburger and
pepperoni (and any optional
toppings you choose) over
sauce.
5. Top with cheese.
6. Bake at 350° for 30
minutes, or until cheese is
melted and slightly brown.

Hobo Joes

Marcia S. Myer
Manheim, PA

Makes 6 servings

Prep. Time: 5 minutes
Cooking/Baking Time: 20–25 minutes

1 lb. ground beef
1 small onion, chopped
1 can vegetable soup
2 Tbsp. ketchup

1. Brown hamburger and onion in a non-stick skillet.
2. Add vegetable soup and ketchup. Mix well.
3. Simmer for 10 minutes.
4. Serve in hamburger buns.

Reuben Rolls

Evelyn Page
Gillette, WY

Makes 8 servings

Prep. Time: 20 minutes
Cooking/Baking Time: 10–15 minutes

8-oz. tube refrigerated crescent rolls
1 cup sauerkraut, drained
1 Tbsp. Thousand Island dressing
4 slices Swiss cheese
8 thin slices cooked corned beef

1. Separate crescent dough into 8 triangles.
2. Rinse the sauerkraut and drain well. Chop into small pieces.
3. In a small mixing bowl, combine kraut and salad dressing.
4. Cut the Swiss cheese into ½" wide strips. Place two cheese strips across the short side of each triangle.
5. Fold corned beef slices in half; place over cheese. Top with kraut mixture.
6. Roll up each crescent from the short side. Place on ungreased baking sheet.
7. Bake at 375° for 10–15 minutes, or until golden brown.

Reubens

Lynne Bandel
Arcadia, IN

Makes 8 servings

Prep. Time: 15 minutes
Cooking/Baking Time: 5 minutes

24-oz. unsliced loaf of rye bread
½ cup Thousand Island dressing
1 lb. cooked corned beef, *or* veggie corned beef, sliced thin *or* chipped
32-oz. can sauerkraut, drained
1 lb. Swiss cheese, thinly sliced

1. Split the loaf of bread in half horizontally.
2. Spread the cut side of each half with half the dressing.
3. Layer half the ingredients—in order—on each half of the loaf.
4. Place under broiler, about 5" below the heat, until cheese is melted.
5. Slice each half in 4 pieces and serve.

A Tip —

I make grilled sandwiches with all sorts of leftovers.

Reuben Casserole

Mary Kathryn Yoder
Harrisonville, MO

Makes 10 servings

Prep Time: 15 minutes
Cooking/Baking Time: 45–60 minutes

2-lb. bag, *or can,*
  sauerkraut
1 lb. cooked corned beef,
  sliced thin
1 cup Thousand Island
  dressing
1 lb. thick sliced baby
  Swiss cheese
12 slices rye bread, cubed
  and buttered

1. Lightly grease a 9 × 13 baking pan. Rinse and drain the sauerkraut. Then spread it over the bottom of the baking pan.
2. Layer the corned beef evenly over the kraut.
3. Spread the dressing over the beef. Top with cheese slices.
4. Scatter the buttered bread cubes over the cheese. Press down into pan.
5. Bake at 350° until heated through, 45–55 minutes, depending upon the temperature of the ingredients when you put them in the pan.

Creamed Dried Beef

Janet Oberholtzer, Ephrata, PA
Alica Denlinger, Lancaster, PA
Vera Martin, East Earl, PA
Beverly High, Bradford, PA
Hazel Lightcap Propst
Oxford, PA

Makes 4 servings

Prep. Time: 2–3 minutes
Cooking/Baking Time: 15 minutes

4 Tbsp. butter
¼ lb. thinly sliced dried
  beef, torn in pieces
4 Tbsp. flour
dash of pepper, *optional*
2½ cups milk
2 Tbsp. grated sharp
  cheese, *optional*

1. In a medium-sized saucepan, melt butter. Stir in dried beef. Brown slightly.
2. Stir in flour and mix well. Brown over medium heat to prevent a raw flour taste.
3. Continuing over medium heat, slowly add milk. Using a whisk or wooden spoon, stir continually until smooth and thickened.
4. Serve over toast, home fries, waffles, or pancakes for breakfast or supper. Or serve it as a topping for baked potatoes, mashed potatoes, or noodles for a main meal.

Variaton: To add a heartier flavor, stir in the cheese just as the sauce smooths out and thickens.

— **Hazel Lightcap Propst**
Oxford, PA

Dried Beef Casserole

Kendra Dreps, Liberty, PA
Ida H. Goering, Dayton, VA
Judy Diller, Bluffton, OH

Makes 6–8 servings

Prep Time: 10 minutes
Chilling Time: 4–8 hours, or overnight
Cooking/Baking Time: 1 hour

2 10¾-oz. cans cream of
  mushroom soup
3 cups milk
2 cups uncooked macaroni
½ lb. shredded dried beef
2 cups cheddar cheese,
  grated
⅓ cup chopped onion,
  optional
2 hard-boiled eggs, sliced,
  optional

1. Butter a 9 × 13 baking pan.
2. In a large mixing bowl, mix soup and milk together until smooth.
3. Stir in all remaining ingredients and blend well. Spoon into baking pan.
4. Cover and refrigerate overnight.
5. Bake uncovered at 350° for one hour, or until heated through and bubbly.

Tip from the Tester: For a different flavor, use a 6-oz. can tuna, or ½ lb. cooked and cubed chicken, instead of the dried beef.

Pork Main Dishes

Brown Sugar and Dijon-Marinated Pork Tenderloin

J. B. Miller
Indianapolis, IN

Makes 4–6 servings

Prep. Time: 5 minutes
Marinating Time: 2–3 hours
Cooking/Baking Time: 15 minutes

½ cup soy sauce
¼ cup sherry vinegar
½ tsp. Dijon mustard
¼ cup brown sugar
2-lb. pork tenderloin

1. Combine the first four ingredients in a large, zip-lock plastic bag to make the marinade.
2. Place tenderloin in marinade and close bag. Surround meat with marinade, and then place in refrigerator for 2 to 3 hours.

3. Heat grill to medium-high. Remove tenderloin from bag, patting dry.
4. Grill tenderloin until desired doneness, 160° for medium. Thinly slice into medallions and serve.

Tips:
1. Be sure grill is hot before placing tenderloin on grill. Tenderloin should have a thin crisp crust.
2. This is especially good served with garlic mashed potatoes or polenta.

Tips from Tester:
1. You can also prepare the tenderloin in your broiler.
2. Use a meat thermometer to be sure the meat is cooked sufficiently.

Barbecued Ribs

Barry Coggin, Jacksonville, FL

Makes 4 servings

Prep. Time: 10–15 minutes
Cooking/Baking Time: 2½–3 hours

2–3 lbs. pork ribs
olive oil
salt and pepper
paprika
barbecue sauce, warmed slightly

1. Rub ribs with olive oil. Sprinkle on all sides with salt, pepper, and a generous amount of paprika.
2. Sear 5 minutes each side on a very hot grill.
3. Wrap ribs in 3 layers of heavy duty aluminum foil so that they're airtight.
4. Turn one grill burner on high. Place ribs on the other side, not directly above fire.
5. Cook 3 hours. Turn 2–3 times.

6. Unwrap on a serving platter. Cut into serving-size pieces.

7. Pour barbecue sauce over top of each piece. Turn and pour additional sauce over.

Pork Chops
Judi Robb
Manhattan, KS

Makes 3 servings

Prep. Time: 20–30 minutes
Cooking/Baking Time: 40–60 minutes

21-oz. can apple pie filling
3 thick pork chops
1 box pork-flavored stuffing mix

1. In large skillet brown pork chops on both sides over high heat. Do not crowd the skillet or the chops will steam in each other's juices rather than brown. To prevent that, brown them 1 or 2 at a time.

2. Meanwhile, prepare stuffing according to directions on box.

3. In a greased 9 × 9 baking dish, spread apple pie filling over the bottom.

4. Place browned pork chops on top of apples.

5. Layer prepared stuffing over pork chops. Cover with foil.

6. Bake, covered, at 350° for 30 minutes. Remove foil and bake 10 more minutes.

7. Check to see if the chops are cooked through in the middle and tender. If not, cover and continue baking up to 20 more minutes if needed.

Pork Chops and Apples
Arlene M. Kopp
Lineboro, MD

Makes 5–6 servings

Prep. Time: 15 minutes
Cooking/Baking Time: 1–1½ hours

5–6 pork chops
2 Tbsp. oil
3–4 apples, cored and sliced
¼ cup brown sugar
1 tsp. cinnamon

1. Brown chops on both sides in oil in a skillet, about 3 minutes on each side. Do not crowd the skillet or the chops will steam in their own juices rather than brown. Brown in batches for good browning results.

2. Meanwhile, place apples in a long greased baking dish. Sprinkle with sugar and cinnamon.

3. Top with browned pork chops.

4. Cover and bake 1–1½ hours, or until chops are tender and cooked through.

Pork Chop Divine
Norma P. Zehr
Lowville, NY

Makes 4 servings

Prep. Time: 10 minutes
Cooking/Baking Time: 20–30 minutes

4 pork chops
salt and pepper to taste
3 Tbsp. butter, *divided*
½ lb. red grapes, halved
½ cup brown sugar

1. Brown chops in non-stick skillet, about 3 minutes on each side, until browned. Resist crowding the skillet because the chops will steam in their own juices if they're too close together. For best results, brown in batches.

2. Meanwhile, melt 2 Tbsp. butter in another skillet or a saucepan. Add grapes and cook over medium-high heat until they burst open.

3. Stir in brown sugar. Add 1 Tbsp. butter. Continue cooking until sauce is heated through. Stir occasionally so sauce doesn't scorch.

4. Pour sauce over chops in non-stick skillet and continue cooking until chops are tender.

5. Serve chops topped with sauce.

Zingy Pork Chops

Jean H. Robinson
Cinnaminson, NJ

Makes 4 servings

Prep. Time: 10 minutes
Cooking/Baking Time: 20–25
minutes

4 boneless pork loin chops
  (about 1 pound)
2 Tbsp. olive oil
½ cup apricot preserves, *or*
  orange marmalade
juice and zest of 1 lemon
¼ tsp. salt
½ tsp. white pepper
1 Tbsp. ground ginger,
  optional

1. Brown chops 3 minutes
per side in a heavy skillet in
about 2 Tbsp. olive oil over
high heat. Do not crowd the
skillet or the chops will steam
in their juices rather than
brown. It's better to brown
them in batches.

2. Remove chops from skillet and keep warm. Reduce
heat to low.

3. Add apricot preserves,
lemon juice, salt and pepper,
and ginger if you wish, to pan
drippings, as well as any juice
from the pork chop plate.

4. When sauce ingredients
are thoroughly blended and
hot, return chops to skillet.
Spoon sauce over chops.
Continue heating until chops
are hot but not over-cooked.

Raspberry Pork Chops

Louise Bodziony
Sunrise Beach, MO

Makes 4 servings

Prep. Time: 10 minutes
Cooking/Baking Time: 25–30
minutes

1 Tbsp. cooking oil
4 boneless pork loin chops,
  ½" thick
¼ cup raspberry preserves
1 tsp. vinegar
¼ cup raspberries

1. Heat oil in large skillet
over medium-high heat until
hot. Add pork chops, but
don't crowd the skillet. Cook
2–3 minutes or until brown,
turning once.

2. Reduce heat to low.
Cover and cook 10–15
minutes, or until pork is
tender and no longer pink.

3. Meanwhile, in a small
saucepan combine preserves
and vinegar. Cook over low
heat 1–3 minutes, or until
thoroughly heated. Stir in
raspberries. Serve over pork
chops.

Pork Chops Supreme

Barb Harvey
Quarryville, PA

Makes as many servings as you need!

Prep. Time: 10 minutes
Cooking/Baking Time: 1½ hours

1 thick pork chop per
  person
1 large onion slice per
  person
1 lemon slice per person
1 Tbsp. brown sugar per
  person
1 Tbsp. ketchup per person

1. Place pork chops in
lightly greased baking dish.
On top of each chop, place
1 large slice onion, 1 slice
lemon, 1 Tbsp. brown sugar,
and 1 Tbsp. ketchup.

2. Cover and bake 1 hour
at 350°. Uncover and bake
half an hour more.

New Mexican Pork Chops

John D. Allen
Rye, CO

Makes 6 servings

Prep. Time: 15–20 minutes
Cooking/Baking Time: 8–10 minutes

6 pork chops, about ¾–1" thick
vegetable oil for browning
8-oz. jar salsa

1. In a large skillet, brown chops in oil until golden. Brown them in batches so as not to crowd the skillet. If the skillet is too full, the chops will steam in their juices rather than brown.
2. Return all chops to the skillet. Add the salsa, turn down the heat, and simmer, covered, for about 8–10 minutes, or until the meat is tender.

Tip from the Tester: There's a lovely amount of juice with this dish, which is perfect to serve over the meat and hot cooked rice as an accompaniment.

Tangy Pork Skillet

Sherri Mayer
Menomonee Falls, WI

Makes 4 servings

Prep. Time: 5 minutes
Cooking/Baking Time: 15 minutes

4 pork loin chops
¼ cup Italian dressing
¼ cup barbecue sauce
1 tsp. chili powder

1. In a large non-stick skillet, brown pork chops on one side over medium-high heat. If the skillet is full, brown the chops in 2 batches so they brown well.
2. Remove browned chops to platter and keep warm.
3. Add remaining ingredients to pan, stirring to blend. Return all chops to pan, and turn them so the browned side is up.
4. Cover and simmer for 5–8 minutes, or until meat is tender.

A Tip —

Allow roasted, broiled, or grilled meat to rest for 10 minutes before slicing and serving so the meat can reabsorb its juices.

Pork Chop and Potato Casserole

Jeanette B. Oberholtzer
Manheim, PA

Makes 4–6 servings

Prep. Time: 15 minutes
Cooking/Baking Time: 1–1½ hours

4–5 medium to large potatoes
salt and pepper
6 pork chops ¾–1" thick
milk to cover potatoes

1. Peel potatoes. Slice medium/thin and arrange in a large greased baking dish. Sprinkle with salt and pepper.
2. Arrange chops on top of potatoes. Sprinkle with salt and pepper.
3. Pour in enough milk to cover potatoes, but not the chops.
4. Bake in 350 degree oven for 1–1½ hours, or until chops and potatoes are tender. Cover loosely with foil if chops are browning before they and the potatoes are tender.

Pork Chops and Rice

Donna Lantgen, Golden, CO

Makes 4 servings

Prep. Time: 5–10 minutes
Cooking/Baking Time: 1 hour

1½ cups dry long-grain rice
2 cups water
10¾-oz. can cream of
  celery soup
1 Tbsp. chicken bouillon
  granules, *or* 1 chicken
  bouillon cube
4 pork chops

1. In a mixing bowl, stir together all ingredients except pork chops. Spoon into a lightly greased 9 × 13 glass baking dish.
2. Place pork chops on top.
3. Cover. Bake at 350° for 1 hour, or until rice and meat are both tender.

Pork Chops on Amber Rice

Esther Porter
Minneapolis, MN

Makes 6 servings

Prep. Time: 15–20 minutes
Cooking/Baking Time: 55 minutes

6 pork chops
1⅓ cups uncooked minute
  rice
1 cup orange juice

¼ cup chopped green onion
10½-oz. can chicken-rice
  soup

1. Brown pork chops in heavy non-stick skillet. Do not crowd the skillet, but brown the chops in batches in order to avoid having the chops steam in each other's juices.
2. Meanwhile, place uncooked rice in a lightly greased 7 × 12 baking dish. Pour orange juice over rice.
3. Arrange browned pork chops on top of rice. Sprinkle green onion over pork chops.
4. Pour chicken rice soup over all.
5. Cover and bake at 350° for 45 minutes. Then uncover and bake 10 minutes longer.

Ham Loaf

Ruth E. Schiefer
Vassar, MI

Makes 8 servings

Prep. Time: 15 minutes
Cooking/Baking Time: 1 hour

1 lb. ground pork
1 lb. ground ham
1 cup milk
1 cup bread crumbs
1 egg
¼ tsp. pepper, *optional*

1. In a large mixing bowl, mix all ingredients together well.
2. Shape into a loaf. Place in a lightly greased baking loaf pan.

3. Bake at 350°, uncovered, for 1 hour.

Tip from Tester: If you wish, spoon ¼ cup ketchup over top of the loaf 15 minutes before the end of the baking time.

Ham Loaf and Hash Brown Casserole

LuAnna Hochstedler
East Earl, PA

Makes 8–10 servings

Prep. Time: 5–10 minutes
Cooking/Baking Time: 60–65 minutes

2 lbs. ready-to-bake ham-
  loaf mixture
10¾-oz. can cream of
  celery soup
2 lbs. hash brown patties
  or cubes, *or* tater tots
2 cups shredded cheese

1. Press ham loaf into bottom of a lightly greased 9 × 13 baking dish.
2. Spread soup over ham loaf.
3. Layer hash brown patties on top.
4. Bake at 350° for 55 minutes. Sprinkle cheese on top.
5. Bake 5 minutes more, or until cheese melts.

Whipped Potatoes and Ham

June S. Groff, Denver, PA
Jeannine Janzen, Elbing, KS

Makes 9 servings

Prep. Time: 45–50 minutes
Cooking/Baking Time: 20–30 minutes
Standing Time: 10 minutes

6 medium-sized potatoes
2–4 cups cooked ham chunks
¼ tsp. garlic salt
1 cup heavy whipping cream
2 cups shredded cheddar cheese

1. Peel potatoes. Cut into chunks and place in a medium-sized saucepan. Add 2" water, cover, and cook over low heat for 20 minutes or so, or until potatoes are break-apart-tender when poked with a fork.
2. Mash potatoes with an electric mixer, adding some of the cooking water to keep them from being too stiff. Mix in garlic salt.
3. Spoon into lightly greased 9 × 13 baking pan.
4. Scatter ham over potatoes.
5. Whip heavy cream until light and fluffy.
6. Gently fold cheddar cheese into whipped cream.
7. Spoon mixture over top of ham.
8. Bake at 350° for 20–30 minutes.
9. Allow to stand 10 minutes before serving to allow potatoes to firm up.

Company Ham and Noodles

Diane Eby
Holtwood, PA

Makes 5–6 servings

Prep. Time: 5 minutes
Cooking/Baking Time: 10 minutes

¼ cup chopped onion
2 Tbsp. butter
10 ozs. fully cooked ham, julienned (about 2 cups)
2 tsp. flour
1 cup sour cream
hot cooked noodles
chopped fresh parsley, *optional*

1. In a skillet over medium heat, sauté onion in butter until tender.
2. Add ham. Cook and stir until heated through.
3. Sprinkle with flour and stir for 1 minute.
4. Reduce heat to low. Gradually stir in sour cream.
5. Cook and stir until thickened, about 2–3 minutes.
6. Serve over noodles. Garnish with parsley if you wish.

Cumberland Stockpot

Esther Porter
Minneapolis, MN

Makes 4 servings

Prep. Time: 10 minutes
Cooking/Baking Time: 60–75 minutes

4 bratwurst
1 small head of red cabbage
1 cup apple juice
3 Tbsp. currant jelly
1 Tbsp. cider vinegar
1 tsp. juniper berries, *optional*

1. Place bratwurst in good-sized saucepan.
2. Shred or chop cabbage coarsely. Add to saucepan with bratwurst.
3. In a small bowl, mix together apple juice, currant jelly, and vinegar. Pour into saucepan containing cabbage and bratwurst.
4. Cover and simmer for 60–75 minutes, or until cabbage is tender.

Sausage, Potato, and Cabbage Stir-Fry

Deborah Heatwole
Waynesboro, GA
Alta Metzler
Willow Street, PA

Makes 6 servings

Prep. Time: 20–25 minutes
Cooking/Baking Time: 20–25 minutes

1 lb. bulk pork sausage
3–4 potatoes, peeled and cubed (about 3 cups)
4 carrots, sliced thin *or* diced, *optional*
½ cup water
salt and pepper
6 cups coarsely chopped cabbage

1. Brown the sausage in a large skillet. Drain off drippings.
2. Add the potatoes, carrots if you wish, and water to the meat in the skillet.
3. Stir up the browned drippings from the bottom of the skillet and mix through the meat and vegetables.
4. Cover and cook until vegetables are almost tender.
5. Add cabbage. Sprinkle with salt and pepper.
6. Cover and cook 5–8 minutes, or until cabbage and potatoes are tender, stirring several times to prevent sticking.

Fresh Sausage and Sauerkraut

Susanne Nobrega
Duxbury, MA

Makes 4–6 servings

Prep. Time: 10 minutes
Cooking/Baking Time: 1 hour

1 lb. fresh sausage, bulk, *or* sliced link sausage
1-lb. bag sauerkraut, rinsed and drained
1 lb. (about 4 cups) fresh shredded cabbage
1 Tbsp. caraway seeds, *optional*
½ cup beer, regular, light, *or* non-alcoholic
¼–½ cup water, if needed

1. In heavy, large skillet, brown the fresh sausage thoroughly.
2. Remove sausage from pan. Do not clean the pan. Add sauerkraut, cabbage, and caraway seeds if you wish. Mix well.
3. Place sausage back in pan on top of the mixed cabbage. Add the beer, pouring all around.
4. Cover. Simmer 45–60 minutes until sausage is cooked through.
5. Check occasionally. If the dish becomes dry, stir in ¼–½ cup water.

Italian Sausage and Potatoes

Maryann Markano
Wilmington, DE

Makes 4 servings

Prep. Time: 20 minutes
Cooking/Baking Time: 30–35 minutes

1 lb. sweet *or* hot Italian sausage, cut on the diagonal in 1½" lengths
1 lb. small red potatoes, each cut in half
1 large onion, cut into 12 wedges
2 red *or* yellow bell peppers, cut into strips
1 Tbsp. olive oil

1. Preheat oven to 450°.
2. Combine all ingredients in large bowl or plastic bag. Toss to coat with oil.
3. Pour mixture onto large, lightly greased jelly-roll pan.
4. Roast for 30–35 minutes, or until potatoes are fork-tender and sausages are lightly browned. Stir halfway through cooking.

A Tip —

Always use a portable oven thermometer inside your oven. Most ovens vary at least 25 degrees from their supposed degree settings which can alter baking times significantly.

Sausage Veggie Casserole

Rhonda Freed
Croghan, NY

Makes 8 servings

Prep. Time: 20–30 minutes
Cooking/Baking Time: 30 minutes

1 lb. pork sausage, cut
  in ¼" slices, *or* bulk
  sausage
2 1-lb. pkgs. frozen vegetable
  of your choice, thawed
10¾-oz. can cream of
  mushroom soup
3 cups leftover mashed
  potatoes (or 6 servings
  instant mashed potatoes)
1 cup shredded cheddar
  cheese

1. Brown sausage in a large skillet.
2. Meanwhile, either lightly steam, or microwave, vegetable until crisp-tender.
3. Prepare instant mashed potatoes according to package directions, if you don't have leftover mashed potatoes.
4. When sausage is browned, spread on bottom of a lightly greased 9 × 13 glass baking dish.
5. Spoon cooked vegetable over top of sausage.
6. Spread mushroom soup over vegetable.
7. Spread mashed potatoes over top.
8. Bake uncovered at 350° for 20 minutes, or until vegetable is done to your liking.

9. Sprinkle cheese evenly over top. Return to oven and bake an additional 10 minutes, uncovered.

Tip from Tester: Add 1 medium-sized onion, chopped, and/or 2 cloves minced garlic to Step 1.

Sausage Sweet Potato De-lish

Cathy Boshart
Lebanon, PA
Jackie Stefl
E. Bethany, NY

Makes 4–6 servings

Prep. Time: 45 minutes
Cooking/Baking Time: 1 hour

4 large sweet potatoes
1 lb. smoked sausage, cut
  in ¼" slices
4 large apples
salt to taste, *optional*
water
½ cup brown sugar

1. Place sweet potatoes in a large saucepan. Add about 1" water. Cover and cook over medium heat until tender. Check occasionally to make sure they don't cook dry.
2. When fully cooked, remove from pan and allow to cool.
3. When cool enough to handle, pull off skins. Cut potatoes into ¼" slices.
4. Place half the potatoes in bottom of a greased casserole.

Cover with all of the sausage, cut in slices.
5. Top with sliced apples, peeled or not peeled. Sprinkle with salt if you wish.
6. Cover with remaining potatoes.
7. Brush with water. Sprinkle with brown sugar.
8. Bake uncovered at 350° for approximately 1 hour, or until heated through.

Variations:
1. Use a 29-oz. can sweet potatoes, drained, instead of the 4 sweet potatoes. Skip Steps 1, 2, and 3.
2. Use kielbasa instead of smoked sausage. Cut the kielbasa into 6 pieces.
3. Brush potatoes in Step 7 with 1–2 Tbsp. prepared mustard instead of water.

—Jackie Stefl
  E. Bethany, NY

Sweet and Sour Kielbasa

Makes 6–8 servings

Prep. Time: 15 minutes
Cooking/Baking Time: 50 minutes

3 lbs. sliced kielbasa
1 bottle chili sauce
20-oz. can crushed
   pineapple in heavy
   syrup, undrained
½ cup brown sugar

   1. Mix all ingredients in a
large mixing bowl. Place in a
lightly greased 9 × 13 baking
pan.
   2. Cover and bake at 350°
for 40 minutes.
   3. Uncover and continue
baking at 350° for 10 more
minutes.

Coke Kielbasa

Shelia Heil
Lancaster, PA

Makes 3–4 servings

Prep. Time: 10 minutes
Cooking/Baking Time: 15 minutes

1-lb. pkg. kielbasa
12-oz. can cola
¼ cup brown sugar
hot cooked rice

   1. Slice kielbasa diagonally
into ⅓"-thick slices.
   2. Place in a medium-sized
saucepan. Stir in cola and
brown sugar.
   3. Simmer over low
heat for about 15 minutes,
uncovered. Stir frequently
to prevent the sauce from
sticking as it thickens.
   4. Serve over rice.

Italian Subs

Susan Kasting
Jenks, OK

Makes 6 servings

Prep. Time: 15 minutes
Cooking/Baking Time: 15 minutes

6 Italian sausages
1 green bell pepper, sliced
   in ¼" strips
1 red bell pepper, sliced in
   ¼" strips
1 medium-sized onion,
   sliced in ¼" rounds
6 hoagie rolls, split

   1. Pan-fry sausages, or
grill, until browned on all
sides.
   2. In a separate pan
sprayed with non-stick
cooking spray, heat to
medium/high heat and sauté
the peppers and onions until
tender-crisp.
   3. Place one sausage and
a generous amount of the pep-
per-onion mix in each hoagie
roll. Serve immediately

A Tip —

   When I purchase bacon, I cook the whole pound, doing it
3-4 slices at a time between paper towels in the microwave.
Whatever I don't use immediately, I freeze in ziplock bags.
It's ready later with a zap in the microwave.

Ham and Cheese Stromboli

Jane Steiner
Orrville, OH

Makes 6 servings

Prep. Time: 20 minutes
Cooking/Baking Time: 20 minutes
Standing Time: 10 minutes

11-oz. tube refrigerated
 French bread
¼–½ lb. cooked ham,
 chipped *or* thinly sliced
small onion, diced,
 optional
8 bacon strips, cooked
 and crumbled, *or* ½ cup
 prepared cooked and
 crumbled bacon
2 cups shredded
 mozzarella cheese

1. Unroll dough on a
greased baking sheet.
2. Place ham over dough to
within ½" of edges. Sprinkle
evenly with onion, bacon,
and cheese.
3. Roll up, jelly-roll style,
starting with a long side.
Pinch seams to seal and tuck
ends under. Place seam-side
down on baking sheet.
4. Bake at 350° for 20
minutes, or until golden
brown.
5. Allow to stand 10
minutes before slicing. Serve
warm.

Cordon Bleu Stromboli

Melody Baum
Greencastle, PA

Makes 6 servings

Prep. Time: 15 minutes
Rising Time: 20 minutes
Cooking/Baking Time: 25–30
* minutes*
Standing Time: 10 minutes

1 loaf frozen bread dough,
 thawed (see package
 directions)
2 Tbsp. butter
8 ozs. thinly sliced deli ham
½ cup shredded Swiss
 cheese
5 ozs. thinly sliced deli
 turkey

1. Roll bread dough into an
8 × 10 rectangle on a baking
sheet.
2. Spread with butter. Top
with a layer of ham, followed
by a layer of cheese, and
finally a layer of turkey.
3. Roll up, jelly-roll style,
starting with the long side.
Pinch seam to seal and tuck
ends under.
4. Place seam-side down on
a greased baking sheet. Place
in a warm place. Cover with
a tea towel, and let rise for 20
minutes.
5. Bake at 350° for 25–30
minutes, or until golden
brown.
6. Allow to stand for 10
minutes before slicing.

Chipped Ham Sandwiches

Betty K. Drescher
Quakertown, PA

Makes 8 servings

Prep. Time: 10 minutes
Cooking/Baking Time: 1 hour

1 lb. chipped ham
1 small onion, chopped
 fine
½ cup ketchup
2–3 tsp. apple cider
 vinegar, depending upon
 your taste preference
3 Tbsp. brown sugar

1. Mix together all ingredients in a mixing bowl. Put in
small roaster pan.
2. Cook uncovered at 300°
for 1 hour, stirring occasionally.
3. Serve in warmed mini-
sandwich rolls.

Poultry Main Dishes

Fancy Baked Chicken

Denise Martin
Lancaster, PA
Flo Mast, Broadway, VA

Makes 8 servings

Prep. Time: 20 minutes
Cooking/Baking Time: 45–60 minutes

---

1 stick (½ cup) butter, melted
¾ cup grated Parmesan cheese
1 tsp. garlic powder
½ tsp. salt
8 boneless, skinless chicken breast halves
1½ cups soft bread crumbs

1. Combine butter, cheese, garlic powder, and salt in a shallow bowl. Mix well.
2. Dip each piece of chicken in mixture. (Reserve remaining butter mixture.)
3. Coat each chicken breast half with bread crumbs.

4. As you finish with each piece, place it in a greased 9 × 13 baking pan. Spoon reserved butter mixture over top.
5. Bake uncovered at 350° for 45–60 minutes.

Variations:

1. Cut each breast half into 6–8 nuggets, each about 1½" square.

2. Place the melted butter in a shallow bowl.

3. Mix cheese, salt, and bread crumbs together in another shallow bowl.

4. Dip each nugget into butter, and then into cheese-crumb mixture.

5. Place in a single layer in baking pan. Bake at 400° for 10 minutes.

6. Serve hot or cold.

— **Flo Mast**
Broadway, VA

Parmesan Chicken

Janet Oberholtzer, Ephrata, PA
Cindy Krestynick
Glen Lyon, PA
Susan Roth, Salem, OR
Sherri Mayer
Menomonee Falls, WI
Mary C. Wirth, Lancaster, PA

Makes 6 servings

Prep. Time: 15–20 minutes
Cooking/Baking Time: 20–35 minutes

---

1 cup grated Parmesan cheese
2 cups fine bread crumbs
5⅓ Tbsp. (⅓ cup) butter, melted
⅓ cup prepared mustard
6 boneless, skinless chicken breast halves

1. Combine Parmesan cheese, bread crumbs, and butter in a shallow bowl.
2. Coat chicken breasts with thin layer of mustard and dip into crumb mixture, coating well.

3. As you finish coating each breast, lay it in a greased 9 × 13 baking pan.

4. Bake uncovered at 400° for 20–35 minutes, or until chicken is cooked through.

Variations:

1. Add 1 Tbsp. garlic powder to Step 1, if you wish.

2. Instead of using only breasts, use 2 legs and thighs combined, 2 breast halves, and 4 wings, skin removed from all of them.

—**Cindy Krestynick**
Glen Lyon, PA

1. Use mayonnaise instead of prepared mustard.

2. Add 1 tsp. Italian seasonings to Step 1, if you wish.

3. You can use frozen breasts, too. Follow the same procedure, but bake 40–50 minutes.

—**Susan Roth**
Salem, OR

1. For a lower fat version, dip chicken in water, instead of mustard or mayonnaise, before coating with crumbs.

2. And skip the bread crumbs and butter in Step 1. Instead, mix ½ cup Parmesan cheese with 1 envelope dry Italian salad dressing mix and ½ tsp. garlic powder. Continue with Steps 3 and 4.

—**Sherri Mayer**
Menomonee Falls, WI

Chicken with Feta Cheese

Susan Tjon
Austin, TX

Makes 6 servings

Prep. Time: 20 minutes
Cooking/Baking Time: 35 minutes

6 boneless chicken cutlets
2 Tbsp. lemon juice, *divided*
½ pkg. (about 3 ozs.) feta cheese, crumbled
1 red *or* green pepper, chopped

1. Preheat oven to 350°. Spray 9 × 13 baking pan with non-stick cooking spray.

2. Place chicken cutlets in bottom of pan. Sprinkle with 1 Tbsp. lemon juice.

3. Crumble feta cheese evenly over the cutlets. Top with remaining tablespoon of lemon juice.

4. Bake uncovered for 35 minutes. Sprinkle with chopped pepper before serving.

A Tip —

Keep cooked chicken in the freezer so it's ready when you need to quickly make a recipe.

Cheesy Chicken Breasts

Cheryl Lapp
Parkesburg, PA

Makes 4 servings

Prep. Time: 5–15 minutes
Cooking/Baking Time: 1 hour

4 chicken breast halves
8 slices bacon
1 egg, beaten
1 cup herb stuffing crumbs
½ lb. Velveeta, *or* your choice of, cheese, sliced

1. Put 2 slices uncooked bacon around each breast.

2. Crush stuffing crumbs with rolling pin to make finer.

3. Place egg in shallow dish. Place stuffing crumbs in another shallow dish. Lightly grease a 9 × 13 baking dish.

4. Dip each piece of chicken in egg and then in stuffing crumbs.

5. Lay each coated piece in baking pan, without them touching each other.

6. Bake uncovered at 350° for 40 minutes.

7. Top each breast half with slice of cheese.

8. Continue baking another 10–20 minutes, or until chicken is brown and cheese has melted.

Corn-Bread Chicken

Kaye Taylor
Florissant, MO

Makes 6 servings

Prep. Time: 10 minutes
Cooking/Baking Time: 30 minutes

8½-oz. pkg. corn-bread mix
1 envelope dry Ranch
  salad dressing mix
1 cup milk
6 4-oz. boneless, skinless
  chicken breast halves
2 Tbsp. oil

1. In large resealable plastic bag, combine corn-bread mix and salad dressing mix.
2. Pour milk into shallow bowl.
3. Dip chicken in milk, then place in bag with dry mixes and shake to coat.
4. In large skillet, heat oil over medium-high heat. Brown half the chicken on both sides. Remove and keep warm. Repeat with second batch. (Doing the chicken in two batches allows each piece to brown rather than steam, which happens when the skillet is crowded.)
5. Place browned chicken in 9 × 13 baking pan and bake uncovered for about 15 minutes, or until juices run clear.

Oven Crisp Chicken

Barbara Yoder
Christiana, PA
Bernice Britez
Morris, PA

Makes 12 servings

Prep. Time: 15 minutes
Cooking/Baking Time: 1 hour
  30 minutes

1 cup buttermilk baking
  mix
1 tsp. salt
2 tsp. paprika
12 chicken legs and thighs,
  skin removed

1. Mix baking mix, salt, and paprika in a zip-lock bag.
2. Either grease, or lay a piece of foil in, the bottom of a 9 × 13 baking pan.
3. Shake 1 piece of chicken at a time in bag until coated.
4. Lay each piece in baking pan. Keep the pieces from touching each other if possible.
5. Bake uncovered at 325° for 1 hour and 30 minutes, or until juices run clear.

Variations:
1. Melt 1 Tbsp. butter in baking pan before adding chicken.
2. Add ¼ tsp. pepper to Step 1.
— **Bernice Britez**
  Morris, PA

Crispy Ranch Chicken

Barb Shirk, Hawkins, WI
Arlene Snyder, Millerstown, PA
Doyle Rounds, Bridgewater, VA
Pat Chase, Fairbank, IA

Makes 6–8 servings

Prep. Time: 10 minutes
Cooking/Baking Time: 20–25
  minutes

¾–2 cups crispy rice cereal
¾ cup grated Parmesan
  cheese
1 envelope dry Ranch
  dressing mix
2 egg whites, beaten
8 boneless, skinless
  chicken thighs, about 5
  ozs. each

1. Preheat oven to 350°.
2. Spray a large baking sheet with non-stick cooking spray.
3. Combine rice cereal, Parmesan cheese, and dry dressing mix in a large bowl.
4. Place beaten egg whites in a medium-sized bowl.
5. Dip each chicken thigh in the egg whites, and then in the cereal.
6. Arrange the coated chicken on the prepared baking sheet.
7. Bake for about 20–25 minutes, or until chicken is golden and juices run clear when meat is pierced with a knife.

Variations:
1. Substitute crushed

cornflakes for the rice cereal.

2. Substitute 1 stick (½ cup) melted butter for the 2 beaten egg whites.

3. Substitute 8 boneless, skinless chicken breast halves, or 1 cut-up fryer, for the thighs.

— **Arlene Snyder**
Millerstown, PA

— **Doyle Rounds**
Bridgewater, VA

— **Pat Chase**, Fairbank, IA

Yummy Quick Chicken

Kathleen A. Rogge
Alexandria, IN

Makes 4 servings

Prep. Time: 15 minutes
Cooking/Baking Time: 25 minutes

½ cup Ranch dressing
1 Tbsp. flour
4 boneless, skinless chicken breast halves
¼ cup cheddar cheese, shredded
¼ cup grated Parmesan cheese

1. Mix dressing and flour in a shallow bowl.
2. Lightly grease a 8 × 8 baking dish.
3. Coat each chicken breast with dressing-flour mixture. As you finish with each piece, place it in baking dish.
4. Mix cheeses together in a small bowl. Sprinkle over chicken.

5. Bake uncovered at 375° for 25 minutes, or until juices run clear when meat is pricked with a fork.

Dressed-Up Chicken

Sue Hamilton
Minooka, IL

Makes 4 servings

Prep. Time: 3 minutes
Cooking/Baking Time: 10–15 minutes

1 lb. boneless, skinless thinly sliced chicken breast cutlets
½ cup Ranch salad dressing
5-oz. pkg. potato chips of your choice

1. Lightly grease a 7 × 11 baking dish.
2. Pour Ranch dressing into shallow bowl.
3. Crush potato chips, but leave rather coarse. Place in another shallow bowl.
4. Coat chicken on both sides with dressing. Shake off extra dressing.
5. Coat both sides with chips.
6. Place on baking sheet and bake uncovered 10–15 minutes.

Tasty Onion Chicken

Amber Swarey, Honea Path, SC
Norma P. Zehr, Lowville, NY

Makes 4 servings

Prep. Time: 15 minutes
Cooking/Baking Time: 20–25 minutes

1 stick (½ cup) butter, melted
1 Tbsp. Worcestershire sauce
1 tsp. ground mustard
2.8-oz. can French-fried onions, crushed
4 boneless, skinless chicken breast halves

1. Lightly grease a 7 × 11 baking dish.
2. In a shallow bowl, combine butter, Worcestershire sauce, and mustard.
3. Place onions in another shallow bowl.
4. Dip chicken, one piece at a time, in butter mixture, then coat with onions. As you finish, place each piece in the baking dish.
5. Drizzle with any remaining butter mixture.
6. Bake uncovered at 400° for 20–25 minutes or until chicken juices run clear when meat is pierced with a fork.

Variation: Simplify by dipping the chicken only in a beaten egg, and then in 2 cans of crushed French-fried onions. Proceed with Step 6 above.

— **Norma P. Zehr**
Lowville, NY

Basil Chicken Strips

Melissa Raber, Millersburg, OH

Makes 2 servings

Prep. Time: 10 minutes
Cooking/Baking Time: 10 minutes

½ lb. boneless, skinless
  chicken breasts, cut into
  ¾"-wide strips
2 Tbsp. flour
3 Tbsp. butter
2 Tbsp. red wine vinegar
  or cider vinegar
½ tsp. dried basil

1. In a large resealable
plastic bag, shake chicken
strips and flour until coated.

2. In a large skillet over
medium high heat, melt
butter. Add chicken. Sauté for
5 minutes.

3. Stir in the vinegar and
basil. Cook until chicken
juices run clear.

COQ au VIN

Chicken Fingers with BBQ Sauce

Jan Pembleton
Arlington, TX

Makes 4 servings

Prep. Time: 20 minutes
*Cooking/Baking Time: 12–15
minutes*

2 Tbsp. honey mustard
2 Tbsp. buttermilk
½ cup dried bread crumbs
1 lb. boneless, skinless
  chicken breasts, cut into
  12 equal strips
6 Tbsp. barbecue sauce
  (hickory-flavored is
  especially good)

1. Preheat oven to 450°.
Place large baking sheet in
oven to preheat.

2. In shallow dish, whisk
together mustard and but-
termilk. Place bread crumbs
in a separate dish.

3. Add chicken, a few
pieces at a time, to mustard
mixture. Turn to coat.

4. Transfer chicken, a few
pieces at a time, to bread
crumbs. Toss to coat.

5. Remove the hot baking
sheet from oven and coat
with cooking spray. Place
chicken on baking sheet,
keeping pieces from touching
each other. Bake 6 minutes.
Flip and bake until golden
brown and cooked through,
about 6 minutes more.

6. Serve with barbecue
sauce on side.

*Tip from Tester: For added
zest, use Italian-flavored or
herb-seasoned bread crumbs.*

Sesame Baked Chicken

Sandra Haverstraw
Hummelstown, PA

Makes 4 servings

Prep. Time: 10 minutes
Cooking/Baking Time: 1½ hours

1 stick (½ cup) butter,
  melted
⅔ cup fine cracker crumbs
  (15 crackers)
¼ cup toasted sesame
  seeds
⅓ cup evaporated milk, *or*
  light cream
1 broiler fryer, cut up

1. Pour melted butter into
9 × 13 baking dish.

2. Mix crumbs and sesame
seeds in a shallow bowl.

3. Place milk in another
shallow bowl. Dip chicken in
milk, one piece at a time.

4. Roll chicken in crumbs,
one piece at a time.

5. When each piece is
coated, dip skin side into
butter. Turn over and bake,
uncovered, at 350° for 1½
hours, or until juices run
clear when meat is pierced
with a fork.

Crunchy Creamy Chicken

Betty Moore, Plano, IL
Arlene Snyder, Millerstown, PA
Orpha Herr, Andover, NY

Makes 6 servings

Prep Time: 45 minutes
Cooking/Baking Time: 30 minutes

3–4-lb. whole chicken, cut up
2 10¾-oz. cans cream of
  chicken soup
8 ozs. sour cream
1 sleeve Ritz, *or* other
  snack, crackers, crushed
1 stick (½ cup) butter

1. Place chicken pieces in large stockpot. Add water to cover about half the depth of the chicken. Cover and simmer gently until chicken begins to fall off the bone. Remove from hot broth and allow to cool.
2. When cool enough to handle, debone chicken. Place meat in greased 9 × 13 baking pan.
3. In a large mixing bowl, blend soup and sour cream. Spread over chicken.
4. Melt butter in a small sauce pan. Stir in crushed crackers. Sprinkle on top.
5. Bake uncovered at 350° for 30 minutes, or until crumbs are brown and casserole is bubbly.

Variation: Instead of a whole chicken, use 4–5 whole chicken breasts. Proceed with Step 1.

— **Arlene Snyder**
  Millerstown, PA

Tip from Tester: Use low-fat or fat-free sour cream if you like.

Creamy Baked Chicken

Norma Grieser
Clarksville, MI

Makes 8 servings

Prep. Time: 15 minutes
Cooking/Baking Time: 1½ hours

10¾-oz. can cream of
  chicken soup
10¾-oz. can cream of
  celery soup
½ cup white, *or* cooking,
  wine
¾ cup shredded cheddar
  cheese
8 chicken breast halves

1. In a good-sized mixing bowl, mix first four ingredients together.
2. Place chicken in a lightly greased 9 × 13 baking pan.
3. Pour creamy mixture over breasts.
4. Cover and bake for 1 hour at 350°. Uncover and bake an additional 30 minutes, or until juices run clear when meat is pierced with a sharp fork.

A Tip —

Slice chicken when it is partly frozen. It is much easier to slice cleanly.

Chicken Breast Bliss

Virginia Blish
Akron, NY

Makes 6 servings

Prep Time: 25 minutes
Cooking/Baking Time: 1 hour

6 chicken breast halves
2 Tbsp. oil, *divided*
10¾-oz. can cream of
  celery soup
2½ cups boiling water
1 envelope dry onion soup
  mix

1. Brown half the chicken breasts in a large skillet in 1 Tbsp. oil. When both sides are lightly browned, place in a greased 9 × 13 baking dish. Repeat with the second half of the breasts.
2. In a large mixing bowl, blend soup, boiling water, and dry onion soup mix together. Pour over chicken breasts.
3. Bake uncovered in a 350° oven for 1 hour.

Tip: You can substitute pork chops for the chicken breasts. And you can use cream of mushroom or cream of chicken instead of the celery soup.

Vanished Chicken

Janice Burkholder
Richfield, PA

Makes 8 servings

Prep. Time: 10–15 minutes
Cooking/Baking Time: 1 hour

1 envelope dry onion soup
   mix
2 Tbsp. brown sugar
½ cup ketchup
1 cup water
3-4 lbs. chicken pieces

1. Mix all ingredients, except chicken, together.
2. Put chicken pieces in a greased 9 × 13 baking dish. Pour sauce over chicken.
3. Bake uncovered for 1 hour at 350°, or grill for 30 minutes using indirect heat. Baste frequently.

Teddy's Italian Chicken

Teddy Decker
Albuquerque, NM

Makes 4 servings

Prep. Time: 5 minutes
Cooking/Baking Time: 37–67 minutes

4 boneless, skinless
   chicken breast halves
14½-oz. can diced tomatoes
14½-oz. can tomato sauce
2 tsp. Italian seasoning, *or*
   1 tsp. dried basil and
   1 tsp. dried oregano
2 cups shredded herb-
   flavored cheese

1. Place chicken breast halves, frozen or thawed, into a greased 7 × 11 baking dish in a single layer.
2. In a medium-sized mixing bowl, stir together diced tomatoes and tomato sauce. Pour over chicken. Sprinkle with seasoning.
3. Bake in 350° oven for 30 minutes if chicken is fresh, or for 1 hour if chicken is frozen. Continue baking until juices run clear when meat is pierced with a fork.
4. Remove pan from oven and turn oven to broil.
5. Sprinkle chicken with cheese. Broil 5–7 minutes, or until cheese melts and bubbles.

Smokey Mountain Chicken

Amber Swarey, Honea Path, SC

Makes 4–6 servings

Prep. Time: 15 minutes
Cooking/Baking Time: 45–60 minutes

1 medium-sized onion,
   sliced
3 lbs. chicken legs and
   thighs, *or* breast halves
½ cup ketchup
½ cup maple syrup
¼ cup vinegar
2 Tbsp. prepared mustard,
   optional

1. Place onions in bottom of greased 9 × 13 baking pan.
2. Arrange chicken in a single layer over top of onions.
3. Combine remaining ingredients in a small bowl. Pour over all, completely coating chicken.
4. Bake uncovered at 350° for 45–60 minutes, basting several times. Chicken is finished when juices run clear after meat is pierced with a fork.

Jerk-Seasoned Chicken and Pepper Saute

Louise Bodziony
Sunrise Beach, MO

Makes 4 servings

Prep. Time: 5–10 minutes
Cooking/Baking Time: 15–20 minutes

1 lb. boneless, skinless
   chicken breast halves,
   cut into ¾"-wide strips
2 tsp. Caribbean jerk
   seasoning
1 pkg. frozen bell pepper
   and onion stir fry
⅓ cup orange juice
2 tsp. cornstarch

1. Spray large non-stick skillet lightly with cooking spray. Heat over medium heat until hot.

2. Add chicken and jerk seasoning. Cook and stir 5–7 minutes, or until chicken is no longer pink.

3. Add pepper and onion stir fry. Cover and cook 3–5 minutes, or until vegetables are crisp-tender. Stir occasionally.

4. Meanwhile, in a small bowl, combine orange juice and cornstarch. Blend until smooth. Add to mixture in skillet; cook and stir until bubbly and thickened.

5. This is good served over cooked rice.

Sweet and Sour Baked Chicken

Charmaine Caesar, Lancaster, PA
Carol Armstrong, Winston, OR
Barbara Smith, Bedford, PA

Makes 6–8 servings

Prep. Time: 10 minutes
Cooking/Baking Time: 1½ hours

¼–½ cup olive oil
3–4 lb. cut-up chicken,
 or 8 breast halves, *or* 8
 chicken legs and thighs
8- *or* 12-oz. jar apricot
 preserves
1 envelope dry onion soup
 mix
8-oz. bottle Italian, *or*
 Russian, salad dressing

1. Coat bottom of 9 × 13 baking pan with olive oil.
2. Place chicken pieces in pan.

3. Place apricot preserves in a medium-sized microwave-safe dish. Cover and microwave on High for 1 minute. Stir. Continue microwaving for 30-second periods, stirring between, until preserves melt.

4. Add onion soup mix and salad dressing to melted preserves. Stir well and then spoon over chicken.

5. Bake in pre-heated oven at 325° for 1–1½ hours, depending on how tender chicken is. Bake until juices run clear when meat is pierced with a fork.

Variations:

1. Skip the olive oil. Instead, lightly grease the baking pan before filling with chicken.

2. Sprinkle the chicken with either salt or garlic salt before topping with sauce.

 —Carol Armstrong
 Winston, OR

3. Use an 8-oz. jar apricot preserves, and add an 8-oz. jar pineapple preserves, to Step 3.

 —Barbara Smith
 Bedford, PA

Sour Cream Basil Chicken
Rika Allen
New Holland, PA

Makes 4 servings

Prep. Time: 5 minutes
Cooking/Baking Time: 30 minutes

2 lbs. skinless boneless
 chicken thighs (about 8
 pieces)
1–2 Tbsp. olive oil, *divided*
1 cup fat free sour cream
¼ cup white cooking wine
1 Tbsp. dried basil

1. Put 1 Tbsp. olive oil in large non-stick skillet. Brown half the chicken over medium-high heat, about 3 minutes on each side. Remove and keep warm while browning the rest of the chicken. (Add additional olive oil when browning second batch of chicken, if needed.)

2. Meanwhile, mix sour cream, wine, and basil together in a small bowl.

3. When all chicken pieces are browned and removed from skillet, place sauce in skillet.

4. Cook over low heat, uncovered, until sauce thickens, about 10 minutes.

5. Return browned chicken to skillet, nestling into the sauce. Heat over low heat until meat is thoroughly warmed.

Lemon Chicken

Ruth Shank
Monroe, GA

Makes 6 servings

Prep. Time: 10 minutes
Cooking/Baking Time: 40–50
  minutes

6 boneless, skinless
   chicken breast halves
¼ cup lemon juice
2 tsp. dried oregano
½ tsp. salt, *or* garlic
   powder
¼ tsp. ground black
   pepper
olive oil

1. Preheat oven to 375°.
2. Place chicken breasts in a greased 9 × 13 baking dish.
3. Mix lemon juice, oregano, salt, and pepper together in a small bowl. Pour over chicken.
4. Place in oven. Brush with olive oil every 10 minutes, turning chicken pieces over occasionally.
5. Bake for 40–50 minutes, or until juices run clear when pricked with a sharp fork.

Lemonade Chicken

Carol L. Stroh
Akron, NY

Makes 4 servings

Prep. Time: 10 minutes
Cooking/Baking Time: 30–35
  minutes
Marinating Time: 8 hours, or
  overnight

1 large can frozen
   lemonade, thawed but
   not diluted
4 boneless, skinless
   chicken breast halves
¾ cup dry bread crumbs
half a stick (4 Tbsp.) butter,
   melted

1. Pour lemonade over chicken in a large plastic bag or covered bowl. Marinate overnight in the refrigerator.
2. Drain chicken. Roll each piece in breadcrumbs. Place in a lightly greased 8 × 8, or 9 × 13 baking pan, depending on size of breasts.
3. Drizzle melted butter over chicken.
4. Bake 30–35 minutes at 350°, or until chicken is done. Chicken is finished baking when the juices run clear when meat is pierced with a sharp fork.

Company Chicken

Elaine Vigoda
Rochester, NY

Makes 6 servings

Prep. Time: 5–7 minutes
Cooking/Baking Time: 25–30
  minutes

1 cup peach jam
¼ cup prepared mustard
1 Tbsp. lemon *or* lime juice
1 Tbsp. curry powder
6 boneless, skinless
   chicken breast halves

1. In a small saucepan, mix jam, mustard, juice, and curry. Simmer 5 minutes. (Or mix together in a microwave-safe bowl. Cover and microwave on High for 1 minute. Stir. If jam hasn't melted, microwave another 30 seconds. Stir. Repeat until jam melts.)
2. Pat chicken dry and place in 9 × 13 baking pan.
3. Pour sauce over chicken.
4. Bake uncovered in a 350-degree oven for 10 minutes.
5. Turn each chicken piece to cover with sauce.
6. Cover and continue baking another 10 minutes.

A Tip —

Warm a lemon to room temperature before squeezing it in order to get more juice from it.

Honey-Glazed Chicken

Laura R. Showalter
Dayton, VA

Makes 6–8 servings

Prep. Time: 10–20 minutes
Cooking/Baking Time: 1½ hours

3 lbs. chicken pieces
5⅓ Tbsp. (⅓ cup) butter, melted
⅓ cup honey
2 Tbsp. prepared mustard
1 tsp. salt
1 tsp. curry powder, *optional*

1. Place chicken skin-side up in a 9 × 13 baking dish. (The dish is just as tasty if you remove skin from chicken!)
2. Combine sauce ingredients in a small bowl. Pour over chicken.
3. Bake uncovered at 350° for 1 hour. Baste ever 15–20 minutes. Cover and continue baking 30 minutes, or until chicken is tender and juices run clear when pierced with a sharp fork.

Tip: If you are unable to baste the chicken while baking, double the sauce so that it almost covers the chicken.

Honey-Baked Chicken Strips

Jan Rankin
Millersville, PA

Makes 3–4 servings

Prep. Time: 20–30 minutes
Cooking/Baking Time: 15 minutes

2 egg whites
1 Tbsp. honey
2 cups cornflake crumbs
¼–½ tsp. salt *or* garlic powder
1 lb. chicken tenders, cut into strips

1. Mix egg whites and honey together in a shallow bowl.
2. Place cornflake crumbs and seasoning in another shallow bowl.
3. Dip chicken strips into egg-white-honey mixture.
4. Then coat each strip with cornflake crumbs.
5. Place each strip on ungreased cookie sheet and bake at 400° for 15 minutes.

Savory Cranberry Chicken

Janice Muller
Derwood, MD

Makes 6 servings

Prep. Time: 10–15 minutes
Cooking/Baking Time: 40–60 minutes

6 boneless, skinless chicken breast halves
16-oz. can whole berry cranberry sauce
8-oz. bottle French salad dressing
1 envelope dry onion soup mix

1. Arrange chicken in an ungreased 9 × 13 baking pan.
2. Combine remaining ingredients in a small bowl.
3. Pour sauce over chicken breasts. Cover with foil.
4. Bake at 350° for 40-60 minutes, or until juices run clear when meat is pierced with a sharp fork.

Orange Chicken

Jan Mast
Lancaster, PA

Makes 6 servings

Prep. Time: 5 minutes
Cooking/Baking Time: 40 minutes

6 boneless, skinless
  chicken breast halves
6-oz. can orange juice
  concentrate, undiluted
1 tsp. paprika
1 tsp. dried rosemary
1 tsp. dried basil

1. Place chicken on a
baking sheet.
2. Broil 3–5 minutes on
each side until golden brown.
3. Remove from oven and
place meat in a 9 × 13 baking
pan. Reduce heat to 350°.
4. Pour orange juice
concentrate over chicken.
Sprinkle with paprika and
then with herbs.
5. Bake uncovered 30
minutes, or until done and
juices run clear when pierced
with a fork.

A Tip —

Use gravy as soon after
you've made it as possible.
Gravy tends to thin as it
sits.

Do-Ahead Chicken

Annabelle Unternahrer
Shipshewana, IN
Krista Hershberger
Elverson, PA
Susan Tjon, Austin, TX
Carol Hershey, Jonestown, PA
Dorothy VanDeest
Memphis, TN
Deborah Heatwole
Waynesboro, GA
Peggy C. Forsythe, Bartlett, TN
Erma Martin, East Earl, PA
Martha Hershey, Ronks, PA

Makes 4–6 servings

Prep. Time: 10–15 minutes
Cooking/Baking Time: 2½ hours

4–6 boneless, skinless
  chicken breast halves
8 very thin slices, *or*
  4-oz. container, dried
  beef (sometimes called
  "chipped, air-dried
  beef," and found in the
  refrigerated meat section
  near the bacon)
4–6 slices lean bacon
10¾-oz. can mushroom soup
8 ozs. sour cream

1. Wrap each chicken
breast half with dried beef.
Secure with slice of bacon.
2. Place chicken in a lightly
greased baking dish, large
enough to accommodate 4–6
chicken breasts.
3. Mix soup and sour
cream in a bowl. Spread over
chicken.
4. Bake uncovered at 300°
for 2½ hours.

Tips:
1. You can make this
ahead of when you need it and
refrigerate it for several hours.
Cover with foil and reheat for
20–30 minutes at 350°.
2. This dish makes a lot of
gravy, and it is good on rice,
pasta, or mashed potatoes.

Tip from Tester: To eliminate
some bacon grease from
accumulating in the dish, pre-
cook the bacon. But stop while
it still bends easily and before it
gets crispy.
—Annabelle Unternahrer
Shipshewana, IN

Variations:
1. Top with buttered bread
crumbs during the last 30
minutes of baking, if you wish.
Mix together ½ cup fine bread
crumbs and 2 Tbsp. melted
butter.
—Carol Hershey
Jonestown, PA
—Erma Martin, East Earl, PA

2. Sprinkle with paprika and
rosemary just before baking, if
you wish.
—Deborah Heatwole
Waynesboro, GA

3. If you don't have time
to have the dish bake for 2½
hours, you can bake it at 350°
for 50 minutes. Cover it for the
first 30 minutes.
—Erma Martin, East Earl, PA

Picante Chicken

Janice Crist
Quinter, KS
Nancy Graves
Manhattan, KS

Makes 4 servings

Prep. Time: 10–15 minutes
Cooking/Baking Time: 30–35 minutes

4 boneless, skinless
  chicken breast halves
16-oz. jar picante sauce
3 Tbsp. brown sugar
1 Tbsp. prepared mustard

1. Place chicken in a greased shallow 2-quart baking dish.
2. In a small bowl, combine the picante sauce, brown sugar, and mustard. Pour over chicken.
3. Bake uncovered at 400° 30–35 minutes, or until chicken juices run clear.
4. Serve over rice if you wish.

Variation: Here's a simpler version: Place chicken in baking dish. Sprinkle with salt and pepper. Spoon picante sauce over top. Proceed with Step 3 above.

— Nancy Graves
Manhattan, KS

Salsa Chicken

Barbara Smith
Bedford, PA

Makes 4 servings

Prep. Time: 10–15 minutes
Cooking/Baking Time: 35–45 minutes

4 boneless, skinless
  chicken breast halves
1 cup salsa
4 tsp. dry taco seasoning
  mix
1 cup cheddar cheese,
  shredded
2 Tbsp. sour cream,
  optional

1. Place chicken in a lightly greased 9 × 13 baking dish.
2. Sprinkle top and bottom of each breast with taco seasoning.
3. Spoon salsa over chicken.
4. Bake covered at 375° for 25–30 minutes, or until chicken is tender and juicy. Sprinkle with cheese.
5. Return to oven and continue baking uncovered for 10 minutes, or until cheese is melted and bubbly.
6. Top with sour cream as you serve the chicken, if you wish.

Honey Mustard Chicken

Rhoda Nissley
Parkesburg, PA

Makes 4 servings

Prep. Time: 5 minutes
Cooking/Baking Time: 20 minutes

½ cup Miracle Whip salad
  dressing
2 Tbsp. prepared mustard
1 Tbsp. honey
4 boneless, skinless
  chicken breast halves

1. In a small mixing bowl, stir salad dressing, mustard, and honey together.
2. Place chicken on grill or rack of broiler pan. Brush with half the sauce.
3. Grill or broil 8–10 minutes. Turn and brush with remaining sauce.
4. Continue grilling or broiling 8–10 minutes, or until tender.

Chicken Cacciatore with Green Peppers

Donna Lantgen
Golden, CO

Makes 6 servings

Prep. Time: 5–10 minutes
Cooking/Baking Time: 1 hour

1 green pepper, chopped
1 onion, chopped
1 Tbsp. Italian seasoning
15½-oz. can diced tomatoes
6 boneless, skinless
  chicken breast halves

1. Mix the first 4 ingredients in a bowl.
2. Put chicken in a lightly greased 9 × 13 glass baking dish.
3. Spoon sauce over top.
4. Bake covered at 350° for 1 hour.

Chicken with Peppers and Onions

Jeanette B. Oberholtzer
Manheim, PA

Makes 4–6 servings

Prep. Time: 15–20 minutes
Cooking/Baking Time: 1 hour

1 frying chicken, cut in
  pieces, *or* 4–6 legs and
  thighs, *or* 4–6 boneless,
  skinless breast halves

salt and pepper
2–3 onions, sliced
1–2 sweet green peppers,
  sliced
18-oz. bottle hickory-
  smoked barbecue sauce

1. Wash chicken and pat dry with paper towel. Arrange in a single layer in a large frying pan. Sprinkle with salt and pepper.
2. Arrange onions and peppers in layers on top of chicken.
3. Pour barbecue sauce over all. Cover and cook on medium-high heat about 45 minutes, or until chicken is tender. Turn chicken once during cooking.
4. Remove cover and continue cooking 15–20 minutes longer, or until sauce is thickened. If sauce cooks down too quickly, add ½ cup water.

Chicken and Green Bean Casserole

Janet Oberholtzer, Ephrata, PA

Makes 6–8 servings

Prep Time: 20–30 minutes
Cooking/Baking Time: 30–60 minutes

3–4 cups diced, cooked
  chicken
16-oz. pkg. frozen cut green
  beans, cooked
2 10½-oz. cans cream of
  chicken soup

½ cup water
2 cups shredded cheddar
  cheese
1 cup buttered bread
  crumbs

1. Layer chicken and green beans in a greased 9 × 13 baking dish.
2. In a mixing bowl, combine soup and water. Pour over chicken and green beans.
3. Sprinkle with cheese and bread crumbs.
4. Bake uncovered at 350° for 30–60 minutes, or until bubbly.

Tip: Use your own leftover chicken, or rotisserie chicken, or canned chicken.

Chicken and Broccoli Bake

Jan Rankin
Millersville, PA

Makes 6 servings

Prep Time: 10–15 minutes
Cooking/Baking Time: 30–35 minutes

16-oz. bag of chopped
  broccoli, thawed
3 cups cooked, cut-up
  chicken breast
2 cans cream of chicken
  soup
2½ cups milk, *divided*
2 cups buttermilk baking
  mix

1. In a large mixing bowl, combine broccoli, chicken, soup, and 1 cup of milk. Pour into a lightly greased 9 × 13 baking pan.

2. Mix together 1½ cups milk and buttermilk baking mix. Spread over top of mixture in pan.

3. Bake at 450° for 30 minutes.

Tip: *To cook the chicken, cut 2 large chicken breast halves into 1"-square chunks. Place in long microwave-safe dish. Cover with waxed paper. Microwave on High for 4 minutes. Turn over each piece of chicken. Cover and microwave on High for 2 more minutes.*

Chicken Broccoli Casserole

Della Yoder, Kalona, IA

Makes 5–6 servings

Prep Time: 30 minutes
Cooking/Baking Time: 35 minutes

5–6 cups cooked chicken (your own leftovers, rotisserie chicken, *or* canned chicken)
2 10-oz. pkgs. broccoli spears, cooked according to pkg. directions
1 envelope dry onion soup mix
1 pint sour cream
10¾-oz. can cream of mushroom soup
grated cheese, *optional*

1. Prepare chicken and broccoli.

2. In a large mixing bowl, blend dry onion soup mix, sour cream, and cream of mushroom soup together.

3. Fold in cooked chicken and broccoli. Spoon into lightly greased 9 × 13 baking pan.

4. Bake at 350° for 30 minutes. Sprinkle with grated cheese, if you wish, and bake for five more minutes.

Chicken Divine

Carlene Horne, Bedford, NH
Carol Lenz, Little Chute, WI

Makes 4 servings

Prep. Time: 20 minutes
Cooking/Baking Time: 45 minutes

4 boneless chicken breast halves, cubed
1-lb. pkg. frozen chopped broccoli
1 cup shredded cheddar cheese, *divided*
10¾-oz. can cream of mushroom soup
½ cup bread crumbs

1. Place half of chicken cubes in shallow microwave-safe dish. Cover with waxed paper. Microwave on High for 4 minutes. Stir. Microwave on High an additional 2 minutes. Remove chicken and repeat process for the rest of the chicken.

2. Place broccoli in microwave-safe dish. Cover and microwave on High for 3½ minutes. Stir. Microwave on High for 2½ minutes.

3. Place broccoli in bottom of lightly greased casserole dish.

4. Layer chicken over top. Sprinkle with half the cheese.

5. Spread mushroom soup over top. Sprinkle with remaining cheese.

6. Sprinkle bread crumbs over all.

7. Bake uncovered at 350° for 45 minutes.

Tip: *You can make this through Step 6 the night before you want to serve it. Refrigerate until ready to bake.*

Variation: *Use cream of chicken soup instead of mushroom. Mix it with 1 cup Miracle Whip and 1 tsp. lemon juice before adding it to the dish in Step 5.*

—**Carol Lenz**
Little Chute, WI

Super Swiss Chicken

Jan Rankin, Millersville, PA
Carla J. Elliott, Phoenix, AZ
Joyce Shackelford, Green Bay, WI
Christie Detamore-Hunsberger
Harrisonburg, VA
Colleen Heatwole, Burton, MI
Lavina Hochstedler
Grand Blanc, MI
Janeen L. Zimmerman
Denver, PA

Makes 6 servings

Prep. Time: 20 minutes
Cooking/Baking Time: 1 hour

6 boneless, skinless
   chicken breasts halves
6 slices of Swiss, *or*
   American, cheese
10¾-oz. can cream of
   chicken soup
soup can of water
half a stick (4 Tbsp.) butter
2 cups herb-seasoned
   stuffing crumbs

1. Place chicken breast halves in a lightly greased 9 × 13 baking dish.
2. Place one slice of cheese on top of each chicken breast.
3. In a medium-sized mixing bowl, combine can of soup with soup can of water. Pour over chicken and cheese.
4. Melt butter in a medium-sized saucepan. Brown stuffing mix in butter. Sprinkle crumbs over casserole.
5. Bake uncovered at 350° for 1 hour.

Variation: Use ½ cup white wine and only half a soup-can of water in Step 3.
— **Joyce Shackelford**
Green Bay, WI

Scalloped Chicken and Stuffing

Rosemarie Fitzgerald
Gibsonia, PA
Chris Kaczynski
Schenectady, NY
Joyce L. Moser, Copenhagen, NY
Karen Waggoner, Joplin, MO

Makes 6 servings

Prep Time: 20–25 minutes
Cooking/Baking Time: 30 minutes

3 whole chicken breasts
10¾-oz. can cream of
   chicken soup
10¾-oz. can cream of
   mushroom soup
1 cup sour cream *or* yogurt
1 box stuffing mix

1. Cut the chicken breasts into 1" chunks. Put half in a microwave-safe 7 × 11 dish. Cover with waxed paper. Microwave on High for 4 minutes. Turn chunks over, cover, and microwave for another 2 minutes on High. Spread cooked chicken in greased 9 × 13 baking pan. Repeat with remaining half of chicken.
2. In a large mixing bowl, blend soups with sour cream. Spread over chicken in pan.
3. Prepare stuffing mix according to package directions. Spread over chicken mixture.
4. Bake uncovered at 350° for 30 minutes, or until heated through and bubbly.

Variation: Use corn-bread stuffing mix for a somewhat different flavor.
— **Karen Waggoner**
Joplin, MO

Tip: Make this dish with leftover chicken or turkey if you have it on hand or in the freezer.
— **Rosemarie Fitzgerald**
Gibsonia, PA

A Tip —

Rice can be baked in the oven along with a meat dish. In a separate greased baking dish, mix rice and water (1 part rice to 2 parts water). Bake for the same time amount as you would cook it on the stove top.

Chicken with Apples and Stuffing

Jean H. Robinson
Cinnaminson, NJ

Makes 6 servings

Prep. Time: 15–20 minutes
Cooking/Baking Time: 60 minutes

6 boneless chicken breasts
  halves, flattened
2 Tbsp. olive oil
1 pkg. chicken-flavored
  stuffing mix
21-oz. can apple pie filling
¼ cup brown sugar

1. Place olive oil in large
skillet. Brown half the
chicken breasts 3 minutes
on each side. Remove and
keep warm. Repeat with the
remaining breasts.
2. Meanwhile, make
stuffing according to package
directions.
3. In a medium-sized
mixing bowl, mix brown
sugar and pie filling together.
Put in bottom of lightly
greased 9 × 13 baking pan.
4. Put chicken on top of
apple mixture.
5. Spoon stuffing over top
of chicken.
6. Cover loosely with
foil and bake at 350° for
45 minutes. Uncover and
bake 15 more minutes until
stuffing is browned.

Chicken Bruschetta Bake

Krista Hershberger
Elverson, PA

Makes 6 servings

Prep. Time: 15 minutes
Cooking/Baking Time: 60 minutes

1½ lbs. boneless, skinless
  chicken breasts, cut into
  cubes
1 tsp. Italian seasoning
28-oz. can Italian-style
  stewed tomatoes, well
  drained
¾ cup shredded
  mozzarella cheese
6-oz. pkg. stuffing mix for
  chicken
1½ cups water

1. Place chicken in lightly
greased 9 × 13 baking dish.
Sprinkle with seasoning.
2. Spread tomatoes over top.
3. Sprinkle with cheese.
4. In a mixing bowl,
combine stuffing mix with
1½ cups water. Spoon over
baking-pan ingredients.
5. Cover and bake for 30
minutes. Remove cover and
bake 30 more minutes.

Chicken with Veggies

Beth Shank
Wellman, IA

Makes 2 servings

Prep. Time:10 minutes
Cooking/Baking Time: 1¼ hours

2 boneless chicken breast
  halves
cut-up carrots *or* baby
  carrots for 2 servings
quartered potatoes (peeled
  or unpeeled) for 2
  servings
salt and pepper to taste
10½-oz. can cream of
  onion soup

1. Put chicken in lightly
greased shallow baking dish.
2. Place vegetables around
and on top of the chicken.
Salt and pepper lightly.
3. Spoon the soup (undi-
luted) over it all and cover
with foil.
4. Bake at 350° for 65–75
minutes, or until vegetables
are tender.

Chicken Potato Dish

Ruth Fisher
Leicester, NY

Makes 10–12 servings

Prep. Time: 30 minutes
Cooking/Baking Time: 1–2 hours

10 chicken thighs, skinned and deboned
8 potatoes
½ tsp. salt
pinch of pepper
1 cup sour cream
10¾-oz. can cream of chicken soup

1. Cut chicken thighs in half. Place in roaster.
2. Peel potatoes and cut into chunks. Scatter over chicken in roaster.
3. Sprinkle with salt and pepper.
4. In a mixing bowl, blend sour cream and chicken soup together.
5. Spoon over chicken and potatoes.
6. Bake covered at 350° for 1–2 hours, or until chicken and potatoes are tender.

A Tip —

Use a kitchen shears to cut up chicken. It is fast, safe, and easy.

Coconut Chicken Curry

Rika Allen, New Holland, PA

Makes 6–8 servings

Prep. Time: 10–15 minutes
Cooking/Baking Time: 1 hour and 20 minutes

5 lbs. skinless chicken thighs, about 10 pieces
2 onions, chopped
3–4 potatoes, peeled *or* unpeeled, and chopped, *optional*
13½-oz. can coconut milk
2–3 tsp. curry powder
1–1½ tsp. salt and dash of pepper

1. Put chicken in large stockpot. Add 3" of water. Bring to boil. Reduce heat to medium and cook for about 20 minutes.
2. Skim off fat.
3. Add onions, and potatoes if you wish.
4. Bring to boil. Reduce heat to medium, and cook 15 minutes, or until onions and potatoes are tender.
5. Add coconut milk, curry powder, salt, and pepper. Uncover, and cook down over medium heat for 20–30 minutes.
6. This is good served over cooked rice.

Tips:
1. For a different flavor, use sweet potatoes instead of white potatoes.
2. Add chopped garlic to Step 3.

Chicken-Rice Bake

Carol Eberly, Harrisonburg, VA
Anna Stoltzfus, Honey Brook, PA
Susan Wenger, Lebanon, PA
Agnes Dick, Vanderhoof, BC

Makes 4–6 servings

Prep Time: 15 minutes
Cooking/Baking Time: 1–2 hours

1 cup uncooked long-grain rice
1 envelope dry onion soup mix
6 chicken pieces, your choice
10¾-oz. can cream of chicken soup
2 soup cans of water
parsley flakes, *optional*

1. Spread rice in bottom of greased 9 × 13 baking pan. Sprinkle onion soup mix over rice.
2. Arrange chicken pieces over all.
3. Combine cream of chicken soup and water in a large mixing bowl. Combine thoroughly. Pour evenly over rice and chicken.
4. Cover and bake in 350° oven for 1–2 hours, or until meat and rice are tender.

Variations:
1. Change the order in which the ingredients are assembled:

1. Put rice in bottom of greased 9 × 13 baking pan.
2. Combine cream of chicken soup and water in a large mixing bowl. Pour over rice.

3. Place chicken pieces on top, pushing them down into the soup.

4. Sprinkle with dry onion soup and parsley flakes.

5. Cover and bake at 350° for 1–2 hours, or at 275° for 3 hours.

— **Anna Stoltzfus**
Honey Brook, PA

2. Substitute 1 can mushroom soup and 1 soup can milk for the 2 cans of water.

— **Susan Wenger**
Lebanon, PA

3. Add 2 cups fresh or frozen vegetables (mixed, or a single variety), and 1 tsp. dried basil, to combined cream soup and water, if you wish.

— **Agnes Dick**
Vanderhoof, BC

Wild Rice Mushroom Chicken

Karen Waggoner, Joplin, MO

Makes 4 servings

Prep. Time: 10 minutes
Cooking/Baking Time: 30 minutes

4 boneless chicken breast halves
2½ Tbsp. butter, *divided*
half a large sweet red pepper, *or* 1 whole small, pepper, chopped
4½-oz. can sliced mushrooms, drained
6-oz. pkg. long-grain and

wild rice mix, cooked according to directions
frozen peas, *optional*

1. In a large skillet, saute chicken in 1½ Tbsp. butter for 7–10 minutes on each side, or until meat is no long pink and juices run clear. Remove chicken and keep warm.

2. Melt 1 Tbsp. butter in skillet. Saute red pepper until tender.

3. Stir in mushrooms; heat through.

4. Add rice. Stir in frozen peas if you wish, and steam until hot.

5. Serve mixture over chicken breasts.

Chicken Noodle Casserole

Cheryl A. Lapp, Parkesburg, PA

Makes 6 servings

Prep Time: 5–10 minutes
Chilling Time: 4–8 hours, or overnight
Cooking/Baking Time: 1 hour

4 cups cooked chicken, cut into small pieces (use your own leftover cooked chicken, rotisserie cooked chicken, *or* canned chicken)
2 cups chicken broth
10¾-oz. can cream of mushroom soup
½ cup Velveeta, *or* your choice of creamy, cheese, cut into small cubes
half a lb. uncooked Kluski,

or **other sturdy, noodles**

1. Mix above ingredients together in a large mixing bowl. Spoon into greased 9 × 13 baking pan. Cover and refrigerate overnight.

2. Bake at 350°, uncovered, for 30 minutes. Cover and continue baking another 30 minutes.

Chicken Fajita Stir Fry

Eileen Eash, Carlsbad, NM

Makes 4 servings

Prep. Time: 5 minutes
Cooking/Baking Time: 12 minutes
Marinating Time: 1 hour

1 lb. chicken tenders
¼ cup Claude's Fajita Marinating Sauce
1 Tbsp. cooking oil
16-oz. bag fiesta blend vegetables, frozen

1. Pour sauce over chicken and marinate at least 1 hour.

2. Brown chicken in oil in skillet (about 5 minutes).

3. Add vegetables and continue cooking an additional 6–7 minutes, or until vegetables are tender.

4. Serve over rice.

Tip from Tester: *Use boneless, skinless chicken breast, sliced in thin strips, if you can't find chicken tenders.*

Easy Chicken Enchiladas

Bernadette Veenstra
Grand Rapids, MI

Makes 4 servings

Prep. Time: 15 minutes
Cooking/Baking Time: 25–30 minutes

4 boneless, skinless chicken breast halves
1 Tbsp. oil
1 cup picante sauce *or* salsa
2 cups cheddar cheese, *divided*
8–10 8" tortillas

1. Cube chicken. Brown in a large skillet in 1 Tbsp. oil until cooked through.
2. Add salsa and simmer for 5 minutes.
3. Add 1¼ cups cheese. Stir until melted. Remove from heat.
4. Divide chicken mixture among tortillas. Roll up, tucking in ends.
5. Place in greased 9 × 13 baking pan. Sprinkle with remaining cheese.
6. Bake in 350 degree oven for 10–15 minutes, or until cheese melts.

Soft Chicken Tacos

Natalia Showalter
Mt. Solon, VA

Makes 5–6 servings

Prep. Time: 15–20 minutes
Cooking/Baking Time: 15 minutes

1 lb. boneless, skinless chicken breasts, cubed
15-oz. can black beans, rinsed and drained
1 cup salsa
1 Tbsp. taco seasoning
6 flour tortillas, warmed

1. In non-stick skillet, cook chicken until juices run clear.
2. Add beans, salsa, and seasoning. Heat through.
3. Spoon chicken mixture down center of each tortilla.
4. Garnish with toppings of your choice.

Guacamole Chicken

Joy Uhler, Richardson, TX

Makes 4 servings

Prep. Time: 5–10 minutes
Cooking/Baking Time: 8–15 minutes

1 lb. chicken tenders, cut into bite-size pieces
8-oz. pkg. guacamole
1 cup sour cream *or* plain yogurt

¾ cup salsa
diced green onions *or* chives

1. Brown chicken pieces in large skillet sprayed with non-stick cooking spray.
2. Mix in guacamole, sour cream, and salsa. Heat until warm.
3. Garnish with onions or chives.
4. Serve over rice.

Pozole

Jonathan Gehman
Harrisonburg, VA

Makes 6 servings

Prep. Time: 25 minutes
Cooking/Baking Time: 1 hour

4 skinless chicken thighs, approximately 1½ pounds
1 Tbsp. oil
1 small onion, chopped coarsely
3 *or* 4 cloves garlic, *or* more if you wish
water to cover, about 5 cups
1 Tbsp. *or* more chili powder, *optional*
2 15-oz. cans hominy, drained and rinsed

1. Brown chicken in oil in heavy 4½-quart stockpot. Turn to brown all sides over medium heat.
2. Add onion and garlic to stockpot. Reduce heat, cooking and stirring until onion turns clear.

3. Add 5 cups water, chili powder if you wish, and hominy. Bring to boil and reduce heat to low. Cover.

4. After 30 minutes, remove chicken. Debone. Cut meat into big chunks and return to pot.

5. Simmer at least 15 more minutes.

Tip: Pozole is traditionally served with fresh raw shredded veggies on top (tomatoes, cabbage, radishes, carrots, hot onions, chiles, etc.) with a squeeze of lime juice. Just put out bowls of chopped veggies and let people add what they want on top of their bowl. Pozole is great by itself, too.

Chicken Puffs

Carolyn Snader, Ephrata, PA

Makes 4 servings

Prep. Time: 30 minutes
Cooking/Baking Time: 20–25 minutes

8-oz. tube crescent rolls
3-oz. pkg. cream cheese with chives, softened
2 Tbsp. milk
2 cups chunked cooked chicken breasts
¼ tsp. celery salt
dash of pepper, *optional*

1. Make 4 rectangles with rolls, using 2 rolls for 1 rectangle.

2. In a good-sized mixing bowl, mix cream cheese and milk together until smooth.

Stir in chicken and the seasonings that you want.

3. Lightly grease a baking sheet.

4. Place ½ cup mixture on center of each rectangle.

5. Bring dough from opposite corners together. Pinch to hold in place. Place puffs on cookie sheet as you finish making them, being careful not to let them touch each other.

6. Bake at 350° for 20–25 minutes.

Barbecued Chicken Pizza

Susan Roth, Salem, OR
Rosalie D. Miller, Mifflintown, PA

Makes 6 servings

Prep. Time: 10–20 minutes
Cooking/Baking Time: 15–20 minutes

10- *or* 12-oz. pkg. refrigerated pizza crust
1 cup barbecue sauce, teriyaki-flavored, *or* your choice of flavors
2 cups cooked, chopped chicken breast (your own leftovers, rotisserie chicken, *or* canned chicken)
20-oz. can pineapple tidbits, drained, *optional*
½ cup green bell pepper, chopped, *optional*
¼ cup red onion, diced *or* sliced, *optional*
2 cups shredded mozzarella cheese

1. Grease large pizza pan. Roll out dough into a 12"–14" circle on pan. Spread barbecue sauce over crust.

2. Spread chopped chicken evenly over sauce.

3. Spoon either pineapple tidbits, or chopped peppers and onions, over chicken.

4. Sprinkle with cheese.

5. Bake at 425° for 15–20 minutes, or until golden brown around edges and with the cheese melted in the middle.

Tip: For a thicker crust, let the pizza dough rise before baking it (up to 1 hour). If you like a thinner crust, bake immediately without letting it rise.

Buffalo Wings

Violette Harris Denney
Carrollton, GA

Makes 8–12 servings

Prep. Time: 20–30 minutes
Cooking/Baking Time: 40–45 minutes

1 stick (½ cup) butter
5-oz. bottle cayenne pepper sauce
1 tsp. celery seed, *optional*
1½ cups potato flakes
2 lbs. chicken wings, rinsed and dried

1. Line baking sheet with foil and spray with non-stick spray.
2. Combine butter, cayenne sauce, and celery seed if you wish, in a shallow microwave-safe dish. Cook 45–60 seconds, or until butter is melted.
3. Blend mixture with a fork. Remove and reserve ½ cup sauce.
4. Place potato flakes in another shallow bowl.
5. Dip each piece of chicken into cayenne sauce. Then roll in potato flakes. Gently pat potato flakes onto chicken.
6. Place wings on prepared sheet pan. (If you wish, the coated wings can be refrigerated for several hours.)
7. Just before baking, drizzle wings with reserved cayenne sauce.
8. Bake uncovered at 425° for 40–45 minutes, until juices run clear when meat is pierced with a fork.

Mom's Cornish Hens

Kay Taylor
Florissant, MO

Makes 4 servings

Prep. Time: 25 minutes
Cooking/Baking Time: 60 minutes

half a stick (¼ cup) butter, *divided*
2 cups carrots, diced
2 cups onion, diced
4 Cornish hens
Lawry's seasoning salt, *or equivalent, optional*
¼ cup water

1. Melt 2 Tbsp. butter in large skillet.
2. Saute diced carrots and onions in skillet until crisp tender.
3. Spread vegetables over bottom of 9 × 13 baking pan.
4. Butter hens inside and out with remaining butter. Sprinkle with seasoning salt if you wish.
5. Place hens in pan on top of vegetables.
6. Add ¼ cup water around the hens.
7. Cover. Bake for 30 minutes at 350°. Uncover. Continue baking for 30 more minutes.

Turkey Loaf

Makes 10 servings

Prep. Time: 15 minutes
Cooking/Baking Time: 1½ hours
Standing Time: 10 minutes

2 lbs. ground turkey
16-oz. can whole berry cranberry sauce, *divided*
1 pkg. dry chicken-flavored stuffing
2 eggs

1. Mix all ingredients in a large bowl, reserving ¼ cup cranberry sauce.
2. When thoroughly mixed, shape into loaf. Place in lightly greased loaf pan.
3. Bake uncovered at 350° for 1 hour.
4. Spread top of loaf with ¼ cup reserved sauce. Return to oven and bake another 30 minutes.
5. Allow to stand for 10 minutes before slicing to serve.

A Tip —

Cook enough for two meals—and you can have a break from meal preparation.

118

Turkey Sausage Patties

Sharon Timpe
Jackson, WI

Makes 4 servings

Prep. Time: 10–15 minutes
Chilling Time: 1 hour
Cooking/Baking Time: 6–8 minutes

1 lb. ground turkey
½ tsp. salt
¼ tsp. white pepper
½ tsp. dried crushed sage
⅛ tsp. crushed red pepper flakes
1 Tbsp. olive oil

1. Combine turkey, salt, pepper, sage, and red pepper flakes in a bowl. Mix gently.
2. Cover and chill 1 hour to blend flavors. Shape into 8 small patties.
3. Heat olive oil in a skillet. Add the patties and cook on both sides until lightly browned and done all the way through, 3–4 minutes per side.
4. Serve immediately.

Turkey Steaks Dijon

Christie Detamore-Hunsberger
Harrisonburg, VA

Makes 4 servings

Prep. Time: 5 minutes
Cooking/Baking Time: 15 minutes

1 lb. turkey steaks
¼ tsp. black pepper, *optional*
1½ Tbsp. butter
1 cup beef broth
1 Tbsp. cornstarch dissolved in 3 Tbsp. water
1½ Tbsp. Dijon-style mustard
⅓ cup chopped onion, *optional*

1. Sprinkle turkey steaks with pepper if you wish.
2. Heat butter in skillet.
3. Brown steaks 3 minutes per side. Remove steaks and keep warm. Drain off drippings from skillet.
4. Slowly add broth to hot pan, stirring to dissolve brown particles from bottom of pan. Stir in cornstarch and water, stirring until thickened. Stir in mustard, and onion if you wish.
5. Reduce heat to medium. Return steaks to skillet and settle into sauce. Tilt pan and spoon sauce over top of steaks.
6. Cover and simmer 2–3 minutes, or just until turkey is done.
7. Place steaks on serving platter, and spoon sauce over before serving.

Turkey Divan Casserole

Leesa DeMartyn
Enola, PA

Makes 6–8 servings

Prep Time: 5–10 minutes
Cooking/Baking Time: 30 minutes

1 head broccoli, cut up *or* 16-oz. pkg. frozen cut-up broccoli, thawed
3 cups cooked turkey, cut in chunks
6 slices cheddar, *or* your choice of, cheese
10¾-oz. can cream of chicken soup
½ cup milk

1. Preheat oven to 350°.
2. Spread broccoli in ungreased 7 × 11 baking dish.
3. Top with turkey and cheese.
4. In a small bowl, mix soup and milk. Pour over turkey and cheese.
5. Bake uncovered until hot and bubbly, about 30 minutes.

Tip: If you wish, top with buttered bread crumbs (2 cups fine bread crumbs, mixed with 2 Tbsp. melted butter) and a sprinkle of paprika.

Seafood Main Dishes

Baked Fish
John D. Allen
Rye, CO

Makes 3–4 servings

Prep. Time: 10–20 minutes
Cooking/Baking Time: 20–30 minutes

1 lb. white fish fillet of
  your choice
¼ cup French dressing
½ cup cracker crumbs
paprika

1. Place the dressing in a shallow dish. Place the cracker crumbs in another shallow dish.
2. Hold the fillet over the dish with the dressing and spoon or brush the dressing over the fish.
3. Continuing to hold the fillet, spoon cracker crumbs over it on top and bottom.
4. Place fillets in a single layer in a greased baking dish.
5. Sprinkle with paprika.

6. Bake uncovered at 375° for 20–30 minutes, or until fish flakes easily. (Length of baking time depends on the kind of fish as well as its thickness.)

Tip from the Tester: Instead of cracker crumbs, use seasoned bread crumbs, if you wish.

Crumb-Topped Fish Filets
Marie Skelly, Babylon, NY

Makes 4 servings

Prep. Time: 10 minutes
Cooking/Baking Time: 10–12 minutes

half a stick (¼ cup) butter,
  melted, *or* olive oil
½ tsp. dried tarragon, *or*
  1½ tsp. fresh tarragon
  leaves
½ tsp. onion salt
1 lb. fish filets
⅔ cup dry bread crumbs

1. In a small bowl or saucepan, mix melted butter, or olive oil, and tarragon.
2. Place fish in lightly greased baking pan. Spoon half of butter mixture over top.
3. Mix remaining butter mixture with bread crumbs. Sprinkle over fish.
4. Bake at 350° for 10–12 minutes, or until fish flakes easily with fork.

Tips from the Tester:
1. I had one non-fish eater at my table when I served this dish. So I put a chicken breast in a smaller pan and fixed that for her with the same topping. She loved it!
2. Make your own bread crumbs with 100% whole wheat bread.
3. When serving, add a sprig of fresh tarragon to the top of each fish fillet.

Parsley Buttered Fish

Shirley Sears
Tiskilwa, IL

Makes 2 servings

Prep. Time: 3 minutes
Cooking/Baking Time: 5–6 minutes

2 Tbsp. butter
2 Tbsp. lemon juice
1 lb. white fish fillets
1 Tbsp. chopped fresh parsley, *or* 1 tsp. dried
salt to taste, *optional*

1. Place butter and lemon juice together in microwave-safe, 8 × 12 glass dish. Microwave on High 30–60 seconds, or until butter is melted. Stir.
2. Coat both sides of fillets with butter sauce.
3. Arrange fish in baking dish.
4. Cover with waxed paper.
5. Microwave on High until fish flakes easily, 5–6 minutes in 1000-watt oven.
6. Sprinkle with parsley, and salt if you wish, before serving.

Baked Fish

Becky Frey
Lebanon, PA

Makes 6–8 servings

Prep. Time: 15–20 minutes
Cooking/Baking Time: 30 minutes

2 lbs. fish of your choice
10¾-oz. can cream of mushroom soup
1¼ cups sour cream, *or* plain yogurt
½ cup buttered crumbs, *or* cracker crumbs
1 Tbsp. poppy seeds

1. Put fish in greased 2-quart casserole dish.
2. In a small bowl, mix soup and sour cream. Pour over fish.
3. Add poppy seeds to crumbs. Sprinkle on top.
4. Cover. Bake at 350° for 30 minutes, or just until fish flakes easily.

Baked Fish Mozzarella

Judy DeLong
Burnt Hills, NY

Makes 6–8 servings

Prep. Time: 10 minutes
Cooking/Baking Time: 10–15 minutes

2 lbs. thick flounder, *or* sole, fillets
salt and pepper to taste
½ tsp. dried oregano
1 cup shredded mozzarella cheese
1 large fresh tomato, thinly sliced

1. Butter large baking dish. Arrange fish in single layer. Sprinkle with salt, pepper, and oregano.
2. Top with shredded cheese and tomato slices.
3. Bake covered at 375° for 10–15 minutes, or until fish flakes easily.

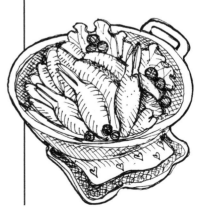

Honey Curry Sole Filets

Jean Turner
Williams Lake, BC

Makes 4 servings

Prep. Time: 10 minutes
Cooking/Baking Time: 15–20 minutes

⅓ cup honey
¼ cup Dijon mustard
¾–1 Tbsp. curry powder
half a stick (¼ cup) butter, melted
4 thick sole fillets

1. Combine first 4 ingredients in a small bowl. Mix well.
2. Lightly spray shallow baking pan. Add sole fillets, slightly overlapping, top side up.
3. Pour honey-curry sauce over top.
4. Bake at 350°, uncovered, 15–20 minutes, depending upon the thickness of the sole, until fish flakes easily. Serve at once.

Tips:
1. This recipe works well with cod and halibut, too.
2. Garnish with fresh parsley before serving.

Tip from the Tester: I also tried the recipe with fresh salmon fillets, and we loved it!

Tilapia with Mango

Sherry Goss Lapp
Lancaster, PA

Makes 4 servings

Prep. Time: 10 minutes
Cooking/Baking Time: 30 minutes

4 6-oz. tilapia fillets
2 Tbsp. soy sauce
⅛ tsp. salt
⅛ tsp. pepper, *or* lemon pepper seasoning
1 Tbsp. butter, cut into chunks
1 mango, *or* slices of dried mango

1. Place tilapia fillets in baking pan.
2. Pour soy sauce over top of fish.
3. Sprinkle salt and pepper over fish. Lay butter on top.
4. Peel the mango and cut into lengthwise pieces. Lay around fish.
5. Bake covered at 400° for 30 minutes. Turn mango slices after 15 minutes of baking.

Seasoned Salmon

Charmaine Caesar
Lancaster, PA

Makes 3 servings

Prep. Time: 10 minutes
Cooking/Baking Time: 15–20 minutes

1 lb. salmon filet
3 Tbsp. lemon juice
2 Tbsp. fresh dill, *or* 2 tsp. dried dill weed
2 Tbsp. minced garlic, *or* powdered garlic to taste
3 slices onion on top

1. Line a 9 × 13 baking pan with foil. Spray foil with non-stick spray.
2. Place fish on foil. Sprinkle with lemon juice.
3. Sprinkle with dill and garlic. Place onion slices on top.
4. Cover with second sheet of foil.
5. Bake at 450° for 15–20 minutes, or until fish flakes easily. (Salmon is still pink after being fully cooked.)

A Tip —

Do not put your good knife in the dishwasher.

Salmon Baked with Rosemary

Susan Sigraves
Lansdale, PA

Makes 4 servings

Prep. Time: 10 minutes
Cooking/Baking Time: 10–15 minutes

2 Tbsp. fresh minced rosemary, *or* 2 tsp. dried rosemary, crumbled
2 cloves of garlic, minced
⅔ cup Italian-seasoned bread crumbs
4 6-oz. salmon steaks
4 Tbsp. olive oil

1. Combine first 3 ingredients in a bowl and mash to a paste.
2. Arrange salmon steaks in a lightly greased baking dish.
3. Press equal amounts of bread-crumb mixture onto top of each salmon steak. Drizzle with oil.
4. Place in 425° oven and roast 10–15 minutes, or until fish is flaky throughout.

Oriental Salmon

Barbara Forrester Landis
Lititz, PA

Makes 6 servings

Prep. Time: 10 minutes
Marinating Time: 20 minutes
Cooking/Baking Time: 15 minutes

¼ cup rice wine vinegar
¼ cup maple syrup
1½ lbs. salmon filet

1. Preheat oven to 450°.
2. Combine rice vinegar and maple syrup in a small bowl.
3. Place salmon in a lightly greased baking dish, skin side up.
4. Pour liquid mixture over fish. Turn fish over to coat, placing skin side down. Let marinate 20 minutes.
5. Bake fish, uncovered, in marinade, for approximately 15 minutes or until it flakes easily.

Tangy Steelhead Trout or Salmon

Marie Skelly
Babylon, NY

Makes 4 servings

Prep. Time: 5 minutes
Cooking/Baking Time: 15 minutes

1¼ lbs. steelhead trout, *or* salmon
2 Tbsp. soy sauce
2 Tbsp. orange juice
1 tsp. sesame oil
1 Tbsp. rice wine vinegar

1. Lay fish skin side down in lightly greased baking dish.
2. In small bowl, combine other ingredients. Pour dressing over fish.
3. Bake at 450° for about 15 minutes, or until thickest part of fillet is flaky.

Quick Wild Salmon Cakes

Willard E. Roth
Elkhart, IN

Makes 4 servings

Prep. Time: 10 minutes
Cooking/Baking Time: 10 minutes

15-oz. can wild-caught
    Alaskan pink salmon
1 large egg
1 cup crushed wheat
    saltines
½ cup chopped onion
additional seasonings,
    optional
1 Tbsp. olive oil

   1. In a medium-sized
mixing bowl, mix salmon,
egg, saltines, and onion with
your hands. Add any other
seasonings that you wish.
   2. Form into four balls and
flatten into cakes.
   3. Heat oil in skillet,
preferably cast-iron. Brown
cakes on medium-high heat
for five minutes. Turn over
and brown an additional five
minutes on medium-high.

Salmon Bundles

Esther Porter
Minneapolis, MN

Makes 4 servings

Prep. Time: 20 minutes
*Cooking/Baking Time: 15–17
minutes*

1 6–7.5-oz. can salmon,
    drained
3-oz. pkg. cream cheese,
    softened
¼ cup chopped green
    onions
2 tsp. lemon juice
8-oz. tube refrigerated
    crescent rolls
½ tsp. dill weed, *optional*

   1. In small bowl, blend
salmon, softened cream
cheese, green onions, and
lemon juice.
   2. Unroll crescent roll
dough onto counter top.
Separate into 4 rectangles.
Press the center diagonal
seam together on each pair
of triangles to make a solid
rectangular crust.
   3. Spoon about ¼ cup
salmon filling near a short
side of the rectangle. Fold the
short side of the dough over
so edges meet. Press edges
with a fork to seal.
   4. Sprinkle with dill weed,
if you wish.
   5. Transfer bundles to
baking sheet. Bake 15–17
minutes, or until golden and
puffy. Serve warm.

Creamed Oysters

Mary W. Stauffer
Ephrata, PA

Makes 4 servings

Prep. Time: 10 minutes
*Cooking/Baking Time: 10–15
minutes*

1 pint oysters
2 Tbsp. butter
2 Tbsp. flour
milk *or* cream
¾ tsp. salt
⅛ tsp. pepper
½ tsp. Worcestershire
    sauce, *optional*

   1. Drain oysters, reserving
liquid in a one-cup measure.
   2. Melt butter in saucepan.
Slowly blend in flour.
   3. Meanwhile, add milk or
cream to oyster liquid so that
the mixture makes 1 cup.
   4. Pour liquid slowly into
butter-flour in saucepan.
Cook over low heat, stirring
constantly until smooth.
   5. When boiling, add
drained oysters. Heat thoroughly but do not boil.
   6. Season with salt, pepper,
and Worcestershire sauce if
you wish.

*Tip: This is delicious served
over toast points, corn-bread
squares, or baked patty shells.*

Grilled Fish Marinade

Darlene Bloom
San Antonio, TX

Makes 2+ cups marinade

Prep. Time: 3 minutes
Marinating Time: 3–4 hours
Grilling Time: 15 minutes

1 cup soy sauce (reduced
  sodium works well)
½ cup lemon juice
half a stick (¼ cup) butter,
  melted
1 clove garlic, minced
3 Tbsp. brown sugar
3 lbs. fish

1. Mix all ingredients together in bowl. Pour into a re-sealable bag.
2. Place 3 lbs. sturdy fish in the bag with the marinade. Place in refrigerator for 2 hours. Turn upside down and continue to marinate in the fridge for another 1–2 hours.
3. Remove fish from bag. Put fish skin side down on a hot grill.
4. After 5 minutes, turn the fish and remove the skin. Continue grilling until fish flakes, up to 10 more minutes.

Richly Herby Scallops

Barbara Jean Fabel
Wausau, WI

Makes 2–4 servings

Prep. Time: 10 minutes
Cooking/Baking Time: 15 minutes

1 stick (¼ lb.) butter
¼ cup fresh chives
¼ cup fresh parsley
1 lb. large scallops
Italian-flavored bread
  crumbs

1. Melt butter in a 9 × 9 baking pan in a 425° oven.
2. Add chives and parsley.
3. Dip each scallop in the herb-butter mixture. Then place in baking pan.
4. Sprinkle heavily with Italian-flavored bread crumbs.
5. Bake uncovered at 425° for 15 minutes.

Stir Fry Scallops

Donna Treloar
Hartford City, IN

Makes 4 servings

Prep. Time: 5 minutes
Cooking/Baking Time: 5 minutes

12–16 large scallops
½ tsp. chili powder
½ tsp. dried oregano
2 Tbsp. olive oil

1. Rinse scallops and dry with paper towel.
2. Mix seasonings in small bowl. Toss and coat scallops.
3. Stir fry in hot olive oil for about 3–5 minutes, just until opaque.

Scallops in Wine Sauce

Doris M. Zipp
Germantown, NY

Makes 2–4 servings

Prep. Time: 10 minutes
Cooking/Baking Time: 10 minutes

1 stick (½ cup) butter
1 lb. scallops
2 Tbsp. flour
½ cup dry white wine
fresh parsley

1. Melt butter in skillet.
2. Add scallops and sauté until barely cooked.
3. Sprinkle flour over scallops. Stir until flour is moistened. Add wine. Stir and simmer just until a creamy sauce appears. Be careful not to overcook the scallops.
4. Garnish with parsley.

Tip: This makes a great sauce and works well served with spaghetti.

Scallops with Spinach and Bacon

Norma Gehman
Ephrata, PA

Makes 4 servings

Prep. Time: 5 minutes
Cooking/Baking Time: 15–20 minutes

4 slices bacon
1 lb. fresh sea scallops
½–1 Tbsp. Old Bay, *or* Cajun, seasoning
10-oz. bag fresh spinach
2 Tbsp. balsamic vinegar

1. In a large skillet, cook bacon until crisp. Remove all but 1 Tbsp. drippings. Drain and crumble bacon and set aside.
2. Rinse scallops and pat dry. Add to drippings in skillet. Add seasoning and stir gently.
3. Cook over medium heat until scallops are browned and opaque, turning once. Remove from pan and keep warm.
4. Add well washed spinach to skillet. Cover and heat 2 minutes or until wilted down.
5. Add vinegar and mix thoroughly.
6. Return scallops to pan. Heat through.
7. Sprinkle bacon over top just before serving.

Crab Imperial

Cheryl A. Lapp
Parkesburg, PA

Makes 4–6 servings

Prep. Time: 5 minutes
Cooking/Baking Time: 20 minutes

1 lb. crabmeat
3 Tbsp. butter
2 whole garlic cloves, chopped fine
¼ tsp. onion powder
16-oz. jar Alfredo sauce

1. Cut crabmeat into small pieces.
2. Melt butter in a large skillet. Saute crab with garlic and onion powder for 10 minutes, or until meat is hot and garlic is softened.
3. Add Alfredo sauce. Simmer over low heat another 10 minutes, stirring frequently. (Thin with ½ cup milk if the sauce seems too thick.)
4. Serve over hot cooked noodles.

Crab Pizza

Sharon Easter
Yuba City, CA

Makes 6–8 servings

Prep. Time: 10 minutes
Cooking/Baking Time: 13–15 minutes

half a stick (¼ cup) butter
6 green onions, sliced thin
8-oz. pkg. cream cheese, cubed
½ lb. flaked crabmeat
prepared pizza crust

1. Melt butter in a large skillet. Add onions and cook until onions soften.
2. Toss cubed cream cheese into skillet. Heat until bubbly and melted, stirring frequently to prevent scorching.
3. Break up crab with a fork. Stir into creamy sauce in skillet. Continue heating over low heat until crab is also hot.
4. Meanwhile, heat a large pizza bread crust on a baking sheet in a 400° oven for 5 minutes. Remove crust from oven.
5. Turn oven to 450°. Spoon crab mixture onto crust. Place pizza in oven and bake 8 minutes.

Shrimp with Sun-Dried Tomatoes

Josie Healy
Middle Village, NY

Makes 3–4 servings

Prep. Time: 10 minutes
Cooking/Baking Time: 10 minutes

2 Tbsp. olive oil
1 lb. cleaned and peeled shrimp
2 cloves garlic, minced
¼ cup white wine
6–8 sun-dried tomatoes, chopped (use dry tomatoes, not in oil)

1. Place olive oil in large skillet and heat. Carefully add shrimp and garlic, being careful not to splatter yourself with the hot oil.
2. Saute, stirring constantly, until shrimp is slightly pink and garlic is softened.
3. Stir in wine and sun dried tomatoes. Cook another 1–2 minutes over low heat.
4. If you'd like more liquid, add ¼ cup water, more wine, or chicken stock.
5. Serve over rice or pasta.

Shrimp Curry

Sharon Swartz Lambert
Harrisonburg, VA

Makes 4–6 servings

Prep. Time: 10 minutes
Cooking/Baking Time: 20 minutes

2 Tbsp. chopped onion
1 Tbsp. curry powder
10¾-oz. can cream of mushroom soup
1 cup sour cream
1 cup cooked shelled shrimp

1. Sweat onion in non-stick skillet.
2. Stir in curry powder and mushroom soup. Let simmer over medium heat for 5 minutes.
3. Add sour cream and cooked shrimp. Heat through.
4. Serve over rice.

Variation: You may use plain yogurt or smooth cottage cheese in place of the sour cream.

A Tip —

When purchasing a new skillet make sure it has weight to it. Heavier skillets distribute heat more evenly.

Tuna with Black Pepper and Artichokes

Stephanie Walker
Keezletown, VA

Makes 4 servings

Prep. Time: 10 minutes
Cooking/Baking Time: 10 minutes

3 6½-oz. jars artichoke hearts, drained and halved
1 lemon, cut into 8 slices
2 cloves garlic, thinly sliced
1½ lbs. fresh tuna, cut into 1" pieces
1½ tsp. salt
1 tsp. black pepper

1. Place artichoke hearts, lemon slices, and garlic cloves in a large non-stick skillet over medium heat. Cook until heated through, about 3 or more minutes.
2. Transfer to a plate.
3. Season tuna on both sides with salt and pepper.
4. Place tuna in hot skillet. Sear for about 1 minute on each side.
5. Return the artichoke mixture to skillet and toss to combine.
6. Serve over cooked rice.

Tip: Look for artichokes packed in oil or water. If you can only find marinated artichokes, rinse well and pat dry.

Baked Tuna Salad

Ruth Shank
Monroe, GA

Makes 4–6 servings

Prep. Time: 10–15 minutes
Cooking/Baking Time: 30–35 minutes

7 cans (6-oz.) chunk light tuna, drained
2 ribs celery, chopped
3 cups Miracle Whip salad dressing
2 Tbsp. dry minced onion
1 scant cup evaporated milk
1–2 8-oz. cans water chestnuts, drained and chopped, *optional*

1. In a large mixing bowl, combine tuna, celery, salad dressing, onion, evaporated milk, and water chestnuts if you wish.
2. Turn into greased baking dish.
3. Bake covered at 350° for 30–35 minutes, or until bubbly and heated through.

Tip: To make Tuna Melts using leftover Baked Tuna Salad:

1. Spread salad on slices of bread. Place on cookie sheet.
2. Layer slices of your favorite cheese on top.
3. Bake uncovered at 400° for 8–12 minutes, or until cheese begins to melt and tuna is heated through.

Tuna Burger Sandwich

Nathan LeBeau
Rapid City, SD

Makes 6 servings

Prep. Time: 15 minutes
Cooking/Baking Time: 15 minutes

6-oz. can tuna, packed in water
¼ cup cheddar cheese, shredded
1 cup chopped celery
small onion, minced, *optional*
¼ cup Miracle Whip salad dressing
6 hamburger buns

1. Layer ingredients on the buns.
2. Wrap in aluminum foil.
3. Place in oven at 350° for 15 minutes. Serve hot.

Tuna Noodle Casserole

Carol Lenz
Little Chute, WI
Rosemarie Fitzgerald
Gibsonia, PA

Makes 6–8 servings

Prep. Time: 15 minutes
Cooking/Baking Time: 30–45 minutes

2 cups dry elbow macaroni
2 6-oz. cans tuna, packed in water
2 10¾-oz. cans mushroom soup
2 cups shredded cheddar cheese
salt and pepper to taste
1 cup frozen peas, *optional*
¾ cup cornflake crumbs, *optional*

1. Cook macaroni according to package directions. Drain. Place cooked pasta in a large mixing bowl.
2. Stir in tuna, soup, cheese, salt and pepper, and peas if you wish. Stir together gently until well mixed. Top with cornflake crumbs if you want.
3. Place in lightly greased 2-quart casserole. Top with cornflake crumbs if you want.
4. Bake uncovered at 350° for 30–45 minutes, or until heated through and bubbly.

Pasta

Pasta with Fresh Tomatoes and Basil

Naomi Cunningham
Arlington, KS

Makes 2 servings

Prep Time: 5 minutes
Standing Time: 2–3 hours
Cooking/Baking Time: 15 minutes

2 large fresh tomatoes, chopped
2 Tbsp. snipped fresh basil, *or* 2 tsp. dried basil
1 garlic clove, minced
¼ tsp. pepper
4 ozs. dry bow tie, *or* other, pasta, cooked and drained
additional fresh basil, *optional*

1. Combine the tomatoes, basil, garlic, and pepper in a mixing bowl.

2. Set aside at room temperature for several hours.
3. Serve over hot cooked pasta.
4. Garnish with additional basil if you wish.

Tomato and Mozzarella Pasta Sauce

Josie Healy
Middle Village, NY

Makes 6 servings

Prep. Time: 10 minutes
Standing Time: 30 minutes

14-oz. can diced tomatoes with garlic and oil
½ lb. fresh mozzarella cheese, cubed
3–4 fresh basil leaves, chopped
salt and pepper to taste

1. Mix all ingredients in a good-sized mixing bowl.
2. Let stand for 30 minutes at room temperature.
3. Serve over 1 lb. cooked pasta of your choice.

A Tip —

Fresh ingredients are always the best. If you substitute less expensive ingredients, test the dish before serving it to guests.

Sophia's Favorite Spaghetti Sauce

Barbara Jean Fabel
Wausau, WI

Makes 4–6 servings

Prep. Time: 10 minutes
Cooking/Baking Time: 30 minutes

6 Tbsp. olive oil
1–2 cloves garlic, crushed
24-oz. can peeled tomatoes
1 Tbsp. minced fresh basil,
 or 1 tsp. dried basil
1 tsp. sugar

1. Heat olive oil in a skillet.
2. Add garlic and heat for 30 seconds. Watch carefully so it doesn't burn.
3. Stir in the tomatoes, basil, and sugar until well blended.
4. Lower heat and cook gently for 30 minutes, stirring occasionally.
5. Serve over a pound of cooked pasta.

Stuffed Pasta Shells

Jean M. Butzer, Batavia, NY
Lori Lehman, Ephrata, PA
Rhoda Atzeff, Lancaster, PA

Makes 12–14 servings

Prep. Time: 30–45 minutes
Cooking/Baking Time: 30–45 minutes

1 lb. shredded mozzarella cheese
15-oz. container ricotta cheese
10-oz. pkg. frozen chopped spinach, thawed and squeezed dry
12-oz. pkg. jumbo pasta shells, cooked and drained
28-oz. jar spaghetti sauce

1. Combine cheeses and spinach in a good-sized mixing bowl.
2. Stuff a rounded tablespoonful into each shell.
3. Arrange filled shells in a greased 9 × 13 baking dish.
4. Pour spaghetti sauce over the shells.
5. Cover and bake at 350° for 30–45 minutes, or until heated through.

Broccoli Noodle Supreme

Virginia Blish, Akron, NY

Makes 6 servings

Prep Time: 10 minutes
Cooking/Baking Time: 15 minutes

3 cups uncooked egg noodles
2 cups broccoli florets
10¾-oz. can condensed cream of chicken-and-broccoli, *or* cream of chicken, soup
½ cup sour cream
⅓ cup grated Parmesan cheese
⅛ tsp. pepper, *optional*

1. Cook noodles in a saucepan according to package directions. Add broccoli during the noodles' last 5 minutes of cooking.
2. Drain and set aside. Keep warm.
3. In the same saucepan, combine soup, sour cream, Parmesan cheese, and pepper if you wish. Cook and stir until heated through.
4. Remove from heat and stir in noodles and broccoli mixture. Mix thoroughly and serve.

Parmesan Noodles

Jan Mast
Lancaster, PA

Makes 4–6 servings

Prep. Time: 7 minutes
Cooking/Baking Time: 10 minutes

8-oz. pkg., *or* 3 cups, uncooked noodles
¾ stick (6 Tbsp.) butter, melted
1 cup Parmesan cheese
¼ tsp. garlic salt
½ cup light cream
1 tsp. parsley, *optional*

1. Cook noodles as directed on package. Drain. Return noodles to stockpot.
2. Stir in remaining ingredients, except parsley. Toss to mix.
3. Just before serving, garnish with parsley if you wish.

Fettuccine with Butter-Herb Sauce

Stacy Stoltzfus
Grantham, PA

Makes 3–4 servings

Prep Time: 5 minutes
Cooking/Baking Time: 8–10 minutes

⅓ lb. uncooked fettuccine noodles
half a stick (4 Tbsp.) butter, melted
1 Tbsp., or more, fresh basil, *or* 1 tsp. dried basil
¼ tsp. dried thyme
¼ cup fresh parsley (do not use dried)
1 Tbsp. chives, *optional*

1. Cook fettuccine noodles according to package directions.
2. Meanwhile blend remaining ingredients in a small pitcher.
3. Drain noodles very well when done and transfer to a serving bowl.
4. Pour melted butter with herbs over noodles. Toss and serve immediately.

Tip: For best flavor, use fresh herbs. Feel free to alter the amounts to your own taste. You may also substitute extra-virgin olive oil for the butter.

Classic Pesto

Leona Yoder
Hartville, OH

Makes about 1½ cups

Prep Time: 10 minutes

2 cups lightly packed fresh basil
1 cup (about 5 ozs.) grated Parmesan cheese
½–⅔ cup extra-virgin olive oil
1–2 cloves garlic, *optional*

1. Whirl basil, Parmesan, half the oil, and, if desired, garlic in a blender or food processor until smooth. Add more oil, if needed.
2. If you're not ready to use the pesto immediately, cover and refrigerate it for up to 5 days. Or freeze it if you want to store it longer.
3. Serve over your favorite cooked pasta, or on bruschetta.

Penne with Herb Cheese and Spinach

Barbara A. Nolan
Pleasant Valley, NY

Makes 4 servings

Prep. Time: 10 minutes
Cooking/Baking Time: 25–30 minutes

½ lb. penne pasta
2 Tbsp. olive oil
2 Tbsp. minced garlic
10-oz. pkg. fresh baby spinach, washed and drained
5–6-oz. container garlic/herb cheese spread
½ cup pasta cooking water
salt and pepper to taste, *optional*

1. Cook pasta according to directions on box. Set aside ½ cup cooking water. Drain the rest of the water off, and keep pasta warm.
2. Heat olive oil in large stockpot.
3. Cook minced garlic until soft, 5–6 minutes. Do not brown.
4. Add spinach and cook until wilted, about 3–4 minutes.
5. Coarsely chop spinach.
6. Add cheese and ½ cup water from pasta to spinach in pan. Cook over medium-low heat, stirring to melt cheese.
7. Add cooked pasta to spinach/cheese mixture.
8. Season with salt and pepper if you wish.
9. Toss gently. Serve immediately.

Alfredo Sauce

Barbara Kuhns
Millersburg, OH

Makes 2½–3 cups

Prep. Time: 3–5 minutes
Cooking/Baking Time: 20 minutes

1 stick (½ cup) butter
1 pint heavy cream
1 tsp. garlic powder
pepper, *optional*
½ cup Parmesan cheese
2 Tbsp. cream cheese,
  softened

1. Lightly brown butter in a small saucepan.
2. Add rest of ingredients and simmer over low heat for 15 minutes, or until all ingredients are well blended.
3. Stir occasionally to prevent sticking and scorching.

Bow-Tie Pasta with Peas and Bacon

J. B. Miller
Indianapolis, IN

Makes 4 servings

Prep Time: 5 minutes
Cooking/Baking Time: 20 minutes

1 lb. uncooked bow tie pasta
3 strips bacon
2–3 ozs. bleu cheese
2 cups frozen peas
salt and pepper

1. Cook pasta in boiling, salted water as directed on package.
2. While the pasta cooks, dice bacon and crumble cheese.
3. In a large skillet, cook bacon over medium-high heat until crisp. Remove and drain bacon, keeping 1 Tbsp. of the pan drippings.
4. When the pasta is done but before draining it, stir frozen peas into pasta cooking water. Drain well and place in large bowl.
5. Add bacon, cheese, and reserved pan drippings to pasta and peas. Toss.
6. Add salt and freshly ground pepper to taste. Mix well and serve.

Tip: Substitute asparagus cut into bite-size pieces for the peas.

Chicken Alfredo Penne

Esther Gingerich
Parnell, IA

Makes 4 servings

Prep. Time: 5–8 minutes
Cooking/Baking Time: 15 minutes

½ lb. uncooked penne
  pasta
1½ cups frozen sugar snap
  peas
15-oz. jar Alfredo sauce
2 cups sliced cooked
  chicken

1. In a large saucepan, cook pasta in boiling water for 6 minutes.
2. Add peas. Return to boil. Cook 4–5 minutes, or until pasta is tender.
3. Drain pasta mixture.
4. Stir in sauce and chicken. Heat over medium heat for a few minutes, just until chicken is heated through. Stir frequently so the penne doesn't stick and scorch.

Chicken Alfredo
Erma Martin
East Earl, PA

Makes 4 servings

Prep. Time: 15 minutes
Cooking/Baking Time: 15–20 minutes

8-oz. pkg. cream cheese, cubed
¾ cup milk, *divided*
½ tsp. garlic powder
salt and pepper to taste
4 skinless, boneless chicken breast halves, cooked and diced

1. In skillet over medium heat, melt cream cheese in about ⅓ cup of the milk, stirring until smooth.
2. Add remaining milk and seasoning. Cook about 3 minutes until thickened.
3. Add diced chicken and cook until chicken is well heated, about 3 minutes.
4. Serve over half a pound (dry) cooked fettuccine or other pasta.

Variation: Add 2–3 cups thawed cut-up (frozen) broccoli to Step 3. Extend cooking time for that Step to 5–7 minutes.

Tip: Begin heating the cooking water for the fettuccine when you begin Step 1.

Vegetable-Turkey Pasta Sauce
Janelle Yoder
Lancaster, PA

Makes 6 servings

Prep. Time: 10 minutes
Cooking/Baking Time: 15 minutes

¾ lb. ground turkey
1 large green pepper, chopped into chunks
1 large onion, chopped
2 ripe tomatoes, chopped
2 cups Alfredo sauce

1. Brown ground turkey in large skillet with pepper and onions.
2. Stir in tomatoes and sauce. Heat through, stirring frequently so the sauce doesn't stick.
3. Serve over cooked spaghetti, linguine, or fettucine.

Tortellini Carbonara
Monica Yoder
Millersburg, OH

Makes 4 servings

Prep. Time: 2 minutes
Cooking/Baking Time: 25 minutes

8 bacon strips, cooked and crumbled, *or* ½ cup prepared cooked and crumbled bacon
1 cup whipping cream
½ cup fresh parsley, chopped
½ cup grated Parmesan, *or* Romano, cheese
9-oz. pkg. cheese tortellini

1. Combine bacon, cream, parsley, and cheese in a large saucepan. Cook over low heat until hot. Stir frequently to prevent sticking and scorching.
2. Meanwhile, cook tortellini according to package directions. Drain and transfer to a serving dish.
3. Drizzle cheese sauce over tortellini and toss to coat.

A Tip —
    If you can read a recipe and follow directions you can cook.

Spaghetti with Clam Sauce

Susan Kasting
Jenks, OK

Makes 4 servings

Prep. Time: 5 minutes
Cooking/Baking Time: 20 minutes

1 lb. uncooked spaghetti
2 sticks (1 cup) butter
3 cloves garlic, minced
2 6-oz. cans chopped
  clams, with juice
½ cup chopped fresh
  parsley

1. Cook spaghetti al dente according to package directions.
2. Meanwhile, melt butter in saucepan. Stir in garlic and sauté briefly.
3. Add clams and parsley. Heat just until hot throughout.
4. Drain spaghetti and return to cooking pot. Pour sauce over noodles and mix through.
5. Let stand for a few minutes so the pasta can absorb some of the sauce.

Variation: Replace 1 stick of butter with ½ cup dry white wine.

Quicky Bolognese Spaghetti

Judi Robb
Manhattan, KS

Makes 4 servings

Prep. Time: 10 minutes
Cooking/Baking Time: 20 minutes

1 onion, chopped
1 lb. lean hamburger
½ lb. uncooked spaghetti
10½-oz. can tomato soup
10¾-oz. can cream of
  mushroom soup

1. Saute onion and hamburger together in large skillet. Drain.
2. While onion and meat are browning, cook spaghetti according to package directions. Drain when finished cooking.
3. Add both soups to browned meat and onion. Cover and simmer for 5 minutes.
4. Add cooked spaghetti to skillet. Stir and serve.

A Tip —

Keep peeled onions covered in a jar when refrigerated.

Bacon Cheeseburger Pasta

Janelle Reitz
Lancaster, PA

Makes 4–6 servings

Prep. Time: 10 minutes
Cooking/Baking Time: 20 minutes

8 ozs. uncooked tube, *or*
  spiral, pasta
1 lb. ground beef
6 bacon strips, diced
10½-oz. can tomato soup
4 ozs. shredded cheddar
  cheese
barbecue sauce, *optional*
prepared mustard, *optional*

1. Cook pasta according to package directions. Drain.
2. Meanwhile, in a skillet, cook beef over medium heat until no longer pink. Drain and set aside.
3. In the same skillet, cook bacon until crisp. Remove with slotted spoon to paper towels. Discard drippings. Break bacon into pieces.
4. Add pasta to skillet. Add soup, bacon, and beef. Heat through.
5. Sprinkle with cheese. Cover and cook until the cheese is melted.
6. Serve with barbecue sauce and mustard as condiments, if you wish.

Cheeseburger Macaroni

Carol Eberly
Harrisonburg, VA

Makes 4 servings

Prep. Time: 10 minutes
Cooking/Baking Time: 15 minutes

1 lb. ground beef
1 cup chopped onion
14½-oz. can stewed
 tomatoes
1 cup water
1 cup uncooked elbow
 macaroni
1½ cups shredded cheddar
 cheese

1. Brown meat and onion in large skillet. Drain.
2. Add tomatoes and 1 cup water. Bring to boil.
3. Stir in macaroni. Cover and simmer 10 minutes, or until done.
4. Stir in cheese.

Simply Lasagna

Janelle Nolt, Richland, PA
Jeannine Janzen, Elbing, KS

Makes 6–8 servings

Prep. Time: 15 minutes
Cooking/Baking Time: 1 hour
Standing Time: 10–15 minutes

1 lb. lean ground beef
28-oz. jar spaghetti sauce
 of your choice, *divided*
8 lasagna noodles,
 uncooked, *divided*
15-oz. container ricotta
 cheese
2 cups grated mozzarella
 cheese

1. Brown ground beef in a skillet. Drain.
2. Arrange in a lightly greased 9 × 13 baking dish: ⅓ jar of sauce, 4 uncooked noodles, all the ricotta cheese, and all the ground beef.
3. Follow that with ⅓ jar of sauce, 4 uncooked noodles, and the remaining sauce.
4. Bake covered at 375° for 1 hour.
5. Top with mozzarella cheese.
6. Allow to stand 10–15 minutes before cutting and serving.

Variations:
 1. Make this a vegetarian dish by dropping the ground beef.
 2. Add ¼ cup grated Parmesan on top of the ricotta cheese in Step 2.

 —Jeannine Janzen
 Elbing, KS

Pigs in Blankets

Ruth E. Martin
Loysville, PA

Makes 6–8 servings

Prep. Time: 30 minutes
Cooking/Baking Time: 45 minutes

1 lb. uncooked lasagna
 noodles
1½ lbs. smoked sausage
1 quart pizza sauce, *divided*
2 cups shredded
 mozzarella cheese

1. Spray a 9 × 13 baking pan with non-stick cooking spray.
2. Cook noodles in boiling water for 10 minutes. Drain and rinse in cold water to cool.
3. Meanwhile, cut sausage into 3" pieces.
4. Put ½ cup pizza sauce in bottom of pan.
5. Wrap each piece of sausage in a cooked noodle. Put into pan seam-side down.
6. When pan is full of wrapped sausage pieces, top all with remaining pizza sauce.
7. Sprinkle with cheese.
8. Bake uncovered at 350 for 35 minutes.

Quick Vegetable Lasagna

Judy Govotsos
Frederickville, MD

Makes 6–8 servings

Prep. Time: 30 minutes
Cooking/Baking Time: 30–40 minutes

28-oz. jar spaghetti sauce of your choice, *divided*
2 9-oz. pkgs. cheese, spinach, *or* cheese-and-spinach, ravioli, thawed, *divided*
½–¾ cup grated carrot
small yellow squash, grated
6 ozs. grated mozzarella cheese, *divided*

1. Spread ¼ cup sauce in lightly greased 9 × 13 baking pan.
2. Layer 1 package ravioli over top.
3. Sprinkle with all the grated carrots and squash.
4. Spoon 1½ cups spaghetti sauce over top.
5. Sprinkle on half the cheese.
6. Layer on second package of ravioli.
7. Spoon over remainder of spaghetti sauce.
8. Sprinkle with rest of cheese.
9. Bake at 350° for 30–40 minutes, or until cheese is golden and bubbling.

Last-Minute Lasagna

Marlene Fonken, Upland, CA

Makes 4–6 servings

Prep. Time: 10–15 minutes
Cooking/Baking Time: 35–45 minutes
Standing Time: 10 minutes

28-oz. jar pasta sauce, *divided*
30-oz. pkg. of cheese, *or* meat-and-cheese, ravioli unthawed, *divided*
10-oz. box frozen chopped spinach, thawed and squeezed dry
8-oz. pkg. shredded mozzarella cheese, *divided*
½ cup grated Parmesan cheese, *divided*

1. Preheat oven to 350°. Spray a 9 × 13 baking pan with non-stick cooking spray.
2. Spoon ⅓ of sauce into bottom of pan.
3. Arrange half of frozen ravioli on top of sauce.
4. Top with half of remaining sauce.
5. Scatter spinach on top.
6. Top with half of each cheese.
7. Top with remaining ravioli, then the remaining sauce, and the rest of the cheeses.
8. Cover with foil and bake 25 minutes.
9. Uncover and bake 5–20 minutes more, or until bubbly.
10. Let sit a few minutes before cutting.

Spinach Ravioli Bake

Susan Segraves, Lansdale, PA

Makes 6 servings

Prep. Time: 15 minutes
Cooking/Baking Time: 50 minutes
Standing Time: 10 minutes

6-oz. bag fresh baby spinach
12-oz. pkg. refrigerated cooked turkey meatballs
28-oz. jar spaghetti sauce
1½ cups water
2 9-oz. pkgs. refrigerated 4-cheese ravioli, *divided*
8-oz. bag shredded mozzarella cheese, *divided*

1. Heat oven to 375°. Rinse spinach and shake off excess water. Heat in large skillet over medium heat 5 minutes, or until wilted.
2. Coarsely chop meatballs and place in large bowl. Add spinach, spaghetti sauce, and 1½ cups water. Stir to combine.
3. Spoon about 2 cups meatball mixture into bottom of lightly greased 2½-quart casserole.
4. Arrange 1 pkg. ravioli over mixture. Sprinkle with ½ cup cheese.
5. Repeat layering using remaining ravioli, meatball mixture, and cheese.
6. Cover with foil. Bake at 375° for 35 minutes.
7. Uncover and bake 5 minutes longer, or until cheese melts.
8. Let stand 10 minutes before serving.

Spaghetti Pizza

Moreen Weaver
Bath, NY

Makes 8–12 servings

Prep. Time: 20 minutes
Cooking/Baking Time: 1 hour

1 lb. angel hair pasta
¾ cup milk
3 eggs, beaten
2-lb. 13-oz. jar your
    favorite pasta sauce
1 lb. shredded mozzarella
    cheese

Optional toppings:
fresh mushrooms, sliced
thinly sliced pepperoni
thinly sliced ham
browned and crumbled
    sausage
lightly sautéed sliced
    onions

1. Cook pasta according to package instructions. Drain well.
2. Mix milk and eggs together in a mixing bowl.
3. Put cooked angel hair pasta into a lightly greased 9 x 13 baking pan. Pour egg mixture over pasta and stir until well coated. Press evenly over bottom of pan.
4. Pour pasta sauce evenly over pasta.
5. Top with cheese.
6. Add any optional toppings that you wish.
7. Bake at 350°, uncovered, for 1 hour.

Super Creamy Macaroni and Cheese

Jean M. Butzer
Batavia, NY
Arlene Leaman Kliewer
Lakewood, CO
Esther Burkholder
Millerstown, PA
Hazel Lightcap Propst
Oxford, PA
Karla Baer
North Lima, OH

Makes 8–10 servings

Prep. Time: 5–10 minutes
Cooking/Baking Time: 1 hour 20 minutes

1-lb. pkg. uncooked elbow
    macaroni
4 cups shredded cheddar
    cheese, *or* ½ lb. cubed
    Velveeta cheese
2 10¾-oz. cans cheddar
    cheese, *or* cream of
    celery, soup
3½ cups milk
1½ cups cooked ham,
    chopped, *optional*
1 tsp. salt, *optional*
¼ tsp. pepper, *optional*

1. Combine all ingredients in a buttered 3-quart casserole or baking dish.
2. Cover and bake at 350° for 1 hour.
3. Stir up from bottom.
4. Bake uncovered an additional 20 minutes.

Tomato-y Mac and Cheese

Dorothy Ladd
Ballston Lake, NY

Makes 3–4 servings

Prep. Time: 20 minutes
Cooking/Baking Time: 20 minutes

2 cups uncooked macaroni
10½-oz. can tomato soup
¾ cup milk
2 cups shredded *or* cubed
    cheese of your choice

1. Cook the macaroni according to package directions, just until al dente.
2. Drain and set aside.
3. Mix together the soup and milk. Heat in a saucepan or microwave until heated through.
4. Stir in cheese. Continue heating until cheese is melted.
5. Stir in cooked macaroni.
6. Spoon mixture into a lightly greased 1½-quart casserole.
7. Bake uncovered at 375° for 20 minutes.

> **A Tip —**
> Wet your knife when cubing cheese to keep it from sticking.

137

Grilling

Grilled or Broiled Chicken Breasts

Judy Houser
Hershey, PA

Makes 8 servings

Prep. Time: 15 minutes
Marinating Time: 2–4 hours
Grilling/Broiling Time: 10–15 minutes

8 boneless, skinless
   chicken breast halves
4 Tbsp. olive oil
4 Tbsp. soy sauce
3 Tbsp. lemon juice, *or*
   wine vinegar
3 garlic cloves, sliced
1 tsp. dried thyme, *or* basil
   leaves, *optional*

1. For marinade, blend together oil, soy sauce, and lemon juice.
2. Place chicken breasts in single layer in glass dish. Sprinkle with garlic and optional herbs. Pour marinade over chicken.

3. Cover and refrigerate for 2–4 hours, turning breasts over from time to time.
4. Preheat **grill.** Place chicken breasts on grill. Baste with marinade. Grill for 5 minutes on one side.
5. Turn and grill for 5–9 minutes on other side. Juices should run clear when pierced with a fork.
6. **To broil**, preheat broiler for 10 minutes. Place breasts on tray. Pour marinade over breasts.
7. Broil close to heat for 3–5 minutes on each side. Juices should run clear when pierced with a fork.

Lemon Grilled Chicken Breasts

Wilma Haberkamp, Fairbank, IA

Makes 4 servings

Prep. Time: 15 minutes
Grilling Time: 4–5 minutes

1¼ lbs. boneless, skinless
   chicken breasts
2 lemons
2 Tbsp. olive oil
½ tsp. salt
½ tsp. coarsely ground
   pepper

1. Prepare grill for direct grilling over medium heat.
2. Pound chicken to uniform ¼" thickness.
3. Grate 1½ Tbsp. lemon peel and squeeze 3 Tbsp. lemon juice into a small bowl.
4. Add oil, salt, and pepper. Whisk until well blended.
5. In large bowl, toss chicken with marinade.
6. Place on grill. Cook 2–2½ minutes.
7. Turn over. Cook 2–2½ minutes more, or until juices run clear.

Grilled Chicken Caesar

Deborah Heatwole
Waynesboro, GA

Makes 4 servings

Prep. Time: 5 minutes
Grilling Time: 15 minutes

4 boneless, skinless
  chicken breast halves
4 tsp. olive, *or* canola, oil
½ tsp. Italian seasoning
½ tsp. garlic salt
½ tsp. black pepper
½ tsp. paprika, *optional*

1. Drizzle oil over chicken. Sprinkle with seasonings.
2. Grill, covered, over medium-hot coals for 12–15 minutes, or until juices run clear. Turn over several times.

Thai Peanut Chicken

Susan Kasting
Jenks, OK

Makes 4 servings

Prep. Time: 10 minutes
Marinating Time: 1 hour
Cooking/Baking Time: 15 minutes

4 boneless, skinless
  chicken breasts
½ cup peanut butter

⅓ cup honey
¼ cup soy sauce
2 Tbsp. curry powder

1. Combine peanut butter, honey, soy sauce, and curry powder.
2. Marinate chicken breasts in mixture for 1 hour.
3. Grill chicken breasts until juices run clear when pierced with a fork.

Sweet and Spicy Chicken

Janice Muller
Derwood, MD

Makes 6 servings

Prep. Time: 3 minutes
Marinating Time: 1 hour
Grilling/Broiling Time: 10–20 minutes

½ cup orange juice
¼ cup honey
1-oz. envelope Italian salad
  dressing mix
6 boneless, skinless
  chicken breast halves

1. Place chicken in a glass rectangular dish.
2. Mix first three ingredients together and pour over chicken. Cover and marinate for 1 hour, turning to coat both sides.
3. Grill or broil until juices run clear when pierced with a fork.

Grilled Sesame Chicken

Jeannine Janzen
Elbing, KS

Makes 4–6 servings

Prep. Time: 5 minutes
Marinating Time: 4–8 hours
Grilling Time: 20–40 minutes

4 to 6 boneless, skinless
  chicken thighs
1 cup soy sauce
½ cup pineapple juice
1 Tbsp. sesame seeds

1. Place chicken in a large resealable plastic bag.
2. Pour soy sauce and pineapple juice into bag. Chill 4–8 hours.
3. Place chicken on grill. Cook 10–20 minutes on each side, or until juices run clear when chicken is pierced with a fork.
4. Sprinkle sesame seeds lightly on both sides of chicken as it grills.

A Tip —

To clear honey out of your measuring cup easily, first spray the measuring cup with cooking spray.

Marinated Grilled Chicken

Dale and Shari Mast
Harrisonburg, VA

Makes 8–10 servings

Prep. Time: 10 minutes
Marinating Time: 8 hours, or overnight
Grilling Time: 20–30 minutes

12 boneless, skinless chicken thighs
1 cup honey barbecue sauce (see page 141)
1 cup raspberry vinaigrette dressing (regular *or* light)

1. Place chicken thighs in a large bowl for marinating.
2. Combine barbecue sauce and dressing in a small mixing bowl.
3. Pour over chicken. Cover, refrigerate, and allow to marinate 8 hours, or overnight.
4. Grill 10–15 minutes per side over medium heat, basting with extra marinade sauce.

Tip: You can combine any vinaigrette dressing with your favorite barbecue sauce for an excellent marinade tailored to your individual taste.

Chicken on the Throne

Meredith Miller, Dover, DE

Makes 2 servings

Prep. Time: 15 minutes
Marinating Time: 1 hour
Grilling Time: 1½–2 hours

3–3½-lb. chicken fryer
3 Tbsp. poultry seasoning
12-oz. can beer, *or* soda
half a medium-sized onion
1 green pepper

1. Rinse chicken in cold water and let drain. Be sure to remove giblets and neck.
2. Rub a light coating of seasoning over skin and pour the remainder into the cavity rubbing in well. Place in plastic bag in refrigerator for 1 hour.
3. Preheat grill to medium heat.
4. Remove top of aluminum beverage can with a can opener. Remove half the drink.
5. Chop onion and pepper and place in can along with the remaining half of drink.
6. Push cavity of chicken over can until chicken's legs reach the bottom of the can on the outside.
7. Place chicken-on-the-can in a foil pan on grill. (This will prevent grease flare-ups.)
8. Close lid and grill until juices run clear when pierced with a fork and leg moves freely when twisted, about 1½–2 hours.

Grilled Turkey Breast

Naomi Ressler, Harrisonburg, VA

Makes 7–9 servings

Prep. Time: 15 minutes
Marinating Time: 4 hours
Grilling Time: 10 minutes or so

5–7-lb. turkey breast
8-oz. bottle light Italian dressing
½ cup soy sauce
2 tsp. onion powder
2 tsp. dry mustard

1. Cut turkey off the bone, slicing down each side of the breast bone. Then cut each half crosswise into serving-size pieces.
2. Combine remaining ingredients in a sizable baking dish. Reserve ½ cup for basting turkey while grilling.
3. Marinate turkey for at least 4 hours in the fridge, pushing meat down into marinade until submerged.
4. Grill over medium heat, basting with marinade until juices run clear. Grill for 5 minutes on one side. Turn over and grill another 5 minutes or so, watching carefully so the meat doesn't dry out or burn.

Tips:
1. Turkey cuts best when it's still partially frozen.
2. I put the breast bone in a large stockpot and nearly cover it with water. I put the lid on

the pot and simmer it to make a great broth for later use. There's also good meat attached, which I cut up into the broth.

Honey Barbecue Sauce—for Poultry or Beef

Lori Lehman, Ephrata, PA

Makes 2½ cups

Prep. Time: 5–10 minutes

1 cup ketchup
½ cup honey
½ cup brown sugar
¼ cup prepared mustard
2 Tbsp. Worcestershire
   sauce
1½ tsp. liquid smoke,
   optional

1. Mix all ingredients together.
2. Spread over chicken or steak before grilling.

Barbecued Chicken Sauce

Paula King, Flanagan, IL

Makes 4–6 servings

Prep. Time: 5 minutes
Cooking/Baking Time: 5 minutes

¼ cup water
½ cup vinegar
1 stick (½ cup) butter
½ tsp. salt
dash paprika
dash pepper

1. Put all ingredients in a small saucepan. Heat on stove top or grill top until butter melts and all ingredients can be mixed together.
2. Keep warm while grilling chicken and baste chicken periodically.

Tip: This amount of sauce will baste one whole cut-up chicken.

Brooks White Sauce Marinade

Deb Herr, Montaintop, PA

Makes 3¼ cups

Prep. Time: 5 minutes
Marinating Time: 3–4 hours
Grilling Time: 10–20 minutes

2 cups white vinegar
1 cup vegetable oil

½ tsp. pepper
2 Tbsp. salt
3 Tbsp. poultry seasoning
1 egg, beaten

1. Pour all ingredients into a 1-quart covered container. Shake vigorously.
2. Pour over chicken breasts to marinate for a few hours, and then grill.

Flank Steak

Sharon Swartz Lambert
Harrisonburg, VA

Makes 2–4 servings

Prep. Time: 10 minutes
Marinating Time: 5-24 hours
Grilling Time: 15 minutes

½–2-lb. flank steak
1 Tbsp. cooking sherry
2 Tbsp. soy sauce
1 tsp. minced fresh garlic
1 tsp. honey

1. Diamond-cut ¼"-wide slashes on both sides of flank steak.
2. Mix marinade ingredients together in a small bowl.
3. Place steak in a long dish. Pour marinade over top. Cover and refrigerate 5–24 hours, or overnight.
4. Grill 5 minutes per side over high heat. (You may need a bit more time, depending on thickness of the meat.)
5. Cut into thin slices on the diagonal.

Vegetable Shish Kebabs

Rosemarie Fitzgerald
Gibsonia, PA

Makes 4 servings

Prep. Time: 15–20 minutes
Grilling Time: 10–15 minutes

1 pint cherry tomatoes
2–3 small zucchini, unpeeled
1 medium red onion
1 lb. fresh mushrooms
16-oz. bottle Catalina salad dressing

1. Clean vegetables. Leave tomatoes whole, but cube zucchini, onion, and mushrooms for skewers.
2. Thread vegetables onto skewers. Thread zucchini through its outside edges and not through the centers of the cubes.
3. Grill, basting with dressing, until vegetables are done to your liking.
4. Serve with Meat Shish Kebabs (next recipe) over cooked rice.

Meat Shish Kebabs

Rosemarie Fitzgerald
Gibsonia, PA

Makes 4 servings

Prep. Time: 5–10 minutes
Marinating Time: 30 minutes or more
Grilling Time: 15–30 minutes

1 lb. cubed beef, pork, *or* chicken
16-oz. bottle Catalina salad dressing

1. Place cubed meat in a long pan. Pour salad dressing over top, submerging the meat in the liquid.
2. Cover and refrigerate for at least 30 minutes.
3. Remove meat from marinade and thread onto skewers.
4. Grill, basting with dressing, until meat is done to your liking.
5. Serve alongside the Vegetable Shish Kebabs (previous recipe) over cooked rice.

Grilled Burgers

Deborah Heatwole
Waynesboro, GA

Makes 12 servings

Prep. Time: 10–15 minutes
Grilling Time: 10–15 minutes

2 lbs. ground beef
¾ cup uncooked rolled, *or* quick, oats
2 eggs
⅓ cup ketchup
1½ tsp. dried onion, *optional*
1 tsp. Worcestershire sauce, *optional*
salt and pepper to taste

1. Mix ground beef thoroughly with the rest of the ingredients.
2. Shape ⅓ cupfuls into patties.
3. Place patties on hot grill. Grill, covered, 5–7 minutes per side, or until centers of burgers are no longer pink.
4. Serve on buns with toppings of your choice.

Grill Pack Dinner

Shelia Heil
Lancaster, PA

Makes 1 serving

Prep Time: 10 minutes
Grilling Time: 45 minutes

¼-lb. burger
1 potato, sliced thin
1 carrot, sliced thin
¼ onion, diced
½ tsp. salt

1. Layer ingredients onto large sheet of double-strength aluminum foil. Wrap up and seal well.
2. Place on baking sheet with sealed edge up.
3. Grill for 45 minutes, or until meat and veggies are done to your liking.

Tip: Make as many packets as the number of people you plan to feed. In fact, it's fun to make an assembly line and have everyone create her/his own package.

Marinade for Beef or Venison

Alta Metzler
Willow Street, PA

Makes 6–8 servings

Prep. Time: 10 minutes
Marinating Time: 24 hours
Cooking/Baking Time: 30–40 minutes

½ cup soy sauce
2 Tbsp. water
¼ cup oil
1 tsp. minced garlic
¼ tsp. pepper
2 tsp. brown sugar

1. Mix all ingredients together well in a small bowl.
2. Place 2 lbs. venison or beef steak in a long bowl.
3. Marinate, covered, in refrigerator for 24 hours, turning meat 1 or 2 times.
4. Grill according to the thickness of the meat and your preferred done-ness.

Steak Marinade

Sharon Shank
Bridgewater, VA

Makes 2+ cups

Prep. Time: 5 minutes
Marinating Time: 8-12 hours

1 cup red wine vinegar
1 Tbsp. garlic powder
½ cup oil
½ cup soy sauce
2 Tbsp. minced onion

1. Mix all ingredients together in a small bowl.
2. Marinate steaks in the sauce for 8–12 hours before grilling.

Many-Meats Marinade

Carole Bolatto
Marseilles, IL

Makes 2½+ cups

Prep. Time: 10 minutes
Marinating Time: 6 or more hours

5-oz. bottle soy sauce
¼ cup brown sugar
1 Tbsp. lemon juice
1½ cups water
¼ cup sherry, *optional*

1. Mix all ingredients together in a medium-sized bowl. Stir well, making sure the brown sugar dissolves.
2. Pour over meat and marinate, covered, in refrigerator for at least 6 hours.

Tip: Try this on poultry, beef, pork, and shrimp.

Southern Pork Marinating/ Basting Sauce

Barbara Sparks
Glen Burnie, MD

Makes 2¾ cups

Prep. Time: 35 minutes
Marinating time: 2 hours
Grilling/Broiling Time: about 15 minutes on each side

1 cup water
2 cups cider vinegar
1–1½ (½–¾ cup) sticks butter
1 tsp. salt
1 tsp. ground red pepper, *or* cayenne

1. Combine all ingredients in a saucepan. Simmer for 30 minutes.
2. Marinate pork chops or ribs in the sauce for 2 hours before grilling or broiling. (Discard sauce used for marinating. Make fresh sauce for basting.)
3. Baste pork chops or ribs with sauce on the grill, or under the broiler.

Grilled Pork Chops

Laura R. Showalter
Dayton, VA

Makes 4 servings

Prep. Time: 10 minutes
Marinating Time: 2 hours
Grilling Time: 20 minutes

1 large onion, sliced
¾ cup lime, *or* lemon, juice
½ tsp. cayenne pepper
1 clove garlic, minced
½ tsp. salt, *optional*
4 pork chops

1. Combine all ingredients except the pork chops in a large re-sealable bag or container with tight-fitting lid. Combine well.
2. Submerge chops in marinade.
3. Seal bag or container and refrigerate at least 2 hours.
4. Remove chops from marinade and grill, covered, over medium-hot heat 8–10 minutes on each side.
5. Bring the marinade to a boil in a small saucepan. Use it to baste the chops if you wish while they grill.

A Tip —

Food is always more tasty when served attractively. Add a garnish and a special touch whenever possible.

Sugar-Crusted Ham

Pat Bechtel
Dillsburg, PA

Makes 6–8 servings

Prep. Time: 10 minutes
Grilling Time: 30 minutes

2 fully cooked ham slices, each about 1" thick
1 cup brown sugar, packed
⅓ cup prepared horseradish
¼ cup lemon juice

1. Score each side of ham ¼" deep in a diamond pattern.
2. Combine remaining ingredients in a small saucepan. Heat to boiling, stirring frequently.
3. Grill ham slices 3" from medium-hot coals, 15 minutes on each side. Baste frequently with the sugar mixture.

Fill and Grill Sizzlers

Shanon Swartz Lambert
Harrisonburg, VA

Makes 6 servings

Prep. Time: 30 minutes
Grilling Time: 10–15 minutes

2 lbs. smoked sausage, *or* Kielbasa
1 cup Muenster cheese, grated
½ cup sauerkraut, drained well
6 bacon slices, *optional*

1. Cut sausage into six 6" pieces. Split lengthwise ¾ through.
2. Mix grated cheese and drained sauerkraut together in a small mixing bowl.
3. Fill each sausage piece with mixture of 2 Tbsp. grated cheese and 1 Tbsp. sauerkraut.
4. Wrap each filled piece with a strip of bacon, if you wish. Secure with a toothpick.
5. Grill or broil 4" from heat until done.
6. Garnish with additional Muenster cheese just before serving.

Flavorful Grilled Salmon

Carol Findling
Carol Stream, IL

Makes 6 servings

Prep. Time: 10 minutes
Marinating Time: 15–30 minutes
Grilling Time: 10–12 minutes

¼ cup Italian dressing, light *or* regular
¼ cup soy sauce
¼ cup Dijon mustard
2 Tbsp. brown sugar
6 salmon fillets (4–6-oz. each, about 1" thick)

1. Place all ingredients except salmon in medium bowl. Whisk until smooth. Set aside ⅓ cup.
2. Pour remaining marinade into sealable plastic bag. Add salmon to bag. Seal tightly. Place in bowl. Refrigerate 15–30 minutes.
3. Remove fillets and discard marinade in bag.
4. Grill skin-side down over indirect heat until opaque throughout, about 10–12 minutes (adjust for thickness of fillet).
5. During last 2 minutes of grilling, brush with reserved marinade.
6. When done, slide spatula between skin and salmon meat and transfer to serving plate.

Tip: This recipe is basic. You can add or eliminate ingredients as you wish; for example orange juice, tequila, herbs, spices, different vinegars, hot peppers, etc. Use your imagination and favorite flavors.

Simply Grilled Salmon

Leann Brown
Lancaster, PA

Makes 3 servings

Prep. Time: 5 minutes
Grilling Time: 15 minutes

2 lbs. salmon steaks *or*
   fillets
½ cup lemon juice
1½ Tbsp. butter
seasoned salt

1. Lay salmon on large piece of foil.
2. Pour lemon juice over top.
3. Lay butter in several slivers over top.
4. Sprinkle evenly with seasoned salt to taste.
5. Close foil and wrap again in second layer so lemon juice will not escape.
6. Grill over medium heat for 15 minutes, or until salmon is flakey but not dry.

Grilled Asparagus Spears

Dale and Shari Mast
Harrisonburg, VA

Makes 6–8 servings

Prep. Time: 7 minutes
Grilling Time: 12 minutes

2 lbs. fresh asparagus
   spears
1 Tbsp. olive oil
seasoned salt

1. Break woody ends off washed asparagus.
2. In a large bowl or Ziploc bag, toss asparagus spears with oil and salt to taste.
3. Place spears directly onto preheated grill on low heat.
4. Grill for 12 minutes, turning spears 2–3 times.
5. Serve hot or at room temperature.

Chili Lime Grilled Corn

Betty Moore
Plano, IL

Makes 8 servings

Prep. Time: 15 minutes
Soaking Time: 3–4 hours
Grilling Time: 25 minutes

8 ears fresh corn with
   husks
1 stick (½ cup) butter,
   softened
1 tsp. grated lime rind
1 tsp. fresh lime juice
chili powder

1. Remove outer husks from corn. Pull back inner husks. Remove and discard silks. Pull husks back up on corn. Soak in cool water for 3 or 4 hours, putting a plate on top of corn to keep under water.
2. Mix butter, lime juice and grated lime rind in a small bowl.
3. Remove corn from water. Grill corn in its husks over medium heat on grill for 25 minutes. Turn often.
4. Carefully remove husks.
5. Spread corn with butter mixture. Sprinkle with chili powder if you wish. Or add ½ tsp. chili powder to butter mixture before spreading on corn.

Grilled Onions with Stuffing

Natalia Showalter
Mt. Solon, VA

Makes 6 servings

Prep. Time: 20 minutes
Grilling Time: 30–45 minutes

1½ cups herb-seasoned stuffing mix
1 cup shredded cheddar cheese
1 tsp. poultry seasoning
5½ Tbsp. (⅓ cup) butter, melted
⅓ cup hot water
6 medium-sized sweet onions

1. Combine first 5 ingredients in a medium bowl. Set aside.
2. Cut each onion into 3 horizontal slices. Spread 2 Tbsp. stuffing mixture between slices and re-assemble onions.
3. Place each onion on a 12" square of aluminum foil coated with cooking spray.
4. Bring corners together and twist to seal.
5. Cook over hot coals 30 minutes, or until tender.

Tip: You can also bake the onions in a lightly greased, covered, 7 × 11 baking dish at 350° for 1 hour, or until tender.

Grilled Cabbage

Jenelle Miller
Marion, SD

Makes 4 servings

Prep. Time: 5–10 minutes
Grilling Time: 40–45 minutes

1 small head of cabbage
half a stick (4 Tbsp.) butter
seasoned salt
4 slices bacon, uncooked

1. Remove outer leaves of cabbage head. Cut cabbage into 4 wedges.
2. Lay each wedge on a square of aluminum foil.
3. Spread 1 Tbsp. of butter over side of wedge.
4. Sprinkle each generously with seasoned salt.
5. Wrap a piece of bacon around each wedge.
6. Wrap tightly in foil.
7. Lay over hot coals. Grill 40–45 minutes, or until tender when jagged with a fork.

Grilled Vegetables

Deborah Heatwole
Waynesboro, GA

Makes 4 servings

Prep. Time: 15–30 minutes, depending on how fast you slice veggies
Grilling Time: 15–25 minutes

4 cups sliced fresh summer squash *and/or* zucchini
4 cups sliced sweet onions, such as Vidalia
3–4 Tbsp. olive, *or* canola, oil
1–2 Tbsp. red wine vinegar
salt and pepper to taste

1. Toss all ingredients in a large bowl until vegetables are evenly coated with oil and vinegar.
2. Spray a grill basket with nonstick cooking spray. Place on grill rack over hot coals.
3. Pour vegetables into basket, replace grill lid, and cook 15–25 minutes, until vegetables reach desired doneness, stirring every 4–5 minutes.

Tip: This is a versatile dish. Add or substitute your favorite garden vegetables, especially those that are in season.

Zucchini on the Grill

Judy Buller
Bluffton, OH

Makes as many servings as yo wish

Prep. Time: 5 minutes
Grilling Time: 5–6 minutes

medium-sized zucchini
olive oil
pepper
seasoning salt
garlic powder

1. Wash, but do not peel zucchini. Slice into long strips about ¼" thick.
2. Brush both sides with olive oil. Gently sprinkle both sides with pepper, seasoning salt, and garlic powder.
3. Place on grill, turning frequently. Each side takes about 3 minutes, but watch carefully so as not to overdo or burn the slices.

Grilled Parmesan Potatoes

Joanna Bear
Salisbury, MD

Makes 4 servings

Prep. Time: 10 minutes
Grilling Time: 18–20 minutes

1 lb. small red potatoes
¼ cup chopped green onions, *optional*
2 tsp. cooking oil
1 Tbsp. Parmesan cheese
1 tsp. dried oregano
½ tsp. garlic salt

1. Cut potatoes in ½" cubes. Place in medium bowl.
2. Add onions, if you wish, and oil. Toss to coat.
3. Place potatoes in center of 12 × 12 sheet of heavy-duty aluminum foil.
4. Combine spices and cheese in a small bowl. Sprinkle over potatoes.
5. Fold foil into pouch, sealing tightly to prevent leaks.
6. Place pouch on a grill over medium hot coals for 18–20 minutes, or until potatoes are tender.

Potato Pockets

Barb Harvey, Quarryville, PA

Makes 4 servings

Prep. Time: 20 minutes
Grilling Time: 20–30 minutes

4 medium-sized potatoes, julienned
3 carrots, julienned
⅓ cup chopped onion
2 Tbsp. butter
salt and pepper, *optional*
½ cup shredded Parmesan, *or* cheddar, cheese

1. Divide potatoes, carrots, and onion equally between four pieces of heavy-duty aluminum foil.
2. Top with butter. Sprinkle with salt and pepper if you wish.
3. Bring opposite short ends of foil together over vegetables and fold down several times. Fold unsealed ends toward vegetables and crimp tightly.
4. Grill, covered, over medium coals for 20–30 minutes, or until potatoes are tender.
5. Remove from grill.
6. Open foil and sprinkle with cheese. Reseal for 5 minutes, or until cheese melts.

A Tip —

In order to prevent peeled potatoes from discoloring, drop them into a cup of cold water with ½ teaspoon cream of tartar dissolved in it. Drain the potatoes when you're ready to use them.

Vegetables

Whole Green Beans in Garlic

Leona Yoder, Hartville, OH
Joyce Shackelford, Green Bay, WI
Doris Ranck, Gap, PA

Makes 4 servings

Prep. Time: 15–20 minutes
Cooking/Baking Time: 20–30 minutes

1 lb. green beans, ends trimmed
2 tsp. butter
⅛ tsp. finely chopped garlic
½ tsp. salt
¼ tsp. pepper
1 tsp. dried oregano, *optional*
⅓ cup shredded Parmesan cheese, *optional*

1. Cook beans in small amount of boiling water in covered saucepan until crisp-tender. Drain.
2. Melt butter in large skillet. Saute beans and garlic in butter until heated through and done to your liking.
3. Season before serving with salt and pepper, and oregano if you wish.
4. Place in serving dish. Just before serving, top with shredded cheese if you wish.

Green Bean and Mushroom Saute

Louise Bodziony
Sunrise Beach, MO
Clara Yoder Byler
Hartville, OH

Makes 4 servings

Prep. Time: 10 minutes
Cooking/Baking Time: 20 minutes

1 lb. fresh, *or* frozen, green beans
¾–1 cup sliced fresh mushrooms
2 Tbsp. butter
2–3 tsp. onion, *or* garlic, powder
4 strips bacon, cooked and crumbled, *optional*

1. Cook green beans in water to cover, just until tender.
2. Meanwhile, in a skillet sauté mushrooms in butter until tender.
3. Stir in onion, or garlic, powder.
4. Drain beans. Add to skillet and toss with mushrooms and seasonings.
5. Place in serving dish. Top with crumbled bacon if you wish.

Green Beans with Bacon and Onions

Deborah Heatwole
Waynesboro, GA
Anne Nolt
Thompsontown, PA

Makes 6 servings

Prep. Time: 5 minutes
Cooking/Baking Time: 30 minutes

---

4 slices bacon
½ cup, or more, chopped
  onions
6 cups water
1 quart fresh, *or* frozen,
  green beans
½ tsp. garlic salt

1. Saute bacon in large skillet. Remove bacon and drain. Reserve drippings.
2. Add onions to drippings. Sauté until tender. Crumble bacon, add to skillet, and set aside.
3. Meanwhile, bring 6 cups of water to a boil in a large saucepan.
4. Add green beans. Return to boil, cook 8–15 minutes, or just until beans are tender. Drain.
5. Pour sautéed onions and crumbled bacon into beans in saucepan.
6. Sprinkle with garlic salt. Mix thoroughly and serve.

Variation: To bake these beans, make these changes beginning with Step 3: Dissolve 1 beef bouillon cube in 1 cup hot water. Add garlic salt. Place beans in lightly greased 1½-qt.

baking dish. Pour liquid over beans. Cover and bake at 350° for 1 hour. Before serving, stir onions and bacon into beans.

—Anne Nolt
Thompsontown, PA

Barbecued Green Beans

Joanna Bear
Salisbury, MD

Makes 12 servings

Prep. Time: 10–15 minutes
Cooking/Baking Time: 4 hours

---

3 quarts green beans
1 onion, diced
1 cup ketchup
1 cup brown sugar
6 slices bacon

1. Microwave beans in microwave-safe dish, or steam lightly in a large stockpot, just until crisp-tender. Drain.
2. Mix onion, ketchup, and brown sugar together in a mixing bowl.
3. Pour over beans. Mix together well.
4. Place beans and sauce in a lightly greased 3- or 4-qt. baking dish or roaster.
5. Either place the uncooked bacon slices over the top of the beans, or chop and mix into beans.
6. Cover and bake at 275° for 4 hours.

Zesty Green Beans

June Grafl
Denver, PA

Makes 4–5 servings

Prep. Time: 2–3 minutes
Cooking/Baking Time: 15–20
  minutes

---

1 lb. fresh, *or* frozen, green
  beans
6 slices bacon, cut in pieces
½ Tbsp. prepared mustard
6 Tbsp. sugar
2 Tbsp. apple cider, *or* red
  wine, vinegar

1. Place beans in large stockpot with about an inch of water. Cover and steam until just-tender.
2. While beans are cooking, sauté bacon in a skillet. When crispy, remove from pan and drain. Reserve drippings. Crumble bacon and set aside.
3. To bacon drippings, add remaining ingredients. Bring to a boil, stirring frequently to mix well.
4. Stir bacon back into sauce.
5. Drain cooked beans. Stir sauce into drained beans.

A Tip —

Don't overcook vegetables.

Au Gratin Green Beans

Donna Lantgen, Golden, CO

Makes 12 servings

Prep. Time: 10 minutes
Cooking/Baking Time: 1–1½ hours

2 lbs. frozen green beans
1–2 cups Velveeta cheese, cubed
½ cup onion, chopped
½ cup milk
1 Tbsp. flour

1. Mix all ingredients together in a large mixing bowl.
2. Spoon into well greased 2- or 3-qt. casserole dish.
3. Cover and bake at 350° for 1–1½ hours, or until beans are done to your liking.

Parmesan Baked—or Grilled—Asparagus

Jean M. Butzer, Batavia, NY
Carol Findling, Carol Stream, IL
Colleen Heatwole, Burton, MI

Makes 4 servings

Prep Time: 5 minutes
Cooking/Baking Time: 15 minutes

1 lb. fresh asparagus
2 tsp. olive oil
¼ tsp. salt
¼ tsp. pepper
¼ cup grated Parmesan cheese

1. Preheat oven to 425°.
2. Place asparagus (trimmed and washed) on a non-stick baking sheet. Drizzle with olive oil and sprinkle with salt and pepper. Toss to coat.
3. Bake 10 minutes. Toss again.
4. Sprinkle with cheese.
5. Return to oven and bake until the cheese melts, about 5 minutes longer.

Variations:

1. After Step 3, place asparagus on serving plate and drizzle with 2–3 Tbsp. balsamic vinegar.

—Colleen Heatwole
Burton, MI

2. After trimming and washing asparagus, brush stalks with oil. Place on pre-heated grill, direct medium, for 6–8 minutes, or until the stem end jags tender. Turn stalks every 2–3 minutes, being careful not to overcook it. (Remember, the asparagus will continue to cook after leaving the grill.) Arrange on platter. Sprinkle with cheese.

—Carol Findling
Carol Stream, IL

Asparagus with Sesame Butter

Doyle Rounds
Bridgewater, VA

Makes 6–8 servings

Prep. Time: 7 minutes
Cooking/Baking Time: about 10 minutes

2 lbs. fresh asparagus
1 cup boiling water
½ tsp. salt
1 Tbsp. cornstarch
¼ cup cold water
half a stick (¼ cup) butter
3 Tbsp. sesame seeds, toasted

1. Place asparagus spears in a large skillet. Add boiling water and salt. Cook covered for 5–7 minutes, or until tender.
2. Remove asparagus and keep warm. Drain cooking liquid, reserving ½ cup in a small saucepan.
3. Combine cornstarch and cold water in a small bowl. Stir into asparagus cooking liquid.
4. Cook and stir over medium heat until thickened and bubbly. Cook and stir 1 minute more.
5. Stir in butter until melted.
6. Spoon over asparagus. Sprinkle with sesame seeds and serve immediately.

Creamed Asparagus

Natalia Showalter
Mt. Solon, VA

Makes 4 servings

Prep. Time: 15 minutes
Cooking/Baking Time: 20 minutes

1 lb. fresh asparagus, cut into 1" pieces
half a stick (¼ cup) butter
¼ cup flour
¼ tsp. salt
dash of pepper
2 cups milk
1 cup shredded cheddar cheese, *optional*
2 hard-boiled eggs, sliced, *optional*

1. Cook asparagus for 4 minutes in boiling water. Drain. Set aside.
2. In a non-stick skillet, melt butter. Stir in flour, salt, and pepper until smooth.
3. Gradually stir in milk. Bring to a boil. Cook, and stir 1 minute until thickened and bubbly.
4. Reduce heat. Stir in cheese if you wish.
5. Add asparagus, and eggs if you wish.
6. This is good served over toast. Just before serving, toast 4 slices of bread. Cut in half diagonally. Place 2 halves on each serving plate. Divide creamed asparagus over toast. Serve immediately

Creamy Asparagus

Norma Grieser
Clarksville, MI

Makes 4 servings

Prep. Time: 15 minutes
Cooking/Baking Time: 30 minutes

1 lb. fresh asparagus
1 onion, chopped
1 can cream of mushroom soup
small can of mushrooms, drained, *optional*
4 ozs. cheddar cheese, shredded
½ cup crushed potato chips, *or* corn chips, *optional*

1. Cook asparagus in ⅓ cup water in a good-sized saucepan until crisp-tender.
2. Meanwhile, wilt chopped onion in a non-stick skillet. Stir in mushroom soup and mushrooms.
3. Add cheese, stirring constantly until it melts. Remove from heat.
4. Mix all ingredients together, including chips if you wish.
5. Spoon into lightly greased 2-quart casserole dish.
6. Bake uncovered at 350° for 30 minutes.

Asparagus Frittata

Bernita Boyts
Shawnee Mission, KS

Makes 4 servings

Prep Time: 10–12 minutes
Cooking/Baking Time: 13–15 minutes

half a stick (4 Tbsp.) butter
¾ lb. fresh asparagus, chopped in 1–1½" pieces
10 baby bella mushrooms, sliced
6 eggs, beaten
salt and pepper to taste

Optional ingredients:
1 tsp. prepared mustard
½ cup Asiago cheese, *or* 1 cup Mexican cheese, shredded

1. Melt butter in large skillet.
2. Saute asparagus and mushrooms in butter just until asparagus is crisp-tender.
3. Beat eggs in a large mixing bowl. Stir in salt and pepper.
4. Pour asparagus, mushrooms, and butter into eggs. Stir together well.
5. If you wish, add any or all of the optional ingredients.
6. Spoon mixture into a lightly greased 8 × 8 baking pan.
7. Put pan in oven and bake uncovered at 375° for 8–12 minutes, or just until eggs are set.

Asparagus Puffs
Anna Stoltzfus
Honey Brook, PA

Makes 10 servings

Prep Time: 20 minutes
Cooking/Baking Time: 20 minutes

8-oz. pkg. cream cheese, softened
4-oz. pkg. bleu cheese, softened
1 egg, beaten
1 loaf Pepperidge Farm white, thinly sliced bread
12-oz. can asparagus spears, drained

1. Beat together cream cheese, bleu cheese, and egg in a small mixing bowl.
2. Remove crusts from bread. Flatten each slice of bread with a rolling pin.
3. Spread each bread slice with about 1 ample Tbsp. creamed mixture and roll around each asparagus spear.
4. Cut each asparagus roll in 3 pieces.
5. Place on a lightly greased baking sheet, making sure they don't touch each other.
6. Bake uncovered at 350° for 20 minutes.

A Tip —

Cook according to the season. Focus on the vegetables and fruits that are ripe for the month you're in. Visit a local farmer's market for inspiration.

Tips:
1. You can use fresh asparagus, cooked just until tender, instead of canned asparagus.
2. Serve any leftover asparagus spears drizzled with butter.

Vegetable Medley
Joan S. Eye
Harrisonburg, VA

Makes 4 servings

Prep Time: 20 minutes
Cooking/Baking Time: 4 minutes
Standing Time: 5 minutes

1½ cups raw broccoli, cut up
1½ cups raw zucchini, cut up
½ cup raw sweet red pepper, cut up
¼ cup raw onion, cut up
2 Tbsp. butter
2 tsp. chicken broth

1. Combine ingredients in a microwave-safe dish.
2. Cover and microwave on High for 4 minutes.
3. Let stand for 5 minutes before serving.

Tip: Substitute other raw vegetables that you prefer.

Spring Veggie Bundles
Cheryl A. Lapp
Parkesburg, PA

Makes 8–10 servings

Prep. Time: 20 minutes
Cooking/Baking Time: 12 minutes

6 green spring onions
1 cup water
2 medium-sized bell peppers, ideally one red and one yellow
3 medium-sized carrots
1 lb. thin asparagus
1⅓ cups chicken broth

1. Trim off long green tops of onions and reserve.
2. Bring water to a boil in a skillet or good-sized saucepan. Add onion greens and boil 1 minute.
3. Drain onions. Submerge in ice water for a few minutes. Drain again. Pat dry.
4. Cut carrots and peppers into long julienne strips. Divide into 8–10 bundles, along with asparagus.
5. Tie each with several of the green onion tops.
6. Place bundles in large skillet. Pour in chicken broth.
7. Cook uncovered, approximately 8–10 minutes, until tender.
8. Remove from skillet and place on serving platter. Pour remaining broth from pan over bundles.

Healthy Veggie Stir Fry
Joy Uhler
Richardson, TX

Makes 2–3 servings

Prep Time: 5–10 minutes
Cooking/Baking Time: 9–10 minutes

¼ cup onion, chopped
1 clove garlic, minced
12-oz. pkg. frozen vegetable mix of broccoli, carrots, sugar snap peas, and water chestnuts
7-oz. block firm tofu, cubed
1½ Tbsp. low-sodium teriyaki marinade and sauce
¼ cup chopped fresh mushrooms, *optional*

1. Use a large non-stick skillet or spray another skillet with non-stick cooking spray.
2. Heat skillet over medium heat.
3. Stir fry onion and garlic for a few minutes until onion begins to wilt.
4. Stir in frozen vegetables. Cover and allow to steam, about 5 minutes.
5. Stir in tofu and sauce. Stir until heated through.
6. Serve over prepared brown rice.

Cheesy Veggies
Judy Wantland
Menomonee Falls, WI

Makes 6 servings

Prep. Time: 5 minutes
Cooking/Baking Time: 35 minutes

16-oz. bag frozen vegetable medley, thawed
10¾-oz. can cream of mushroom soup
⅓ cup sour cream
2 cups shredded mozzarella, *or* cheddar, cheese
6-oz. can fried onion rings, *divided*

1. Preheat oven to 350°.
2. In a large mixing bowl, mix all ingredients together using only half the fried onion rings.
3. Spoon into a lightly greased 2-quart baking dish.
4. Bake covered for 30 minutes.
5. Sprinkle remaining onion rings on top. Bake uncovered an additional 5 minutes, or until onions are crispy.

A Tip —

Using freshly ground black pepper and freshly picked herbs to add an extra pop of flavor.

Inspired-by-Hollandaise Sauce
June Grafl
Denver, PA

Makes 1 cup

Prep. Time: 5–10 minutes
Cooking/Baking Time: 5 minutes

½ cup mayonnaise
½ cup plain yogurt
1 tsp. honey mustard
1 tsp. lemon juice

1. Mix all ingredients in a small saucepan.
2. Heat over low heat for 5 minutes, stirring constantly, until heated through.
3. Serve over asparagus, snap peas, or broccoli.

Sauce for Greens and Potatoes
Esther J. Yoder
Hartville, OH

Makes 1⅓ cups

Prep. Time: 4 minutes
Cooking/Baking Time: 6–7 minutes

2 Tbsp. flour
2 Tbsp. oil
1 cup milk
2 Tbsp. vinegar
½ tsp. salt

1. Blend oil and flour in saucepan over medium heat. Stir continually until bubbly.

2. Add milk and stir constantly until a smooth white sauce forms.

3. Continue gently boiling and stirring for 2 minutes.

4. Add vinegar and salt. Remove from heat. Let cool 3-4 minutes.

5. Serve over cooked potatoes, fresh spinach, or endive.

Seasoning for Vegetables

Wafi Brandt
Manheim, PA

Makes 5-6 servings

Prep. Time: 2 minutes
Cooking/Baking Time: 22–32 minutes

2 Tbsp. butter
½ tsp. garlic powder
1 Tbsp. fresh, *or* ½ tsp. dried, basil
¼ tsp. salt
1 lb. cooked vegetables (broccoli, carrots, or potatoes are especially good)

1. Melt butter over low heat. Stir in garlic powder, basil, and salt.

2. Pour over drained, cooked vegetables.

Italian Herb Mix

Leona Yoder, Hartville, OH

Makes ¼–⅓ cup

Prep. Time: 20 minutes

3 Tbsp. dried basil
1 Tbsp. dried oregano
1 Tbsp. parsley
¾ tsp. rosemary, scant
dash of cayenne pepper

1. Mix all together in a small mixing bowl.

2. Use as a rub for red meats, or mix into marinating vegetables.

Seasoned Crumbs

Vera H. Campbell, Dayton, VA

Makes 2 cups

Prep. Time: 10 minutes

4 slices day-old white bread, crusts removed
1 tsp. dried oregano
¼ tsp. dried thyme
¼ tsp. paprika

1. Break bread into pieces and whirl in blender to make fine crumbs.

2. Mix with seasonings.

3. Store in refrigerator in an airtight container.

4. Use for topping casseroles or for breading fish or chicken.

Corn with Bacon

Mary Jane Musser
Narvon, PA

Makes 6 servings

Prep Time: 10 minutes
Cooking/Baking Time: 35 minutes

4 cups fresh, *or* frozen, corn
1 tsp. salt
¼ tsp. pepper
1½ tsp. sugar
1 cup finely diced uncooked bacon

1. Place corn in a 1½-quart greased baking dish.

2. Stir in salt, pepper, and sugar.

3. Spread bacon over top of corn.

4. Bake uncovered at 350° for 35 minutes, or until bacon is crisp.

Baked Corn

Makes 6 servings

Prep. Time: 20 minutes
Cooking/Baking Time: 30–45
*   minutes*

3 eggs
2 cups fresh *or* frozen corn,
    creamed *or* simply cut
    off the cob
2 cups milk
1 Tbsp. butter, melted
salt and pepper to taste

1. In a large mixing bowl,
beat eggs well.
2. Stir in the remaining
ingredients.
3. Pour into a lightly
greased 1½- or 2-quart
greased casserole.
4. Bake uncovered at 325°
for 30–45 minutes, or until
knife inserted in center
comes out clean.

Corn Bake

Donna Conto
Saylorsburg, PA
Marla Folkerts
Holland, OH
Barbara Walker
Sturgis, SD

Makes 8 servings

Prep. Time: 10 minutes
Cooking/Baking Time: 1 hour

15-oz. can creamed corn
15-oz. can whole corn with
    juice
1 cup uncooked broken
    spaghetti noodles, *or*
    macaroni
1 cup shredded mozzarella
    cheese
¼ tsp. pepper

1. Lightly grease a 2-quart
baking dish.
2. Put all ingredients in
dish and stir together well.
3. Bake at 350° for 30
minutes, covered.
4. Uncover and bake 30
minutes more.

Corn and Green Chilies Casserole

Janice Muller
Derwood, MD

Makes 6 servings

Prep. Time: 7 minutes
Cooking/Baking Time: 25 minutes

2 10-oz. pkgs. frozen corn
2 Tbsp. butter
8-oz. pkg. cream cheese,
    softened
1 Tbsp. sugar
4-oz. can chopped green
    chilies, drained

1. Cook corn and butter
on High for 5 minutes in a
microwave-safe container.
2. Cut cream cheese into
chunks and stir into corn
until well blended.
3. Stir in sugar and green
chilies.
4. Spoon into a lightly
greased 1-quart baking dish.
5. Cover and bake at 350°
for 25 minutes.

Baked Hominy
Sharon Shank
Bridgewater, VA

Makes 8 servings

Prep Time: 5–10 minutes
Alternate Cooking Time: 2–3 hours
Baking Time: 30 minutes

8 cups water
2 tsp. salt
2 cups uncooked hominy, *or* 2 cans of cooked hominy
2 Tbsp. butter, melted
1–1½ cups grated cheese of your choice
1 cup sour cream
pepper to taste
¼ cup milk, *optional*
bacon bits, *optional*

1. Cook water, salt, and uncooked hominy in a large stockpot on medium heat for 2–3 hours or until soft. If you use 2 cans of cooked hominy, skip Step 1.

2. In a large mixing bowl, mix rest of ingredients into prepared hominy.

3. Place in a greased 9 × 13 baking dish. Bake uncovered at 350° for 30 minutes.

Tip: This is a good side dish to serve with roast beef, or any main dish meat.

Roasted Baby Carrots
Melanie Mohler
Ephrata, PA

Makes 4–5 servings

Prep. Time: 5–10 minutes
Cooking/Baking Time: 10–15 minutes

1 lb. baby carrots
1 Tbsp. olive oil
1 Tbsp. dried dill weed
salt

1. Preheat oven to 475°.

2. If using thick baby carrots, slice in half lengthwise. Otherwise leave as is.

3. In a large bowl, combine olive oil and dill. Add carrots and toss to coat.

4. In a 10 × 15 baking pan, spread carrots in a single layer.

5. Roast, uncovered, about 10 minutes or until carrots are just tender, stirring once.

6. Sprinkle with salt before serving.

Tangy Carrots
Carol L. Stroh
Akron, NY
Orpha Herr
Andover, NY

Makes 4 servings

Prep Time: 10 minutes
Cooking/Baking Time: 12–15 minutes

1 lb. carrots, diced
3 Tbsp. butter
1 Tbsp. brown sugar
1 Tbsp. Hot and Spicy, *or* Dijon, mustard
⅛ tsp. salt

1. Place carrots in saucepan with 1" of water.

2. Bring to a boil, reduce heat, and simmer 7–9 minutes, or until carrots are crisp-tender. Drain.

3. Add the butter, brown sugar, mustard, and salt to the pan with the carrots.

4. Cook and stir over medium heat until sauce is thickened and carrots are coated.

Variation: For a sweet and sour twist on this dish, increase brown sugar to ¼ cup, add ¼ cup red wine or apple cider vinegar, and drop the mustard.

—**Orpha Herr**
Andover, NY

Glazed Carrots with Bacon

Charlotte Shaffer, East Earl, PA

Makes 2–3 servings

Prep Time: 20–30 minutes
Cooking/Baking Time: 15 minutes

3 bacon slices
1 small yellow onion,
   chopped
3 Tbsp. light brown sugar,
   firmly packed
1 lb. carrots, trimmed, pared,
   sliced, cooked, drained

1. In good-sized skillet,
sauté bacon until crispy.
Remove bacon and drain.
Reserve 1–2 Tbsp. drippings.
2. Saute onion in bacon
drippings for 5 minutes.
3. Stir in sugar and carrots.
Cook over fairly high heat,
stirring frequently until heated
and glazed (5–10 minutes).
Remove from heat.
4. Sprinkle with bacon and
serve.

Bacon-Touched Carrots and Turnips

Becky Frey
Lebanon, PA

Makes 6 servings

Prep. Time: 10 minutes
Cooking/Baking Time: 20 minutes

2 slices bacon, diced
1 medium onion, sliced
3 medium carrots,
   julienned
2 turnips, julienned
   (approximately 2 cups)
salt and pepper to taste
snipped parsley, *optional*

1. Cook bacon in saucepan.
Remove from pan and drain.
Reserve drippings.
2. Stir fry vegetables in
bacon drippings until crisp-
tender, about 5 minutes.
3. Cover and cook on low
8–10 minutes, or until as
tender as you like.
4. Sprinkle with salt and
pepper. Garnish with bacon,
and also parsley if you wish,
just before serving.

Guava Carrot Sugar Snaps

Diann Dunham
State College, PA

Makes 6–8 servings

Prep. Time: 5–10 minutes
Cooking/Baking Time: 8 minutes

1 lb. baby carrots
2 Tbsp. butter
½ tsp. seasoned salt
½ lb. fresh sugar snap
   peas, rinsed
¼ cup guava jelly

1. Place carrots, butter,
and seasoned salt in large
microwave-safe bowl. Cover
and microwave on High 4
minutes, or until carrots
begin to soften.
2. Meanwhile, snip ends of
snap peas if needed.
3. Stir snap peas into
carrots. Cover and microwave
on High 4 more minutes, or
until vegetables are as tender
as you like.
4. Stir in jelly and serve.

A Tip —

Add a Tablespoon or two of milk when cooking
cauliflower; the cauliflower will remain attractively white.

Carrots Au Gratin

Mary Kathryn Yoder
Harrisonville, MO
Judy Newman
St. Mary's, ON

Makes 8 servings

Prep Time: 20 minutes
Cooking/Baking Time: 20–25 minutes

4 cups sliced carrots
1 cup shredded cheese
1 can cream of celery soup
¼ cup bread crumbs
1 Tbsp. melted butter

1. Cook carrots in a small amount of water in a saucepan, covered. When just-tender (5–10 minutes), place in large mixing bowl.
2. Stir in the cheese and soup. Pour into lightly greased 2-quart baking dish.
3. Mix the bread crumbs and butter together in a small bowl. Sprinkle over carrot mixture.
4. Bake uncovered at 350° for 20–25 minutes, or until browned.

Broccoli with Garlic and Lemon

Jan Moore, Wellsville, KS
Leona Yoder, Hartville, OH

Makes 4–5 servings

Prep. Time: 10 minutes
Cooking/Baking Time: 10–15 minutes

4½ cups fresh broccoli florets
¼–½ cup water
1 Tbsp. extra-virgin olive oil
1 garlic clove, crushed, *or* 1½ tsp. jarred minced garlic
juice and grated peel from half a lemon
grated Parmesan cheese, *optional*

1. Place broccoli and water in a good-sized saucepan. Cover and cook over medium-high heat, stirring occasionally for several minutes until broccoli is crisp-tender. Add more water if necessary to prevent scorching, but only a small amount.
2. Drain excess liquid from skillet. Push broccoli to one side and add olive oil and garlic to the other side. Cook for about 10–20 seconds, or until garlic begins to turn color and smell fragrant.
3. Toss all together.
4. Stir in lemon juice and peel.
5. When ready to serve, top with Parmesan cheese if you wish.

Cheesy Broccoli

Esther J. Mast
Lancaster, PA
Jan Rankin
Millersville, PA

Makes 6–8 servings

Prep. Time: 20 minutes
Cooking/Baking Time: 20 minutes

2 10-oz. pkgs. frozen broccoli
1 stick (½ cup) butter, melted, *divided*
8-oz. pkg. Velveeta cheese, grated, *divided*
36–38 Ritz crackers (about ⅔ tube), crushed

1. Place broccoli in a medium-sized saucepan, along with about ¼ cup water. Cover and steam, stirring occasionally, until crisp-tender, about 5–10 minutes.
2. Drain broccoli and place in lightly greased 1½-quart casserole.
3. Pour half of melted butter over broccoli.
4. Stir in most of the cheese. Reserve the rest for sprinkling on top of fully mixed casserole.
5. In a mixing bowl, combine the remaining butter with the crushed crackers. Sprinkle over broccoli mixture.
6. Top with reserved cheese.
7. Bake uncovered at 325° for 20 minutes.

Broccoli with Orange Sauce

Gaylene Harden
Arlington, IL
Miriam Christophel
Goshen, IN

Makes 4 servings

Prep. Time: 5 minutes
Cooking/Baking Time: 10 minutes

2 10-oz. pkgs. frozen
  broccoli spears
half a stick (¼ cup) butter
1 tsp. cornstarch
½ cup orange juice
1 Tbsp. freshly grated
  orange peel

1. Cook broccoli according
to package directions.
2. Meanwhile, melt butter
in a saucepan. Whisk in
cornstarch until smooth.
3. Gradually stir in orange
juice over heat. Add orange
peel. Bring to a boil and cook
and stir for 2 minutes, or
until sauce thickens.
4. Drain broccoli. Drizzle
with sauce just before serving.

Sugar Snap Pea Crunchies

Joy Uhler
Richardson, TX

*Makes 4–12 servings
(salad/veg. or snack/appetizer)*

Prep Time: 6–8 minutes

½ lb. fresh sugar snap
  peas, washed
1 Tbsp. sesame oil
2 tsp. toasted sesame seeds
¼ tsp. salt, *optional*

1. Pinch off ends and any
strings from each pod.
2. Place in mixing bowl.
3. Toss raw peas with
sesame oil.
4. Sprinkle toasted sesame
seeds over all and toss
together.
5. Serve as a vegetable side
dish, a salad, or as finger food
for a snack or appetizer.

Tips:
  *1. Store these peas in an air-
tight container. Just take the lid
off and eat or serve. Refrigerate
if you won't be eating the peas
immediately. Serve chilled or at
room temperature.*
  *2. You can find the oil and
seeds in the Asian food section
of your grocery store.*

Baked Spinach and Tomatoes

Kathleen A. Rogge
Alexandria, IN

Makes 6 servings

Prep. Time: 20–25 minutes
Cooking/Baking Time: 45 minutes

4 slices bacon
2 10-oz. pkgs. frozen
  chopped spinach, thawed
  and squeezed dry
salt and pepper to taste
¼ lb. sliced Swiss cheese,
  divided
3 fresh tomatoes, halved

1. Saute bacon until
crisp in a skillet. Drain and
crumble. Set aside.
2. Spread spinach in a
lightly greased 1½-quart
baking dish. Sprinkle with
salt and pepper.
3. Layer half the cheese
over the spinach.
4. Top with tomato halves.
5. Layer on the rest of the
cheese.
6. Sprinkle with bacon.
7. Bake uncovered at 375°
for 45 minutes.

Spinach Souffle

Orpha Herr
Andover, NY

Makes 6–8 servings

Prep. Time: 20 minutes
Cooking/Baking Time: 45 minutes
Standing Time: 5–10 minutes

2 cups cottage cheese
3 eggs, beaten
3 10-oz. pkgs. frozen
　spinach, thawed and
　squeezed dry
1½ cups shredded cheddar
　cheese, *divided*
½ tsp. salt
dash of ground nutmeg,
　optional

1. In large mixing bowl,
beat together cottage cheese
and eggs.
2. Stir in spinach, 1¼ cups
cheddar cheese, salt, and
nutmeg if you wish.
3. Spoon into a lightly
greased 8 × 12 baking pan.
4. Bake uncovered at 350°
until set, about 45 minutes.
5. Sprinkle with remain-
ing cheese. Let stand 5–10
minutes so cheese can melt
and soufflé can firm up.

Absolutely Creamy Spinach

Vicki J. Hill, Memphis, TN

Makes 9 servings

Prep. Time: 5 minutes
Cooking/Baking Time: 8–30
*　minutes*

4 10-oz. pkgs. frozen
　chopped spinach, thawed
　and squeezed dry
8-oz. pkg. cream cheese
1 stick (½ cup) butter
fine bread crumbs
paprika, *optional*

1. Place spinach in lightly
greased 2-quart baking dish.
2. Soften cream cheese and
butter in microwave for 1
minute. Beat until combined.
Pour over spinach.
3. Sprinkle with crumbs
and paprika.
4. Heat uncovered in oven
at 350° for 20–30 minutes, or
in the microwave, covered,
for 8–10 minutes.

Spinach Spaghetti Cabrini

Diane Eby
Holtwood, PA

Makes 8–10 servings

Prep. Time: 15–20 minutes
Cooking/Baking Time: 45 minutes

9 ozs. spaghetti, broken
　into pieces
1 stick (½ cup) butter,
　melted
10-oz. pkg. raw spinach,
　washed and chopped, *or*
　frozen chopped spinach,
　thawed and squeezed
　dry
4 cups shredded Monterey
　Jack cheese
2 cups sour cream
dash of oregano, *optional*
¼ tsp. salt, *optional*

1. Cook spaghetti al dente
according to package directions. Drain off water. Return
cooked spaghetti to cooking
pot.
2. Add the rest of the
ingredients to the spaghetti
and stir together in the
stockpot.
3. Spoon into a large,
lightly greased baking dish.
4. Bake uncovered at 350°
for 45 minutes.

Kale or Collard Greens

Judy Houser
Hershey, PA

Makes 2–4 servings

Prep. Time: 10 minutes
Cooking/Baking Time: 5 minutes

1 lb. kale *or* collard greens
2–3 garlic cloves, minced
2 tsp. olive oil
½–¾ tsp. salt
water

1. Wash the greens. Then remove stems and chop the leaves into ½"-wide strips.
2. Saute garlic in oil for 30 seconds in a large skillet or saucepan. Do not let it brown.
3. Add the kale or collard greens and salt. Toss to mix.
4. Cover and cook over medium-low heat for 3–4 minutes.
5. Add water, 1 Tbsp. at a time, if necessary, to keep greens from sticking.

Easy Baked Beans

Annabelle Unternahrer
Shipshewana, IN
Joan Brown
Warriors Mark, PA
Jean M. Butzer
Batavia, NY

Makes 9–10 servings

Prep. Time: 10–15 minutes
Cooking/Baking Time: 60 minutes

1½ cups ketchup
½ cup brown sugar
1 small onion, chopped
2 Tbsp. prepared mustard, *or* 1 tsp. dried mustard
3 16-oz. cans baked beans

1. Mix ketchup, brown sugar, onion, and mustard until blended. Stir in beans.
2. Pour into 2½ quart greased casserole.
3. Bake in preheated 350° oven for 1 hour, or until heated through and bubbly.

Variations:
1. For a more hearty meal, add 1 lb. browned hamburger in Step 1.
2. Cut 6–8 slices bacon into 1"-wide pieces and arrange on top of baking dish just before placing in oven.

—**Joan Brown**
Warriors Mark, PA

3. Use 2 15-oz. cans butter beans, rinsed and drained, instead of 3 cans baked beans.

—**Jean M. Butzer**
Batavia, NY

Country-Style Baked Beans

Rhoda Atzeff
Lancaster, PA

Makes 8 servings

Prep Time: 10–15 minutes
Cooking/Baking Time: 12–15 minutes
Standing Time: 5 minutes

2 16-oz. cans pinto beans, drained
1 cup chopped ham
½ cup Bull's Eye Original barbecue sauce
½ cup finely chopped onion
2 Tbsp.–¼ cup molasses, depending on your taste preference

1. Combine ingredients in a lightly greased 1½-quart casserole. Cover with waxed paper.
2. Microwave on High 12–15 minutes, or until thoroughly heated, stirring every 5 minutes.
3. Let stand 5 minutes before serving.

Best Baked Limas

Cheryl A. Lapp
Parkesburg, PA

Makes 6–8 servings

Prep. Time: 15 minutes
Soaking Time: overnight
Cooking/Baking Time: 70 minutes

1 lb. dried lima beans
4 cups water
2 cups ketchup
1 cup King molasses, *or*
 your favorite variety
1 cup dark brown sugar
1 lb. bacon

1. Soak lima beans in 4 cups water overnight in a large stockpot.
2. In the morning, do not drain, but cook, covered, for 45 minutes in soaking water.
3. Meanwhile, saute bacon in a large skillet until crispy. Drain off drippings. Break cooled bacon into small pieces.
4. Add all ingredients to beans in stockpot and mix together well.
5. Pour into 3½–4-quart baking dish or roaster. Cover.
6. Bake 20–25 minutes at 350°, or until hot and bubbly throughout.

Pineapple Baked Beans

Shelia Heil
Lancaster, PA

Makes 10 servings

Prep Time: 5 minutes
Cooking/Baking Time: 1 hour

2 16-oz. cans baked beans
¼ cup packed brown sugar
2 Tbsp. ketchup
2 tsp. prepared mustard
8-oz. can crushed
 pineapple, undrained

1. In a large bowl, combine beans, brown sugar, ketchup, and mustard.
2. Transfer to a lightly greased 2-quart baking dish.
3. Bake uncovered at 350° for 30 minutes.
4. Stir in pineapple and bake uncovered 30 minutes longer.

Chili Bean Hot Dish

Darla Sathre, Baxter, MN

Makes 4 servings

Prep. Time: 10 minutes
Cooking/Baking Time: 20–30 minutes

15-oz. can chili beans
15-oz. can whole-kernel
 corn, drained
8-oz. pkg. (2 cups) grated
 cheese, your choice of
 flavor
2 cups corn chips, slightly
 crushed

1. In a 1½-quart ungreased casserole dish, mix together the beans, corn, and cheese.
2. Top with corn chips, pressing down gently.
3. Bake uncovered at 350° for 20–30 minutes.

A Tip —

For convenient and economically priced bacon, buy bacon ends and pieces. Chop into small pieces in a food processor and sauté until crisp. Drain well in a sieve, then freeze. The bacon is handy for seasoning many dishes, baked potatoes, salads, and omelets.

Corn Chips Chili Pie

Lynne Bandel, Arcadia, IN

Makes 4–6 servings

Prep. Time: 15–20 minutes
Cooking/Baking Time: 15–20 minutes

3 cups corn chips, *divided*
1 large onion, chopped
1 cup cheddar cheese, grated, *divided*
19-oz. can chili, with *or* without beans

1. Place 2 cups corn chips in a lightly greased baking dish.
2. Arrange onion and half of grated cheese over the corn chips.
3. Pour chili over onion and cheese.
4. Top with remaining corn chips and grated cheese.
5. Bake uncovered at 350° for 15 to 20 minutes.

Quick Bean Quesadillas

Sue Pennington
Bridgewater, VA

Makes 4 servings

Prep. Time: 10 minutes
Cooking/Baking Time: 30 minutes

1 cup refried beans
11.5-oz. pkg. flour tortillas for burritos (8 count)
½ cup Mexican cheese and salsa dip
½ cup guacamole, your favorite variety
½ cup thick and chunky salsa

1. Spread ¼ cup refried beans over each of 4 tortillas.
2. Place one bean-topped tortilla in 10" skillet over medium heat. Spread 2 Tbsp. dip over beans. Top with additional tortilla. Heat 5 minutes.
3. With large pancake turner, turn quesadilla. Heat 1–2 minutes longer. Remove to plate and keep warm.
4. Repeat with remaining tortillas and dip.
5. Cut each quesadilla into 8 wedges.
6. Serve with guacamole and salsa.

Bean Burritos

Rebecca Meyerkorth
Wamego, KS

Makes 12 burritos

Prep. Time: 15 minutes
Cooking/Baking Time: 20–25 minutes

1 can refried beans
1 cup salsa of your choice
1 cup cooked rice
2 cups (8 ozs.) shredded cheddar cheese, *divided*
12 flour tortillas (6–7")

1. Combine beans, salsa, rice, and 1 cup cheese in a bowl.
2. Spoon about ⅓ cup off-center on each tortilla. Fold the sides and ends of tortilla over filling and roll up.
3. Arrange burritos in a lightly greased 9 × 13 baking pan.
4. Sprinkle with remaining cheese.
5. Cover and bake at 375° for 20–25 minutes, or until heated through.

Quesadillas

Carol Findling
Carol Stream, IL

Makes 2 servings

Prep. Time: 15 minutes
Cooking/Baking Time: 20 minutes

olive oil
half a medium-sized
  onion, sliced
half a green pepper, seeded
  and membrane removed,
  cut into strips
2 8" tortillas
Monterey Jack cheese,
  shredded, to taste
optional toppings: cut-up
  fresh tomatoes, hot salsa,
  yogurt *or* sour cream

1. Heat a 10" skillet or
sauté pan over medium heat.
Add small amount of olive oil.
2. Add onion and green
pepper. Sauté about 5 minutes, or until onion is soft and
slightly browned.
3. Place shredded cheese
on half of each tortilla. Add
cooked onion and green
pepper on top of cheese. Fold
in half.
4. Add small amount of
olive oil to sauté pan. Place
folded filled tortillas in pan.
Cook over medium heat until
slightly browned.
5. Turn tortillas to brown
other side.
6. When browned, cut each
tortilla into 4 triangles.
7. Serve with optional
toppings if you wish.

Roasted Plum Tomatoes

Betti Russer
Lancaster, PA

Makes 4 servings

Prep. Time: 10 minutes
Cooking/Baking Time: 30 minutes

8 plum tomatoes (about 1½
  lbs.)
1 Tbsp. olive oil
¼ tsp. dried thyme
½ tsp. salt
¼ tsp. pepper

1. Preheat oven to 425°.
2. Core tomatoes. Slice
each one lengthwise. Place in
a mixing bowl.
3. Toss tomatoes with olive
oil and seasonings.
4. Arrange tomatoes in a
single layer, with cut sides up,
on a rimmed baking sheet.
5. Bake until softened,
about 30 minutes.

Fried Ripe Tomatoes

Mary W. Stauffer
Ephrata, PA

Makes 4 servings

Prep. Time: 10 minutes
Cooking/Baking Time: 10 minutes

2 firm ripe, *or* partly ripe,
  tomatoes
2 Tbsp. sugar
2 Tbsp. flour
2 Tbsp. fine bread crumbs
1–2 Tbsp. olive oil

1. Core and slice, but do
not peel, tomatoes.
2. Mix sugar, flour, and
crumbs together in a low
mixing bowl.
3. Dip tomato slices, one by
one, into this mixture. Saute
in a large skillet in oil until
browned.
4. Flip and brown on the
other side.

A Tip —

A little sugar brings out the flavor of most foods. Brown
sugar cuts the acid in tomato dishes.

Bacon Cabbage Surprise

Jonathan Gehman
Harrisonburg, VA

Makes an adaptable number of servings!

Prep. Time: 10 minutes if cooking for 3–4 persons
Cooking/Baking Time: 15 minutes

bacon, 1 *or* 2 strips per person
onion, cut in thick slices, ¼ cup per person,
garlic, minced, 1 small clove per person
cabbage, cut in thin strips, 1 cup per person
carrots, shredded, ¼ cup per person

1. Cut bacon in ½" wide squares. Place in non-stick pan large enough to hold all ingredients. Saute over medium heat until browned but not crispy. Drain off all but 2 Tbsp. drippings.
2. Turn heat to low. Add onion and garlic and cook until transparent.
3. Add carrot and cabbage, stirring to coat with bacon drippings. Mix all ingredients together well.
4. The dish is done when the cabbage begins to wilt.

Serbian Cabbage

Patricia Howard, Breen Valley, AZ

Makes 6 servings

Prep. Time: 20 minutes
Cooking/Baking Time: 30 minutes

1 medium head cabbage
13-oz. can evaporated milk
1 cup dry bread crumbs
1 stick (½ cup) butter

1. Shred cabbage. Place in lightly greased 4-quart casserole.
2. Pour milk over cabbage.
3. Sprinkle with bread crumbs and then dot with butter.
4. Cover and bake at 350° for 30 minutes.

Baked Sauerkraut

Annabelle Unternahrer
Shipshewana, IN

Makes 6–8 servings

Prep. Time: 20 minutes
Cooking/Baking Time: 1 hour

4 slices bacon
1 quart sauerkraut
¾ cup brown sugar
15-oz. can diced tomatoes
1–3 tsp. dried minced onion

1. Brown bacon in skillet. When crispy, remove and drain. Reserve drippings. Set bacon aside.
2. In a large mixing bowl, combine sauerkraut drained of most of its juice, brown sugar, tomatoes, and onion. Stir in bacon drippings.
3. Bake uncovered in lightly greased 2-quart baking dish at 350° for about 1 hour.
4. Top with bacon crumbles during last 20 minutes of baking time.

Creamy Onions

Darla Sathre
Baxter, MN

Makes 4–6 servings

Prep Time: 15 minutes
Cooking/Baking Time: 30 minutes

6 large onions, cut in quarters
10½-oz. can cream of celery soup
8-oz. container French onion dip
½ cup shredded cheddar cheese

1. Cook quartered onions in water in a good-sized saucepan until tender, but not falling apart. Drain.
2. Place drained onions in lightly greased 1½-quart baking dish.
3. In a mixing bowl, blend together the soup, dip, and cheese. Pour over onions.
4. Bake uncovered at 350° for about 20 minutes.

Vegetables

Cheesy Onions
Melissa Sensenig
Newmanstown, PA

Makes 7–8 servings

Prep Time: 15 minutes
Cooking/Baking Time: 45 minutes

3 *or* 4 large sweet onions
10¾-oz. can cream of
  chicken soup
½ cup shredded cheddar
  cheese
½ cup shredded Swiss
  cheese
1 cup crushed potato chips

1. Cut onions into bite-size
chunks.
2. Mix all ingredients
together in a large mixing
bowl except potato chips.
Pour into a lightly greased
9 × 13 baking dish.
3. Top with crushed chips.
4. Bake at 350°, uncovered,
for 45 minutes, or until
onions are tender.

Tip: Not only is this a satisfy-
ing side dish, it also makes a
good topping for baked potatoes
and sausage sandwiches.

Sweet Onion Bake
John D. Allen
Rye, CO

Makes 6 servings

Prep. Time: 20 minutes
Cooking/Baking Time: 45 minutes

5 cups chopped sweet
  onions, preferably Walla
  Walla
half a stick (¼ cup) butter,
  melted
1 cup long-grain rice,
  cooked
8-oz. carton sour cream
1 cup shredded Swiss, *or*
  cheddar, cheese, *divided*

1. Saute the onions in a
large skillet until tender.
2. Remove from heat and
stir in rice and sour cream.
3. Spread half the mixture
in a lightly greased 8 × 12
baking dish.
4. Top with half the cheese.
5. Repeat layers.
6. Cover and bake at 350°
for 30 minutes.
7. Uncover and bake for 15
minutes more, or until top is
lightly browned.

Vidalia Casserole
Mary Lynn Miller
Reinholds, PA

Makes 4–6 servings

Prep Time: 15 minutes
Cooking/Baking Time: 20–25
  minutes

4–5 Vidalia, *or* sweet,
  onions, sliced ¼" thick
half a stick (¼ cup) butter
¼ cup sour cream
¾ cup grated Parmesan
  cheese
10 butter-flavored crackers,
  crushed

1. In a skillet over medium
heat, saute onions in butter
until tender. Remove from
heat.
2. Stir in sour cream.
3. Spoon half of mixture
into a lightly greased 1-quart
baking dish. Sprinkle with
cheese.
4. Top with remaining
onion mixture and crackers.
5. Bake uncovered at 350°
for 20–25 minutes.

A Tip —

To chop onions painlessly, place your cutting board on a
front unheated burner. Turn on the rear burner and chop
the onions. The heat from the back burner will pull the
"teary" oils away from you.

Middle-Eastern Lentil Dish

Rika Allen
New Holland, PA

Makes 4 servings

Prep. Time: 10 minutes
Cooking/Baking Time: 30 minutes

½ lb. dry lentils
2 onions, chopped
3–4 tsp. curry powder, depending on your taste preference
1 tsp. cinnamon
1 tsp. salt
dash of pepper

1. Put lentils in a 3-quart saucepan. Cover with water.
2. Cover and bring to a boil. Reduce heat, and cook until lentils become slightly soft, about 10–12 minutes. Drain off water.
3. Meanwhile, saute onions in large skillet until clear, about 5 minutes.
4. Add curry powder, cinnamon, salt, and pepper to onions. Stir fry for a few minutes.
5. Add lentils and cook over low heat until heated through.

Tips

Serve over rice or with pita.
May use 1 Tbsp. olive oil instead of cooking spray.
May add chopped and cooked carrots with lentils.
May add garlic (minced) with onions.

Something Special Zucchini

Mary C. Wirth
Lancaster, PA

Makes 4 servings

Prep Time: 15 minutes
Cooking/Baking Time: 50 minutes

2 medium zucchini, *divided*
1 large sweet, *or* Vidalia, onion, *divided*
2 medium tomatoes, *divided*
2 green peppers, *divided*
6 slices cheese of your choice
salt and pepper, *optional*

1. Slice zucchini diagonally into ⅛"-thick slices.
2. Slice onion and tomatoes into ⅛"-thick slices.
3. Seed and slice green peppers into strips.
4. Layer half the ingredients into a lightly greased 2-quart shallow baking dish.
5. Repeat the layers, using all remaining ingredients.
6. Sprinkle with salt and pepper if you wish.
7. Cover tightly and bake at 375° for 45 minutes.
8. Layer cheese on top.
9. Bake uncovered 2–5 more minutes, or until cheese has melted.

Zucchini Casserole

Virginia R. Bender
Dover, DE

Makes 6 servings

Prep. Time: 30 minutes
Cooking/Baking Time: 1 hour

4 cups grated fresh zucchini
1 medium onion, grated
2 Tbsp. flour
4 eggs
½–¾ cup grated cheddar cheese
black pepper, *or* seasoning salt, to taste, *optional*

1. Place grated zucchini and onion into lightly greased 2-quart baking dish and mix together gently.
2. Sprinkle flour over all.
3. Beat eggs in a mixing bowl. Pour over all. Stir.
4. Sprinkle with grated cheese, and seasonings if you wish.
5. Bake uncovered at 350° for 1 hour.

A Tip —

Wrap cut-up onions or peppers in a paper towel before placing them in a ziplock bag and refrigerating. The paper towel absorbs moisture and delays spoiling.

Zucchini Patties

Eileen M. Landis, Lebanon, PA

Makes 2 servings

Prep. Time: 10 minutes
*Cooking/Baking Time: 12–15
minutes*

1 egg, beaten
1 cup grated fresh
   zucchini, unpeeled
2 Tbsp. cracker crumbs
1 Tbsp. chopped onion
¾ cup grated cheddar
   cheese

1. Beat egg in a good-sized
mixing bowl.
2. Stir in remaining
ingredients. Scoop out ⅓ cup
batter and form into patty.
Continue with rest of batter
to form about 4 patties total.
3. Cook patties in lightly
greased skillet until browned on
both sides. Serve immediately.

Cranberry Sauced Beets

Carol L. Stroh, Akron, NY

Makes 4 servings

Prep Time: 10 minutes
Cooking/Baking Time: 7 minutes

1 cup whole berry
   cranberry sauce
2 tsp. Dijon mustard
1 tsp. finely grated orange
   peel

2 16-oz. cans sliced beets,
   drained

1. In a medium-sized
saucepan, combine cranberry
sauce, mustard, and orange
peel.
2. Cook over medium heat,
stirring occasionally until
mixture comes to a boil.
3. Stir in beets.
4. Cover and cook 5
minutes.

Steamed Mushrooms

Jean Binns Smith
Bellefonte, PA

Makes 4 servings

Prep Time: 5 minutes
Cooking/Baking Time: 20 minutes

1 lb. small mushrooms,
   left whole *or* sliced
2 Tbsp. butter
¼ tsp. salt
⅛ tsp. paprika
½ cup milk

1. Place mushrooms in top
of double boiler. Be sure to
place them **over, not in** hot
water.
2. Dot mushrooms with
butter.
3. Sprinkle with salt and
paprika.
4. Pour milk around edge
of double boiler pan holding
the mushrooms.
5. Cover and steam 20
minutes, or until tender.

Tips:
   *1. This is especially good as
a side dish with roast beef and
mashed potatoes.*
   *2. I've found that the broth
makes a good soup stock.*

Grilled Mushrooms

Doyle Rounds
Bridgewater, VA

Makes 4 servings

Prep. Time: 5 minutes
*Cooking/Baking Time: 10–15
minutes*

½ lb. whole fresh medium-
   sized mushrooms
half a stick (¼ cup) butter,
   melted
½ tsp. dill weed
½ tsp. garlic salt

1. Thread mushrooms onto
skewers.
2. Combine butter, dill,
and garlic salt. Brush over
mushrooms.
3. Grill over hot coals for
10–15 minutes, basting and
turning every 5 minutes.

*Note: If using wooden skewers,
soak them in water for 30
minutes before threading on the
mushrooms.*

Broiled Eggplant
Carol L. Stroh
Akron, NY

Makes 4 servings

Prep Time: 15 minutes
Cooking/Baking Time: 5–6 minutes

2 beaten eggs
2 tsp. canola oil
1 medium-sized eggplant, peeled and sliced ¼" thick
1⅓ cups flavored bread crumbs
2 cups shredded mozzarella, *or* Monterey Jack, cheese, *optional*
2 cups tomato sauce, *optional*

1. Lightly oil unheated broiler pan.
2. Beat eggs and 2 teaspoons oil together in a shallow dish.
3. Dip eggplant in egg mixture, then coat with bread crumbs.
4. Place on greased broiler pan. Broil 4" from heat, 2 minutes per side, or until golden.
5. If desired, spread cheese on top and broil for another minute, or until cheese melts.
6. Serve plain or with tomato sauce.

I like to serve this crispy right out of the broiler, with tomato sauce on the side for dipping.

Maple-Glazed Squash
Jean Turner
Williams Lake, BC

Makes 6–8 servings

Prep Time: 10–15 minutes
Cooking/Baking Time: 50–55 minutes

2 acorn squash
salt and pepper
⅔ cup maple syrup
½ cup soft bread crumbs
half a stick (¼ cup) butter, softened

1. Trim off ends of acorn squash, then cut crosswise into 1" slices. Discard seeds.
2. Season squash with salt and pepper.
3. Arrange a single layer of squash in a large shallow baking pan. Cover and bake at 350° for 30–35 minutes.
4. Combine syrup, crumbs, and butter in a small mixing bowl. Spread over squash.
5. Bake uncovered for 15–20 minutes, basting occasionally.

Bean Sprouts
Roseann Wilson
Albuquerque, NM

Makes 2 servings

Prep. Time: 5 minutes
Cooking/Baking Time: 8–10 minutes

1 clove garlic, minced
2 Tbsp. oil
1 lb. fresh bean sprouts
salt and pepper

1. Cook garlic in oil in a large skillet or saucepan until translucent.
2. Add bean sprouts. Stir fry 4–5 minutes.
3. Add salt and pepper to taste.

Savory Rice
Barb Harvey, Quarryville, PA
Carna Reitz, Remington, VA

Makes 6 servings

Prep. Time: 5 minutes
Cooking/Baking Time: 30 minutes

½ to ¾ stick (4–6 Tbsp.) butter
1 cup uncooked long-grain rice
2½ cups water
3 beef bouillon cubes
1 Tbsp. fresh parsley
1 Tbsp. fresh basil

1. Melt butter in good-sized saucepan over medium heat.
2. Add rice, water, and bouillon cubes. Cover and bring to a boil.
3. Turn heat to low and cook 20–25 minutes until rice is soft, stirring once.
4. Just before serving, stir in fresh herbs.

Variations:

1. Substitute 2½ cups chicken broth for the water and beef bouillon cubes.
2. Drop the fresh basil. Replace with 1 tsp. dried onion and 1 tsp. seasoned salt.

—**Carna Reitz**
   Remington, VA

Flavored Rice
Pat Schmidt
Newton, KS

Makes 8 servings

Prep Time: 10 minutes
Cooking/Baking Time: 1–1¼ hours

10½-oz. can beef broth
10½-oz. can French onion soup
1 cup uncooked long-grain rice
4-oz. can mushrooms, drained, *optional*
small can sliced water chestnuts, drained, *optional*

1. Combine above ingredients in a mixing bowl.
2. Spoon into a lightly greased 1½-qt. baking dish.
3. Cover and bake at 325° for 1–1¼ hours, or until rice is soft and has absorbed the liquid.

Rice-Vermicelli Pilaf
Jan Mast
Lancaster, PA

Makes 4 servings

Prep. Time: 5 minutes
Cooking/Baking Time: 30 minutes

half a stick (¼ cup) butter
1 cup uncooked long-grain rice
½ cup uncooked vermicelli, broken into short pieces
2¾ cups chicken broth
2 Tbsp. parsley

1. Melt butter in a saucepan. Add rice and noodles, stirring until browned, about 3 minutes.
2. Stir in broth and bring to a boil.
3. Reduce heat, cover, and simmer 20–25 minutes, or until rice is tender.
4. Stir in parsley before serving.

A Tip —

Always rinse rice before cooking it to remove the excess starch that makes cooked rice gummy. I also like to fry my rice in a little olive oil right before cooking to give it a pleasant flavor and texture.

Homemade Seasoned Rice Mix

Doris Beachy, Stevens, PA

Makes 3¼ cups mix

Prep Time: 10 minutes
Cooking/Baking Time: 20 minutes

---

3 cups uncooked long-grain rice
6 tsp. instant bouillon granules
¼ cup dried parsley flakes
2½ tsp. onion powder
¼ tsp. dried thyme

1. Combine all ingredients in a storage container with a tight lid.
2. To prepare rice as a side dish, combine 2 cups water and 1 Tbsp. butter in a saucepan.
3. Bring to a boil. Stir in 1 cup mix.
4. Reduce heat, cover, and simmer for 15–20 minutes, or until liquid is absorbed.

Perfect Brown Rice

Jeanette B. Oberholtzer
Manheim, PA

Makes 4 servings

Prep Time: 10 minutes
Cooking/Baking Time: 1 hour

---

1 cup uncooked brown rice
1 small onion, finely chopped
2 tsp. instant chicken bouillon
2 cups hot water
½ cup chopped raw carrots, *optional*
½ cup chopped raw, *or* frozen, string beans, *optional*

1. Put rice into lightly greased 1½-quart baking dish. Add chopped onion.
2. Dissolve bouillon in hot water and pour over rice. Stir in carrots and string beans if you wish.
3. Cover with foil and bake in 350° oven for 1 hour.

Persian Rice

Lizzie Ann Yoder
Hartville, OH

Makes 6 servings

Prep. Time: 10 minutes
Cooking/Baking Time: 40–60 minutes

---

1 cup uncooked brown rice
1 cup orange juice
2 cups water
½ cup raisins
¼ tsp. grated orange rind, *or* dried orange bits
1 Tbsp. chopped fresh parsley

1. Place rice in dry skillet and cook over moderate heat until slightly toasted.
2. Stir to prevent burning. Add orange juice, water, and raisins.
3. Cover tightly and simmer over low heat until rice is tender, 40–60 minutes.
4. Remove from heat. Fluff rice with fork and stir in orange rind and parsley.

Brazilian Rice

Jeanette B. Oberholtzer
Manheim, PA

Makes 8 servings

Prep Time: 15 minutes
Cooking/Baking Time: 40 minutes

2 Tbsp. olive oil
1 small onion, finely
    chopped
1 clove garlic, minced,
    optional
2 cups uncooked long-grain
    rice
2 Roma tomatoes, chopped
1 tsp. salt
hot water

1. Heat olive oil in 3-quart saucepan. Add onion, and garlic if you wish. Saute until golden brown.
2. Add rice. Cook and stir a few minutes to coat with oil.
3. When rice begins to brown, stir in tomatoes and salt.
4. Add enough hot water to cover rice, plus an inch above the rice.
5. Cover and simmer over low to moderate heat for about 30 minutes. The rice is finished when it's absorbed all the liquid.

Jennifer's Mexican Rice

Carolyn Spohn
Shawnee, KS

Makes 4 servings

Prep. Time: 10 minutes
Cooking/Baking Time: 40–45 minutes

small onion, finely
    chopped
1–2 cloves garlic, minced,
    optional
2 tsp. canola oil
1 cup basmati, *or* other
    long-grain, rice
1 tsp. chili powder
2 cups water
2 tsp. tomato, *or* vegetable,
    bouillon
½ cup frozen peas, *optional*

1. In a good-sized saucepan, saute onion, and garlic if you wish, in oil until softened.
2. Add rice and stir to coat with oil. Add chili powder and stir over heat until fragrant.
3. Add water and tomato bouillon. Bring to boil.
4. Cover. Reduce heat and cook until rice is done and water is absorbed.
5. If you wish to add the peas, stir them in about 10 minutes into the cooking time.
6. Stir rice with a fork to fluff just before serving.

Barberton Hot Sauce

F. Elaine Asper
Norton, OH

Makes 6–8 servings

Prep. Time: 20 minutes
Cooking/Baking Time: 45 minutes

1 onion, chopped
2 Tbsp. butter
¼–½ tsp. paprika,
    according to your taste
    preference
3 cans Rotel tomatoes with
    jalapenos
½ cup uncooked long-grain
    rice

1. Saute onion in butter in a good-sized saucepan. Add paprika to taste.
2. Process tomatoes briefly in blender.
3. Add tomatoes and rice to onion.
4. Cover and cook until rice is tender, about 45 minutes. Check the rice every 10–15 minutes to see whether water is needed to keep it from sticking and scorching. Add ¼ cup at a time if necessary.

Fried Rice

Bernita Boyts
Shawnee Mission, KS

Makes 2 servings

Prep Time: 3–5 minutes
Cooking/Baking Time: 6–8
minutes

¼ cup chopped onion, *or*
  sliced green onions
5 baby bella mushrooms,
  sliced
2 tsp. olive oil
¾ cup frozen peas
3 cups cooked brown rice

1. In a large skillet or
saucepan, saute onion and
bellas in olive oil for about 2
minutes. Onions should be
translucent and mushrooms
somewhat dark.
2. Stir in frozen peas and
cook for a minute.
3. Add cooked rice and
continue cooking over low
heat until dish is hot through.
Stir frequently to prevent
sticking.

Tips:
1. Turn this into an entrée
by topping with cut-up leftover
meat or fish.
2. Stir in any leftover
vegetables that you want to add
in Step 2.

Microwave Sour Cream-Chilies Rice

Stephanie Walker
Keezletown, VA

Makes 4 servings

Prep. Time: 10 minutes
Cooking/Baking Time: 15 minutes
Standing Time: 4 minutes

2 cups uncooked long-grain
  rice
2 cups vegetable, *or*
  chicken, broth
4 ozs. shredded cheddar
  cheese, *divided*
½ cup sour cream
4-oz. can chopped green
  chilies, drained

1. Mix rice and broth in
2-quart microwave-safe dish.
Cover tightly and microwave
on High 9–10 minutes, or
until rice is tender and liquid
is absorbed.
2. Stir in half the cheese,
and all the sour cream and
chilies.
3. Cover tightly and
microwave on High another
2–3 minutes.
4. Sprinkle with remaining
cheese. Cover and let stand
about 4 minutes.

Oven Parmesan Chips

Erma Martin, East Earl, PA
Nettie J. Miller, Millersburg, OH
Robin Schrock, Millersburg, OH
Carol L. Stroh, Akron, NY

Makes 4–6 servings

Prep. Time: 10 minutes
Cooking/Baking Time: 15–25
minutes

half a stick (¼ cup) butter,
  melted
⅓ tsp. garlic powder
½ tsp. salt
⅛ tsp. pepper
2–3 Tbsp. grated Parmesan
  cheese
4 medium-sized baking
  potatoes, unpeeled

1. Melt butter on baking
sheet.
2. Sprinkle seasonings and
grated cheese evenly over
butter.
3. Cut potatoes into ¼" slices.
4. Lay potato slices in
single layer on top of buttery
mixture. Then turn each slice
over so both sides are coated.
5. Bake at 425° for 15–25
minutes, or until potatoes are
tender and golden.

Variations:
1. Instead of 4 baking
potatoes, use 8 medium-sized
unpeeled red potatoes, cut in half.

*—***Janet Oberholtzer**
Ephrata, PA

2. Drop the garlic powder
and add 1 finely minced garlic

clove instead. *For an interesting additional flavor, add ⅛ tsp. ground nutmeg to Step 2.*

—**Carol L. Stroh**
Akron, NY

Tip: These are decadently delicious served with sour cream as a condiment.

—**Nettie J. Miller**
Millersburg, OH

Herb-Roasted Potatoes

Jean M. Butzer
Batavia, NY

Makes 4 servings

Prep. Time: 10 minutes
Cooking/Baking Time: 35–45 minutes

⅓ cup Dijon mustard
2 Tbsp. olive oil
1 clove garlic, chopped
½ tsp. Italian seasoning
6 medium-sized red-skin potatoes (about 2 lbs.), cut into chunks

1. Mix all ingredients except potatoes in a small bowl.
2. Place potatoes in a lightly greased 9 × 13 baking pan. Toss with mustard mixture.
3. Bake uncovered at 425° for 35–45 minutes, or until potatoes are fork-tender. Stir occasionally during baking to prevent potatoes from sticking and scorching.

Seasoned Oven Potatoes

Lucille Hollinger, Richland, PA
June Grafl, Denver, PA
Esther Burkholder
Millerstown, PA
Jamie Schwankl, Ephrata, PA
Leona Yoder, Hartville, OH

Makes 4–6 servings

Prep. Time: 10 minutes
Cooking/Baking Time: 30–40 minutes

4 good-sized potatoes, peeled and cut into wedges *or* cubes
1 Tbsp. olive oil
¼ tsp. salt, *or* seasoned salt
¼ tsp. pepper
garlic salt

1. In a large re-sealable plastic bag, mix oil, salt, and pepper.
2. Add potatoes and shake to coat. Place in a lightly greased 9 × 13 baking pan.
3. Bake at 425° for 20 minutes.
4. Turn and sprinkle with garlic salt.
5. Bake 10–20 minutes longer, or until potatoes are fork-tender and browned.

Variations:

1. Skip the garlic salt and instead use ½ tsp. dried basil and ½ tsp. dill weed.

—**June Grafl**, Denver, PA

2. Skip the salt, pepper, and garlic salt and instead use 2 tsp. Season-All and 1 tsp. pizza

seasoning *(which includes basil, oregano, marjoram, garlic powder, thyme, red pepper, and savory).*

—**Jamie Schwankl**
Ephrata, PA

3. Skip the salt, pepper, and garlic salt and instead use half an envelope dry onion soup mix.

—**Leona Yoder**
Hartville, OH

Scored Potatoes

Ida H. Goering, Dayton, VA
Carolyn A. Baer, Conrath, WI

Makes 4 servings

Prep Time: 10 minutes
Cooking/Baking Time: 50 minutes

4 large baking potatoes
2 Tbsp. butter, melted
⅛ tsp. paprika
1 Tbsp. minced fresh parsley
salt and pepper to taste

1. Cut scrubbed potatoes in half lengthwise. Slice widthwise six times, but not all the way through.
2. Fan potatoes slightly. Place in a lightly greased shallow baking dish.
3. Brush each potato with butter.
4. Sprinkle each with paprika, parsley, salt, and pepper.
5. Bake uncovered at 400° for 50 minutes, or until tender.

Half-Baked Potatoes

Shelia Heil
Lancaster, PA

Makes 4 servings

Prep Time: 5 minutes
Cooking/Baking Time: 35–45 minutes

4 baking potatoes
½ stick (4 Tbsp.) butter

1. Cut unpeeled potatoes in half lengthwise. Place in lightly greased baking pan.
2. Dot with butter and bake at 350° for 35–45 minutes, cut side up. When potatoes form a puffy brown top, they're ready to eat.

Jeanne's Baked Potato Topping

Natalia Showalter
Mt. Solon, VA

Makes 10 servings

Prep. Time: 10 minutes
Chilling Time: 2–4 hours

8-oz. pkg. cream cheese, softened
1 cup sour cream
¼ cup finely chopped onion
2 Tbsp. prepared horseradish
2 Tbsp. fresh minced parsley
1 Tbsp. lemon juice, *optional*
½ tsp. salt, *optional*

1. In mixing bowl, combine cream cheese and sour cream.
2. Mix in onion, horseradish, parsley, and your choice of seasonings.
3. Serve over piping hot baked potatoes.
4. Garnish with shredded cheddar cheese, if you wish.

Tip: *If you can, make this ahead of time and chill for several hours before using. The extra time will allow the flavors to blend.*

Baked Potato Reuben

Jean M. Butzer
Batavia, NY

Makes 4 servings

Prep. Time: 10 minutes
Cooking/Baking Time: 1 hour and 15 minutes

4 baking potatoes
2 cups sauerkraut, drained
2 cups corned beef, chopped fine
Russian salad dressing
1 cup Swiss cheese, grated

1. Bake potatoes until tender. Split lengthwise and squeeze potato to open it.
2. Cover each potato with ½ cup sauerkraut, ½ cup corned beef, and salad dressing to taste.
3. Cover each with ¼ cup of the grated cheese.
4. Place in baking dish. Bake uncovered at 400° until cheese melts, about 15 minutes. Serve immediately.

Tip: *To bake potatoes, rub with oil, place in a shallow baking pan. Bake at 400° for one hour or until tender.*

A Tip —

To bake potatoes quickly, place them in boiling water for 10-15 minutes. Pierce skins with a fork and then bake them in a pre-heated oven.

Swiss Potatoes

Jan Pembleton
Arlington, TX
Nathan LeBeau
Rapid City, SD

Makes 8 servings

Prep. Time: 45 minutes
Cooking/Baking Time: 1½ hours

6 medium red potatoes, uncooked, unpeeled, and sliced ¼" thick, *divided*
1½ cups Swiss, *or* cheddar, cheese, grated, *divided*
¼–1 tsp. salt, according to your taste preferences, *divided*
¼ tsp. pepper, *divided*
3 Tbsp. butter, *divided*
½ pint whipping cream

1. Create layers in a lightly greased 2-quart casserole in this order: half the potatoes, half the cheese, half the salt and pepper.
2. Dot with half the butter.
3. Repeat layers.
4. Pour cream over all.
5. Bake uncovered at 300° for 1½ hours.

Variation: For a somewhat different texture, cube the potatoes instead of slicing them.
— **Nathan LeBeau**
Rapid City, SD

Scalloped Potatoes

Eleanor Larson
Glen Lyon, PA

Makes 6–8 servings

Prep Time: 15–20 minutes
Cooking/Baking Time: 1 hour and 15 minutes

¼ cup onions, chopped
half a stick (¼ cup) butter
¼ cup flour
1½ tsp. salt, *optional*
¼ tsp. pepper, *optional*
2½ cups milk
5 large potatoes, uncooked and sliced (your choice about whether to leave the skins on or not), *divided*

1. Cook onions in butter in a saucepan until tender.
2. Stir in flour, and salt and pepper if you wish. Blend well.
3. Gradually stir in milk, stirring constantly.
4. Cook until thickened and bubbly. Cook 1 minute more. Remove from heat.
5. Place half of sliced potatoes into a greased 2-quart casserole.
6. Cover with half the sauce.
7. Repeat layers.
8. Bake covered in a 350 degree oven for 45 minutes. Stir.
9. Continue baking, uncovered, for 30 more minutes, or until potatoes are bubbly and brown.

Potatoes Supreme

Ruth Zendt
Mifflintown, PA

Makes 8–10 servings

Prep Time: 20–30 minutes
Cooking/Baking Time: 25–30 minutes

8–10 medium-sized potatoes, uncooked, peeled, and cubed
10¾-oz. can cream of chicken soup
3 cups shredded cheddar cheese, *divided*
8-oz. container sour cream
3 green onions, chopped
salt and pepper to taste, *optional*

1. Place potatoes in a saucepan and cover with water. Bring to a boil.
2. Cover and cook until almost tender. Drain.
3. In a large mixing bowl, blend soup, 1½ cups cheese, sour cream, onions, and salt and pepper if you wish.
4. Stir in potatoes.
5. Place mixture in a greased 9 × 13 baking dish. Sprinkle with remaining cheese.
6. Bake uncovered at 350° for 25–30 minutes, or until heated through.

Baked Potato Salad

Barbara Smith
Beaford, PA
Janice Yoskovich
Carmichaels, PA

Makes 6 servings

Prep. Time: 30–40 minutes
Cooking/Baking Time: 60 minutes

8 medium-sized potatoes, cooked, peeled, and cubed
½ lb. Velveeta cheese, cut into small cubes, *or* 1½ cups hot pepper Monterey Jack cheese, grated
1 cup mayonnaise, *optional*
½ cup chopped onion
½–1 lb. bacon fried crisp, crumbled, according to your taste preferences

1. Place potatoes in a lightly greased 9 × 13 baking pan.
2. Combine cheese, mayonnaise, and onion in a small mixing bowl.
3. Pour over potatoes. Mix well.
4. Top with crumbled bacon.
5. Bake uncovered at 350° for 60 minutes, or until cheese is bubbly and brown around edges.

Party Mashed Potatoes

Peggy Clark, Burrton, KS
Elaine Patton
West Middletown, PA
Freda Imler, Eldon, MO
Ruth Hofstetter, Versailles, MO

Makes 10–12 servings

Prep. Time: 30 minutes
Cooking/Baking Time: 45–60 minutes

5 lbs., *or* 9 large, potatoes
8-oz. pkg. cream cheese, softened
1 cup sour cream
2 tsp. onion salt
2 Tbsp. butter, softened
¼ tsp. pepper, *optional*

1. Peel potatoes, cut in pieces, and boil in salted water until tender.
2. Drain. Mash until smooth.
3. Add remaining ingredients and beat until light and fluffy.
4. Spread potatoes into greased 9 × 13 baking dish. **At this point, you can bake the potatoes, or cover and refrigerate for a week until you're ready to bake and serve. Or you can cover tightly and freeze for 2–4 weeks, until ready to bake and serve.**
5. When ready to bake, dot with butter. Bake uncovered, unfrozen potatoes at 350° for 45–60 minutes, or until potatoes are hot through and bubbly on top.

Variation: Drop the onion salt, butter, and pepper. Instead, stir in 1 tsp. diced chives in Step 3. Top with ¼ cup breadcrumbs just before baking.

—**Elaine Patton**
West Middletown, PA

Tip: This makes a big portion. Instead of baking the whole batch at once, you can simply spoon out the amount you need, bake it, and continue to store the rest in the fridge for up to a week.

—**Freda Imler**, Eldon, MO

Creamy Potato Bake

Dorothy VanDeest
Memphis, TN

Makes 6 servings

Prep. Time: 20–25 minutes
Cooking/Baking Time: 30 minutes

3 cups mashed potatoes
8-oz. carton sour cream
5–6 slices bacon, cooked and crumbled
3 small green onions, chopped
4 ozs. shredded cheddar cheese

1. Evenly spread potatoes in a lightly greased 6 × 10 baking dish.
2. Top with sour cream. Sprinkle with bacon and green onions. Top with cheese.
3. Bake potatoes uncovered at 300° for 30 minutes.

Lite Mashed Potatoes

Susan Kasting, Jenks, OK

Makes 6 servings

Prep. Time: 10 minutes
Cooking/Baking Time: 20 minutes

4 medium potatoes, peeled
   and coarsely chopped
4 stalks celery, coarsely
   chopped
3 whole cloves garlic
3 Tbsp. butter
½ cup chicken stock *or* milk

1. Place first 3 ingredients
in a pot of water. Boil until
potatoes are tender.
2. Lift out celery and garlic
and place in food processor.
Pulse until smooth.
3. Mash potatoes with
butter. Add celery to mashed
potatoes and mix together,
adding milk/chicken stock as
needed.

Horseradish Mashed Potatoes

Barbara Nolan
Pleasant Valley, NY

Makes 6–8 servings

Prep Time: 15 minutes
Cooking/Baking Time: 20 minutes

3 lbs. peeled potatoes cut
   into large chunks
5⅓ Tbsp. (⅓ cup) butter,
   softened
¾ cup hot milk, *or* half-
   and-half
1 tsp., *or* less, salt
2–4 Tbsp. prepared
   horseradish, according
   to your taste preference

1. Place potatoes in a
large stockpot. Add an inch
of water or more. Cover
and bring to a boil. Simmer
partially covered for 20
minutes, or until potatoes are
tender.
2. Drain off all water.
3. Beat potatoes with a
potato masher until almost
smooth.
4. Add remaining ingredi-
ents and mash until smooth.

Potato Puff

Sharon Swartz Lambert
`Harrisonburg, VA

Makes 4–6 servings

Prep. Time: 45 minutes
Cooking/Baking Time: 30 minutes

2 cups mashed potatoes
2 Tbsp. grated Parmesan
   cheese
1 Tbsp. melted butter
2 Tbsp. chopped onion
3 eggs

1. In a large mixing bowl,
combine potatoes and cheese.
2. Stir in butter and onion.
3. Separate eggs. Beat
egg yolks and add to potato
mixture.
4. Beat whites until stiff.
Fold into potato mixture.
5. Turn into a deep, lightly
greased 2-quart casserole.
6. Bake uncovered at
350° for 30 minutes, or until
a knife inserted in center
comes out clean.

A Tip —

For especially creamy
mashed potatoes, use an
electric mixer to mash
them.

Stove-Top Roasted Red Potatoes

Bonnie Goering
Bridgewater, VA

Makes 6 servings

Prep. Time: 5–10 minutes
Cooking/Baking Time: 30 minutes

2–3 lbs. small red potatoes
half a stick (¼ cup) butter
salt to taste
pepper to taste
1–2 Tbsp. freshly chopped
   parsley

1. Wash potatoes well. Using a vegetable peeler, cut a ribbon of skin off just around the middle of each potato.
2. Melt butter in large skillet. Lay in potatoes in a single layer.
3. Sprinkle with salt and pepper.
4. Cook, covered, over medium heat.
5. Stir frequently. Cook until potatoes are fork-tender and browned.
6. Add parsley and cook a few minutes more.

Potatoes and Green Beans

Edna E. Moran
Gulfport, MS

Makes 2 servings

Prep. Time: 15 minutes
Cooking/Baking Time: 20–25 minutes

1 strip bacon, fried and
   crumbled
4 small new potatoes,
   washed, unpeeled, and
   cut in half
2 cups fresh green beans,
   snapped
1 Tbsp. dried chopped
   onions
salt and pepper to taste
water

1. Place bacon in 2-quart saucepan. Add in this order: potatoes, beans, onions, salt, and pepper.
2. Cover with water. Cover pan and simmer until done to your liking.

The potatoes and beans do not shrink while cooking!

Amish Fried Potatoes

Alice Miller
Stuarts Draft, VA

Makes 6 servings

Prep. Time: 30 minutes
Cooking/Baking Time: 40 minutes

1 Tbsp. butter
1–2 Tbsp. vegetable oil
6 medium-sized potatoes,
   cooked, peeled, and
   diced
1 tsp. salt
¼ tsp. pepper
¼ cup milk

1. Place butter and oil in large skillet. Heat skillet before adding potatoes.
2. When skillet is hot, add potatoes (be careful not to splash yourself with the hot butter and oil).
3. Saute until potatoes on bottom of skillet become golden brown. Then turn with a metal spatula, making sure that the potatoes on top are now on the bottom.
4. Add salt and pepper. Turn potatoes again when those on the bottom turn golden brown.
5. Turn 2 more times until all potatoes are golden brown.
6. Pour in milk and mix through potatoes.
7. Continue sautéing just until the milk is hot and blended into potatoes.

A Tip —

Don't grind or shake salt, pepper, spices, or dried herbs over steaming cooking pots. The steam will cause mildew in the containers. If you do shake the seasonings over a steaming pot, leave the containers' lids off for about 10 minutes before closing them.

Scalloped Fall Bake

Kathleen A. Rogge
Alexandria, IN
Jeanette B. Oberholtzer
Manheim, PA
Irene J. Dewar, Pickering, ON

Makes 6–8 servings

Prep. Time: 25 minutes
Cooking/Baking Time: 40 minutes

3 large tart, unpared apples
4 medium sweet potatoes,
  cooked and skinned
half a stick (¼ cup) butter,
  divided
1 tsp. salt
½ cup honey, *or* brown
  sugar
1 tsp. zest of orange, *optional*

1. Slice apples and potatoes into ½" thick slices.
2. In a skillet, saute apples in 2 Tbsp. butter until light brown.
3. Arrange alternate layers of potatoes and apples in a greased 2-quart baking dish. Sprinkle each layer with salt.
4. Melt remaining butter in skillet. Stir in honey, and orange zest if you wish, and blend.
5. Pour over potatoes and apples.
6. Bake uncovered at 375° for 40 minutes.

Variation: Add ½ cup pecan pieces to top of baking dish, just before pouring sauce over all.

—**Jeanette B. Oberholtzer**
Manheim, PA

Baked Sweet Taters

Suellen Fletcher
Noblesville, IN

Makes 6–8 servings

Prep. Time: 45 minutes
Cooking/Baking Time: 10 minutes

6 medium-sized sweet
  potatoes
1 tsp. cinnamon
½ tsp. nutmeg
3 Tbsp. butter, softened
¼ cup brown sugar
mini marshmallows,
  optional
pecans, *optional*

1. Peel sweet potatoes, rinse in cold water and boil until very tender. Drain.
2. Mash until smooth
3. Add cinnamon, nutmeg, butter, and brown sugar. Blend well with mixer.
4. Spoon into a serving dish and serve.
5. Or, if you wish, spoon into a lightly greased baking dish. Top with marshmallows and pecans. Slide under the broiler to brown toppings. Watch carefully so they don't burn!

Candied Yams

Jamie Schwankl
Ephrata, PA
Alica Denlinger
Lancaster, PA

Makes 6–7 servings

Prep Time: 5 minutes
Cooking/Baking Time: 40–50
  minutes

1 tsp. salt
half a stick (¼ cup) butter
¾ cup water
½–1 cup brown sugar,
  according to your taste
  preference
2 Tbsp. cornstarch
40-oz. can of yams,
  drained

1. Combine salt, butter, and water in a good-sized saucepan over medium heat.
2. In a small bowl, stir together brown sugar and cornstarch. Add to saucepan, mixing well.
3. Add the yams. Cook for 10 minutes, or until sauce starts to thicken.
4. Spoon potatoes and sauce into a lightly greased 2-quart baking dish.
5. Bake uncovered at 350° for 30–40 minutes

Maple Sweet Potatoes

Betti Risser
Lancaster, PA

Makes 8–10 servings

Prep. Time: 10 minutes
Cooking/Baking Time: 50–60 minutes

7 medium-sized sweet potatoes, peeled and cut into chunks
1 tsp. salt
half a stick (¼ cup) butter, cut up
¼–⅓ cup real maple syrup, depending upon your taste preference
2 cups miniature marshmallows

1. Bring sweet potatoes, salt, and water to a boil in a large saucepan. Cook 15–20 minutes, or until tender. Drain.
2. Mash potatoes, or press through a ricer.
3. Stir in butter and maple syrup.
4. Spoon mixture into a lightly greased 9 × 13 baking dish.
5. Bake at 350° for 20 minutes.
6. Top evenly with marshmallows and bake 8 more minutes, or until marshmallows are puffed and golden.

Cranberry-Apple Sweet Potatoes

Charlotte Shaffer
East Earl, PA

Makes 6–8 servings

Prep Time: 15–30 minutes
Cooking/Baking Time: 20–25 minutes

5–6 medium, uncooked sweet potatoes, peeled, and cut into bite-size pieces *or* two 18-oz. cans sweet potatoes, drained and cut into bite-size pieces
21-oz. can apple pie filling
8-oz. can whole berry cranberry sauce
2 Tbsp. apricot preserves
2 Tbsp. orange marmalade

1. If you're starting with uncooked sweet potato pieces, place them in stockpot. Add an inch or more of water. Cover and simmer until tender. Drain.
2. Spread pie filling in a lightly greased 8 × 8 baking dish.
3. Arrange cooked or canned sweet potatoes over top.
4. In a small mixing bowl, stir together cranberry sauce, apricot preserves, and orange marmalade.
5. Spoon over sweet potatoes.
6. Bake uncovered at 350° for 20–25 minutes.

Variation: When finished baking, sprinkle with 1½ cups mini marshmallows. Broil 4 minutes, just until marshmallows are lightly browned. Watch carefully to prevent burning!
—Charlotte Shaffer
East Earl, PA

Baked Sweet Potato Fries

Joan S. Eye
Harrisonburg, VA

Makes 4 servings

Prep Time: 20 minutes
Cooking/Baking Time: 30–35 minutes

4 medium-sized sweet potatoes, unpeeled and scrubbed
1 tsp. olive oil
dash cayenne pepper
salt to taste

1. Cut unpeeled sweet potatoes lengthwise into ⅓" slices. Cut slices into sticks.
2. In a large bowl, combine olive oil and cayenne pepper. Add sweet potatoes and toss until well coated.
3. Transfer to lightly greased baking sheet.
4. Bake 15 minutes at 450°.
5. Turn fries over. Continue roasting until golden, about 15–20 more minutes.
6. Sprinkle with salt before serving.

Salads

Spinach Salad

Ann Bender, Ft. Defiance, VA
Jackie Stefl, E. Bethany, NY
Joyce Shackelford, Green Bay, WI
Laura R. Showalter, Dayton, VA

Makes 4 servings

Prep Time: 10–15 minutes

8 ozs. fresh spinach leaves, washed
¼ cup chopped walnuts, *or* sliced almonds, *or* pecan halves, toasted
1 cup sliced fresh strawberries
1 small can mandarin oranges, drained
berry vinaigrette, *or* poppy seed, *or* oil and vinegar dressing

Toss all ingredients in a large salad bowl just before serving.

Variations:

1. Mix 1½ Tbsp. sugar and ¼ cup chopped pecans in hot skil-let. Stir continually until sugar melts and coats pecans. When pecans are toasted and well coated with melted sugar, remove from pan and cool. Add to other ingredients above and toss.

2. Brown 3 bacon slices until brown and crisp. Cool, and then crumble. Add to other ingredients above and toss.

— **Laura R. Showalter**
Dayton, VA

Berry Vinaigrette

Barbara Walker, Sturgis, SD

Makes 1½ cups

Prep Time: 5–8 minutes

3–4 Tbsp. seedless raspberry jam, depending on your taste preference
⅔ cup extra-virgin olive oil
⅓–½ cup wine vinegar, depending on your taste preference

¼ tsp. salt
¼ tsp. pepper

1. Melt the jam in the microwave in a small microwave-safe jar. Heat on High for 10 seconds. Stir. Repeat, if necessary, until melted.

2. Add rest of ingredients and shake to blend.

3. Pour over salad just before serving and toss. If you don't use it all, just save it in the jar for the next time.

Poppy Seed Dressing

Jackie Stefl
E. Bethany, NY

Makes 3½+ cups

Prep Time: 5 minutes

1 cup honey
6 Tbsp. cider vinegar
3 Tbsp. Dijon mustard
2 cups canola oil
2 Tbsp. poppy seeds

1. Mix furiously in blender.
2. Serve a portion over Spinach Salad. Store the rest in the fridge.

Rose's Balsamic Vinaigrette

Rose Hankins
Stevensville, MD

Makes 1 cup

Prep Time: 5 minutes

¼ cup balsamic vinegar
¾ cup extra-virgin olive oil
2 Tbsp. lemon juice
1 Tbsp. Italian seasoning
1 tsp. garlic powder *or* salt

1. Mix together well.
2. Store in refrigerator.

Flavorful Oil and Vinegar Dressing

Laura R. Showalter
Dayton, VA
Ruth Hofstetter
Versailles, MO

Makes ½ cup dressing

Prep Time: 3 minutes

¼ cup extra-virgin olive oil
2 Tbsp. sugar
2 tsp.–2 Tbsp. vinegar, your choice of amounts
1 tsp. parsley flakes *or* leaves
½ tsp. salt
½ tsp. pepper

1. Place all ingredients in jar with tight-fitting lid.
2. Cover and shake until ingredients are blended.
3. Pour over Spinach Salad. Toss. Serve immediately.

Tips:
1. This is also good on cucumbers and onions, or fresh tomatoes.
2. It keeps covered in the fridge for several weeks.

Mom's Vinaigrette Dressing

Mary C. Wirth
Lancaster, PA

Makes ⅓–½ cup

Prep Time: 5–10 minutes

3 Tbsp. extra-virgin olive oil
1½–2 Tbsp. red wine vinegar
1 Tbsp. minced parsley
¾ tsp. garlic salt
½ tsp. sugar
⅛ tsp. dried oregano, *optional*

1. Mix all ingredients together well.
2. Chill 2 hours or more if you wish, although it can be served immediately after mixing.
3. Serve over sliced tomatoes, cucumbers, or Vidalia onions.

Sweet and Sour Salad Dressing

Cynthia Morris, Grottoes, VA
Carol Eberly, Harrisonburg, VA

Makes 1⅔ cups

Prep Time: 5 minutes

½ cup packed brown sugar
½ cup vegetable oil
⅓ cup apple cider vinegar
⅓ cup ketchup
1 Tbsp. Worcestershire
   sauce

  1. In a bottle or jar, combine all dressing ingredients.
  2. Cover and shake well to mix.
  3. Store in the fridge until ready to use.

Oriental Salad Dressing

Brenda J. Hochstedler
East Earl, PA

Makes ⅔–1 cup

Prep. Time: 5 minutes

¼ cup vinegar
⅓ cup sugar
⅓ cup extra-virgin olive oil
1 chicken-flavored Ramen
   noodle seasoning packet
1 Oriental-flavored Ramen
   noodle seasoning packet

  1. Blend all ingredients well.
  2. Chill.
  3. Pour over your favorite salad just before serving.

Cole Slaw Dressing/ Veggie Dip

Annabelle Unternahrer
Shipshewana, IN

Makes 2½ cups

Prep. Time: 5–10 minutes

2 cups Miracle Whip
½ cup sour cream
½ cup vinegar
1 cup sugar
1 tsp. celery seed

  1. Mix all together until well blended.
  2. When ready to make slaw, pour over shredded cabbage, using only enough dressing to moisten cabbage.
  Or serve as a dip for fresh vegetables cut up as finger food.

Tip: Dressing can be stored in the refrigerator for up to 3 weeks.

Spinach Salad Caprese

Jan Moore. Wellsville, KS

Makes 4 servings

Prep Time: 10–20 minutes

6 cups fresh spinach
12 cherry tomatoes, halved
½ cup chopped fresh basil
4 ozs. fresh mozzarella
   cheese, cubed
¼ cup light olive oil

  1. Gently combine all ingredients.
  2. Toss to mix.
  3. Serve immediately.

Irish Pub Salad

Willard E. Roth, Elkhart, IN

Makes 4 servings

Prep. Time: 15–20 minutes

4 cups baby spinach, washed
½ cup sliced cucumbers
2 medium–sized tomatoes, sliced
2 hard–cooked eggs sliced
4 ozs. Irish cheddar cheese, cubed

1. Place washed spinach in salad bowl for serving.
2. Cover, in order, with cucumbers, tomatoes, eggs, and cheese.
3. Mix gently with salad dressing just before serving (or serve on the side).

Irish Pub Salad Dressing

Willard E. Roth, Elkhart, IN

Makes ¾ cup dressing

Prep. Time: 3 minutes

½ cup light mayonnaise
2 Tbsp. white wine vinegar
1 Tbsp. whole-grain Dijon mustard
1 Tbsp. fresh tarragon
1 tsp. salt
1 tsp. freshly ground pepper

1. Whisk all ingredients together until smooth.
2. Pour over salad and toss.

Refreshing Summer Salad

Kathleen A. Rogge
Alexandria, IN

Makes 4 servings

Prep Time: 20 minutes
Cooking Time: 10 minutes

2 lbs. fresh asparagus, tough ends trimmed
2 oranges, preferably Valencia
1 Tbsp. orange juice
¼ cup extra-virgin olive oil
1 cup crumbled bleu cheese

1. Fill a large bowl with ice water; set it aside.
2. Bring large pot of water to a boil. Add asparagus to boiling water and cook until crisp tender, about 4 minutes.
3. Transfer asparagus to ice bath and let sit for 1 minute. Drain and set aside.
4. Meanwhile, peel oranges, cutting off white pith. Cut between membranes to release segments. Set aside.
5. In a small bowl or jar, whisk or shake together the orange juice and olive oil.
6. To serve, divide asparagus, bleu cheese, and oranges among 4 salad plates. Drizzle each with about 1 Tbsp. of the dressing.

Mixed Vegetables Salad

Kathleen Johnson, Rolfe, IA

Makes 4 servings

Prep Time: 20–30 minutes

1½ cups raw cauliflower, cut into small pieces
½ cup celery, diced
1 cup raw carrots, shredded
1½ cup raw broccoli, cut into small pieces
low-calorie Italian dressing

1. Mix vegetables in a bowl.
2. Mix in just enough dressing to coat vegetables.

Cauliflower-Broccoli Salad

Melanie Thrower
McPherson, KS

Makes 4–5 servings

Prep Time: 15 minutes

half a small head (about 1½ cups) cauliflower, chopped
half a bunch (about 1½ cups) broccoli, chopped
¼ cup raisins
¼ cup shelled and lightly salted sunflower seeds
½ cup light Italian dressing

Mix all ingredients together in a large bowl and serve.

Strawberry Romaine Salad

Rose Hankins
Stevensville, MD

Makes 4 servings

Prep Time: 15 minutes

8 cups Romaine lettuce
1 pt. fresh strawberries
half a red onion
½ cup sunflower seeds,
  roasted
favorite salad dressing

1. Divide torn lettuce leaves among 4 individual salad bowls.
2. Slice 3–4 berries into each bowl.
3. Layer thin slices of onions over top.
4. Sprinkle with seeds.
5. Just before serving, drizzle with dressing.

Raspberry Walnut Salad

Jan Moore
Wellsville, KS
Lucy O'Connell
Northampton, MA

Makes 4 servings

Prep Time: 10 minutes

6 cups mixed salad greens
¼ cup raspberry walnut
  vinaigrette
1 cup fresh raspberries
¼ cup feta cheese *or* bleu
  cheese
¼ cup chopped walnuts

1. Mix greens and vinaigrette in a large bowl.
2. Divide mixture between 4 serving plates.
3. Top each plate of greens with raspberries, cheese, and walnuts.
4. Serve immediately.

Variation: Dress with balsamic vinaigrette.
—**Lucy O'Connell**
Northampton, MA

Apple Bleu Cheese Salad

Judy Houser
Hershey, PA

Makes 6 servings

Prep Time: 15–20 minutes

⅓ cup broken walnuts, *or*
  pecans
1 bunch red *or* green leaf
  lettuce
1–2 apples
3 ozs. crumbled bleu cheese
⅓ cup raisins, *optional*
Greek salad dressing

1. Toast coarsely chopped nuts in dry skillet over medium heat. Stir frequently to prevent burning. Set toasted nuts aside to cool.
2. Wash lettuce and tear into salad bowl.
3. Dice unpeeled apples.
4. Add apples to lettuce, along with nuts and crumbled cheese, and raisins if you wish.
5. Drizzle with Greek dressing when ready to serve.

A Tip —

Fresh lemon juice will remove onion scent from your hands.

Simple Caesar Salad

Joyce Shackelford
Green Bay, WI

Makes 4–6 servings

Prep Time: 10 minutes

6 cups torn Romaine lettuce
½ cup Caesar croutons
2 bacon strips, cooked and crumbled
¼ cup shredded Parmesan cheese
⅓ cup Caesar salad dressing

1. In a large bowl, combine Romaine, croutons, bacon, and cheese.
2. Add dressing and toss to coat.

Ed's Bleu-Cheese Salad

Andrea Zuercher, Lawrence, KS

Makes 4 servings

Prep Time: 15 minutes

1 small bunch Romaine lettuce
2 Tbsp. olive oil, *or more or less to taste*
salt and pepper to taste
4 ozs. bleu cheese, crumbled
juice of half a lemon, *or more to taste*
¼ cup grated Parmesan cheese, *optional*

1. Wash lettuce and tear into bite-size pieces. Place in salad bowl.
2. Drizzle with olive oil. Toss.
3. Season leaves with salt and pepper to taste.
4. Add bleu cheese. Toss. Set aside until near serving time. (Refrigerate if more than 15 minutes).
5. When ready to serve, add lemon juice, and Parmesan cheese if you wish, and toss again.

Tip: If you want to use pre-packaged greens, this recipe works for one regular-size bag. Adjust proportions for more or less lettuce.

Bulgarian Salad

Gail Martin
Elkhart, IN

Makes 2 servings

Prep Time: 8–10 minutes

1 tomato, diced
2 spring onions, chopped
¼ cup chopped parsley
half a green bell pepper, chopped, *optional*
salt and pepper, *optional*
vinaigrette dressing Bulgarian, *or other*, feta cheese

1. Mound tomato, onion, and parsley on 2 salad plates. Add chopped green pepper if you wish.
2. Sprinkle with salt and pepper if you wish.
3. Drizzle with dressing.
4. Crumble feta over top.

Tomato Salad
Doris Bachman
Putnam, IL

Makes 3 servings

Prep Time: 15 minutes

2 tomatoes, peeled *or*
  unpeeled
1 green pepper
1 small onion

1. Chop tomatoes, pepper, and onion. As you do, place in a mixing bowl.
2. Stir together gently.
3. Pour dressing over vegetables.

Tomato Salad Dressing:
1 Tbsp. vinegar
2 Tbsp. lemon juice
1 Tbsp. sugar
salt and pepper to taste

1. Place ingredients in jar with tightly fitting lid.
2. Cover and shake until well blended.

A Tip —

A sharp knife is a safe knife. Keep your knives sharp!

Quick Greek Salad
Melanie Mohler
Ephrata, PA

Makes 4 cups

Prep Time: 10 minutes

3–4 tomatoes
1–2 cucumbers
4-oz. pkg. feta cheese,
  crumbled
drizzle of olive oil
pepper

1. Chop tomatoes and cucumbers. Place in large bowl.
2. Toss with crumbled feta cheese.
3. Drizzle with olive oil.
4. Season with pepper.
5. Toss again and serve immediately.

Cucumber Salad
Doris Beachy
Stevens, PA

Makes 6 servings

Prep Time: 10 minutes
Chilling Time: 6 hours

2 large cucumbers
small onion
1 tsp. salt
2 cups vinegar
1 cup water
1½ cups sugar, *or* Splenda

1. Slice cucumbers and onion in thin slices into large bowl.
2. Stir in salt. Let stand 3–4 minutes.
3. In a separate bowl, mix vinegar, water, and sugar together until well blended.
4. Pour dressing over cucumbers. Cover with lid.
5. Refrigerate for 6 hours to allow dressing to penetrate the cucumbers.

Waldorf Salad with Broccoli
Frances L. Kruba
Dundalk, MD

Makes 2 servings

Prep Time: 10–15 minutes
Chilling Time: 1–2 hours

3 Tbsp. mayonnaise
1 Tbsp. honey
1 tsp. cider vinegar
1½ cups fresh broccoli,
  chopped
¾ cup chopped apple
2 Tbsp. raisins, *optional*
1 Tbsp. pecans, chopped,
  optional

1. In a medium-sized bowl, combine mayonnaise, honey, and vinegar. Whisk together until smooth.
2. Stir in broccoli and apple. Add raisins and pecans if you wish.
3. Refrigerate for an hour or two before serving.

Orange Pecan Salad

Mary Lynn Miller, Reinholds, PA

Makes 4 servings

Prep Time: 10 minutes

2 oranges, peeled and
  sectioned, *or* 11-oz. can
  mandarin oranges,
  drained
1 head, *or* bunch, leaf
  lettuce, torn
¼ cup pecan halves,
  toasted
½ cup peach yogurt
3 Tbsp. mayonnaise

1. Toss oranges, lettuce,
and pecans in a large salad
bowl. Set aside.
2. Combine yogurt and
mayonnaise in a small bowl.
3. Pour dressing over salad
just before serving. Toss.

Fresh Peach Salad

Barbara Sparks
Glen Burnie, MD

Makes 4–6 servings

Prep. Time: 20 minutes
Chilling Time: 2 hours, or more

¼ cup sugar
1 Tbsp. mayonnaise
1 cup sour cream
9 fresh peaches, peeled
  and sliced
lettuce leaves

1. Mix together sugar,
mayonnaise, and sour cream
in a small bowl.
2. Pour over peaches in a
large mixing bowl.
3. Cover and chill for at
least 2 hours to allow flavors
to blend.
4. Serve on a bed of let-
tuce, either on a large platter,
or on individual salad plates.

Dreamy Creamy Coleslaw

Nancy Wagner Graves
Manhattan, KS

Makes 6–8 servings

Prep Time: 5 minutes
*Standing/Chilling Time: 60
  minutes*

½–⅔ cup sugar, depending
  upon your taste
  preference
1 tsp. salt
⅓ cup vinegar
1 cup whipping cream
1½ lbs. shredded green
  cabbage

1. In a large bowl, blend
sugar, salt, vinegar, and
whipping cream. Refrigerate
for 30 minutes.
2. Meanwhile, shred
cabbage.
3. After dressing ingre-
dients have blended for 30
minutes, mix cabbage into
dressing, blending well.
4. Cover and chill for 30
more minutes before serving.

A Tip —

  We eat with our "eyes" as well as our mouths. Vary the
colors and textures of food you serve at a meal.

Pat's Southern-Style Coleslaw

Norma I. Gehman
Ephrata, PA

Makes 5–6 servings

Prep Time: 20 minutes

half a small head of
   cabbage (4 cups)
   shredded
¼ cup shredded carrot
¼ cup dill pickle relish
½ cup mayonnaise
salt and pepper to taste

1. Mix shredded cabbage and carrot together in a good-sized bowl.
2. Blend dill pickle relish and mayonnaise together in a small bowl.
3. Blend dressing and seasonings into vegetables.
4. Serve immediately, or chill if you'll be serving it later.

Greek Cabbage Slaw

B. Gautcher
Harrisonburg, VA

Makes 10 servings

Prep. Time: 20 minutes
Standing/Chilling Time: 12 hours

1 medium-sized head of
   cabbage head, shredded
1 medium-sized onion,
   grated
¾ cup sugar
1 tsp. salt, *optional*
½ cup oil
½ cup vinegar

1. Put shredded cabbage in stainless steel or glass bowl.
2. Sprinkle onion on top.
3. Layer on sugar, salt if you wish, oil, and vinegar, in that order. **Do not stir.**
4. Put in cool place and let stand for at least 12 hours.
5. Stir before serving.

Mountaineer Salad

Kathleen A. Rogge
Alexandria, IN

Makes 8 servings

Prep Time: 20 minutes

small head of cabbage,
   grated *or* sliced thin
½ cup peanuts
1 cup crushed pineapple,
   undrained

2 cups mini marshmallows
⅓ cup mayonnaise, *or*
   more

1. Combine first 4 just before serving.
2. When well mixed, stir in ⅓ cup mayonnaise. Add more if you'd like a creamier salad.
3. Serve immediately.

Tip: The peanuts get soft if you make this too far in advance of serving the salad.

Cranberry Coleslaw

Carolyn A. Baer
Conrath, WI

Makes 6 servings

Prep Time: 15 minutes
Chilling Time: 45 minutes

¼ cup mayonnaise
1–2 Tbsp. honey
1 Tbsp. vinegar
¼ cup fresh chopped
   cranberries, *or* snipped
   dried cranberries
small head (5 cups)
   cabbage, shredded

1. Stir together mayo, honey, and vinegar. Stir in cranberries.
2. Place shredded cabbage in large serving bowl. Pour dressing over cabbage. Toss to coat.
3. Cover and chill 45 minutes.

Poppy Seed Coleslaw

Esther Becker
Gordonville, PA

Makes 8–10 servings

Prep Time: 10–15 minutes
Chilling Time: 1 hour

16-oz. bag tri-color coleslaw mix
8¼-oz. can mandarin oranges, drained
8-oz. can pineapple chunks, drained
½ cup poppy seed salad dressing
½ cup sour cream

1. In a large mixing bowl, combine coleslaw mix and fruit.
2. In a small bowl, stir together poppy seed dressing and sour cream.
3. Pour over slaw. Mix and toss.
4. Chill in refrigerator for an hour.

German Bean Salad

Chris Kaczynski
Schenectady, NY

Makes 6 servings

Prep Time: 5 minutes
Cooking Time: 10 minutes

2 cans French-style green, or yellow, beans
2 small onions
6 slices bacon
⅓ cup vinegar
2½ Tbsp. sugar

1. Heat beans. Drain and keep warm.
2. Cut onions into slices. Separate into rings, and put in bowl with beans.
3. Dice bacon and fry until crisp. Remove bacon, but reserve drippings.
4. Add vinegar and sugar to drippings in skillet. Heat to boiling, stirring well.
5. Meanwhile, crumble bacon and stir into beans and onions.
6. Pour vinegar-sugar mixture over vegetables and bacon. Toss lightly to coat thoroughly.
7. Serve warm or at room-temperature.

Roasted Red Potato Salad

Mary Puskar
Forest Hill, MD

Makes 10 servings

Prep Time: 30 minutes
Baking Time: 30–35 minutes

5 lbs. red potatoes, skins on, quartered
2–3 chopped hard-cooked eggs
1 bunch spring onions, chopped
1 lb. bacon
16-oz. jar Miracle Whip salad dressing

1. Bake potatoes at 425° in a baking pan sprayed with non-stick cooking spray for 30–35 minutes, or until tender.
2. Meanwhile, cook bacon in a large skillet until crisp. Do in several batches so as not to crowd skillet. Drain bacon. When cooled, crumble. Set aside.
3. Mix all ingredients in a large mixing bowl. Toss well and serve.

Tips:
1. I like to microwave the bacon. Put pieces one-layer deep on a paper plate. Cover with another paper plate. Microwave on High, 1 minute per slice of bacon.
2. As you finish one batch, drain off drippings, set bacon aside to cool, and continue with the rest.

Baked Potato Salad

Lynne Bandel
Arcadia, IN

Makes 8–10 servings

Prep. Time: 45 minutes
Cooking/Baking Time: 1 hour

8 potatoes, boiled and
   cubed
1 lb. Velveeta cheese,
   cubed
2 cups mayonnaise
1 cup diced onion

1. Mix together all ingredients in a large mixing bowl.
2. Spoon into a 9 × 13 baking dish. Bake at 350° for 1 hour, uncovered.
3. Serve hot, at room temperature, or chilled.

Tip: You can make this a day ahead of when you need it and refrigerate it in the meantime.

A Tip —

   Using a wide blade peeler makes peeling potatoes a breeze.

White or Sweet Potato Salad

Irma H. Schoen
Windsor, CT

Makes 4 servings

Prep. Time: 15 minutes
Cooking/Baking Time: 20 minutes
Chilling Time: 1–2 hours

4 white, *or* sweet, potatoes
⅓–½ cup light olive oil
¼ cup balsamic vinegar
1 tsp. dried oregano
⅓ cup chopped celery,
   optional

1. Wash potatoes, but don't peel them. Place in saucepan with about an inch of water. Cover and steam.
2. If you're using white potatoes, steam until tender, and then allow them to cool enough to handle. Slice or cube.
3. If you're using sweet potatoes, steam until just under done, and then peel when cooled. Slice or cube.
4. Mix oil, vinegar, oregano, and celery if you wish, in a separate bowl.
5. Place potatoes in good-sized mixing bowl. Gently fold in dressing.
6. Chill well before serving.

Variation: Add ½ tsp. salt and ¼ tsp. pepper to Step 4.

BLT Salad

Bernadette Veenstra
Grand Rapids, MI

Makes 12–16 servings

Prep Time: 30 minutes
Cooking Time: 15 minutes

16-oz. pkg. rigatoni, *or*
   penne, pasta
1 lb. sliced bacon
7-oz. bag fresh spinach,
   roughly chopped
1 pt. cherry tomatoes,
   quartered
1 tsp. salt
¼ tsp. black pepper
8 ozs. mozzarella cheese,
   cubed, *optional*

1. Cook pasta according to package directions. Drain and rinse under cold water. Transfer to a large bowl.
2. Dice bacon into small pieces. Saute over medium heat. Place bacon on paper towel-lined plate. Pour all drippings into a small bowl.
3. Return 1 Tbsp. drippings to skillet and heat. Stir spinach into hot drippings until it wilts, about 1 minute. Transfer spinach to pasta.
4. Add ½ Tbsp. drippings to skillet and heat. Stir tomatoes into drippings in skillet. Cook for 2 minutes. Transfer tomatoes to spinach and pasta and toss.
5. If pasta seems dry, add up to 1½ Tbsp. more of the drippings.
6. Add salt, pepper, bacon, and cheese if desired. Refrigerate until serving time.

Tortellini Summer Salad

Norma P. Zehr
Lowville, NY

Makes 4–6 servings

Prep Time: 15 minutes
Cooking Time: 10 minutes
Cooling Time: 30 minutes

9-oz. pkg. cheese tortellini, cooked and cooled
1 cup julienned, fully cooked ham
¾ cup frozen peas, thawed
½ cup Swiss cheese, cut in cubes
2 cups Ranch dressing

1. Cook tortellini according to package directions until done. Drain and cool.
2. Combine all ingredients in a large mixing bowl and toss.
3. Chill until ready to serve.

Variation: Add several tablespoons minced onion in Step 2 for extra flavor.

A Tip —

Don't be afraid to alter recipes to your liking.

Veggie Pasta Salad

Linda E. Wilcox
Blythewood, SC

Makes 4–6 servings

Prep Time: 5 minutes
Cooking Time: 8–10 minutes
Chilling Time: 2–4 hours

8 ozs. uncooked rotini pasta
1½ cups cauliflower florets, *or* 1½ cups broccoli florets
1½ cups sliced carrots
1½ cups snow peas
½–¾ cup light Italian dressing

1. Cook pasta according to package directions, adding the veggies to the saucepan 3 minutes before pasta is done.
2. Drain and run cold water over mixture to stop cooking.
3. Transfer drained pasta-veggie mixture to large mixing bowl.
4. Pour dressing over and chill 2–4 hours.

Tips:
1. Grate some Parmesan cheese over the salad, just before serving.
2. Serve over lettuce.

Crab Pasta Salad

Lauren Eberhard
Seneca, IL

Makes 8–10 servings

Prep. Time: 20 minutes
Cooking/Baking Time: 10–15 minutes
Chilling Time: 1 hour

8-oz. pkg. crabmeat
1-lb. pkg. rotini, *or* your choice of pasta
1 cup frozen peas
2 carrots, grated
1 bottle favorite salad dressing, *or* cole slaw dressing

1. Prepare pasta as directed on package. Rinse and cool.
2. Cut crabmeat into 1" pieces.
3. Thaw peas and grate carrot.
4. Mix all together in a large bowl.
5. Stir in dressing one hour before serving. Refrigerate and allow flavors to blend.

Tip: If you wish, place lettuce leaves in large salad bowl and put salad on top. Or put 1 Bibb lettuce leaf on each dinner or salad plate and top with a scoop of salad.

Pea and Crab Salad

Rebecca Meyerkorth
Wamego, KS
Ruth Ann Bender
Cochranville, PA

Makes 4–6 servings

Prep. Time: 15 minutes
Cooking/Baking Time: 5 minutes
Chilling Time: 2–3 hours

10-oz. pkg. frozen peas, thawed
8-oz. pkg. crabmeat, flaked
6–8 bacon strips ((turkey or pork), cooked, drained, and crumbled
½ cup mayonnaise
¼ tsp. onion powder, *or* 6 minced green onions

1. Combine peas, crab, and bacon in large bowl.
2. Mix mayonnaise and onion powder or slices together. Then fold in crab mixture.
3. Refrigerate at least 2 hours before serving to allow the flavors to blend.

Tips:
1. Scoop salad onto a bed of lettuce to serve, if you want.
2. Garnish with any or all of the following, if you wish: chopped fresh parsley, paprika, hard-boiled sliced eggs, tomato wedges.

Tuna Salad

Vera Martin
East Earl, PA

Makes 2–3 servings

Prep Time: 15 minutes

6-oz. can tuna, drained and flaked
1 Tbsp. mayonnaise
1½ tsp. onion flakes
salt and pepper to taste
lettuce leaves
green pepper, *optional*
radish, *optional*

1. Combine tuna, mayonnaise, onion flakes, salt and pepper to taste in a medium-sized bowl.
2. When ready to serve, place lettuce leaves on a plate and put tuna mixture in center of lettuce.
3. If you wish, place pepper rings and radish roses around the tuna salad.

Grandma's Zippy Deviled Eggs

Nan Decker
Albuquerque, NM

Makes 6–12 servings

Prep Time: 15 minutes
Cooking/Baking Time: 25 minutes

6 hard-boiled eggs, peeled
¼ tsp. salt
¼ tsp. pepper
½ tsp. dry mustard
½ tsp. cider vinegar
about 3 Tbsp. mayonnaise *or* salad dressing
half a stuffed green olive on top of each egg, *optional*

1. Cut hard-boiled shelled eggs in halves.
2. Slip out yolks. Mash yolks with fork in a small mixing bowl.
3. Mix yolks with salt, pepper, mustard, vinegar, and mayonnaise or salad dressing.
4. Refill egg whites with egg yolk mixture, heaping it up lightly.

Tip: Stuffed olives on top make the eggs look festive for any special occasion.

Southern Deviled Eggs

Suellen Fletcher
Noblesville, IN

Makes 6 servings

Prep Time: 15 minutes
Cooking Time: 15 minutes

6 eggs
salt and pepper to taste
1½–2 Tbsp. sugar
3 Tbsp. sweet pickle relish
up to 3 Tbsp. mayonnaise

1. Place the eggs in a good-sized saucepan. Cover with water. Bring water to a boil over high heat.
2. When the water begins to boil, take the pan off the heat. Let stand for 10 minutes.
3. Plunge eggs into cold water. Let stand for 5 minutes.
4. Peel carefully.
5. Slice eggs from end to end.
6. Place yolks in a medium-sized bowl.
7. Mash yolks well using a fork.
8. Stir in about ¾ tsp. salt and ¼ tsp. pepper, and relish, and mayonnaise a tablespoon at a time. Mix well. The filling should be a medium to thick consistency. To thin, stir in an additional teaspoon or so of mayonnaise.
9. Spoon the yolk mixture back into the egg whites. Chill until ready to serve.

Pickled Eggs and Red Beets

Kathy Bless
Fayetteville, PA

Makes 4 servings

Prep Time: 20 minutes
Cooking Time: 15 minutes
Chilling Time: 4–8 hours, or overnight

4 large eggs
16-oz. can small whole red beets, drained and juice reserved
½ cup apple cider vinegar
1 cup sugar
1 stick cinnamon

1. Place the eggs in a saucepan of cold water. Cover and heat to boiling. When the water begins to boil, remove pan from heat.
2. After 10 minutes, pour off hot water. Plunge eggs into cold water. Allow to stand for 5 minutes. Gently peel eggs.
3. Drain the juice from the beets into a one-cup measure. Add water to fill the cup, if needed. Pour into another saucepan. Set aside beets.
4. Add vinegar, sugar, and cinnamon stick to beet juice. Bring to a boil, and then remove from heat.
5. Allow the pickling liquid to cool a bit. Marinate the peeled hard-boiled eggs and beets in the pickling liquid for several hours, or overnight, in the refrigerator.

Fresh Pickles

Arleta Petersheim, Haven, KS

Makes about 5 cups

Prep Time: 15 minutes
Chilling Time: 8 hours, or overnight

6 small to medium-sized cucumbers
1 cup water
¼ cup vinegar
1 Tbsp. salt
½ cup sugar

1. Wash, peel, and slice fresh cucumbers into ¼"-thick slices.
2. In a small bowl, mix other ingredients together. Pour over sliced cucumbers.
3. Cover. Refrigerate 8 hours, or overnight.

Tip: Add some onion slices to the brine for more flavor.

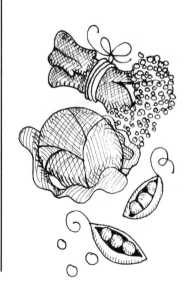

Barb's Fresh Pickles

Carna Reitz
Remington, VA

Makes 1–2 cups

Prep. Time: 5–10 minutes
Chilling Time: 1–12 hours

½ cup white vinegar
½ cup water
½ cup sugar
1 tsp. dill weed
1–2 cucumbers, sliced
  about ¼" thick

1. Mix first 3 ingredients in a medium-sized mixing bowl. Stir until sugar is dissolved.
2. Mix in dill and cucumber slices.
3. Cover. Refrigerate for at least 1 hour for lightly flavored pickles, or up to 1 day for more pickled pickles.

Tip: When the pickle slices are all eaten, you can use the leftover liquid for up to 3 more batches of fresh pickles.

10-Day Candied Pickles

Naomi Ressler
Harrisonburg, VA

Makes 1 quart

Prep Time: 30 minutes
Standing Time: 10 days

1 quart whole kosher dill
  pickles
½ cup apple cider vinegar
2 Tbsp. pickling spices
3 cups sugar

1. Drain pickles and cut into ½" thick slices.
2. Put vinegar and spices in a large glass bowl. Place pickles on top of vinegar and spices. **Do not stir.**
3. Pour the sugar on top of the pickles. **Do not stir.**
4. Cover and let stand at moderate room temperature for 10 days.
5. When the process is finished, either serve or refrigerate the pickles. Leftovers should be refrigerated to keep them crisp.

My mother used this recipe for years. She currently lives in a retirement community, but her crisp, delicious pickles are much in demand at all carry-in meals. They've become known as "Ida's Pickles."

Hot/Sweet Pickles

Jan Pembleton
Arlington, TX

Makes about 5 cups

Prep Time: 30 minutes
Chilling Time: 24 hours

half a jar sliced jalapenos,
  juice reserved
2½ cups sugar
42-oz. jar kosher dill
  pickles, whole (not spicy)
6–8 cloves garlic

1. In a large glass bowl, combine juice from jalapenos and sugar. Stir, dissolving sugar as much as possible.
2. Drain pickles. Cut into 1" thick slices. Stir into sweetened jalapeno juice.
3. Peel and cut up garlic into medium-sized chunks.
4. Stir into rest of mixture. Mix well.
5. Put mixture back into pickle jar. Cover and refrigerate, shaking occasionally.
6. The pickles will be ready in 24 hours.

New Dill Slices

Mary E. Wheatley
Mashpee, MA

Makes 4–5 cups

Prep Time: 20–30 minutes
Standing Time: 1 hour
Chilling Time: 2–9 hours

4–6 medium-sized pickling
cucumbers (about 1 lb.)
1 Tbsp., plus 1 tsp., kosher
salt, *divided*
cold water
3 Tbsp. cider vinegar
½ tsp. dill seed
1 garlic clove, thinly sliced
bay leaf and fresh dill
sprigs, *optional*

1. Cut cucumbers into ⅛"
thick slices.
2. In a large bowl, toss
cucumbers with 1 Tbsp. salt.
Let stand 1 hour, tossing
occasionally. Rinse and drain
3 times with cold water.
3. Meanwhile, in a sauce-
pan, combine vinegar with
dill seed, garlic, 1 tsp. salt,
and 1 cup water, along with
bay leaf if used. Bring to boil.
Boil 1 minute. Cool to room
temperature.
4. With your hands,
squeeze out excess moisture
from pickle slices. Place in a
small (glass) bowl. Add fresh
dill sprigs, if you wish, and
cooled brine.
5. Cover. Refrigerate for at
least one hour before serving,
or for 8 hours, or overnight.

Carrot-Pineapple-Nut Salad

Jeanette B. Oberholtzer
Manheim, PA

Makes 6–8 servings

Prep Time: 20 minutes
Chilling Time: 1–2 hours

1 lb. carrots, grated
8-oz. can pineapple tidbits,
in their own juice
½ cup raisins
lettuce leaves
sunflower seeds

1. Mix carrots, pineapple,
and raisins together. Refrigerate 1–2 hours before serving.
2. Place a lettuce leaf on 6
or 8 individual salad plates.
3. Top with fruit-vegetable
mixture.
4. Sprinkle generously, or
to your liking, with sunflower
seeds.

*Variation: We like our salads
topped with a mound of cottage
cheese.*

Carrot and Fruit Salad

Becky Frey
Lebanon, PA
Miriam Nolt
New Holland, PA

Makes 15 servings

Prep Time: 20–30 minutes
Cooling Time: 4 hours or more

2 .6-oz. pkgs. orange
gelatin
1½ tsp. unflavored gelatin
4 cups boiling water
20-oz. can crushed
pineapples, drained with
juice reserved
2 11-oz. cans mandarin
oranges, drained with
juice reserved
3 large carrots, grated
reserved pineapple and
mandarin orange
juice, plus cold water if
needed, to make 3 cups

1. Mix gelatins together.
Add to boiling water and
dissolve.
2. Pour into a large mixing
bowl. Add remaining ingredients and mix well.
3. Pour into a serving bowl.
4. Cover and refrigerate
until firm.

Pineapple Cottage Cheese Salad

Vera Campbell
Dayton, VA

Makes 6–8 servings

Prep Time: 15 minutes
Cooling Time: 4 hours or more

.3-oz. pkg. lemon gelatin
1 cup boiling water
⅔ cup unsweetened
   evaporated milk
1 cup crushed pineapple,
   undrained
¼ cup Miracle Whip salad
   dressing
1 cup cottage cheese

1. Dissolve gelatin in boiling water. Cool slightly.
2. Place all ingredients in a good-sized mixing bowl and mix well.
3. Pour into a mold or serving dish. Cover and chill until set.

A Tip —

Try out a recipe you've never had before. It is fun to see the family react to it.

Grapefruit Salad

Becky Frey
Lebanon, PA

Makes 8 servings

Prep Time: 20 minutes
Cooling Time: 6–8 hours

---

2 1-lb. cans grapefruit
   segments, drained with
   juice reserved
water
2 .3-oz. pkgs. lemon gelatin
8-oz. pkg. cream cheese,
   softened
milk
½ cup chopped nuts
maraschino cherries,
   optional

1. Measure juice from two cans grapefruit. Add enough water to equal 3½ cups liquid.
2. Pour half the liquid into a saucepan. Bring to a boil.
3. Stir in gelatin. When dissolved, stir in remaining liquid.
4. Arrange half the grapefruit slices in a salad mold or 8" square baking pan.
5. Cover with half the gelatin mixture.
6. Cover and chill until firm.
7. Meanwhile, in a mixing bowl, stir 2–3 Tbsp. milk into cream cheese until it spreads easily. Stir nuts into mixture.
8. When fruit and gelatin are very firm, spread cream cheese mixture over top.
9. Arrange remaining grapefruit segments on top. Cover with remaining gelatin.
10. Cover and chill until firm.
11. Unmold on bed of lettuce, if you wish (or cut into squares).
12. Just before serving, garnish with maraschino cherries, if you wish.

Tips:
1. Put pan or mold into the freezer to hasten the firming up of the first half of the salad.
2. Chill remaining gelatin until syrupy but easily pourable.
3. You can use freshly peeled grapefruit segments instead of canned. Be sure to remove the membrane if you do.

Aunt Cora's Jello Salad

Mary Jane Hoober
Shipshewana, IN

Makes 5 servings

Prep. Time: 25 minutes
Cooling/Baking Time: 5–6 hours

5-oz. can evaporated milk, refrigerated for several hours so it whips
.3-oz. pkg. raspberry gelatin
3-oz. pkg. cream cheese, at room temperature
1 cup water
1 small can crushed pineapple, undrained

1. Refrigerate can of evaporated milk for at least 2 hours before proceeding!
2. Place dry gelatin, cream cheese, and 1 cup water in saucepan. Bring to a boil. Continue boiling until cheese, gelatin, and water become smooth. Stir constantly.
3. Cool to room temperature.
4. Stir in pineapple with juice. Cover and chill in refrigerator. Check every 30 minutes to see if mixture is congealing.
5. Meanwhile, pour cold evaporated milk into a mixing bowl. Whip until soft peaks form.
6. When gelatin mixture begins to gel slightly, fold in whipped evaporated milk.
7. Cover and chill until firm.

Strawberry Fruit Salad

Rebecca Meyerkorth
Wamego, KS

Makes 6–8 servings

Prep. Time: 15 minutes
Chilling Time: 1 hour, or more

1 qt. fresh strawberries, stemmed and halved
20-oz. can pineapple chunks, drained
4 firm bananas, sliced
13½-oz. pkg. strawberry glaze
11-oz. can mandarin orange slices, drained, *optional*

1. In a large bowl, gently mix strawberries, pineapple, and bananas together.
2. Fold in the glaze.
3. Chill for at least one hour before serving.

Fruit Salad with Yogurt Dressing

Judy Buller, Bluffton, OH

Makes 4–6 servings

Prep Time: 15 minutes

1 large apple, unpeeled and diced
1 cup grapes, halved if they're large
2 bananas, sliced
1 orange, peeled and sectioned
6-oz. container lemon yogurt

1. In a good-sized mixing bowl, combine apple, grapes, bananas, and orange.
2. Add yogurt and stir gently to coat fruit.

Tips:
  1. The yogurt keeps the fruit from turning brown.
  2. You may substitute any other fruit or flavor of yogurt.

Fizzy Apple Salad

Krista Hershberger
Elverson, PA

Makes 10 servings

Prep Time: 10 minutes
Cooling Time: 4 hours

2 .6-oz. pkgs. cherry gelatin
4 cups boiling water
4 cups ginger ale
4 cups shredded apples

1. Dissolve gelatin in hot water. Pour into mixing bowl.
2. Stir in ginger ale and shredded apples.
3. Pour into serving dish or salad mold. Chill until firm.

Fruity Raspberry Salad

Arlene Snyder, Millerstown, PA

Makes 6 servings

Prep Time: 20 minutes
Cooling Time: 4 hours

8-oz. can crushed pineapple
10-oz. pkg. frozen
   unsweetened red
   raspberries, thawed
.3-oz. pkg. raspberry
   gelatin
1 cup applesauce

1. Drain pineapple and raspberries, reserving juices.
2. Add enough water to juices to measure 1 cup. Pour into a saucepan and bring to a boil.
3. Stir in gelatin until dissolved.
4. Stir in pineapple, raspberries, and applesauce.
5. Pour into a serving dish or salad mold. Cover and refrigerate until set.

Yogurt-Sauce Salad

Melanie Mohler
Ephrata, PA

Makes 2 servings

Prep Time: 5–10 minutes

½ cup plain, *or* flavored,
   applesauce
½ cup plain yogurt
½ tsp. ground cinnamon
1 Tbsp. raisins
cut-up fruit, such as apples,
   peaches, strawberries,
   blueberries, *or* bananas,
   optional

1. Mix together applesauce and yogurt in a medium-sized mixing bowl.
2. Stir in cinnamon and raisins.
3. Stir in any additional fruit that you choose.

My daughter, Anissa (5), created this recipe and it's never been the same twice! She enjoys experimenting with new ingredients, although certain variations we've encouraged her not to repeat (such as the kiwi and peanut butter combo).

Chunky Applesauce

Stacy Stoltzfus
Grantham, PA

Makes 2–3 servings

Prep. Time: 10 minutes
Cooking Time: 20 minutes

4 cups McIntosh apples,
   peeled, sliced, and cored
   (or your favorite sauce
   apple)
⅓ cup water
sugar to taste

1. If you have an apple peeler/slicer/corer gizmo, use it to prepare your apples. If not, peel, core, and slice your apples very thin.
2. Place in a heavy-duty cooking pot and add the water. Place over medium-low heat. Cover and cook until apples are softened with a few chunks remaining. You may need to add small amounts of water to prevent sticking.
3. Add sugar to taste.
4. Serve hot, warm, or cold. Or freeze in freezer containers.

Tips:
   1. In general, 1 pound of apples makes 1 cup of apple-sauce.
   2. This recipe may be multiplied to make plenty for serving immediately, freezing, or canning.

Creamy Applesauce Deluxe

Anne Nolt
Thompsontown, PA
Michelle High
Fredericksburg, PA

Makes 8–10 servings

Prep. Time: 10 minutes
Cooking/Baking Time: 4 minutes
Chilling Time: 2 hours or more

.6-oz. pkg. gelatin, your choice of flavor
2 cups boiling water
8-oz. pkg. cream cheese, softened
1 quart applesauce
1 tsp. lemon juice

1. Dissolve gelatin in boiling water in a large saucepan or mixing bowl.
2. Blend in softened cream cheese until smooth.
3. Add applesauce and lemon juice.
4. Blend together well. Pour into serving bowl. Cover and chill through.

Variation: Drop the cream cheese for an equally refreshing dessert.

— Michelle High
Fredericksburg, PA

Cranberry Applesauce

Sharon Brubaker
Myerstown, PA
Carolyn Snader
Ephrata, PA
Lina Hoover
Ephrata, PA

Makes 8–10 servings

Prep Time: 15 minutes
Chilling Time: 4–5 hours

.6-oz. pkg. raspberry, strawberry, *or* cherry gelatin
2 cups boiling water
16-oz. can jellied cranberry sauce
3 cups applesauce

1. Dissolve gelatin in boiling water.
2. Blend cranberry sauce and applesauce with mixer on slow speed. Add gelatin mix and blend.
3. Pour mixture into serving dish or mold. Chill 4–5 hours, or until set.
4. Serve plain, or topped with whipped cream or frozen whipped topping, thawed.

Pineapple Cranberry Relish

Jean A. Shaner
York, PA
Patricia Andreas
Wausau, WI

Makes 10–12 servings

Prep Time: 25 minutes
Chilling Time: 4–5 hours, or overnight

1 bag whole cranberries
2 oranges (keep rind on 1 orange)
20-oz. can crushed pineapple, drained with juice reserved
1½ cups sugar
.3-oz. pkg. strawberry, *or* lemon, gelatin
boiling water

1. Grind cranberries and oranges (including the rind of one of the oranges) in a food processor. Pour into a good-sized mixing bowl.
2. Mix drained pineapples and sugar into ground fruit.
3. Place reserved pineapple juice in a 1-cup measure. Add boiling water to fill cup.
4. Stir in gelatin until dissolved.
5. Stir into other ingredients and refrigerate for several hours or overnight.

A Tip —

Recipes using fresh cranberries can be made all year if you purchase them in season (around the holidays) and freeze them right in the bag or other closed container.

Festive Cranberry Pineapple Salad

Peggy Clark, Burrton, KS
Melanie Mohler, Ephrata, PA
Pat Bishop, Bedminster, PA
Barbara Yoder, Christiana, PA
Cheryl Martin, Turin, NY
Krista Hershberger, Elverson, PA

Makes 8–10 servings

Prep. Time: 20 minutes
Chilling Time: 5½–6½ hours

20-oz. can crushed
   pineapple, undrained
.6-oz. pkg. sugar-free
   raspberry gelatin
16-oz. can whole berry
   cranberry sauce
1 medium apple, chopped
⅓ cup chopped walnuts

1. Drain pineapple, reserving liquid in 1-quart liquid measuring cup. Remove 1 Tbsp. of the crushed pineapple. Set aside for garnish.
2. Add enough cold water to reserved liquid to measure 3 cups. Pour into large saucepan.
3. Bring to a boil. Remove from heat.
4. Stir in gelatin until completely dissolved. Stir in cranberry sauce, breaking the cranberries up with a whisk or wooden spoon.
5. Pour into large bowl. Refrigerate 1½ hours, or until slightly thickened.
6. Stir in remaining pineapple, apple, and walnuts. Pour into medium-sized serving bowl.

7. Refrigerate 4–5 hours, or until firm. Top with reserved crushed pineapple just before serving.

Variations:
1. Use a 12-oz. pkg. fresh cranberries, ground, instead of can of cranberry sauce.
2. Add a second chopped apple to Step 6.
3. Fold in 1–2 cups whipped cream in Step 6.

   —Barbara Yoder
   Christiana, PA

4. Use a can of jellied cranberry sauce, instead of whole berry sauce.
5. To the drained pineapple juice in Step 2, add ¾ cup orange juice and 1 Tbsp. lemon juice, and then add water to measure 3 cups liquid.

   —Cheryl Martin
   Turin, NY

6. Instead of the apple, use 1 cup finely chopped celery to Step 6.

   —Krista Hershberger
   Elverson, PA

Creamy Cranberry Salad

Becky Frey
Lebanon, PA

Makes 6–8 servings

Prep Time: 15–20 minutes
Cooking Time: 5 minutes
Chilling Time: 3½–5 hours

.3-oz. pkg. raspberry
   gelatin
1 cup boiling water
16-oz. can whole berry
   cranberry sauce
1 pint sour cream, *or* plain
   yogurt
½ cup nut of your choice,
   chopped
frozen whipped topping,
   thawed, *or* whipped
   cream, *optional*

1. Dissolve gelatin in water. Stir in cranberry sauce. Cover and chill until of syrupy consistency.
2. Fold in sour cream or yogurt, and nuts if you wish.
3. Pour into a mold or serving bowl.
4. Chill for 3–4 hours, or until firm.
5. To serve, garnish with whipped cream, if you wish.

Desserts

Crisps and Cobblers

Peach Cobbler

Eileen Eash, Carlsbad, NM
June S. Groff, Denver, PA
Sharon Wantland
Menomonee Falls, WI

Makes 10 servings

Prep. Time: 30 minutes
Cooking/Baking Time: 60–70 minutes

8 cups sliced fresh, *or* frozen, peaches
1 stick (½ cup) butter, softened
¾ cup sugar
1 cup flour
cinnamon (¼ tsp.)-sugar (½ tsp.)

1. Place peaches in ungreased 9 × 13 baking dish.

2. In a medium-sized mixing bowl, cream butter and sugar together, either with a spoon or an electric mixer.

3. Add flour and mix well. Sprinkle over peaches.

4. Top with cinnamon-sugar mix.

5. Bake at 325° for 60–70 minutes, or until top is golden brown.

6. Serve warm with milk or ice cream, if you wish.

Nutty Peach Crisp

Pat Chase, Fairbank, IA
Dorothy A. Shank, Sterling, IL
Vera Campbell, Dayton, VA
Carol Lenz, Little Chute, WI

Makes 12–16 servings

Prep. Time: 5–10 minutes
Cooking/Baking Time: 1 hour
Standing Time: 15 minutes

29-oz. can peach slices and syrup
18¼-oz. pkg. dry cake mix
(butter brickle, yellow, *or* butter pecan)
1 cup flaked coconut
1 cup chopped pecans *or* walnuts
1 stick (½ cup) butter, melted

1. Layer ingredients as listed in an ungreased 9 × 13 baking dish.

2. Bake at 325° for 55–60 minutes, or until golden brown.

3. Allow to stand for 15 minutes before serving.

4. Serve warm with milk, whipped cream, or ice cream, if you wish.

A Tip —

I always keep 1-cup measuring cups in my sugar and flour canisters. That way I can reach in and measure what I need from that one cup.

Cherry Crumble
Jeanne Allen, Rye, CO

Makes 6 servings

Prep. Time: 15–30 minutes
Cooking/Baking Time: 35–45 minutes

10⅔ Tbsp. (⅔ cup) butter, softened
¾ cup brown, *or* granulated, sugar
1½ cups flour
1 cup dry quick oats
1 can cherry pie filling, *or* flavor of your choice
extra butter, *optional*
whipped topping *or* cream, *optional*

1. In a large mixing bowl, mix all ingredients together except cherry pie filling, extra butter, and topping.
2. Reserve 1½ cups of the crumbs for topping.
3. Line an ungreased 9 × 9 baking pan with remaining crumbs.
4. Spoon cherry pie filling over top of crumbs.
5. Top with reserved crumbs.
6. Dot with extra butter, if you wish.
7. Bake at 350° for 40–45 minutes, or until golden brown.
8. Serve warm or cold, with whipped topping or cream, if you wish.

Edy's Easy Cherry Cobbler
Carolyn Spohn, Shawnee, KS

Makes 4–6 servings

Prep. Time: 15 minutes
Cooking/Baking Time: 30 minutes

15-oz. can red tart cherries
1 cup sugar, *divided*
1 cup buttermilk baking mix
½ cup milk

1. Drain juice from cherries into glass measuring cup. Add ½ cup sugar and heat in microwave until sugar is dissolved.
2. In a small mixing bowl, combine baking mix with remaining ½ cup sugar and ½ cup milk. Mix until all ingredients are moistened.
3. Spray 9 × 9 baking pan with non-stick cooking spray. Spread biscuit mixture in bottom.
4. Spread cherries evenly over this.
5. Carefully pour juice and sugar mixture over top.
6. Bake at 350° for 25–30 minutes, or until lightly browned. The cobbler is finished when a toothpick inserted into the center of the cake comes out clean. (The crust will rise to the top, and the cherries and their syrup will be underneath.)

Deep Dish Fruity Delight
Carol Eveleth, Wellman, IA
Bernice Hubers, Demotte, IN
Jean A. Shaner, York, PA
Carol L. Stroh, Akron, New York
Moreen Weaver, Bath, NY
Patricia S. Echard
Singers Glen, VA
Mary Lynn Miller, Reinholds, PA

Makes 15 servings

Prep. Time: 10 minutes
Cooking/Baking Time: 30–40 minutes

20-oz. can crushed pineapple, drained
21-oz. can cherry pie, apple pie, *or* blueberry pie filling
18¼-oz. box yellow cake, *or* angel food cake, mix
1 stick (½ cup) butter, melted
½–1 cup chopped nuts

1. Heat oven to 350°. Grease a 9 × 13 baking pan.
2. Spread pineapple over bottom of pan.
3. Top with pie filling.
4. Sprinkle dry cake mix over fruit.
5. Drizzle melted butter over cake mix.
6. Top with nuts.
7. Bake at 350° for 30–35 minutes, or until well browned.

Variation: Add 1 cup flaked or grated coconut to Step 6 if you wish.

—**Moreen Weaver**, Bath, NY

Blueberry Raspberry Crunch

Darla Sathre
Baxter, MN

Makes 12 servings

Prep. Time: 15 minutes
Cooking/Baking Time: 25–30 minutes

21-oz. can blueberry pie filling
21-oz. can raspberry pie filling
18¼-oz. pkg. white cake mix
½ cup chopped walnuts
1 stick (½ cup) butter, melted

1. Combine pie fillings in a lightly greased 9 × 13 baking pan.
2. In a mixing bowl, combine dry cake mix, walnuts, and butter. Sprinkle over pie filling.
3. Bake at 375° for 25–30 minutes, or until golden brown. Serve warm or cold.

Blackberry Cobbler

Virginia R. Bender
Dover, DE

Makes 6 servings

Prep. Time: 15 minutes
Cooking/Baking Time: 40 minutes

½ cup sugar
1 cup flour
½ cup milk
1 tsp. baking powder
2 cups blackberries

1. Mix sugar, flour, milk, and baking powder together in a medium-sized mixing bowl until well blended.
2. Pour into a lightly greased 9 × 9 baking dish.
3. Spoon fresh or frozen blackberries over top.
4. Bake at 350° for 40 minutes, or until a toothpick inserted in center comes out clean. Crust will rise to the top.
5. Serve warm.

Grandma's Apple Crisp

Louise Bodziony
Sunrise Beach, MO
Shelley Burns
Elverson, PA
Ruth Ann Penner
Hillsboro, KS
Darla Sathre, Baxter, MN

Makes 9 servings

Prep. Time: 20 minutes
Cooking/Baking Time: 40 minutes

6–8 apples
1 cup dry quick oats
¾ cup brown sugar
½ cup flour
½ tsp. cinnamon, *optional*
1 stick (½ cup) butter

1. Peel, core, and slice apples. Place in buttered 8" or 9" square baking pan.
2. In a mixing bowl, stir together dry oats, brown sugar, flour, and cinnamon if you wish.
3. Cut in butter with 2 knives or a pastry cutter until small crumbs form.
4. Sprinkle crumb topping over apples.
5. Bake at 350° for 40 minutes, or until lightly browned.

Variation: You can use pears, apricots, peaches, or rhubarb instead of apples.

— **Ruth Ann Penner**
Hillsboro, KS

— **Darla Sathre**
Baxter, MN

A Tip —

To clean Pyrex and stainless steel containers, take them outside and spray with oven cleaner. Let stand for an hour. Bring them back in and wash in hot soapy water.

Puddings

Vanilla Pudding
Rhonda Freed, Croghan, NY

Makes 8–10 servings

Prep. Time: 15 minutes
Cooking/Baking Time: 25 minutes
Chilling Time: 2–4 hours

8 cups whole milk, *divided*
¾ cup cornstarch
1¼ cups sugar
2 eggs
2 tsp. vanilla

1. In a 3- or 4-qt. microwave-safe bowl, heat 6 cups milk in microwave on High until scalded, approximately 8–10 minutes.
2. Meanwhile, blend remaining milk, the cornstarch, sugar, and eggs in blender until smooth.
3. Whisk blended ingredients into scalded milk.
4. Microwave on High for 5 minutes. Remove carefully with potholders and mix with whisk.
5. Microwave on High for 4 minutes and stir. Decrease cooking time by a minute each time until the pudding is a bit thinner than you want. (It will continue to thicken as it cools.)
6. Remove from microwave. Stir in vanilla.
7. While still hot, cover with plastic wrap, pressing plastic against the surface of the pudding to prevent a skin from forming.

I am at least the fourth generation (that I know of and remember) to make this recipe. My mom adapted it for the microwave, which saves standing and stirring over a double boiler on a hot stovetop!

Variation: Pour the finished pudding into popsicle molds. Freeze for Pudding Pops.

Grape-Nut Pudding
Esther J. Mast, Lancaster, PA

Makes 4–6 servings

Prep. Time: 10 minutes
Chilling Time: 8–10 hours, or overnight, optional

1 box instant vanilla
  pudding
2 cups skim milk
1 cup Grape-Nuts cereal
3 cups miniature
  marshmallows, *optional*
8-oz. container frozen
  whipped topping, thawed

1. Mix all ingredients together in a large bowl.
2. Chill in refrigerator for 8–10 hours or overnight to allow Grape-Nuts to soften. Or if you prefer a crunchier texture, serve as soon as thickened.

Crumbs for Pudding
Wafi Brandt, Manheim, PA

Makes 8–10 servings

Prep. Time: 5 minutes
Cooking/Baking Time: 30–45 minutes

1 cup flour
1 cup coconut
1 cup chopped pecans
1 stick (½ cup) butter,
  melted
⅓ cup brown sugar

1. Mix all ingredients together in a 9 × 13 pan.
2. Bake at 350° until brown. Stir every 15 minutes.
3. Sprinkle on pudding or ice cream.

Caramel Custard

Nadine L. Martinitz, Salina, KS

Makes 8 servings

Prep. Time: 20 minutes
Cooking/Baking Time: 40–45 minutes
Standing/Cooling Time: 30 minutes–2 hours

1½ cups sugar, *divided*
6 eggs
2 tsp. vanilla extract
3 cups milk

1. In a heavy saucepan over low heat, cook and stir ¾ cup sugar just until melted and golden. Stir frequently to prevent burning.
2. Divide caramelized sugar into eight 6-oz. custard cups. Tilt each cup after you've poured in the sugar to coat bottom of cup. Let stand for 10 minutes.
3. In a large mixing bowl, beat eggs, vanilla, milk, and remaining sugar until combined but not foamy. Divide among the eight custard cups, pouring over caramelized sugar.
4. Place the cups in two 8" square baking pans. Pour boiling water in pans to a depth of 1".
5. Bake at 350° for 40–45 minutes, or until a knife inserted in center of custards comes out clean. Remove cups from pans to cool on wire racks.
6. To unmold, run a knife around rim of cup and invert custard onto dessert plate.
7. Serve warm or chilled.

Quick Chocolate Pudding

Shirley Thieszen
North Newton, KS

Makes 4 servings

Prep. Time: 5 minutes
Cooking/Baking Time: 10–15 minutes

⅓ cup sugar
2 Tbsp. cornstarch
2 Tbsp. dry cocoa powder (not hot chocolate mix)
2 cups milk
1 tsp. vanilla
1 Tbsp. butter, *optional*

1. Place sugar, cornstarch, dry cocoa, and milk in a 1-qt. saucepan.
2. Cook over low heat until thickened, stirring constantly.
3. Stir in vanilla, and butter if you wish.
4. Serve warm or cold.

Tapioca Pudding

Laura Irene Shirk
Womelsdorf, PA

Makes 6 servings

Prep. Time: 20 minutes
Cooking/Baking Time: 10–15 minutes
Cooling Time: 3–4 hours

⅔ cup sugar
6 Tbsp. granulated tapioca
5½ cups milk
2 eggs, well beaten
2 tsp. vanilla
ground cinnamon, *optional*

1. In a large mixing bowl, mix sugar, granulated tapioca, milk, and eggs with a hand-held mixer, until well blended.
2. Pour into large saucepan. Let stand for 15 minutes.
3. Cook on medium high heat, stirring constantly until mixture comes to a full boil.
4. Remove from heat. Mixture will thicken as it cools.
5. When cooled slightly, gently stir in vanilla. Stir occasionally until beginning to thicken.
6. Place in refrigerator and chill until firm.
7. If you wish, sprinkle with cinnamon just before serving.

Orange Tapioca

Karla Baer
North Lima, OH

Makes 6–8 servings

Prep. Time: 10 minutes
Cooking/Baking Time: 15–20
minutes
Chilling Time: 3–4 hours

3–4 fresh oranges
1 cup sugar, *divided*
1 qt. water
½ cup granulated tapioca
¼ tsp. salt, *optional*
1 small can frozen orange
juice concentrate

1. Several hours before
preparing tapioca, peel
oranges. Cut into small
pieces. Sprinkle with 3 Tbsp.
sugar. Chill.
2. Pour water and tapioca
into medium-sized saucepan.
Cook over medium/medium-
high heat until tapioca is
clear, about 15 minutes. Stir
frequently.
3. Stir remaining sugar,
salt if you wish, orange juice
concentrate, and chilled
oranges into tapioca.
4. When well blended,
pour into a serving dish.
5. Cover and chill until
firm.

Strawberry Dessert

Glenda Weaver
Manheim, PA
Joyce Nolt
Richland, PA

Makes 6–8 servings

Prep. Time: 15–20 minutes
Cooking/Baking Time: 4–8 hours

4 cups water
⅔ cup granulated tapioca
1–1½ cups sugar, according
to your taste preferences
2 qts. crushed strawberries
8-oz. container frozen
whipped topping, thawed

1. Place water and tapioca
in a large saucepan. Stir.
Bring to a boil.
2. Cook until mixture is
clear and slightly thickened.
3. Stir in sugar.
4. Cool.
5. Add crushed strawber-
ries, mixing well.
6. Fold in whipped topping.
7. Refrigerate until thoroughly chilled and thickened.

Peach Tapioca Dessert

Sharon Shank
Bridgewater, VA

Makes 12 servings

Prep. Time: 15 minutes
Cooking/Baking Time: 10–15
minutes
Chilling Time: 2–3 hours

2 qts. water
¾ cup minute tapioca
12-oz. can frozen orange
juice concentrate
1 cup sugar
½ tsp. salt
2 qts. sliced peaches, fresh
or frozen
1½–2 cups bananas *and/or*
grapes, *optional*

1. In a large saucepan, cook
water and tapioca together,
stirring constantly, until
tapioca softens and becomes
clear.
2. Remove from heat and
stir in the orange juice, sugar,
and salt.
3. Mix together well until
the sugar is dissolved.
4. Stir in the peaches, and
the bananas and grapes if you
wish.
5. Refrigerate. Stir after 1
hour to make sure the fruit is
well distributed throughout
the tapioca as it gels.

Rhubarb Tapioca

Doris Ranck
Gap, PA

Makes 5 servings

Prep. Time: 5 minutes
Cooking/Baking Time: 10 minutes
Cooling Time: 1 hour

1 qt. rhubarb
1 cup water
1 Tbsp. minute tapioca
.3-oz. pkg. strawberry
    gelatin
¾ cup sugar

1. Cut rhubarb into thin slices. Place in a medium-sized saucepan.
2. Add water and minute tapioca.
3. Cook until rhubarb is soft. Remove from heat.
4. Stir in gelatin and sugar.
5. Allow to cool and thicken before serving.

Berry Delight

Willard E. Roth
Elkhart, IN

Makes 4 servings

Prep. Time: 10 minutes
Chilling Time: 2–3 hours

3½-oz. pkg. instant vanilla
    pudding
1½ cups 2% milk
1 cup vanilla yogurt
¼ tsp. almond extract
4 cups fresh berries, sliced

1. In a medium-sized mixing bowl, whisk pudding with milk.
2. Stir in yogurt and almond flavoring.
3. Layer ⅓ of pudding into glass serving bowl. Top with half the berries.
4. Top with half the remaining pudding. Top with remaining berries.
5. Spoon remaining pudding on top.
6. Refrigerate until ready to serve.

Strawberry Yogurt Dessert

Joyce Shackelford
Green Bay, WI

Makes 8–10 servings

Prep. Time: 10 minutes
Chilling Time: 2–3 hours

14-oz. can sweetened
    condensed milk
6-oz. container strawberry
    yogurt
2 Tbsp. lemon juice
8-oz. container frozen
    whipped topping, thawed
4 cups sliced fresh
    strawberries

1. In a large bowl, combine milk, yogurt, and lemon juice.
2. Fold in whipped topping and berries.
3. Chill until ready to serve.

Tips:
1. To prevent the berries from getting soggy, prepare this 2–3 hours before serving.
2. This is also delicious using peach yogurt and fresh peaches—or a combination using whatever fresh fruit is in season.

A Tip —

Some really good dishes can be very easy to make. Learn to enjoy the pleasure of simple foods.

Fruit Pudding

Carol Hershey, Jonestown, PA

Makes 12 servings

Prep. Time: 5 minutes
Cooking/Baking Time: 15 minutes
Cooling Time: 30–60 minutes

3-oz. pkg. vanilla pudding,
 regular not instant
3-oz. pkg. orange, *or*
 lemon, tapioca pudding,
 regular, not instant
13-oz. can mandarin
 oranges, juice reserved
20-oz. can pineapple
 chunks, juice reserved
2–3 bananas, sliced

1. Drain juice from canned
fruits into large measuring
cup, and add water to make
3 cups.
2. Cook puddings together
according to package directions
with juice/water mixture until
thickened and bubbly.
3. Cool slightly and add
fruit.

*Tip: If you can't find either
orange or lemon tapioca, and
use vanilla tapioca instead, add
1 heaping Tbsp. orange juice
concentrate to Step 2.*

Buttermilk-Plus Salad

Carla J. Elliott, Phoenix, AZ
Sharon Swartz Lambert
Harrisonburg, VA

Makes 8–10 servings

Prep Time: 15 minutes
Chilling Time:
 30 minutes–2 hours

3-oz. pkg. instant vanilla
 pudding
1 cup buttermilk
8-oz. container whipped
 topping, thawed
2 11-oz. cans mandarin
 oranges, drained
half a pkg. ribbon cookies
 with chocolate stripes,
 crushed

1. Combine pudding mix
and buttermilk in a medium-
sized mixing bowl.
2. Refrigerate until about
30 minutes before serving.
3. Fold in whipped topping,
oranges, and crushed cookies.
4. Garnish with whole
cookies.

*Variation: Instead of the
cookies, stir one 15-oz. can
pineapple tidbits, drained, into
mixture in Step 3. Drop Step 4.*

 —Sharon Swartz Lambert
 Harrisonburg, VA

Tips:
 *1. For additional flavor and
texture, add grated coconut,
and/or miniature marshmallows, in the amounts you wish,
in Step 3.*

 *2. Make this the same day
you plan to serve it. And it's
best to add the cookies 30–60
minutes before serving the salad.*

Cookies 'N Cream Fluff

Ruth Hofstetter
Versailles, MO

Makes 6 servings

Prep. Time: 5–10 minutes

2 cups cold milk
3-oz. pkg. instant vanilla
 pudding mix
8-oz. carton frozen
 whipped topping,
 thawed
15 chocolate cream-filled
 sandwich cookies,
 broken into chunks
additional broken cookies,
 optional

1. In a bowl, whisk milk and
pudding mix for 2 minutes, or
until slightly thickened.
2. Fold in whipped topping
and cookies.
3. Spoon into dessert dishes.
4. When ready to serve, top
with additional cookies if you
wish.

Frozen Berry Fluff

Vera Martin
East Earl, PA
Norma Greiser
Clarksville, MI
Michelle High
Fredericksburg, PA

Makes 20 servings

Prep. Time: 15 minutes
Freezing Time: 4–6 hours

21-oz. can strawberry, raspberry, *or* cherry pie filling
14-oz. can sweetened condensed milk
20-oz. can crushed pineapple, drained
32 ozs. frozen whipped topping, thawed

1. Stir pie filling, milk, and drained pineapple together in a large mixing bowl.
2. Fold in whipped topping.
3. Spread into 9 × 13 baking pan.
4. Cover and freeze for 4–6 hours.
5. When partly frozen cut into squares.
6. Thaw slightly before serving.

Variation: Instead of spreading into a long baking pan and freezing the dessert, spoon it into a serving bowl and chill 3–4 hours before serving.

— **Michelle High**
Fredericksburg, PA

Snicker Apple Salad

Jennifer Archer
Kalona, IA

Makes 10–12 servings

Prep Time: 15–20 minutes

3-oz. pkg. instant vanilla pudding
1 cup milk
8-oz. container whipped topping, thawed
6 apples, peeled *or* unpeeled, diced
6 Snicker bars, diced *or* broken

1. Mix pudding with milk in a large mixing bowl.
2. Fold in whipped topping.
3. Fold in chopped apples and Snickers.
4. Cover and refrigerate until ready to serve.

Cranberry Mallow Dessert

Louise Bodziony
Sunrise Beach, MO

Makes 6–8 servings

Prep. Time: 10 minutes

16-oz. can whole berry cranberry sauce
2 cups miniature marshmallows
8-oz. can crushed pineapple, drained
1 tsp. lemon juice
2 cups frozen whipped topping, thawed

1. In a large bowl, combine cranberry sauce, marshmallows, pineapple, and lemon juice.
2. Fold in whipped topping.
3. Transfer to a serving dish. Cover and refrigerate until serving.

Rice Pudding

Becky Frey
Lebanon, PA

Makes 8 servings

Prep. Time: 20 minutes
Cooking/Baking Time: 1½–2 hours

2 qts. milk
1 cup uncooked minute rice
dash of salt
½–1 cup sugar, depending on your taste preferences
1 tsp. vanilla
cinnamon, *optional*

1. Heat milk in a saucepan, or in the microwave until scalding.
2. Meanwhile, put rice in a small saucepan. Add salt and cover with water.
3. Cover pan. Bring rice to a boil. Turn off burner. Keep pan covered.
4. Let rice stand until it absorbs water, about 5 minutes.
5. Stir sugar into rice until well blended.
6. Stir rice into scalded milk.
7. Place in 3½–4-qt. lightly greased casserole dish.
8. Bake at 350° until light brown crust appears, about 30–45 minutes.
9. Skim off crust. Stir in vanilla.
10. Continue baking until a dark crust appears, about another 60–75 minutes.
11. Remove from oven and skim off crust. Cool.
12. Serve plain, or sprinkle with cinnamon.

Tips:
1. If pudding seems too thin, just bake longer after skimming off second crust. But the rice will continue to absorb liquid as it cools, so don't over-bake.
2. If you use lower fat milk, a crust will form, but it won't brown.
3. This recipe can easily be doubled. You'll likely have to bake it longer for the same results.

Festive Fruit and Rice

Sarah Miller
Harrisonburg, VA

Makes 8–10 servings

Prep. Time: 10 minutes
Cooking/Baking Time: 20 minutes
Chilling Time: 1–2 hours

2 cups water
1 cup long-grain rice, uncooked
1 cup raisins
3 bananas, sliced
8-oz. container frozen whipped topping, thawed

1. Bring water to a boil in a medium-sized saucepan.
2. Stir in rice.
3. Cover and simmer 14 minutes. (Stir after 7 minutes of cooking, but don't lift the lid otherwise!)
4. Remove from heat. Fluff rice with fork. Cover and let stand 3–4 minutes.

5. Cool rice until chilled.
6. An hour before serving, stir in raisins and bananas.
7. Fold in whipped topping.
8. Refrigerate until ready to serve.

Landis Pineapple Bread Pudding

Barbara Forrester Landis
Lititz, PA

Makes 8 servings

Prep. Time: 10–15 minutes
Cooking/Baking Time: 1 hour

¾ stick (6 Tbsp.) butter, softened and *divided*
1 cup sugar
4 eggs
5 slices sturdy bread
20-oz. can crushed pineapple, drained

1. Preheat oven to 350°.
2. In a large mixing bowl, cream together half a stick (4 Tbsp.) butter and sugar.
3. Slightly beat eggs and stir into creamed mixture.
4. Butter bread slices. Tear or cut into cubes.
5. Fold buttered cubed bread and drained pineapple into creamy mixture.
6. Pour into a buttered 2-qt. casserole.
7. Bake at 350° for one hour.
8. Allow to stand for 10 minutes before serving. It's great served with a dollop of whipped cream on top of each serving!

Cookies & Bars

Easy Brownies

Donna Klaassen
Whitewater, KS

Makes 36 brownies

Prep. Time: 15 minutes
Cooking/Baking Time: 25–30 minutes

1 stick butter (½ cup), softened
1 cup sugar
4 eggs
1 cup flour
1 can chocolate syrup
½ cup chopped walnuts, *optional*

1. With an electric mixer, cream butter and sugar together in a medium-sized mixing bowl.
2. Add eggs one at a time and beat after each addition.
3. Stir in flour, blending well.
4. Stir in chocolate syrup, blending well.
5. If you wish, stir in nuts.
6. Pour into a lightly greased 9" square baking pan.
7. Bake at 350° for 25–30 minutes.
8. When cooled, cut into squares with a plastic knife. (A plastic knife won't drag crumbs while cutting.)

Pecan Puffs

Mary Ann Bowman
East Earl, PA
Suzanne Nobrega, Duxbury, MA
Jean H. Robinson
Cinnaminson, NJ
Stacy Stoltzfus, Grantham, PA

Makes 30 puffs

Prep Time: 20 minutes
Baking Time: 10–15 minutes

1 stick (½ cup) butter, softened
2 Tbsp. granulated sugar
1 tsp. vanilla, *optional*
1 cup flour
1 cup pecans, finely chopped
½ cup confectioners, *or* granulated, sugar, *optional*
¾ cup shredded coconut, *optional*

1. Cream butter with a mixer. Add sugar, and vanilla if you wish, and continue creaming until smooth.
2. Stir in flour and nuts until well mixed.
3. Using a teaspoon, break off a piece of dough and roll into a small ball. Place on greased baking sheet. Continue with rest of dough.
4. Bake at 350° for 10–15 minutes. Watch carefully so they don't burn.
5. If you wish, when cookies are finished baking, roll one-at-a-time in confectioners sugar, granulated sugar, or in shredded coconut, while still warm. Allow to cool without touching other cookies.

Dina's Shortbread

Chris Kaczynski
Schenectady, NY

Makes 5–6 dozen cookies

Prep. Time: 30 minutes
Cooking/Baking Time: 20 minutes

4 sticks (1 lb.) butter, softened
1 cup confectioners sugar
3 cups sifted flour
¾ cup cornstarch

1. Preheat oven to 350°.
2. Cream the butter with an electric mixer. Add the sugar gradually. Blend well but don't overwork.
3. Gradually add flour and cornstarch.
4. Turn the dough out onto a lightly floured board. Pat out to a ¼" thickness. Do not roll out.
5. Using a cookie cutter or a glass, cut in 1½" circles. Prick each with a fork.
6. Place on baking sheet and bake for 20 minutes, or until top is a pale golden color.

A Tip —

Measure carefully especially when baking. When you have mastered the basics don't be afraid to create.

Devil's Food Cookies

Lucille Amos
Greensboro, NC

Makes 4 dozen cookies

Prep. Time: 15 minutes
Cooking/Baking Time: 10–13 minutes

18¼-oz. box devil's food cake mix
2 eggs
2 Tbsp. butter, softened
6 Tbsp. water
½ cup miniature semi-sweet chocolate chips

1. In large bowl, beat together cake mix, eggs, butter, and water. The batter will be thick.
2. Stir in chocolate chips.
3. Drop by tablespoonfuls 2" apart onto greased baking sheets.
4. Bake at 350° for 10–13 minutes, or until just baked. Cool 2 minutes before moving to wire racks for further cooling.

German Chocolate Cake-Mix Cookies

Monica Yoder, Millersburg, OH

Makes 3 dozen cookies

Prep. Time: 15 minutes
Cooking/Baking Time: 7–9 minutes

18¼-oz. box German chocolate cake mix
½ cup oil
2 eggs, slightly beaten
1 cup semisweet mini chocolate chips
½ cup dry oatmeal, quick *or* rolled

1. Combine all ingredients in the order listed in a large mixing bowl.
2. Drop by rounded teaspoonfuls, 2" apart, onto ungreased baking sheet.
3. Bake at 350° for 7–9 minutes, until just baked.

Gooey Butter Cookies

Kaye Taylor
Florissant, MO
Carol Sherwood
Batavia, NY

Makes 3–4 dozen cookies

Prep. Time: 20 minutes
Cooling Time: 30 minutes
Cooking/Baking Time: 12 minutes

1 stick (½ cup) butter, softened
8-oz. pkg. cream cheese, softened
1 tsp. vanilla
1 egg
18¼-oz. box yellow cake mix

1. Beat butter, cream cheese, vanilla, and egg with an electric mixer until fluffy.
2. Add cake mix until well blended.
3. Refrigerate 30 minutes.
4. Break off dough by tea-spoonfuls. Shape into small balls. Roll in confectioners sugar. Place on ungreased cookies sheet.
5. Bake at 350° for 12 minutes.

Variation: Instead of a yellow cake mix, use an 18¼-oz. box of moist chocolate cake mix. You'll have **Chocolate** *Gooey Butter Cookies!*

—**Carol Sherwood**
Batavia, NY

Lemon Snowflakes

Kay Taylor
Florissant, MO
Arleta Petersheim
Haven, KS
Lena Sheaffer
Port Matilda, PA

Makes 5–6 dozen cookies

Prep. Time: 15 minutes
Cooking/Baking Time: 10–12 minutes

18¼-oz. box lemon cake mix
1 egg
8-oz. carton frozen whipped topping, thawed
confectioners sugar

1. Combine cake mix, egg, and whipped topping in an electric mixer bowl.
2. Beat on medium speed until blended. Batter will be very sticky.
3. Drop by teaspoonfuls into confectioners sugar. Roll lightly to coat. Place on ungreased cookie sheet. Keep cookies about an inch apart, so they don't spread into each other.
4. Bake at 350° for 10–12 minutes, or until lightly browned.

Lemon Crisp Cookies

Diane Eby
Holtwood, PA

Makes 3 dozen cookies

Prep. Time: 15 minutes
Cooking/Baking Time: 10–12 minutes

1 stick (½ cup) butter, melted
1 cup crispy rice cereal
18¼-oz. box lemon cake mix
1 egg

1. Mix all ingredients together in a large mixing bowl.
2. Drop by tablespoonfuls onto ungreased baking sheets. Keep an inch between cookies so they don't spread into each other.
3. Bake at 350° for 10–12 minutes.

Tip: You can substitute yellow cake mix, plus 1 Tbsp. lemon extract, for the lemon cake mix.

Lemon Squares

Mary Kathryn Yoder
Harrisonville, MO

Makes 15 servings

Prep. Time: 10 minutes
Cooking/Baking Time: 30 minutes
Cooling Time: 1–2 hours

1 box angel food cake mix
21-oz. can lemon pie filling
⅛ cup confectioners sugar

1. Mix cake mix and pie filling together with an electric mixer.
2. Pour into a lightly greased 9 × 13 baking pan.
3. Bake at 350° for 30 minutes. Let cool.
4. Sprinkle confectioners sugar over top.
5. Cut into bars.

Easy Cake-Mix Cookies

Mary Kathryn Yoder
Harrisonville, MO

Makes 24 medium-sized cookies

Prep. Time: 12–15 minutes
Cooking/Baking Time: 10 minutes

18¼-oz. box cake mix of
  your choice
2 eggs
2 Tbsp. butter, softened
2 Tbsp. water

1. In a large mixing bowl, mix all ingredients together.
2. If you wish, stir in ½-1 cup broken nuts, or M&Ms, or shredded coconut. Or add nothing extra!
3. Drop by tablespoonfuls onto ungreased baking sheets. Allow about an inch around each cookie so they don't spread into each other.
4. Bake at 350° for 10 minutes.

A Tip —

A small ice cream scoop works well for making uniformly-sized cookies.

Even Easier Cake-Mix Cookies

Peggy Clark
Burrton, KS

Makes 24 medium-sized cookies

Prep. Time: 12–15 minutes
Cooking/Baking Time: 8–10 minutes

18¼-oz. box cake mix of
  your choice
½ cup vegetable oil
2 eggs

1. With an electric mixer, mix all ingredients until blended. Scrape bowl well while mixing so all ingredients are thoroughly incorporated.
2. Using a teaspoon, drop batter by spoonfuls onto an ungreased cookie sheet, keeping the cookies 2" apart.
3. Bake at 350° for 8–10 minutes.

Cherry Cream Cheese Tarts

Louise Bodziony
Sunrise Beach, MO

Makes 24 tarts

Prep. Time: 20 minutes
Chilling Time: 1 hour
Cooking/Baking Time: 20–25 minutes

3-oz. pkg. cream cheese,
  softened
1 stick (½ cup) butter,
  softened
1 cup flour
21-oz. can cherry pie filling

1. Blend cream cheese and butter until smooth in a mixing bowl.
2. Stir in flour just until blended.
3. Chill, covered, for one hour in the fridge.
4. Shape dough into 24 1" balls. Press into ungreased mini muffin cups to make a shallow shell.
5. Spoon one tablespoon pie filling into each center.
6. Bake at 325° for 20–25 minutes.
7. Remove from muffin cups when they reach room temperature.

Apple Butter Cookies

Cathy Boshart
Lebanon, PA

Makes 3–4 dozen cookies

Prep. Time: 30–35 minutes
Cooking/Baking Time: 13–15 minutes

6 cups flour
4 sticks (2 cups) butter
¾ cup cold water
4 tsp. vanilla
¼–½ cup apple butter

1. Place flour in a large mixing bowl. Cut butter in chunks and place in bowl with flour. Using a pastry cutter, cut butter into flour until the entire mixture resembles small peas.
2. Add water gradually, stirring as you go. Stir in vanilla.
3. When the dough forms a ball, gather it all together. Place on a lightly floured surface. Roll out very thin.
4. Cut into 2½" squares.
5. Place ½ tsp. apple butter on each square. Pull 4 corners to center and pinch tightly together.
6. Place filled cookies on an ungreased baking sheet. Bake at 375° for 13–15 minutes, or until cookies are lightly browned.

Caramel Apple Burritos

Peggy Clark
Burrton, KS

Makes 5 servings

Prep. Time: 10–15 minutes
Cooking/Baking Time: 5–7 minutes

3 large tart apples, peeled and sliced
10 caramels
5 8" flour tortillas, warmed

1. Place apple slices in a non-stick saucepan.
2. Cover and cook over medium heat for 3–4 minutes, or until tender. Reduce heat.
3. Add caramels. Cook and stir continually until caramels are melted.
4. Spoon apple mixture below the center on each tortilla. Fold sides and ends over filling.
5. Roll up. Place filled burritos on plate and serve immediately.

Apple Enchiladas

Eileen Eash
Carlsbad, NM

Makes 6 servings

Prep. Time: 15–20 minutes
Cooking/Baking Time: 20 minutes

21-oz. can apple pie filling
6 8" flour tortillas
1 tsp. cinnamon
5⅓ Tbsp. (⅓ cup) butter
½ cup maple syrup
¼ cup water

1. Divide pie filling among tortillas. Spread so the tortillas are evenly covered.
2. Sprinkle each with cinnamon.
3. Roll up. Place seam side down in a lightly greased 8" square baking dish.
4. Simmer butter, syrup, and water in saucepan for 3 minutes, stirring constantly.
5. Pour over enchiladas.
6. Bake at 350° for 20 minutes.
7. Serve warm with ice cream or whipped topping, if you wish.

Turtle Bars
Meredith Miller
Dover, DE

Makes 24 servings

Prep Time: 20 minutes
Baking Time: 20 minutes
Cooling Time: 30 minutes

2 cups flour
1¾ cups light brown sugar, *divided*
2½ sticks (1¼ cups) butter, *divided*
1¼ cup pecan halves
1 cup chocolate chips

1. Mix together flour, 1 cup brown sugar, and 1 stick butter (softened to room temperature) until crumbly. Pat firmly into a 9 × 13 glass baking pan.
2. Place pecan halves evenly over crust.
3. Heat ¾ cup brown sugar and 1½ sticks butter in a saucepan. Boil 1 minute, stirring constantly. Pour over pecan crust and bake at 325° for 20 minutes.
4. Sprinkle chocolate chips over hot bars immediately after removing from oven. Let set 2 minutes, then swirl chips as they melt, leaving some whole.
5. Cool and cut into bars.

Almost Snickers
Ruth Zendt
Mifflintown, PA

Makes 9 servings

Prep. Time: 10 minutes
Freezing Time: 4 hours or more

22-oz. container frozen vanilla yogurt, softened
1 cup frozen whipped topping, thawed
3-oz. box chocolate sugar-free instant pudding
¼ cup peanut butter
⅓ cup Grape-Nuts cereal

1. Mix together the first four ingredients in a large bowl.
2. Pour into an 8 × 8 or 9 × 9 pan. Sprinkle Grape-Nuts over top.
3. Cover and freeze until firm throughout.
4. Thaw slightly to cut into bars.

Tip: *Choose your own flavors of yogurt and pudding.*

Double Chip Bars
Joyce Nolt
Richland, PA

Makes 48 bars

Prep. Time: 20 minutes
Cooking/Baking Time: 25–30 minutes
Cooling Time: 2 hours

1 stick (½ cup) butter
1½ cups graham cracker crumbs
1 can sweetened condensed milk
2 cups semi-sweet chocolate chips
1 cup peanut butter chips

1. Place butter in a 9 × 13 baking pan. Place in 350° oven until melted. Remove from oven.
2. Sprinkle crumbs over butter.
3. Pour milk evenly over crumbs.
4. Sprinkle with chips. Press down firmly.
5. Bake at 350° for 25–30 minutes, or until golden brown.
6. Allow to cool before cutting into bars.

A Tip —

To easily and cleanly crush crackers, put them in a plastic bag. Then crush them with a rolling pin.

Peanut Butter Squares

Arlene M. Kopp
Lineboro, MO
LaRee Eby
Portland, OR

Makes 4 dozen bars

Prep. Time: 20 minutes
Chilling Time: 1 hour

2 sticks (1 cup) butter, melted
1 cup crunchy peanut butter
1½ cups graham cracker crumbs
3 cups confectioners sugar
12-oz. bag chocolate chips, melted

1. In a large mixing bowl, mix butter, peanut butter, graham cracker crumbs, and sugar thoroughly.
2. Pat into a greased 9 × 13 pan.
3. Spread melted chocolate on top. (To melt chips, place in a microwave-safe bowl. Microwave on High for 1–1½ minutes, until chips are melted when stirred.)
4. Chill for an hour and then cut into squares.

Grandma Herr's Easy Butter Crunch

Alica Denlinger
Lancaster, PA

Makes a jelly-roll pan full

Prep Time: 10 minutes
Cooking Time: 20 minutes

2 sticks (1 cup) butter
1 cup sugar
1½ cups blanched almonds, cut into sticks
6 ozs. chocolate bits

1. Melt butter in heavy skillet.
2. Stir in sugar.
3. Add almonds and cook, stirring constantly until golden brown and nuts begin to pop (about 12 minutes).
4. Spread evenly in jelly-roll pan. Sprinkle immediately with chocolate bits. As they melt, spread over mixture.
5. When cool, break into pieces.

Tip: This keeps well in the refrigerator, especially during the summer months.

This was a favorite Christmas-time recipe from my grandma. She loved to bake and spoil us with her treats!

Unbaked Peanut Butter Cookies

Vera Martin, East Earl, PA
Anita Troyer, Fairview, MI
Rebecca Meyerkorth
Wamego, KS
Jan Mast, Lancaster, PA
Rachel Olinger, Parkesburg, PA

Makes 3–4 dozen cookies

Prep. Time: 15–20 minutes
Chilling Time: 15 minutes

⅔ cup sugar
⅔ cup light corn syrup
1 cup peanut butter, plain *or* chunky
2½ cups Rice Krispies
2½ cups Cheerios
1½ cups chocolate chips, *optional*

1. Heat sugar and syrup in a saucepan until sugar is dissolved, about 2 minutes. Stir constantly. Remove from heat.
2. Mix peanut butter into hot sugar syrup.
3. Mix Rice Krispies and Cheerios together in a large mixing bowl.
4. Stir sugar-peanut butter syrup into the Cheerios and Rice Krispies mixture.
5. Drop mixture by spoonfuls onto waxed paper or press into a 9 × 13 pan.
6. If you want, melt the chocolate chips in the microwave, just until spreadable.
   Place in a microwave-safe container. Microwave on High for 1–1½ minutes. Drizzle over the cookies, or spread over the pan of cookies.

7. Chill until firm, approximately 15 minutes, before serving, storing, or cutting into squares.

Variations:

1. Use ⅓ cup granulated sugar and ⅓ cup brown sugar.

2. Use all Rice Krispies and no Cheerios.

— **Anita Troyer**, Fairview, MI

3. Use ¾ cup chocolate chips and ¾ cup butterscotch chips.

— **Rebecca Meyerkorth** Wamego, KS

— **Jan Mast**, Lancaster, PA

— **Rachel Olinger** Parkesburg, PA

Honey-Peanut Bar Cookies

Sherry Goss Lapp
Lancaster, PA

Makes 12–16 cookies

Prep. Time: 15 minutes
Chilling Time: 1 hour

½ cup sugar
½ cup honey
½ cup peanut butter
3 cups Cheerios
½ cup salted peanuts

1. In a small heavy saucepan, combine sugar and honey. Cook and stir over medium heat until sugar is dissolved. Remove from heat.
2. Stir in peanut butter until blended.

3. Stir in Cheerios and peanuts. Stir to coat.
4. Spread into lightly greased 9 × 9 pan.
5. Cover and chill for 1 hour before cutting.

Homemade Granola Bars

Sandra Haverstraw
Hummelstown, PA

Makes 36 servings

Prep. Time: 10 minutes
Cooking/Baking Time: 10–12 minutes

¼ cup honey
½ cup peanut butter
2 Tbsp. butter, softened
1 tsp. vanilla
2 cups granola cereal

1. Combine honey, peanut butter, butter, and vanilla in a mixing bowl.
2. Mix granola into honey mixture.
3. Spread into a greased 9" square baking pan.
4. Bake at 350° for 10 minutes, or until firm.
5. Remove from oven and cut into bars while still warm.

Peanut Butter Cookies

Juanita Lyndaker
Croghan, NY
Stacy Stoltzfus
Grantham, PA
Joleen Albrecht
Gladstone, MI
Doris Bachman
Putnam, IL

Makes 1–1½ dozen cookies

Prep. Time: 15 minutes
Cooking/Baking Time: 10 minutes

1 cup peanut butter
1 cup sugar
1 egg
additional sugar

1. Mix the first 3 ingredients together in a medium-sized mixing bowl.
2. Break dough off with a teaspoon and shape into balls.
3. Roll each ball in granulated sugar.
4. Place on greased baking sheet. Press down with a fork, making a criss-cross pattern.
5. Bake at 350° for 8–10 minutes, or until golden brown.

A Tip —

You can decrease the sugar in almost any cookie or bar recipe without sacrificing taste. Reduce the amount by ¼ cup to start.

Cakes

Almond Cake (or Torte)

Janet Batdorf
Harrisburg, PA

Makes 8 servings

Prep. Time: 20 minutes
Cooking/Baking Time: 20–25 minutes

1 cup flour
1 cup sugar
2 eggs, slightly beaten
1 tsp. almond flavoring
1 stick (½ cup) butter, melted

1. Grease and flour a round 8" or 9" baking pan, or line the pan with waxed paper.
2. In a large mixing bowl, sift together flour and sugar.
3. Stir in eggs and mix.
4. Stir in flavoring and butter. Blend thoroughly
5. Pour into baking pan. Bake at 350° for 20–25 minutes.

Tips:
1. Sprinkle top with slivered almonds before baking.
2. Dust with confectioners sugar before serving.

Dollie's 1916 Pound Cake

Anne Townsend
Albuquerque, NM

Makes 12–15 servings

Prep. Time: 15 minutes
Cooking/Baking Time: 50–55 minutes

2 sticks (1 cup) butter, softened
1⅔ cups sugar
½ tsp. mace
5 eggs
2 cups flour
1 tsp. vanilla, *optional*

1. Cream together butter, sugar, and mace with an electric mixer.
2. Add one egg at a time and beat after each addition until fully incorporated.
3. Add flour, and vanilla if you wish, and mix well.
4. Spray bundt pan with cooking spray. Spoon mixture into pan.
5. Bake at 350° for 50 minutes. If tester inserted in center of cake comes out clean, remove cake from oven. If it doesn't, continue baking for several more minutes until tester comes out clean.
6. Cool about 10 minutes before removing from pan.

In about 1950, a dear elderly neighbor in Washington, D.C. made this cake for our family. She had had the recipe since 1916!

Mace, the covering on nutmeg, makes it a bit unusual, but delicious, and a pleasant aroma permeates the house as it bakes.
We usually enjoy the cake served plain, but it also serves as a good base for fruit toppings.

Tip from Tester: I served this with fresh raspberries, and everyone loved it!

Dark Chocolate Indulgence Cake

Sharon Wantland
Menomonee Falls, WI

Makes 8 servings

Prep. Time: 15 minutes
Cooking/Baking Time: 30 minutes

1 pkg. (6 squares) Baker's bittersweet chocolate
1½ sticks (¾ cup) butter
4 eggs
1 cup sugar
½ cup flour

1. Heat oven to 350°.
2. Melt butter and chocolate together. Cool and set aside.
3. In a mixing bowl, beat eggs and sugar until smooth.
4. Add chocolate and flour and stir until smooth.
5. Pour into a 9" round greased and floured pan.
6. Bake 30 minutes.

Optional Toppings: Sprinkle with confectioners sugar, or drizzle melted chocolate on top.

Quick Chocolate Fudge Cake

Jena Hammond
Traverse City, MI
Shirley Sears, Tiskilwa, IL
Janessa Hochstedler
East Earl, PA
Lori Lehman, Ephrata, PA
Naomi Ressler
Harrisonburg, VA

Makes 15–24 servings

Prep. Time: 10 minutes
Cooking/Baking Time: 35–40 minutes

18¼-oz. box chocolate fudge cake mix, *or* German chocolate cake mix
2 eggs
21-oz. can cherry pie filling
1 tsp. vanilla *or* almond extract, *optional*

1. Place dry cake mix, eggs, pie filling, and extract if you wish in a large mixing bowl. Stir with spoon until well blended. Batter will be rather stiff.
2. Place batter in a lightly greased 9 × 13 baking pan.
3. Bake at 350° for 35–40 minutes, or until tester inserted in center of cake comes out clean.
4. Serve warm or cold. Serve with a mound of whipped cream, whipped topping, or ice cream if you like. Or ice with the Chocolate Frosting below.

Variation: If you'd like more pieces, and a bar-like result

rather than a piece of cake, place the batter in a 10 × 15 jelly-roll pan. Bake at 350° for 20–30 minutes.

Chocolate Frosting

Naomi Ressler
Harrisonburg, VA

Prep. Time: 10 minutes

5 Tbsp. butter
1 cup sugar
⅓–½ cup milk, depending upon the consistency of frosting you'd like
1 cup chocolate chips

1. Combine butter, sugar, and milk in a saucepan.
2. Bring to a boil, stirring constantly. Boil for 1 minute.
3. Remove from heat. Immediately stir in chocolate chips, stirring until the chips melt and the frosting is smooth.
4. Spread over cake.

Chocolate Chip Cake

Sharon Easter, Yuba City, CA

Makes 12–15 servings

Prep. Time: 5–10 minutes
Cooking/Baking Time: 35–45 minutes

18¼-oz. box chocolate cake mix
¼ cup oil
2 eggs
1¼ cups water
3-oz. box instant chocolate pudding mix
1 cup (6 ozs.) chocolate chips

1. Preheat oven to 350°.
2. Lightly grease a 9 × 13 baking pan.
3. In large mixing bowl, combine all ingredients except chocolate chips. Mix well.
4. Stir in chips.
5. Pour batter into prepared pan.
6. Bake for 35–45 minutes, or until a tester inserted in the center of the cake comes out clean.
7. Serve plain, frosted, or with powdered sugar sprinkled on top.

Tip: This is a versatile cake. You can use different cake mixes, and substitute white chips if chocolate chips are not a good complement to a cake mix of another flavor. And you can choose a different flavor of pudding mix to enhance a cake mix that isn't chocolate.

Apple German Chocolate Cake

Sue Pennington
Bridgewater, VA

Makes 12–15 servings

Prep. Time: 10–15 minutes
Cooking/Baking Time: 40–45 minutes

21-oz. can apple pie filling
18¼-oz. pkg. German chocolate cake mix
3 eggs
¾ cup coarsely chopped walnuts
½ cup miniature semisweet chocolate chips

1. Place pie filling in blender. Cover and process until the apples are in ¼" chunks.
2. Pour into mixer bowl.
3. Add dry cake mix and eggs. Beat on medium speed for 5 minutes.
4. Pour into a greased 9 × 13 baking pan.
5. Sprinkle with nuts and chocolate chips.
6. Bake at 350° for 40–45 minutes, or until a toothpick inserted in the center comes out clean. Cool completely on rack before cutting.

Cinnamon Apple Cake

Wanda Beaman
Harrisonville, MO

Makes 15 servings

Prep. Time: 15 minutes
Cooking/Baking Time: 30–40 minutes

18¼-oz. pkg. super-moist spice cake mix
21-oz. can apple pie filling
3 eggs
3 Tbsp. sugar
1 tsp. ground cinnamon

1. Heat oven to 350°. Grease or spray bottom only of 9 × 13 baking dish.
2. Place dry cake mix, pie filling, and eggs in a large bowl. Using an electric mixer, beat on low speed for 2 minutes. Batter will be thick.
3. Spread half of batter in prepared pan.
4. In a small bowl, stir together sugar and cinnamon. Sprinkle half of mixture over batter in pan.
5. Spread remaining batter in pan.
6. Sprinkle with remaining sugar and cinnamon mixture.
7. Bake at 350° for 30–40 minutes, or until tester inserted in center of cake comes out clean.
8. Serve with whipped topping or ice cream, if you wish.

Spicy Apple Cake

Colleen Heatwole
Burton, MI

Makes 18–24 servings

Prep. Time: 10–15 minutes
Cooking/Baking Time: 35–40 minutes

18¼-oz. pkg. yellow cake mix
2 cups applesauce
2 eggs
1½ tsp. pumpkin pie spice

1. Preheat oven to 350°.
2. Mix all ingredients together in large bowl.
3. Spray a 9 × 13 baking pan with non-stick cooking spray.
4. Pour batter into baking pan. Bake at 350° for 35–40 minutes, or until toothpick inserted in center comes out clean.
5. Cool completely before dusting with confectioners sugar, or frosting with your favorite vanilla or lemon cream icing.

Tip: If you don't have pumpkin pie spice, you can easily make your own. For 2 tsp. pumpkin pie spice, combine 1 tsp. cinnamon, ½ tsp. ginger, ¼ tsp. cloves, and ¼ tsp. nutmeg.

Sour Cream Peach Cake

Carol L. Stroh
Akron, NY

Makes 20 servings

Prep. Time: 15 minutes
Cooking/Baking Time: 40–45 minutes

18¼-oz. pkg. orange-
   flavored cake mix
21-oz. can peach pie filling
½ cup sour cream
2 eggs
confectioners sugar, *or*
   whipped topping

1. Heat oven to 350°.
2. Mix dry cake mix, pie filling, sour cream, and eggs with a fork in an ungreased 9 × 13 baking pan, reaching into the corners until all ingredients are well mixed and moistened.
3. Stir batter vigorously with fork for one minute.
4. Scrape down sides with rubber spatula. Spread batter evenly in pan.
5. Bake 40–45 minutes, or until top springs back when touched lightly in center.
6. Cool.
7. Sprinkle with confectioners sugar, or spread with whipped topping just before serving.

Pear Bundt Cake

Orpha Herr
Andover, NY

Makes 16 servings

Prep. Time: 15 minutes
Cooking/Baking Time: 50–55 minutes

15¼-oz. can pears
18¼-oz. pkg. white cake mix
1 egg
2 egg whites
2 tsp. confectioners sugar

1. Remove pears from syrup to chop. Reserve syrup.
2. Place chopped pears and syrup in a mixing bowl. Add dry cake mix, 1 egg, and egg whites.
3. Beat with electric mixer on low speed for 30 seconds, and then on high for 4 minutes.
4. Grease and flour a 10" bundt or fluted tube pan. Pour batter into prepared pan.
5. Bake at 350° for 50–55 minutes, or until tester inserted in center of cake comes out clean.
6. Cool for 15 minutes before removing from pan to cooling rack to cool completely.
7. Dust with confectioners sugar before slicing and serving.

Blueberry Swirl Cake

Lori Lehman
Ephrata, PA

Makes 15 servings

Prep. Time: 15 minutes
Cooking/Baking Time: 30–40 minutes

3-oz. pkg. cream cheese
   softened
18¼-oz. box white cake mix
3 eggs
3 Tbsp. water
21-oz. can blueberry pie
   filling

1. Beat cream cheese in a large mixing bowl until soft and creamy.
2. Stir in dry cake mix, eggs, and water. Blend well with cream cheese.
3. Pour into a greased 9 × 13 baking pan.
4. Pour blueberry pie filling over top of batter.
5. Swirl blueberries and batter with a knife by zig-zagging through batter.
6. Bake at 350° for 30–40 minutes, or until tester inserted in center comes out clean.

Spicy Pumpkin Cake

Janessa Hochstedler
East Earl, PA

Makes 16 servings

Prep. Time: 20 minutes
Cooking/Baking Time: 40–45 minutes

18¼-oz. pkg. spice cake mix
½ cup water
½ cup oil
3 large eggs
half an 8-oz. pkg. cream cheese, softened
1 cup canned pumpkin
6 squares semi-sweet baking chocolate coarsely chopped, *optional*

1. Preheat oven to 350°.
2. Using an electric mixer, blend together cake mix, water, oil, and eggs.
3. Add cream cheese and pumpkin. Beat on medium speed until well blended.
4. Stir in chopped chocolate if you wish.
5. Pour into a greased bundt or 12-cup fluted tube pan.
6. Bake for 40–45 minutes, or until a tester inserted into center of cake comes out clean.

Tip: This is delicious with cream cheese frosting!

Butter Rum Cake

Cheryl Lapp, Parkesburg, PA

Makes 8–10 servings

Prep. Time: 10 minutes
Cooking/Baking Time: 40 minutes
Cooling Time: 15 minutes

18¼-oz. pkg. Plus Butter Cake mix
1 cup water
half a stick (¼ cup) butter, softened
3 eggs
2 tsp. rum extract
1 cup finely chopped pecans

1. Heat oven to 350°.
2. Grease and flour a 10" angel food, or 12-cup fluted tube, pan.
3. In a large mixing bowl, use an electric mixer to blend all ingredients except nuts until moistened. Then mix at the highest speed for 2 minutes.
4. Stir in nuts.
5. Pour batter into pre-pared pan. Bake at 350° for 40 minutes.
6. If you wish, top with Rum Glaze (next to this recipe).

A Tip —

I substitute ½ cup of applesauce and ½ cup of oil when a recipes calls for 1 cup of oil. This makes things moist and healthier.

Rum Glaze

Prep Time: 5–10 minutes

⅓ cup sugar
5⅓ Tbsp. (⅓ cup) butter
2 Tbsp. water
2 tsp. rum extract

1. Mix all ingredients together in a saucepan.
2. Bring to boil, stirring frequently to blend and to prevent scorching.
3. After mixture boils, pour half around edge of baked cake while it's still in the baking pan.
4. Allow to cool 5 minutes.
5. Poke top of cake at several places with a long fork. Pour remaining glaze over the cake top.
6. Allow to cool for 10 minutes before removing from pan.

Pineapple Angel Food Cake

Marlene Fonken, Upland, CA
Esther Mast, Lancaster, PA
Peggy Clark, Burrton, KS

Makes 12 servings

Prep. Time: 5–10 minutes
Cooking/Baking Time: 35 minutes

1 box angel food cake mix
20-oz. can crushed
  pineapple, undrained
1 tsp. vanilla, *optional*

1. Mix ingredients together until well mixed.
2. Pour into either an ungreased 9 × 13 baking pan, into an ungreased tube pan, or into 2 ungreased bread pans.
3. If using a long baking pan, bake at 350° for 30–35 minutes. If using a tube pan, bake at 350° for 45 minutes.
4. If cake was baked in a tube pan, invert to cool.

Variations:

1. I bake the cake in a tube pan. I like to freeze the baked and cooled cake, and then cut it into slices when firm. I wrap the individual slices in plastic so I can serve it like ice cream to a large crowd.

—Esther Mast, Lancaster, PA

2. I bake the cake in a long pan or bread pans. I top the pieces or slices with a mound of whipped topping as I serve it.

—Marlene Fonken, Upland, CA

Cheesecake

Rhonda Freed
Croghan, NY

Makes 8 servings

Prep. Time: 15 minutes
Cooking/Baking Time: 50 minutes
Cooling Time: 15 minutes

2 8-oz. pkgs. cream cheese, softened
3 eggs
1 cup sugar, *divided*
2 tsp. vanilla, *divided*
1 cup sour cream
pie filling of your choice, *optional*

1. In a large mixing bowl, beat softened cream cheese, eggs, ¾ cup sugar, and 1 tsp. vanilla with electric mixer until smooth.
2. Pour into 9" glass pie plate.
3. Bake at 350° for 35 minutes on the second to bottom rack of oven.
4. Remove from oven and cool 15 minutes. (Do not turn the oven off.)
5. In a small bowl, beat together sour cream, ¼ cup sugar, and 1 tsp. vanilla with electric mixer.
6. Pour over top of cake.
7. Bake at 350° for 15 more minutes.
8. Cool completely. Store in refrigerator.
9. If you wish, top with pie filling of your choice to serve.

Blueberry Cheesecake

Betty Moore
Avon Park, FL

Makes 8 servings

Prep. Time: 10 minutes
Cooking/Baking Time: 25–30 minutes
Chilling Time: 4 hours

8-oz. pkg. cream cheese, softened
½ cup sugar
2 eggs, beaten
1 graham cracker crust
21-oz. can blueberry pie filling

1. Preheat oven to 325°.
2. In a mixing bowl, combine cream cheese, sugar, and eggs. Beat with an electric mixer until fluffy.
3. Pour mixture into pie crust.
4. Bake 25–30 minutes. Cool.
5. Spread with half the blueberry pie filling. Chill 2–3 hours before serving.
6. Pass the remaining pie filling with the wedges of pie for anyone who wants to add more topping.

Variation: Use any flavor of pie filling that you wish.

Chocolate Chip Cheesecake

Chris Kaczynski
Schenectady, NY

Makes 16 servings

Prep. Time: 15 minutes
Cooking/Baking Time: 45–50 minutes
Chilling Time: 3–4 hours

3 eggs, beaten
¾ cup sugar
3 8-oz. pkgs. cream cheese, softened
1 tsp. vanilla
24-oz. roll refrigerated chocolate chip cookie dough

1. Preheat oven to 350°.
2. Place all ingredients except cookie dough in large mixing bowl. With electric mixer, blend together until creamy. Set aside.
3. Slice cookie dough into ¼"-thick slices. Set aside 9 slices.
4. Lay remaining slices in bottom of 9 × 13 baking pan. Pat the slices together to form a solid crust.
5. Spoon in cream cheese mixture. Spread out over cookie crust.
6. Arrange the reserved 9 cookie slices on top of cream-cheese mixture.
7. Bake at 350° for 45–50 minutes. Allow to cool to room temperature.
8. Chill in refrigerator. When firm, cut into squares.
9. If you wish, when serving, top with whipped cream or chocolate topping.

Lemon Cheese Pie

Jere Zimmerman
Elaine Patton
West Middletown, PA
Esther Gingerich
Parnell, IA

Makes 8 servings

Prep. Time: 10 minutes
Cooling Time: 1 hour

8-oz. pkg. cream cheese, softened
2 cups milk, *divided*
3.5-oz. box instant lemon pudding
9" graham cracker pie crust

1. In a good-sized mixing bowl, beat cream cheese until soft and creamy.
2. Add ½ cup milk and blend until smooth.
3. Add dry pudding mix and blend until smooth.
4. Blend in 1½ cups milk until well incorporated.
5. Beat slowly for 1 minute.
6. Pour into graham cracker crust.
7. Refrigerate at least 1 hour before serving.

Cream Puffs

Dorcas Alpirez
Willards, MD

Makes 8 servings

Prep. Time: 15 minutes
Cooking/Baking Time: 30 minutes
Standing Time: 5 minutes

½ cup water
half a stick (¼ cup) butter, no substitutes
½ cup all-purpose flour
2 eggs
ice cream, *or* prepared pudding
confectioners sugar

1. In a saucepan, bring water and butter to a boil.
2. Add flour all at once, stirring until a smooth ball forms.
3. Remove from heat. Let stand for 5 minutes.
4. Add eggs, one at a time, beating well after each addition. Continue beating until mixture is smooth.
5. Drop by rounded tablespoonfuls, 3" apart, onto greased baking sheet.
6. Bake at 400° for 30–35 minutes, or until golden brown. Remove to wire racks.
7. Immediately slice tops off puffs (keep the tops) and discard soft dough from inside.
8. Fill puffs with your choice of filling. Lay tops back on. Dust with confectioners sugar, if you wish.

Pies

Grandma's Apple Pie

Andrea Zuercher
Lawrence, KS

Makes 8 servings

Prep. Time: 30 minutes
Cooking/Baking Time: 45 minutes

6 cups pared and sliced
  apples (about 6 medium-
  sized tart apples; Granny
  Smith work well)
6-oz. can frozen 100% juice
  apple juice concentrate,
  thawed
1½ Tbsp. cornstarch
1 Tbsp. water
1 tsp. cinnamon
3 Tbsp. butter, *optional*
10" double pie crust,
  unbaked

1. Place sliced apples in
saucepan with juice concentrate.
2. Bring to a boil. Reduce
heat, and then simmer,
covered, for 5 minutes.
3. In a small bowl, dissolve
cornstarch in water.
4. Gently stir into the
apples.
5. Bring to a boil. Reduce
heat. Simmer, covered, for
10–15 minutes. Apples will
begin to soften as mixture
becomes thickened. Stir
occasionally so it does not
scorch.

6. Gently stir in cinnamon.
7. Fill bottom pie crust
with apples.
8. Dot with butter if you
wish.
9. Cover with top crust.
Pinch crusts together. With
a sharp knife, cut 6–8 steam
vents across the top crust.
10. Place pie pan on a
baking sheet in case the
filling cooks out. Bake at 350°
for about 45 minutes, or until
top crust is lightly browned.

Cinnamon Apple Crumb Pie

Carol Eberly, Harrisonburg, VA

Makes 6–8 servings

Prep. Time: 10–15 minutes
*Cooking/Baking Time: 50–55
  minutes*

21-oz. can apple pie filling
9" unbaked pie crust
½ tsp. ground cinnamon
4 Tbsp. butter, *divided*
1½–2 cups crushed pecan
  shortbread cookies

1. Pour pie filling into pie
crust.
2. Sprinkle with cinnamon.
Dot with 1 Tbsp. butter.
3. Melt remaining butter.
4. Place cookie crumbs in
a small bowl. Stir in melted
butter until coarse crumbs
form.
5. Sprinkle over filling.
6. Cover edges of pastry
loosely with foil.

7. Bake at 450° for 10
minutes.
8. Reduce heat to 350°.
Remove foil. Bake for 40–45
minutes, or until crust is
golden brown and filling is
bubbly.
9. Cool on wire rack before
cutting and serving.

Sour Cream Apple Pie

Carna Reitz
Remington, VA

Makes 6–8 servings

Prep. Time: 5–10 minutes
*Cooking/Baking Time: 30–40
  minutes*

½ cup sour cream
¼ cup sugar
1 egg
21-oz. can apple pie filling
9" unbaked pie crust

1. In a small mixing bowl,
stir together sour cream,
sugar, and egg. Pour into pie
crust.
2. Spoon pie filling over
sour cream mixture.
3. Bake at 375° for 30–40
minutes, or until filling is
firm and crust is slightly
golden on the edges.

Variations: *You can substitute
cherry, blueberry, or other fruit
pie fillings for the apple filling.*

Almond Pear Tort
Martha Mullet
Sugarcreek, OH

Makes 8 servings

Prep. Time: 20–25 minutes
Cooking/Baking Time: 20 minutes

**pastry for 9" single-crust
pie**
**¾ cup plus 2 tsp. sugar,
*divided***
3 Tbsp. all-purpose flour
**4 cups sliced peeled fresh
pears (about 4 medium-
sized pears)**
3 Tbsp. sliced almonds

1. Roll out pastry into a
10" circle. Fold lightly into
quarters, and place on an
ungreased baking sheet
with sides. (The sides are
important in case the pastry
develops a tear and the filling
leaks out while baking.)
2. In a small bowl, com-
bine ¾ cup sugar and flour.
3. Add pears. Toss to coat.
4. Place pear mixture in
center of pastry, spreading to
within 2" of edges. Fold edges
up and slightly crimp.
5. Sprinkle with remaining
sugar.
6. Bake at 450° for 15
minutes, or until pears are
tender.
7. Sprinkle with almonds.
Bake 5 minutes longer.
8. Cool slightly before
cutting into wedges.

Mom's Fresh Fruit Pie
Stacy Stoltzfus, Grantham, PA
Jean A. Shaner, York, PA
Janet Oberholtzer, Ephrata, PA
Eunice Fisher, Clarksville, MI
Carolyn Lehman Henry
Clinton, NY
Monica ByDeley
Annville, PA

Makes 8 servings

Prep. Time: 15 minutes
Chilling Time: 4–8 hours

**3–4 cups fresh fruit of
your choice: berries,
peaches, *or* a mixture of
fruits**
9" baked pie shell
**.3-oz. pkg. strawberry
gelatin (or other flavor
to match the fruit)**
**¾–1¼ cups sugar,
depending on the
sweetness of the fruit**
**3 rounded Tbsp.
cornstarch**
2 cups warm water
whipped topping, *optional*

1. Wash and pat dry fresh
fruit. Slice if necessary.
2. Arrange fruit in baked
pie shell and set aside.
3. In a saucepan mix the
gelatin, sugar, and cornstarch.
Add 2 cups warm water.
Cook and stir until thickened
and clear.
4. Pour over fruit. Refrigerate several hours until set.
5. When time to serve, top
with whipped topping if you
wish.

Fresh Peach Pie
Jan Mast
Lancaster, PA

Makes 8 servings

Prep. Time: 15 minutes
Chilling Time: 3–5 hours
*Cooking/Baking Time: 5–10
  minutes*

½–¾ cup sugar
2 Tbsp. clear gel
**¼ cup peach-flavored
gelatin***
1 cup water
**1 qt. fresh peaches, peeled
and sliced**
**9" prepared, pastry *or*
graham cracker, crust**
**frozen whipped topping,
thawed, *optional***

1. Mix the sugar, clear gel,
and gelatin in a small mixing
bowl. Stir in water.
2. Microwave to a full boil.
Cook briefly at that heat until
gel become clear.
3. Cool at room tempera-
ture for several hours.
4. Fold in peaches.
5. Spoon into baked pie
shell.
6. Refrigerate 1 hour or
more before serving.
7. If you wish, top with
whipped topping just before
serving.

* *A .3-oz. box of gelatin is ⅓
cup, which you can use. I think
it makes a thicker filling than
is ideal.*

Raspberry Custard Pie

Laura R. Showalter
Dayton, VA

Makes 6–8 serivngs

Prep. Time: 7–10 minutes
Cooking/Baking Time: 45–55 minutes
Cooling Time: 30 minutes

9" unbaked pie shell
3 cups fresh black raspberries
¾ cup sugar
3 Tbsp. flour
¾ cup half-and-half
½ tsp. cinnamon, *optional*

1. Wash berries. Dry by blotting with a paper towel. Place in pie shell.
2. Mix remaining ingredients in a small mixing bowl until smooth. Pour over berries.
3. Bake at 375° for 15 minutes. Turn oven back to 300°. Bake 30–40 minutes more, or until center is set.
4. Allow to cool before slicing and serving.

Variation: Use peaches or other berries instead of raspberries.

Summertime Berry Dessert

Natalia Showalter
Mt. Solon, VA

Makes 8 servings

Prep. Time: 15 minutes
Chilling Time: 1–8 hours

half an 8-oz. pkg. cream cheese, softened
¼–⅓ cup sugar
½ cup whipping cream
9" graham cracker crust
3–4 cups fresh blueberries, strawberries, huckleberries, *or* raspberries, washed and drained

1. In a mixing bowl, blend cream cheese and sugar until well combined and creamy.
2. Whip cream. Fold into cream cheese-sugar mixture.
3. Spread whipped cream mixture into graham crust. Chill until ready to serve.
4. Just before serving top with fresh berries.

Grandma's Spring Rhubarb Pie

Eleya Raisn
Oxford, IA

Makes 6 servings

Prep. Time: 30 minutes
Cooking/Baking Time: 45 minutes

1 cup sugar
3 Tbsp. flour
2 egg yolks, beaten
3 cups diced rhubarb
9" unbaked pie crust

1. In a mixing bowl, stir sugar, flour, and egg yolks together until crumbly. Set aside ¾ cup of the crumbs for topping.
2. Stir cut-up rhubarb into remaining crumbs.
3. Spoon rhubarb mixture into pie shell.
4. Sprinkle reserved crumbs on top of pie filling.
5. Bake at 400° for 25 minutes.
6. Reduce heat to 350° and bake an additional 20 minutes, or until rhubarb filling is bubbling.
7. Allow to cool before slicing and serving.

A Tip —

Cooking with someone else is always more fun than cooking solo.

Easy Lime Pie

Trudy Kutter, Corfu, NY
Janie Canupp, Millersville, MD

Makes 6–8 minutes

Prep. Time: 15 minutes
Chilling Time: 4 or more hours

14-oz. can sweetened
condensed milk (not
evaporated)
half a 12-oz. container
frozen whipped topping,
thawed, *plus more if you
choose*
½ cup key lime juice
grated lime rind, *optional*
9" graham cracker pie crust
2 kiwis, *optional*

1. In a large mixing bowl,
mix condensed milk with
thawed dairy topping until
blended.
2. Fold in lime juice and
rind and blend well.
3. Pour into crust and chill
for at least 4 hours.
4. Peel kiwi and slice over
pie just before serving, if you
like. Add a dollop of whipped
topping to the top of each
piece when serving, if you
wish.

A Tip —

To get the most juice
from a lime or lemon,
heat it in the microwave
for 10 seconds, then
squeeze it.

Key Lime—or
Lemon—Pie

Denise Martin, Lancaster, PA
Naomi Ressler, Harrisonburg, VA
Judy DeLong, Burnt Hills, NY
Erma Martin, East Earl, PA
Jan Pembleton, Arlington, TX

Makes 8 servings

Prep. Time: 15 minutes
Cooling Time: 2 hours

.3-oz. box lime gelatin
¼ cup boiling water
2 8-oz. containers key lime
yogurt
8-oz. container frozen
whipped topping, thawed
9" graham cracker crust

1. In a large mixing bowl,
dissolve gelatin in boiling
water. Whisk in yogurt.
2. Fold in whipped topping.
Pour into crust.
3. Refrigerate 2 hours.

Variations:
*1. This pie is equally deli-
cious with a reduced-fat crust,
sugar-free gelatin, and non-fat
yogurt and whipped topping.*

— Erma Martin
East Earl, PA

*2. Substitute lemon gelatin
for the lime. Substitute lemon-
light yogurt for the key lime.
Follow all other directions
above for a Lemon Pie.*

—Jan Pembleton
Arlington, TX

Yogurt Pie

Sarah Miller, Harrisonburg, VA
Shirley Sears, Tiskilwa, IL
Trudy Kutter, Corfu, NY
Betty Moore, Plano, IL
Joyce Kaut, Rochester, NY
Ruth Shank, Monroe, GA

Makes 6 servings

Prep. Time: 5 minutes
*Cooling Time: 5–9 hours, or
overnight*

¼ cup water
.3-oz. box gelatin, your
choice of flavor
2 6-oz. containers yogurt,
your choice of flavor
8-oz. container frozen
whipped topping,
thawed
9" graham cracker crust

1. Boil water. Stir in gelatin
until dissolved. Allow to cool
unto syrupy but not firm.
2. In a large mixing bowl,
combine partially-gelled
gelatin, yogurt, and thawed
whipped topping.
3. Pour into crust.
4. Allow to cool until firm,
from 4–8 hours, or overnight.

*Variation: Skip the water
and gelatin. Instead use 1
pint cut-up fruit, such as
strawberries or blueberries.
Mix the fruit with the yogurt
and thawed whipped topping.
If you use canned fruit, be sure
to drain it well before mixing it
with the other ingredients.*

—Joyce Kaut, Rochester, NY
—Ruth Shank, Monroe, GA

Cookies 'n Cream Pie

Sheila Horst
Bowmansville, PA

Makes 6–8 servings

Prep. Time: 15 minutes
Freezing Time: 6–8 hours, or overnight

1½ cups half-and-half
3.4-oz. pkg. instant vanilla, *or* French vanilla, pudding mix
8-oz. carton frozen whipped topping, thawed
1 cup crushed cream-filled chocolate sandwich cookies
9" chocolate crumb pie crust

1. In a mixing bowl, combine the half-and-half and dry pudding mix. Beat on medium speed for 1 minute. Let stand for 5 minutes.
2. Fold in whipped topping and crushed cookies.
3. Spoon into crust.
4. Freeze until firm, for about 6–8 hours or overnight.
5. Remove from freezer 10 minutes before serving.

Sugar-Free Double-Chocolate Cream Pie

Peggy Clark
Burrton, KS

Makes 6–8 servings

Prep. Time: 15–20 minutes
Standing/Chilling Time 30–60 minutes:

1½ cups milk, *divided*
3-oz. pkg. dark chocolate sugar-free pudding
8-oz. container light frozen whipped topping, thawed, *divided*
9" graham cracker crust
3-oz. pkg. white chocolate sugar-free pudding

1. In a small mixing bowl, mix ¾ cup milk with dark chocolate pudding mix.
2. Fold half of whipped topping into dark chocolate pudding.
3. Place dark chocolate pudding into crust.
4. In another small mixing bowl, mix remaining ¾ cup milk with white chocolate pudding mix.
5. Fold remaining whipped topping into white chocolate pudding.
6. Spoon white chocolate pudding over top of dark chocolate pudding, being careful not to mix the two.
7. Refrigerate until ready to eat.

Easy Peanut Butter Pie

Kendra Dreps, Liberty, PA

Makes 6 servings

Prep. Time: 10 minutes
Chilling Time: 2–4 hours

8-oz. pkg. cream cheese, softened
1 cup peanut butter
1 cup confectioners sugar
8-oz. pkg. frozen whipped topping, thawed
1 graham cracker crust
peanut butter cups, chopped, *optional*

1. In a large mixing bowl, cream the cream cheese and peanut butter together until smooth.
2. Stir in the confectioners sugar until well incorporated.
3. Fold in the whipped topping.
4. Pile into pie crust.
5. If you wish, top with chopped peanut butter cups.
6. Refrigerate 2–4 hours before serving.

Peanut Butter and Banana Pie

Jenny R. Unternahrer
Wayland, IA

Makes 8 servings

Prep. Time: 15 minutes
Chilling Time: 2–4 hours

9" pie crust, baked and
  cooled
⅓–½ cup creamy natural
  peanut butter
2 bananas, sliced
3-oz. pkg. sugar-free instant
  vanilla pudding
1¾ cups milk

1. Spread peanut butter on
bottom and sides of baked pie
crust. Use as much or as little
as you like.
2. Layer banana slices on
top of the peanut butter and
around the sides of the pie
shell.
3. Mix pudding and milk
together according to pudding
package instructions.
4. Pour pudding over
bananas, covering all of them.
5. Refrigerate 2–4 hours, or
until set.

Tip: *If you prefer a fuller
pie you can use another half
package of pudding and 7 ozs.
milk, adding to the milk and
pudding in the recipe.*

Crunchy Peanut Butter Ice Cream Pie

Mary Ann Bowman
East Earl, PA
Susan Wenger
Lebanon, PA
Joanna Bear
Salisbury, MD

Makes 6–8 servings

Prep. Time: 15 minutes
Freezing Time: 4–6 hours

⅓–½ cup crunchy peanut
  butter
⅓–½ cup light corn syrup
2–3 cups Rice Krispies
1 qt. vanilla ice cream,
  slightly softened
toppings of your choice—
  whipped topping, broken
  nuts, cut-up fresh fruit,
  mini- M&M's, mini-
  chocolate chips, *or* chopped
  peanut butter cups

1. In a mixing bowl, beat
peanut butter and corn syrup
together until well blended.
2. Stir in rice krispies.
3. Using a spoon, or your
buttered fingers, press mixture
into a 9" buttered pie pan.
4. Fill pie shell with
softened ice cream.
5. Freeze 4–6 hours, or
until firm.
6. When ready to serve,
garnish with the toppings of
your choice.
7. To make serving easier,
set the filled pie plate in
warm water for 1 minute
before cutting the pie.

Tips from the Tester:
  *1. On the one pie I made, I
added a layer of chocolate syrup
over the crust before spooning
in the vanilla ice cream. Then
I drizzled more chocolate syrup
on top of the ice cream.*
  *2. For the second pie, I used
chocolate ice cream. In fact, you
can use any flavor of ice cream
that you wish and that you find
compatible with the peanut-
butter-flavored crust.*

Variations:
  *1. Instead of the corn syrup,
use half a stick (¼ cup) butter
and 2 Tbsp. brown sugar.*
  *2. Instead of Rice Krispies,
use 4½ cups sugar-coated
cornflakes, crushed.*

—**Joanna Bear**, Salisbury, MD

Creamy Peanut Butter Ice Cream Pie

Anita Troyer
Fairview, MI

Makes 6–8 servings

Prep. Time: 15 minutes
Freezing Time: 8 hours or overnight

4 cups (1 qt.) vanilla ice cream, softened
⅓ cup peanut butter
¾ cup frozen whipped topping, thawed
graham cracker crust
chocolate syrup

1. In a large mixing bowl, mix ice cream and peanut butter together until smooth.
2. Fold in whipped topping until well distributed.
3. Pour into crust and freeze until ready to serve.
4. Drizzle chocolate syrup over top just before serving.

Pie Crust

Christine Weaver
Reinholds, PA
Gwendolyn Chapman
Gwinn, MI

Makes 1 9" 2-crust pie

Prep. Time: 10 minutes

2½ cups flour
½ tsp. salt
¾ cup shortening
6–7 Tbsp. cold water

1. Place flour and salt in large bowl. Cut in shortening with pastry blender or 2 knives until mixture resembles coarse meal or tiny peas.
2. Add water a little at a time and mix lightly with fork until pastry holds together when pressed into a ball.
3. Divide dough into 2 balls, 1 using about ⅔ of the dough, and the other using about ⅓ of the dough.
4. Roll out larger ball of dough on floured countertop until dough is 2" larger than pie pan.
5. Lightly fold circle of dough in half. Then lightly fold in half again so that the resulting shape is a ¼ circle.
6. Lay crust into pie pan. Open up folds. Press crust loosely but firmly into the pan.
7. For a pre-baked shell, prick the bottom and sides of the dough with a sharp fork. Then bake the unfilled crust at 425° for 10 minutes.

If your recipe directs you to bake a filled crust, spoon or pour the filling into the crust, and then bake according to the pie recipe instructions.

A Tip —

Buy sturdy kitchen tools. Buy ones that fit well into your hands. Take care of them and they will last a very long time.

Fruit Salads

Strawberry Jello
Cynthia Morrix, Grottoes, VA

Makes 8 servings

Prep. Time: 20–30 minutes
Chilling Time: 4–6 hours

2 .3-oz. boxes wild
  strawberry gelatin,
  divided
1½ cups boiling water
2 pints frozen strawberries,
  thawed, juice reserved,
  divided
1–1½ cups cold water
8-oz. pkg. cream cheese,
  softened
1 pkg. Dream Whip, *or* 2
  cups frozen whipped
  topping, thawed

1. In a large mixing bowl,
mix 1½ boxes dry gelatin
with 1½ cups boiling water.
Stir until dissolved.
2. Drain strawberry juice
into a measuring cup. Set
aside ½ cup for Topping. To
remaining strawberry juice,
add enough cold water to
equal 1½ cups. Stir into hot
water with dissolved gelatin.
3. Add strawberries and
mix.
4. Pour into large serving
bowl. Chill until firm.

Topping
1. Pour reserved half box
of dry gelatin into a small

saucepan. Mix with reserved
½ cup strawberry juice.
2. Cut cream cheese into
small chunks. Add to mixture
in saucepan. Stir over low
heat until blended.
3. Let cool to room tem-
perature.
4. Fold in Dream Whip or
whipped topping.
5. Pour over gelatin mixture.
6. Cover and refrigerate for
2–3 hours or more.

*My mom always makes this for
my birthday!*

Whipped
Strawberry Jello
Ruth Ann Hoover
New Holland, PA

Makes 8–10 servings

Prep. Time: 30 minutes
Chilling Time: 3–4 hours

2 .3-oz. pkgs. strawberry
  gelatin
2 cups frozen strawberries
1 cup miniature
  marshmallows
8-oz. container frozen
  whipped topping, thawed

1. Mix gelatin according to
package directions.
2. When gelatin begins to
set, beat.
3. Fold in strawberries and
marshmallows.
4. Fold in whipped topping.
5. Refrigerate until set. It's
then ready to serve.

Peach Bavarian
Erma Martin
East Earl, PA

Makes 8–10 servings

Prep. Time: 30 minutes
*Chilling Time: 8 hours, or
  overnight*

16-oz. can sliced peaches
2 .3-oz. pkgs. peach, *or*
  apricot, gelatin
½ cup sugar
2 cups boiling water
1 tsp. almond extract
8-oz. container frozen
  whipped topping,
  thawed
additional peach slices,
  optional

1. Drain peaches, reserving
⅔ cup juice. Chop peaches
into small pieces. Set aside.
2. In a large mixing bowl,
dissolve gelatin and sugar in
boiling water.
3. Stir in reserved peach
juice. Cover and chill in
the fridge until slightly
thickened.
4. Stir extract into whipped
topping. Gently fold into
gelatin mixture. Fold in
peaches.
5. Pour into 6-cup mold.
Cover and chill overnight.
6. Unmold when ready
to serve. Garnish with
additional peach slices, if you
wish.

Rhubarb Strawberry Sauce

Betty K. Drescher
Quakertown, PA

Makes 8 servings

Prep. Time: 15 minutes
Cooking/Baking Time: 10 minutes
Chilling Time: 3–4 hours

¾ cup sugar
3 Tbsp. quick tapioca
1 cup boiling water
2 cups rhubarb, sliced ¼"
   thick
.3-oz. box strawberry
   gelatin
1 cup cold water
1½ cups sliced
   strawberries, *optional*

1. Combine sugar and tapioca in saucepan.
2. Stir in 1 cup boiling water. Let stand 5 minutes.
3. Bring mixture to boil.
4. Add 2 cups rhubarb. Simmer 5 minutes.
5. Remove pan from heat. Add gelatin, stirring to dissolve.
6. Stir in 1 cup cold water.
7. Chill until set, about 3–4 hours.
8. If you wish, stir in fresh strawberries after mixture sets.

Cranberry Mousse

Kathleen A. Rogge
Alexandria, IN

Makes 6–8 servings

Prep. Time: 20 minutes
Cooking/Baking Time: 5 minutes
Chilling Time: 3–4 hours

1 cup cranberry juice
   cocktail
.3-oz. pkg. raspberry-
   flavored gelatin
16-oz. can jellied cranberry
   sauce
1 cup heavy cream

1. In a good-sized saucepan, heat cranberry juice cocktail to boiling.
2. Stir in gelatin until dissolved.
3. Stir in cranberry sauce.
4. Chill until mixture is thickened.
5. Meanwhile, whip cream in chilled bowl until stiff peaks form. Reserve about ½ cup for garnishing mousse before serving.
6. Fold whipped cream into thickened cranberry mixture.
7. Spoon into serving dish. Chill until firm.
8. Garnish with additional whipped cream just before serving.

Lightly Lemon Fruit Salad

Dorothy A. Shank, Sterling, IL
Shirley Unternahrer Hinh
Wayland, IA

Makes 8–10 servings

Prep Time: 10 minutes
Cooling Time: 4 hours or more

.6-oz. box lemon, *or*
   apricot, gelatin
20-oz. can crushed
   pineapple, not drained
8-oz. container whipped
   topping, thawed
2 cups buttermilk

1. Put gelatin and pineapple into microwave-safe bowl. Microwave on High for 3 minutes.
2. Stir. Let stand 2 minutes.
3. Fold in whipped topping.
4. Stir in buttermilk.
5. Place in a serving bowl. Cover and refrigerate until set.

We always made this recipe with apricot gelatin and called it "Mayme Lorene's Apricot Salad." Mayme Lorene found this recipe and learned to make it with her Grandma Unternahrer. Mom, Mayme's grandmother, was a good cook and taught us all so much about baking, sewing, preserving… life… family. Patricia Unternahrer was a regular participant in Good Books' cookbooks. We lost Mom this last February and miss her much.

—**Shirley Unternahrer Hinh**
Wayland, IA

Pistachio Salad

Jeanne Allen, Rye, CO
Janie Canupp
Millersville, MD

Makes 4–6 servings

Prep. Time: 10 minutes
Cooling Time: 4 hours

20-oz. can crushed
  pineapple, undrained
3-oz. pkg. pistachio instant
  pudding
1 bag miniature
  marshmallows
8-oz. container frozen
  whipped topping,
  thawed
maraschino cherries,
  optional

1. Mix first three ingre-
dients together in a large
mixing bowl.
2. Chill until firm, about
3–4 hours.
3. Fold the whipped top-
ping into the mixture. Place
in a serving bowl.
4. Cover and return to
refrigerator.
5. Garnish with mara-
schino cherries if you wish,
just before serving.

*Variation: Substitute ½ cup
chopped nuts and ½ cup miniature marshmallows instead of 1
bag miniature marshmallows.*

—**Janie Canupp**
Millersville, MD

Lemon Souffle

Susan Kasting
Jenks, OK

Makes 12 servings

Prep. Time: 20 minutes
*Cooling Time: 8 hours, or
overnight*

2½ cups water
2 .3-oz. pkgs. lemon gelatin
1 cup sugar
2 lemons, juice and zest
2 cups heavy whipping
  cream
1 prepared angel food cake

1. Bring water to a boil.
Dissolve gelatin in boiling
water.
2. Stir in sugar, lemon
juice, and zest.
3. Chill just until mixture
thickens.
4. Whip cream in chilled
bowl until stiff peaks form.
5. Fold into thickened
gelatin.
6. Break up angel food
cake into 1"–2" pieces Place in
large bowl.
7. Fold gelatin mixture into
cake pieces.
8. Place in serving bowl,
cover, and refrigerate overnight.

Refreshing Raspberry Citrus

Dale Peterson
Rapid City, SD
Marguerite Baumgartner
Versailles, MO

Makes 5 servings

Prep. Time: 10–15 minutes
Cooling Time: 4 hours

.3-oz. pkg. raspberry
  gelatin
1 cup boiling water
1 cup vanilla ice cream
3 Tbsp. orange juice
8¾-oz. can crushed
  pineapple with juice
½ cup walnuts

1. Dissolve gelatin in
boiling water.
2. Pour into mixing bowl.
Stir in ice cream and orange
juice until dissolved.
3. Stir in pineapple and
nuts.
4. When well mixed, pour
into a serving dish or salad
mold. Cover and refrigerate
until firm.

Variations:
  *1. Add 1 banana, sliced, in
Step 3. Drop orange juice, if
you wish.*
  *2. Use pecans instead of
walnuts, if you wish.*

—**Marguerite Baumgartner**
Versailles, MO

Orange Supreme Tapioca Pudding

Jennifer Eberly, Harrisonburg, VA
Peggy Clark, Burrton, KS
Janet Derstine, Telford, PA
Anne Nolt, Thompsontown, PA
Arlene Snyder, Millerstown, PA
Janelle Nolt, Richland, PA
Beth Shank, Wellman, IA

Makes 4–6 servings

Prep Time: 30 minutes
Chilling Time: 4 hours or more

3-oz. box instant tapioca
  pudding
.3-oz. box orange gelatin
3-oz. box instant vanilla
  pudding
2 cups hot water
15-oz. can mandarin
  oranges, *or crushed
  pineapples*
8-oz. container whipped
  topping, thawed

1. Combine dry tapioca
pudding, dry gelatin, and dry
pudding, along with hot water,
in a medium-sized saucepan.
2. Bring to a boil. Cook
over medium heat until thick
and bubbly, about 3 minutes.
Stir constantly.
3. Cool to room temperature.
4. Fold in mandarin
oranges and whipped topping.
5. Cover and chill for at
least 2 hours.

*Variation: Use 2 boxes of
vanilla pudding and drop the
tapioca pudding.*
  —**Anne Nolt**
    Thompsontown, PA

—**Arlene Snyder**
  Millerstown, PA
—**Janelle Nolt**, Richland, PA
—**Beth Shank**, Wellman, IA

Mandarin Orange Sherbet Dessert

Lori Lehman
Ephrata, PA
Mary Ann Bowman
East Earl, PA

Makes 8 servings

Prep. Time: 2 hours
Chilling Time: 8 hours

.3-oz. pkg. orange gelatin
1 cup boiling water
1 pint orange sherbet
16-oz. can mandarin
  oranges, drained
1 cup whipped topping,
  thawed

1. Dissolve gelatin in water.
Place in mixing bowl.
2. Add sherbet and
oranges. Place in fridge until
mixture begins to thicken,
about 20 minutes.
3. Fold in whipped topping.
4. Spoon into serving
dish. Cover and chill 8 hours
before serving.

*Variation: Instead of folding
the whipped topping into the
dessert, use it as a topping just
before serving.*
  —**Mary Ann Bowman**
    East Earl, PA

Sunshine Salad
Mary Lynn Miller
Reinhelds, PA

Makes 8–10 servings

Prep Time: 10–15 minutes
Chilling Time: 2 hours, or more

20-oz. can pineapple
  tidbits
11-oz. can mandarin
  oranges
3.4-oz. pkg. instant lemon
  pudding
1 cup stemmed and
  quartered strawberries
1 cup sliced ripe bananas

1. Drain pineapples and
oranges, reserving liquid.
2. In a large bowl, combine
pudding mix with reserved
fruit juices.
3. Fold in pineapple,
oranges, and strawberries.
4. Cover and chill for at
least 2 hours.
5. Fold in bananas just
before serving.

5-Cup Spring Salad

Barbara Yoder
Christiana, PA
Hazel Lightcap Propst
Oxford, PA
Carna Reitz
Remington, VA
Carolyn A. Baer
Conrath, WI

Makes 6–8 servings

Prep Time: 5 minutes
Chilling Time: 8 hours or overnight

1 cup sour cream
1 cup flaked coconut
11-oz. can mandarin oranges, drained
1 cup pineapple tidbits, drained
1 cup miniature marshmallows
2 Tbsp. chopped walnuts, *optional*
1 Tbsp. brown sugar, *optional*

1. Mix the first 5 ingredients together in a serving bowl.
2. Cover and refrigerate overnight.
3. If you wish, just before serving garnish with walnuts and brown sugar.

Variations:
Add 1 cup seedless grapes to the salad.
Coconut can be an optional ingredient.
—**Carna Reitz**, Remington, VA

Substitute fruit cocktail for the mandarin oranges.

Add 1 cup large-curd cottage cheese, if you wish.
—**Carolyn A. Baer**
Conrath, WI

Creamy Grape Salad

Nettie J. Miller
Millersburg, OH

Makes 8–10 servings

Prep Time: 20–30 minutes
Chilling Time: 1–2 hours, or more

8-oz. pkg. cream cheese, at room temperature
2 cups sour cream
½ cup brown sugar
½ tsp. vanilla
6 cups stemmed and washed seedless grapes, red *or* green

1. In a large mixing bowl, blend the first three ingredients together until smooth.
2. Add vanilla.
3. Fold in grapes.
4. Cover and chill in the refrigerator for 1–2 hours, or more.

Baked Cranberry Sauce

Carolyn Lehman Henry
Clinton, NY

Makes 6–8 servings

Prep. Time: 5 minutes
Cooking/Baking Time: 45 minutes

12-oz. pkg. fresh cranberries
12-oz. jar orange marmalade
¾ cup sugar
¼ cup water
1 cup chopped pecans

1. Preheat oven to 350°.
2. In a 9 × 13 glass baking dish, combine cranberries, orange marmalade, sugar, and water.
3. Bake uncovered for 45 minutes.
4. Stir in pecans.
5. Serve warm or chilled.

A Tip —

Don't be afraid to ask the experienced cooks in your church and community for their recipes. At age 64, I still do.

Marinated Strawberries

Barbara Sparks
Glen Burnie, MD

Makes 4 servings

Prep. Time: 20–25 minutes
Chilling Time: 2 hours

3 pints fresh strawberries
½ cup superfine *or* granulated sugar
juice of 2 large oranges and zest of 1
⅓ cup orange-flavored liqueur
whipped topping *or* whipped cream, *optional*
1 Tbsp. chopped fresh mint leaves, *optional*

1. Hull strawberries and place in large bowl. If berries are large, cut in half. Do not overcrowd.
2. Sprinkle with sugar and orange zest. Add juice and liqueur. Carefully fold into berries.
3. Cover bowl. Refrigerate for about 2 hours, stirring carefully once or twice.
4. Serve chilled, topped with whipped topping or cream and mint leaves, if you wish.

Chocolate Strawberry Salad

Lucy O'Connell
Northampton, MA

Makes 8 servings

Prep Time: 15 minutes

2 lbs. fresh strawberries, sliced and slightly mashed
1 cup milk chocolate chips *or* chunks
½ cup sugar, *or* to taste
½ cup toasted coconut, *optional*

1. Combine berries, chocolate, and sugar.
2. Top with toasted coconut, if you wish.

Fruit Dip Salad

Natalia Showalter
Mt. Solon, VA

Makes 20 servings

Prep. Time: 15–20 minutes
Chilling Time: 1–2 hours

8-oz. pkg. cream cheese, at room temperature
¾ cup confectioners sugar, *or* to taste
1 tsp. lemon juice
1 pt. whipping cream, whipped
4 lbs. fresh grapes, strawberries, and nectarines, mixed
½ cup chopped pecan pieces, *optional*

1. Combine first 3 ingredients in large mixing bowl.
2. Fold in whipped cream.
3. Cut fruit into bite-sized chunks.
4. Gently stir fruit into dressing.
5. Cover and chill 1–2 hours.
6. Just before serving, stir in chopped pecans, if you wish.

Tip: If you use only grapes in this recipe, substitute brown sugar for the confectioners sugar.

Ice Cream

Ice Cream Dessert

Violette Harris Denney
Carrollton, GA
Naomi Ressler, Harrisonburg, VA
Karla Baer, North Lima, OH

Makes 12–15 servings

Prep. Time: 20 minutes
Freezing Time: 6–8 hours, or
overnight

2 stacks Oreo cookies from
a 1-lb. 2-oz.-pkg.
half gallon vanilla ice
cream, softened
8-oz. container frozen
whipped topping, thawed
1 cup roasted peanuts
chocolate syrup to pour on
top

1. Place a portion of the
cookies in a zip-lock bag.
Roll with a rolling pin until
crushed. Place crumbled
cookies in a 8 × 10 baking
pan or casserole dish. Repeat
until all cookies are crushed.
2. Spoon ice cream evenly
over cookie crumbs, being careful not to disturb the crumbs.
3. Spread whipped topping
over ice cream.
4. Sprinkle with peanuts.
5. Pour chocolate syrup
over top.
6. Freeze for 6–8 hours.

Variation:
1. Set aside ¾ cup crumbs
after completing Step 1.

2. In large bowl, mix rest of
crumbs with softened ice cream.
3. Fold in whipped topping.
4. Spoon into 8 × 10 dish or
pan. Score top of dessert into 8
serving-size pieces.
5. Sprinkle with reserved
crumbs.
6. Cover. Freeze until solid.
7. Soften slightly before cutting into squares and serving.

—**Naomi Ressler**
Harrisonburg, VA

—**Karla Baer**, North Lima, OH

*Tip: Keep on hand for guests and
serve as needed. It will keep well
in the freezer for several weeks.*

Chocolate Mint Delight

Eileen Eash, Carlsbad, NM

Makes 6 servings

Prep. Time: 15 minutes
Cooling Time: 20 minutes

.3-oz. pkg. lime gelatin
1 cup boiling water
2 cups vanilla ice cream,
softened
½–¾ tsp. peppermint
extract, according to
your taste preference
¼ cup chocolate chips
1 cup frozen whipped
topping, thawed

1. In a large mixing bowl,
dissolve gelatin in boiling
water.
2. Stir in ice cream until
melted.

3. Stir in peppermint
flavoring and chocolate chips.
4. Chill about 20 minutes,
or until mixture is partially
set.
5. Fold in whipped topping.
6. Chill until ready to serve.

*Tip from Tester: To simplify,
you could substitute mint chocolate chip ice cream instead of
vanilla ice cream, peppermint
extract, and chocolate chips.*

Gladys' Christmas Dessert

Arlene Leaman Kliewer
Lakewood, CO

Makes 8–10 servings

Prep. Time: 5 minutes
Freezing Time: 4–5 hours or more

2-qt. box pineapple, *or*
raspberry, sherbet,
softened
10-oz. pkg. frozen
raspberries with juice,
thawed
2–3 bananas, mashed
½–¾ cup broken nuts,
according to your taste
preference

1. Mix all ingredients
together in a large mixing
bowl.
2. Spoon into a bowl or
baking pan. Cover and freeze
until firm throughout.
3. Remove from freezer to
soften enough to eat partially
frozen.

Cranberry Ice
Patricia Howard
Green Valley, AL

Makes 6 servings

Prep. Time: 10 minutes
Cooking/Baking Time: 10 minutes
Freezing Time: 3–4 hours or more

2 cups raw cranberries
1 cup very hot water
additional water
1 cup sugar
2 cups tart apples, grated

1. In a medium-sized saucepan, cook cranberries in 1 cup partially boiling water until skins burst, about 5 minutes. Strain through a medium sieve. Discard skins.
2. Measure and add enough water to make 2 cups pulp and juice. Return to pan and cook 2 minutes.
3. Stir in sugar and simmer gently until it dissolves. Stir frequently.
4. Cool until room temperature.
5. Stir in 2 cups grated tart apples. Pour into refrigerator tray and freeze for 1–2 hours.
6. Stir. Return to freezer and continue freezing until firm.
7. To serve, place in refrigerator until partially thawed. Stir, or scratch up with fork tines before placing in serving bowl or individual dessert bowls.

Low-Fat Homemade Ice Cream
Denae Villines, Whitewater, KS

Makes 3 servings

Prep. Time: 10 minutes
Freezing Time: 4–8 hours, or overnight

3-oz. box sugar-free, fat-free instant pudding, any flavor
2 cups fat-free milk
8-oz. container frozen fat-free whipped topping, thawed

1. In a large mixing bowl, mix pudding and milk until smooth and creamy.
2. Fold in whipped topping.
3. Place in serving bowl or casserole dish.
4. Freeze for 4–8 hours, or until solid.

I think chocolate is the best!

Ice Cream
Mary Kathryn Yoder
Harrisonville, MO

Makes 10 servings

Prep. Time: 15–20 minutes
Freezing Time: 4 hours

½ gallon chocolate milk
14-oz. can sweetened condensed milk
12-oz. container frozen whipped topping, thawed

1. Mix chocolate milk and sweetened condensed milk together in a good-sized mixing bowl.
2. Stir in whipped topping until well blended.
3. Pour into serving bowl or casserole dish. Cover.
4. Freeze until firm, about 4 hours.

Sherbet Ice Cream
Sara Bucher
Lisbon Falls, ME

Makes 20–24 servings

Prep. Time: 5 minutes
Chilling Time: 60 minutes
Turning Time: 20 minutes

14-oz. can sweetened condensed milk
20-oz. chunked *and/or* crushed pineapple
2 liters orange soda

1. Combine milk and pineapple in a large bowl. Chill for at least 60 minutes in refrigerator. (Also chill soda in fridge.)
2. When ready to turn sherbet in the ice cream freezer, pour soda into freezer.
3. Stir in combined milk and pineapple.
4. Turn until frozen.

Sauces & Toppings

Hot Fudge Sauce

Sharon Wantland
Menomonee Falls, WI

Makes 4 servings

Prep. Time: 10 minutes

12-oz. pkg. semi-sweet
  chocolate chips
1 cup half-and-half
1 Tbsp. butter
1 tsp. vanilla

1. Combine chocolate chips
and half-and-half in an 8-cup
glass microwave-safe bowl.
Microwave on High for 1–1½
minutes until chips melt
when stirred.
2. Cool until just-warm.
Stir in butter and vanilla.

Aunt Dorothy's Chocolate Sauce

Karen Kay Tucker
Manteca, CA
Jeanette B. Oberholtzer
Manheim, PA

Makes 3 cups

Prep. Time: 15 minutes
Cooking/Baking Time: 10 minutes
Cooling Time: 1 hour

12-oz. can evaporated milk
2 cups sugar
3 1-oz. squares unsweetened
  baking chocolate, broken
  in pieces
1 tsp. vanilla

1. Mix together evaporated
milk and sugar in a 2-quart
saucepan.
2. Add chocolate pieces.
Heat to boiling over medium-
high heat, stirring constantly
since the mixture can burn
easily.
3. Turn heat back to
medium/medium-low to keep
mixture at a low boil for five
minutes. Stir continually.
4. Remove from heat. Stir
in 1 tsp. vanilla.
5. Transfer chocolate sauce
to a mixing bowl. Beat two
minutes (not less) with an
electric mixer. This is to
insure a smooth sauce.
6. Cool to room tempera-
ture. Store in refrigerator in a
covered container.
7. Serve over ice cream,
angel food cake, or pound
cake.

Praline Sauce

Vicki J. Hill
Memphis, TN

Makes 2 cups

Prep. Time: 5 minutes
Cooking/Baking Time: 5–10
  minutes
Cooling Time: 30–60 minutes

½ cup packed brown sugar
½ cup light corn syrup
1 stick (½ cup) butter
½ cup chopped pecans
1 tsp. vanilla

1. In a 1-quart saucepan,
combine sugar, syrup, and
butter. Cook over medium
heat, stirring occasionally
until mixture comes to a full
boil.
2. Boil 1 minute. Remove
from heat.
3. Stir in nuts and vanilla.
4. Let cool.
5. Serve over ice cream,
cream puffs, pound cake, or
any other dessert you'd like to
enhance!

*Tip: You can heat the first
3 ingredients together in a
microwave-safe bowl on High
for 1-minute bursts. Stir after
each minute until it boils.*

Sugar-Free Blueberry Sauce

Esther J. Yoder
Hartville, OH

Makes about 6 cups

Prep. Time: 5–10 minutes
Cooking/Baking Time: 15 minutes
Cooling Time: 30–60 minutes

2 lbs. frozen, *or* fresh, blueberries
1 tsp. salt
1 tsp. lemon juice
1½ cups water, *divided*
½ cup cornstarch
¼ cup sugar substitute

1. Mix blueberries, salt, lemon juice, and ½ cup water in a large saucepan. Bring to a boil.
2. In a small bowl, stir cornstarch into 1 cup water until smooth.
3. Immediately stir cornstarch/water into saucepan.
4. Boil for a few minutes, until sauce thickens and clears.
5. Add sugar substitute when sauce has cooled to room temperature.
6. Serve over ice cream, pound cake, angel food cake, waffles, or pancakes.

Tip from Tester: If you refrigerate the sauce, you may need to add a bit of water before serving since it thickens when cooled.

Orange Fruit Dressing

Mary Kathryn Yoder
Harrisonville, MO

Makes 2 cups

Prep. Time: 10 minutes
Cooking/Baking Time: 5 minutes
Cooling Time: 30–60 minutes

1½ cups orange juice
1½ Tbsp. lemon juice
1 cup sugar
1½ Tbsp. cornstarch
fruit of your choice

1. Mix orange juice and lemon juice together in a small saucepan. Bring to a boil.
2. Meanwhile, mix sugar and cornstarch together in a small bowl. Slowly add to boiling juice, stirring continually.
3. Cook several minutes until slightly thickened, stirring frequently.
4. Cool to room temperature, and then chill in refrigerator.
5. Pour over, or fold into, a mixture of chopped raw apples, sliced bananas, strawberries, oranges, pears, and pineapple.

Tips:
1. It only takes a small amount of the sauce to dress a small bowl of fruit.
2. The sauce freezes well.

Sauteed Apples

Barbara Sparks
Glen Burnie, MD

Makes 4–6 servings

Prep. Time: 20 minutes
Cooking/Baking Time: 20 minutes

2 Tbsp. butter
6–8 apples, peeled, sliced and cored
1 Tbsp. cinnamon
¾ cup sugar, *or* less

1. Melt butter in large skillet.
2. Stir in apple slices.
3. Sprinkle cinnamon and sugar over apples.
4. Cover and cook over medium heat, occasionally stirring to prevent sticking.
5. When apples are just soft they are ready to serve. Do not overcook!
6. Serve these as a topping on French toast, pancakes, or vanilla ice cream. Or serve them as a side dish to your favorite pork recipe.

Candies

Creamy Chocolate Fudge

Chris Kaczynski
Schenectady, NY

Makes 64 pieces

Prep Time: 15 minutes
Cooling Time: 1–2 hours

8-oz. pkg. cream cheese, softened
1 lb. confectioners sugar, sifted
12-oz. pkg. semi-sweet chocolate chips
2 tsp. vanilla
½ cup chopped walnuts, *optional*

1. Grease an 8 × 8 or 9 × 9 square pan.
2. In a good-sized mixing bowl, stir cream cheese and confectioners sugar together until well blended.
3. Place chocolate chips in a microwave-safe bowl. Microwave on High for 1–1½ minutes, or until chips show that they are melted when stirred.
4. Add melted chips to sugar mixture.
5. Stir in vanilla, and walnuts if you wish, mixing well.
6. Spread in prepared pan.
7. Chill in refrigerator for 1–2 hours, or until firm enough to cut into squares. Store in refrigerator.

Chocolate Peanut Butter Fudge

Melanie Mohler
Ephrata, PA

Makes 24 pieces

Prep Time: 20 minutes
Cooling Time: 2–3 hours

1 lb. white chocolate wafers
1 lb. milk chocolate wafers
18-oz. jar peanut butter

1. Melt white chocolate wafers in a microwave-safe bowl on High for 2 minutes. Stir. Microwave on High another minute. Stir. Microwave on High in 30-second intervals until chocolate is smooth when stirred. (Be sure to stir. Chocolate may retain its shape but still be melted.) Set melted white chocolate aside.
2. In a separate microwave-safe bowl, repeat same procedure with milk chocolate wafers.
3. Stir half the peanut butter into each bowl of melted chocolate.
4. Coat a 7 × 11 baking dish with non-stick cooking spray.
5. Pour one of the chocolates into the baking dish.
6. Pour the other melted chocolate on top.
7. Use a knife to swirl the two chocolates together into a design.
8. Refrigerate 2–3 hours, or until hard enough to cut into pieces.

Peanut Butter Fudge

Jamie Schwankl
Ephrata, PA

Makes 48 pieces

Prep Time: 10 minutes
Cooking Time: 10 minutes
Cooling time: 2–3 hours

2 sticks (1 cup) butter
1 cup peanut butter
1 tsp. vanilla
pinch of salt
3 cups confectioners sugar

1. Melt butter in a medium-sized saucepan over medium heat.
2. Turn heat to low and stir in peanut butter, vanilla, and salt. Mix with a wooden spoon until smooth.
3. Remove from heat.
4. Stir in confectioners sugar with wooden spoon.
5. Spread in a lightly greased 9 × 13 pan to cool.
6. Refrigerate 1–2 hours to harden.
7. Cut into squares.

Tip: Do not stir ingredients with a mixer.

Peanut Butter Marshmallow Fudge

Jean A. Shaner
York, PA

Makes 25–30 pieces

Prep Time: 7 minutes
Cooking Time: 7 minutes
Cooling Time: 2 hours

3 cups sugar
¾ cup skim milk
1 Tbsp. butter
7-oz. jar marshmallow crème
18-oz. jar peanut butter

1. Boil sugar, milk, and butter for 3 minutes in a medium-sized saucepan.

2. Remove from heat.

3. Stir in marshmallow crème and peanut butter.

4. Place in a buttered 8 × 11, or 10 × 10 pan or dish.

5. Refrigerate for 2 hours, or until firm enough to cut into pieces.

Rocky Road Fudge

Kathleen A. Rogge
Alexandria, IN
Alyssa Reitz
Remington, VA

Makes 36 pieces

Prep Time: 10 minutes
Cooking Time: 2–5 minutes
Cooling Time: 3–4 hours

12-oz. pkg. semi-sweet chocolate chips
1 *or* 2 cups butterscotch chips, whichever you prefer
1 cup crunchy peanut butter
1 Tbsp butter, *optional*
10.5-oz. pkg. mini-marshmallows
1 cup salted peanuts, *or* other nuts

1. Grease an 8 × 8 or 9 × 9 metal baking pan. Line with plastic wrap.

2. In 4-quart saucepan, combine chocolate chips, butterscotch chips, peanut butter, and butter if you wish. Cook over medium heat 2–3 minutes, or just until ingredients are melted, stirring constantly. Remove from heat.

3. Stir marshmallows, and nuts if you wish, into warm fudge mixture.

4. Pour into lined pan, spreading evenly.

5. Cover with plastic wrap and refrigerate until firm, at least 3 hours.

6. Invert fudge onto cutting board. Remove plastic wrap. Cut into 36 pieces. If not serving right away, keep refrigerated.

A Tip —

Read the whole recipe before beginning to cook.

Try These Truffles

Leann Brown
Lancaster, PA

Makes 8 servings

Prep Time: 30 minutes
Cooling Time: 1 hour

12-oz. bag of swirled
  chocolate chips (peanut
  butter, *or* raspberry, *or*
  caramel)
half a 9-oz. container of
  frozen whipped topping,
  thawed
half a 12-oz. bag of semi-
  sweet chips, *or* coating
  chocolate
2 Tbsp. paraffin wax, *or*
  Crisco
confectioners sugar, *optional*
crushed peanuts *or*
  almonds, *optional*

1. Place the swirled chocolate chips in a microwave-safe
bowl. Microwave at 70%
power for 30 seconds. Stir.
Repeat if chips are not fully
melted.
2. Set melted chips aside
to cool to room temperature.
Do not put in refrigerator to
speed process; chocolate will
get too hard again.
3. When melted chocolate
reaches room temperature,
mix in whipped topping.
Refrigerate until chocolate
stiffens.
4. Scoop out with teaspoon
and form into small balls.
Place on waxed-paper-lined
baking sheets. Place in
refrigerator.

5. Place semi-sweet
chips, or coating chocolate,
along with wax or Crisco,
in a microwave-safe bowl.
Microwave on High for 1½–2
minutes, or until melted.
6. Place each chocolate
ball on a thin-tined fork and
lower into melted chocolate.
When finished, place again
on waxed-paper-lined baking
sheet.
7. If you wish, sprinkle
with confectioners sugar or
roll in crushed nuts.
8. Refrigerate if it's
summer-time; otherwise,
store and serve at room
temperature.

Tips:
  *1. If you use raspberry chips,
dark chocolate is the best
coating. For peanut butter and
caramel chips, milk chocolate
is best.*
  *2. From the tester: Allow
plenty of time to make these.
They taste wonderful and
deserve to look as elegant as
they taste!*

A Tip —
  Clean up your kitchen
as you go. Don't wait until
there is a mountain of
dishes to do.

Peanut Butter Snowballs

Jenny R. Unternahrer
Wayland, IA

Makes 18 servings

Prep. Time: 30 minutes
Cooling Time: 1–2 hours

2 cups confectioners sugar
½ cup creamy peanut
  butter
¾ stick (6 Tbsp.) butter,
  softened
1 lb. almond bark

1. Combine sugar, peanut
butter, and butter in a large
mixing bowl. Mix well.
2. Use a 1" cookie scoop to
dip out and roll mixture into
balls. Place balls on waxed-
paper-lined baking sheet.
3. Chill balls for 30
minutes, or until firm.
4. Place almond bark in a
microwave-safe bowl. Microwave on High for 2 minutes.
Stir. Microwave on High
another minute. Stir. Microwave on High in 30-second
intervals until chocolate is
smooth when stirred.
5. Using a fork with thin
tines, lower balls one-by-one
into melted almond bark.
6. Place coated balls on
waxed-paper-lined baking
sheet to harden.

Crunchy Peanut Bark

Doyle Rounds
Bridgewater, VA

Makes 10 dozen

Prep Time: 10 minutes
Cooking Time: 5 minutes
Chilling Time: 1 hour

2 lbs. white confectionery coating
1 cup peanut butter
3 cups crispy rice cereal
2 cups dry roasted peanuts
2 cups miniature marshmallows

1. Place confectionery coating and peanut butter in a large microwave-safe bowl. Microwave at 50% power about 5 minutes.
2. Stir in remaining ingredients.
3. Drop by heaping tablespoonfuls onto waxed-paper-lined baking sheet.
4. Allow to cool thoroughly before serving or storing.

Tip: White confectionery coating is found in the baking section of most grocery stores or bulk food stores. It is sometimes labeled "almond bark" or "candy coating." It comes in blocks or disks.

Bird's Nest Candy

Susan Tjon
Austin, TX

Makes 36 pieces

Prep Time: 20 minutes
Cooling Time: 1 hour

12-oz. bag semi-sweet chocolate chips
½ cup milk chocolate chips
1 cup chopped cashews
1 cup chow mein noodles

1. Place both varieties of chocolate chips in microwave-safe bowl. Microwave on High for 1–1½ minutes. Stir. Microwave on High for 30-second intervals, until chips melt when stirred.
2. Stir in cashews and chow mein noodles. Toss until well coated.
3. Drop by teaspoonfuls onto waxed-paper-covered baking sheets.
4. Refrigerate until hardened, or allow to stand on countertop until firm.

Tip: You may substitute dark chocolate, white chocolate, or peanut butter chips for the semi-sweet chocolate chips, and use any nut of your choice.

I've made this using dark chocolate at Halloween. The kids think the candies look like a "ball of spiders."

Peanut Clusters

Barbara Walker
Sturgis, SD

Makes 36–40 pieces

Prep Time: 15 minutes
Cooling Time: 1 hour

half a 12-oz. pkg. chocolate chips
12-oz. pkg. peanut butter chips
12-oz. jar dry roasted peanuts

1. Place chocolate and peanut butter chips in a microwave-safe medium-sized bowl. Microwave on High for 1–1½ minutes. Stir. Continue microwaving on High for 30-second intervals, stirring after each time until chips are melted.
2. Stir in peanuts.
3. Drop by teaspoonfuls onto waxed-paper-covered baking sheets.
4. Refrigerate, or let stand on countertop, until firm.

Chocolate Grape-Nuts Candy

Darla Sathre
Baxter, MN

Makes 7 dozen

Prep Time: 15 minutes
Cooking Time: 1½ minutes
Cooling Time: 1 hour

12-oz. pkg. chocolate chips
1 can sweetened condensed milk
1 cup Grape-Nuts cereal
1 cup shredded *or* grated coconut
1 cup chopped walnuts

1. Combine chocolate chips and sweetened condensed milk in a microwave-safe bowl. Microwave on High for 1–1½ minutes, or until chips indicate that they're melted when stirred.
2. Add remaining ingredients and stir together quickly.
3. Drop by small spoonfuls onto waxed paper.
4. Let cool on countertop before eating or storing.

A Tip —

Use the paper from inside cereal boxes instead of waxed paper.

Peanut Butter Chews

Joanne Martin
Stevens, PA

Makes 25 pieces

Prep Time: 10–20 minutes

1 cup peanut butter, creamy *or* crunchy
1 cup light corn syrup
1 cup confectioners sugar
2 cups dry powdered milk
1 cup raisins, *optional*

1. Measure all ingredients and mix together in a large bowl.
2. Roll into 1" balls and place on a waxed-paper-lined baking sheet, or press into a greased 9 × 9 pan.
3. If using the latter method, allow to cool, and then cut into pieces.

My children loved to make this recipe by themselves at an early age because it was very easy for them. They used their—just-washed!—hands to mix it.

Toasted Pecan Cranberry Bark

Arlene Snyder
Millerstown, PA

Makes 15–20 servings

Prep Time: 30 minutes
Cooking Time: 18–20 minutes
Cooling Time: 1–2 hours

1 cup pecan halves
20-oz. pkg. white chocolate chips, *or* candy coating
¾ cup dried cranberries
¼ tsp. ground nutmeg

1. Preheat over to 325°.
2. Place pecans in a single layer on a baking sheet.
3. Bake 10–15 minutes until lightly toasted, stirring once. Cool.
4. Place chocolate chips or coating in a microwave-safe bowl. Microwave on High for 2 minutes. Stir. Microwave on High another minute. Stir. Microwave on High for 30-second intervals until chocolate is smooth when stirred.
5. Stir toasted pecans, cranberries, nutmeg, and melted chocolate together in a large mixing bowl.
6. Spread mixture ¼" thick on parchment-lined baking sheet.
7. Refrigerate until cool.
8. Break into pieces to serve or store.

Creamy No-Cook Mints

Janelle Reitz, Lancaster, PA

Makes 80–85 mints

Prep Time: 40–45 minutes

3-oz. pkg. light cream
  cheese, softened
¼ tsp. mint flavoring
2 drops green food
  coloring, *optional*
4¼ cups confectioners
  sugar
super-fine granulated sugar

1. Mix cream cheese, mint flavoring, and coloring if you wish in mixer on low speed until smooth (about 30 seconds).
2. Gradually add confectioners sugar while continuing to mix on low speed.
3. Mix about 1½ minutes, or until mixture becomes very stiff.

To shape mints:

1. Dip individual flexible candy molds in superfine sugar, coating the inside.
2. Press in mint mixture.
3. Turn out onto waxed paper covered with superfine sugar.
4. Repeat until mixture is used up.

OR:

1. Shape mixture into ¾" balls (about 1 tsp.).
2. Roll each ball in super-fine sugar.
3. Place on waxed-paper covered with superfine sugar.

4. Flatten slightly with thumb to form ¼" disks.
5. If you wish, press back of fork lightly on disks to form ridges.

Store finished mints in a tightly covered container in refrigerator. The mints also freeze well.

We served these mints at our wedding reception!

Cracker Candy

Anna Musser, Manheim, PA
Vicki J. Hill, Memphis, TN
Joan Brown, Warriors Mark, PA
Erma Martin, East Earl, PA
Pat Bishop, Bedminster, PA

Makes 10 servings

Prep. Time: 15 minutes
Cooking/Baking Time: 8–10
  minutes
Chilling Time: 2 hours

1 cup brown sugar
2 sticks (1 cup) butter
40 or more saltines, *or* club
  crackers
¾ cup chocolate chips, *or*
  M&Ms, *optional*
2 cups chopped nuts,
  optional

1. Boil brown sugar and butter together for 2–3 minutes.
2. Line an 11 × 15 baking pan with aluminum foil.
3. Lay 40 crackers on foil.
4. Pour butter and sugar mixture over crackers.
5. Bake at 425° for 5 minutes.
6. If you wish, immediately sprinkle chocolate chips or M&Ms over top after the crackers are baked.
7. Let stand for a few minutes, and then spread out with knife.
8. If you wish, immediately sprinkle with nuts.
9. Cool in fridge.
10. Peel crackers off foil and break into pieces.

English Toffee

Sharon Easter
Yuba City, CA

Makes 20 servings

Prep. Time: 20 minutes
Cooking Time: 10 minutes
Chilling Time: 1 hour

1 cup, *or* more, chopped
  walnuts *or* almonds,
  divided
1⅞ sticks (15 Tbsp.) butter
1½ tsp. water
½ cup brown sugar
½ cup granulated sugar
6-oz. pkg. chocolate chips

1. Lightly grease 2 8" pie
or cake pans. Sprinkle with
chopped nuts. Set aside.
2. In heavy cast-iron skillet
combine butter, water, and
sugars. Bring slowly to a boil
and cook for 5–8 minutes,
stirring constantly.
3. Pour gently over nuts so
as not to disturb them.
4. Sprinkle chocolate chips
over top and spread as they
melt.
5. Sprinkle remaining nuts
on top of chocolate.
6. Put in refrigerator to
harden.
7. Break up into small
pieces to serve.

Graham Cracker Chews

Lynne Bandel
Arcadia, IN

Makes 8 servings

Prep. Time: 15 minutes
Baking Time: 5–7 minutes
Cooling Time: 1 hour

graham crackers
1½ sticks (¾ cup) butter
1 cup pecan pieces
1 cup brown sugar

1. Cover lightly greased
baking sheet with graham
crackers.
2. Melt butter in a large
skillet.
3. Stir pecans into butter
and brown them, stirring
frequently.
4. Pour buttered nuts over
graham crackers.
5. Bake at 350° for 5–7
minutes.
6. Allow to cool.
7. Remove from baking
sheet, breaking the chews
into pieces.

Peanut Butter Cups

Barb Harvey
Quarryville, PA

Makes 24 servings

Prep. Time: 15 minutes
Cooking Time: 2 minutes
Cooling Time: 10–15 minutes

1⅓ cups graham cracker
  crumbs
2⅓ cups confectioners
  sugar
2 sticks (1 cup) butter,
  melted
1 cup chunky peanut
  butter
2 cups milk chocolate
  chips

1. Mix first 4 ingredients
together in a good-sized
mixing bowl.
2. Pat into lightly oiled
9 × 13 pan.
3. Place chocolate chips
in a microwave-safe bowl.
Microwave on High for 1–1½
minutes, or until chips are
clearly melted when stirred.
Continue microwaving on
High for 30-second intervals
if more time is needed to melt
the chips.
4. Pour melted chocolate
over peanut mixture. Spread
with a knife to cover.
5. Refrigerate 10–15
minutes.
6. Cut into squares. Do not
allow candy to get too cold or
chocolate will crack.

Snacks and Beverages

Honey Mustard Pretzels

Janice Burkholder, Richfield, PA
Melissa Sensenig
Newmanstown, PA

Makes 20 servings

Prep Time: 20 minutes
Cooking Time: 2 hours

2 lbs. broken sourdough
   pretzels
¾ cup vegetable oil
½ cup prepared mustard
½ cup honey
¼ cup sour cream powder
   (sold in bulk-food stores)

1. Break pretzels as fine as possible into a large bowl. Set aside.
2. Combine remaining ingredients in a bowl.
3. Pour mixture over pretzels. Mix thoroughly to coat every piece.
4. Spread coated pretzels in a jelly-roll pan or baking sheet with 1" sides.

5. Bake at 200°, stirring every 15–20 minutes for 2 hours.
6. Cool completely. Store in airtight container until ready to serve. Delicious served warm or cold!

Seasoned Pretzels or Crackers

Eileen Eash, Carlsbad, NM
Marie Raber, Millersburg, OH
Trudy Kutter, Corfu, NY
Ruth Shank, Monroe, GA
Karen Kay Tucker, Manteca, CA
Barbara Gautcher
Harrisonburg, VA

Makes 15 servings

Prep Time: 15 minutes
Baking Time: 1 hour

20-oz. bag large thick
   pretzels, *or* nuggets, *or*
   oyster crackers
1 envelope, *or* 2 Tbsp., dry
   Ranch dressing mix
½ cup canola oil

1 ½ tsp. dill weed
1 ½ tsp. garlic powder

1. Break large pretzels into bite-sized pieces. Place in large mixing bowl.
2. Mix remaining ingredients in another bowl and pour over pretzels. Stir well.
3. Pour mixture into jelly-roll pan or cookie sheet with 1" sides.
4. Bake at 200° for 1 hour, stirring every 15 minutes.
5. Allow to cool. Keep in tightly closed container until ready to serve.

Snappy Taco Crackers

Jennifer Archer, Kalona, IA

Makes 8 servings

Prep. Time: 5 minutes
Cooking/Baking Time: 15–20 minutes

3 10-oz. pkgs. oyster crackers
¾ cup vegetable, *or* olive, oil
1 envelope dry taco seasoning
½ tsp. garlic powder
½ tsp. chili powder

1. Place crackers in large roasting pan or 9 × 13 baking pan. Drizzle with oil.
2. Combine the seasonings in a small bowl. Sprinkle over crackers. Toss to coat.
3. Bake at 350° for 15–20 minutes, or until golden brown. Stir half-way through baking time.

Crunchy Taco-Flavored Snacks

Sharon Miller
Holmesville, OH

Makes 24 servings

Prep Time: 5–10 minutes
Baking Time: 45 minutes

1 stick (½ cup) butter, melted
1.25-oz. envelope dry taco seasoning
8 cups cereal, such as corn squares, rice squares, toasted oats
3 cups pretzel sticks
1 cup peanuts, *or* other nuts

1. Combine melted butter and dry taco seasoning in a small saucepan.
2. Mix cereal, pretzels, and nuts in a large bowl.
3. Pour butter mixture over dry ingredients. Transfer to 2 large baking sheets with 1" sides.
4. Bake in preheated 250° oven for 45 minutes. Stir every 15 minutes.
5. Let cool and store in airtight containers.

Payday Mix

Moreen Weaver, Bath, NY

Makes 16 servings

Prep Time: 20 minutes
Cooking Time: 10 minutes

6 cups Rice Chex cereal
2 cups salted peanuts (without skins)
1 cup light corn syrup
1 cup sugar
1¾ cups peanut butter
1 tsp. vanilla, *optional*

1. Mix cereal and peanuts together in a large bowl. Set aside.
2. Combine corn syrup and sugar in a medium-sized saucepan. Cook on medium heat until mixture boils, stirring constantly.
3. Remove from heat. Immediately add peanut butter, and vanilla if you wish. Stir until peanut butter is melted.
4. Stir into cereal and peanuts, stirring the sauce in as you pour so that the cereal and peanuts are evenly and thoroughly coated.
5. Spread on foil to cool, breaking mix into smaller pieces.
6. When cooled, store in airtight container.

Our family was on our way home from vacation when we stopped half-way at a friend's house for the night. The next morning, she made this snack for us to eat on the way home. It's been a favorite ever since!

Crispix Snack

Mary Jane Hoober
Shipshewana, IN

Makes 25–30 servings

Prep. Time: 10 minutes
Cooking/Baking Time: 1 hour

1 cup brown sugar
1 stick (½ cup) butter
½ cup light corn syrup
1-lb. box Crispix cereal
1 cup broken pecans, *or*
  more or less, according
  to your preference

1. Melt brown sugar,
butter, and corn syrup
together in a medium-sized
saucepan. Don't allow to boil.
Stir frequently.
2. Put Crispix and pecans
into a large roaster or baking
sheet with 1" sides.
3. Pour sauce over dry
ingredients, stirring the
Crispix and peanuts as you
pour to make sure everything
is well coated.
4. Bake at 250° for 1 hour,
stirring every 15 minutes.
5. Spoon out onto waxed
paper to cool.
6. Store in tightly covered
container.

Puppy Chow

Lena Sheaffer
Port Matilda, PA

Makes 15 servings

Prep Time: 20 minutes
Cooking Time: 5–7 minutes

1 stick (½ cup) butter
1 cup peanut butter
1 cup chocolate chips
9 cups cereal (Chex,
  Cheerios, *or* a mixture)
2 cups confectioners sugar

1. Melt butter, peanut
butter, and chocolate chips
together in a medium-sized
saucepan.
2. Place cereal in a large
bowl. Pour sauce over cereal,
stirring it in as you pour
to make sure cereal is well
coated.
3. When cereal is cool,
put cereal and confectioners
sugar in a Ziploc bag.
4. Make sure bag is
securely locked. Coat cereal
evenly by shaking it together
with the sugar.
5. Store in airtight con-
tainer or Ziploc bags.

Delightfully Peanuty Snack Mix

Rhonda Freed
Croghan, NY

Makes 25–30 servings

Prep. Time: 20 minutes
Cooking/Baking Time: 5 minutes

2 3-oz. boxes vanilla cook-
  and-serve pudding
1 cup honey
1 cup peanut butter
2 cups peanuts
13-oz. box (14 cups) Kix
  cereal

1. Mix dry vanilla pudding
mix and honey in medium-
sized saucepan. Bring to a
boil, stirring constantly. Boil
1 minute.
2. Remove from stove and
add peanut butter.
3. Mix peanuts and Kix
together in a very large bowl.
4. Pour honey mixture
over cereal, mixing the sauce
in as you pour so that the
dry ingredients are all well
coated.
5. Allow to cool completely.
Store in a tightly sealed
container.

Caramel Corn

Joyce Bergen, Goessel, KS
Brenda Lyndaker, Croghan, NY

Makes 20 servings

Prep. Time: 20 minutes
Cooking/Baking Time: 10 minutes

10 cups popped popcorn
1 stick (½ cup) butter
½ cup brown sugar
8 large marshmallows, cut
    into pieces

1. Place popcorn in a large bowl.
2. Place butter, brown sugar, and marshmallows in a medium-sized saucepan. Heat over low heat until all ingredients melt, stirring frequently.
3. Pour sauce over popcorn, stirring as you pour to make sure popcorn is fully coated.

Baked Caramel Corn

Colleen Heatwole, Burton, MI

Makes 20–24 servings

Prep Time: 20 minutes
Baking Time: 1 hour

2 sticks (1 cup) butter
2 cups brown sugar
½ cup light corn syrup
¼ tsp. cream of tartar
½ tsp. baking soda

Base:
1½–2 cups unpopped
    popcorn

1. Pop popcorn first, dividing popped corn into two large bowls for easier mixing.
2. Combine butter, brown sugar, corn syrup, and cream of tartar in a medium-sized saucepan. Bring to a boil over low to medium heat, and then boil for 5 minutes, stirring frequently.
3. Add ½ tsp. baking soda to sauce. *Immediately* remove from heat and drizzle over the two large bowls of popcorn.
4. Stir to coat all popcorn as fully as possible. (Ask a friend to help if one's nearby; see story below.)
5. Spray 2 baking pans (at least 9 × 13) with non-stick cooking spray. Divide coated popcorn between 2 baking pans.
6. Bake 1 hour at 200°. Stir popcorn every 15 minutes.
7. Serve warm or at room temperature.

My daughter and I make this recipe together. I pop the corn in an air popper while she stirs up the sauce. You need to have the soda standing by to add it quickly when the syrup is finished boiling.

When it's time to pour the sauce onto the popcorn, Jen pours, and I stir in order to coat the popcorn evenly.

Cooking with someone else is always more fun than cooking solo.

This snack is requested by our friends at Super-Bowl parties and college gatherings.

Amish Peanut Butter

Ruthie Yoder
Goshen, IN

Makes 2 cups

Prep Time: 5–10 minutes

1¼ cups light corn syrup
1 cup creamy peanut
    butter
½ cup marshmallow creme

1. Mix all ingredients together in a good-sized mixing bowl.
2. If it is too stiff to spread on bread or fresh fruit, add a bit of water to make it spread more easily.

Every summer I supervise 15–20 students in a summer clean-up project. Sometimes I bring one or two loaves of freshly made bread and Amish Peanut Butter for their snack. They love it! At the end of the summer I give them each a pint as a thank-you gift.

Stuffed Tortilla Pie

Amanda Becker
Denver, PA

Makes 6–8 servings

Prep Time: 10 minutes
Baking Time: 5 minutes

**1 can pie filling of your
   choice**
**8-oz. pkg. cream cheese,
   softened**
2 large flour tortillas

1. Preheat oven to 350°.
2. Spread cream cheese over each tortilla, making sure to cover the edges.
3. Spread pie filling over half the surface of each tortilla, leaving the edges free of the filling.
4. Fold tortilla in half. Press edges closed.
5. Lay tortillas on large lightly greased baking sheet.
6. Bake for 5 minutes.
7. Cut into wedges and serve.

Pocket Apple Pies

Norma Saltzman
Shickley, NE

Makes 8 servings

Prep Time: 15–20 minutes
Baking Time: 15–20 minutes

1 Tbsp. sugar
¼ tsp. cinnamon
**1-lb 1.3-oz. can refrigerated
   Grands extra-rich, *or*
   flaky, biscuits**
**1 cup cinnamon-and-spice
   apple pie filling and
   topping**
**1 Tbsp. and 1 tsp. butter,
   melted**

1. Heat oven to 375°.
2. Spray cookie sheet.
3. Combine sugar and cinnamon in a small bowl. Set aside.
4. Separate dough into 8 biscuits.
5. Press or roll each to form a 5" round. Place each on cookie sheet.
6. Stir apple pie filling to break it up a bit. Place 2 Tbsp. pie filling on half of the surface of each flattened biscuit.
7. Fold biscuit dough over filling. Press edges with fork to seal. Prick top of each 3 times with fork.
8. Brush each filled pocket with melted butter. Sprinkle with sugar-cinnamon mixture.
9. Bake at 375° for 15–20 minutes, or until golden brown.
10. Remove from cookie

sheet immediately. Cool 5 minutes before serving. Serve warm.

Tip: These are really good served with vanilla ice cream.

Frozen Yogurt Pops

Jenelle Miller
Marion, SD

Makes 12 servings

Prep Time: 10 minutes
*Freezing Time: 8 hours, or
   overnight*

1 cup strawberry yogurt
¾ cup orange juice
**2 cups sliced strawberries,
   frozen *or* fresh**
**2 tsp. sugar, *or* maybe
   more if you use fresh
   berries**

1. Blend all ingredients in blender until very smooth, about 2 minutes.
2. Pour mixture into 12 small paper cups.
3. Cover each cup with a piece of foil.
4. Poke a hole in the foil with a knife and stick a popsicle stick through.
5. Freeze overnight.

Note from the tester: This makes a delicious smoothie straight from the blender, in case your children can't wait for the pops to freeze.

Orange Pecans

Vicki J. Hill
Memphis, TN

Makes 4 cups

Prep Time: 5 minutes
Cooking Time: 15–20 minutes
Cooling Time: 30 minutes

juice of 1 large orange
rind of 1 large orange,
    grated
1 cup sugar
4 cups pecan halves

1. Place orange juice, rind, and sugar in a medium-sized saucepan. Bring to a quick boil over medium-high heat.
2. Add pecans. Mix syrup and nuts thoroughly.
3. Cook over medium heat until all syrup is absorbed by the nuts, stirring constantly.
4. Remove from heat and continue to stir until pecans separate.
5. Turn onto waxed paper to harden and cool.
6. Break up before serving or storing in an airtight container.

This is something we enjoy at the holidays. You can't eat just one! Really!

Sugared Pecans

Janet Derstine
Telford, PA

Makes 6 cups

Prep Time: 15 minutes
Baking Time: 30 minutes
Cooling Time: 30 minutes

1 egg white, beaten
1 Tbsp. water
1 lb. pecan halves
1 cup sugar
1 ½ tsp. salt
1 tsp. cinnamon

1. Heat oven to 300°.
2. Beat egg white until stiff in a good-sized mixing bowl.
3. Fold water and pecans into egg white.
4. In a small bowl, mix sugar, salt, and cinnamon together. Sprinkle over pecan mixture and mix well.
5. Spread on a non-stick cookie sheet. Bake for 30 minutes, stirring once or twice.
6. Remove from oven. Stir and separate pecans. Cool before serving or storing in an airtight container.

A Tip —

When testing new recipes have your family rate them. Write comments, along with the date that you made the recipe, in the page margins next to the recipe.

Bagel Pizzas

Miriam Nolt, New Holland, PA

Makes 4–6 servings

Prep Time: 10 minutes
Baking Time: 8–10 minutes

6 bagels, sliced and warmed
    or lightly toasted
1½ cups tomato pizza sauce
1½ cups shredded
    mozzarella cheese
3 tsp. dried oregano

1. Preheat oven to 350°.
2. Arrange bagel halves on baking sheet. Top each one with pizza sauce.
3. Then top each with cheese, and then oregano.
4. Bake until cheese is melted, about 8 to 10 minutes.

Caramelized Pear, Onion, and Gorgonzola Cheese Pizza

Kathy Hertzler, Lancaster, PA

Makes 8 servings

Prep Time: 25 minutes
Baking Time: 20 minutes

1 fresh *or* frozen (pre-baked) whole-wheat pizza crust
2 firm but ripe pears
2 Tbsp. butter
1 large yellow onion
¼ lb. Gorgonzola cheese
½ cup chopped hazelnuts, *optional*

1. Thinly slice (¼" thick) pears and saute over medium heat in 2 Tbsp. butter for 5 minutes.
2. Thinly slice onion and add to pears. Turn heat to low. Saute slowly for 10 minutes, or until onion is soft but the pears still hold their shape. The onions should be caramel-colored, but not browned.
3. Scatter mixture evenly over pizza crust.
4. Crumble Gorgonzola cheese and scatter evenly over pears and onions.
5. Add hazelnuts if you wish.
6. Bake following the packaged pizza crust instructions.
7. Cut into 16 appetizer or snack-sized wedges.

This can actually be a "meal pizza." My husband and I can polish off one of these for dinner.

Spinach Cheese Roll-Ups

June S. Groff, Denver, PA

Makes 12 servings

Prep. Time: 20 minutes
Cooking/Baking Time: 10–12 minutes

8-oz. tube refrigerated crescent rolls
⅔ of an 8-oz. block of cream cheese, softened
half an envelope dry Ranch salad dressing mix
4 slices deli ham
½ cup packed fresh baby spinach

1. Separate crescent dough into 4 rectangles. Seal perforations.
2. Spread cream cheese over each rectangle. Sprinkle dry salad dressing mix evenly over each rectangle.
3. Top each with ham and spinach.
4. Roll up each rectangle tightly, jelly-roll style, starting with a short side. Pinch seams to seal.
5. Cut each roll into 6 slices.
6. Place slices, cut-side down, on greased baking sheets.
7. Bake at 400° for 10–12 minutes. Serve warm.

Tip: You can make the rolls through Step 4, 24 hours ahead of when you want to serve them. Refrigerate until ready to bake. Slice just before baking and proceed through Steps 5–7.

Lacy Parmesan Crisps

Gwendolyn P. Chapman
Gwinn, MI

Makes 6 servings

Prep. Time: 10 minutes
Cooking/Baking Time: 7–10 minutes

3-oz. piece Parmesan cheese, grated

1. Put oven rack in middle position and preheat oven to 375°. Line non-stick baking sheet with greased tinfoil or Silpat.
2. Arrange mounds (approximately 1 Tbsp. rounded) of cheese 3" apart. Flatten each mound lightly to form a 3" round.
3. Bake until golden, 7–10 minutes.
4. Transfer with spatula to rack. Cool 5 minutes before serving or storing.

Natalia's Soft Pretzels

Laura R. Showalter, Dayton, VA

Makes 8–10 servings

Prep. Time: 60–70 minutes
Cooking/Baking Time: 5–7 minutes

2¼ cups warm water
2 Tbsp. yeast
6–6 ½ cups unbleached flour, *divided*
½ cup brown sugar
1 tsp. salt
6 cups very hot water
¼ cup baking soda
pretzel salt and melted butter, *optional*

1. Dissolve yeast in 2¼ cups warm water. Pour into a large mixing bowl.

2. Stir in 2 cups flour. Add sugar and salt.

3. Continue adding flour, stirring until dough is too stiff to stir. Then roll out onto counter and knead until dough is smooth and soft.

4. Place dough in large, lightly greased mixing bowl. Cover with a tea towel. Place in a warm place.

5. Let dough rise 20–30 minutes.

6. While dough is rising, grease 2 large baking sheets, or cover them with parchment.

7. Just before the end of the dough's rising time, bring 6 cups water to a boil in a large stockpot. Stir baking soda into water until dissolved. Pour into a wide bowl.

8. When dough has finished rising, divide dough in half. Divide each half into 6 portions.

9. Roll each portion into a 16"-long rope. Form each into a pretzel shape.

10. Dip each pretzel into hot soda water. Lay briefly on bread cloth or towel to absorb excess moisture.

11. Place on greased, or parchment-covered, baking sheets.

12. Sprinkle with pretzel salt if you wish.

13. Bake at 400° for 5–7 minutes, or until golden brown.

14. Brush with melted butter if you wish. Serve warm.

15. You can freeze any extra pretzels after they're baked.

Tips:

1. The pretzels are best if you replace 2 cups white flour with 2 cups freshly ground whole wheat flour.

2. The possibilities for serving these soft pretzels are many: Serve with cheese sauce or hot mustard. Sprinkle with cinnamon sugar, or sour cream and onion powder. Form them into breadsticks and sprinkle them with herbed Parmesan cheese when they come out of the oven. Then dip in pizza sauce. Add raisins to the dough and drizzle with icing when they've cooled a bit from baking.

Iced Tea— Brewed or Sun

Stacy Stoltzfus, Grantham, PA

Makes 16 servings

Prep. Time: 5 minutes
Cooking/Baking Time: 20 minutes, or 6–8 hours

4 cups, *or 1 gallon,* water
3 regular, *or decaf,* tea bags
3 flavored tea bags (mint, raspberry, peach, etc.), *or 1 pint tightly packed fresh mint leaves and stems, washed thoroughly*
⅓ cup sugar, *or to taste*

To make Brewed Tea:

1. Bring 4 cups water to a boil in a large saucepan.

2. Place tea bags, or fresh mint tea, in a 1-gallon pitcher or non-reactive large bowl (non-breakable when heated quickly).

3. Pour boiling water over tea.

4. Cover. Steep approximately 10 minutes.

5. Remove tea bags, or tea, and stir in sugar. Stir until sugar is dissolved.

6. Add enough water to make 1 gallon.

7. Pour over ice or refrigerate until cold.

To make Sun Tea:

1. Place tea bags in a gallon jar. (I haven't had good luck with fresh tea using this method.) Cover with water to make one gallon.

2. Cover jar. Place in the

warm sun for several hours (6–8) until tea is the strength you like.

3. Add sugar and stir to dissolve.

4. Pour over ice or refrigerate until cold.

Summer Iced Tea

Sharon Wantland
Menomonee Falls, WI

Makes 16–18 servings

Prep. Time: 15 minutes
Chilling Time: 4–5 hours

8 tea bags
4 cups boiling water
1 cup sugar, *or more,* depending on your taste preference
6-oz. can frozen lemonade, thawed
6-oz. can frozen orange juice, thawed
10 cups water
1 cup pineapple juice

1. Steep the tea bags in the boiling water for 5 minutes. Discard tea bags.

2. Combine all ingredients in a very large pitcher, jar, or bowl. (You may need to divide the ingredients evenly between 2 containers to blend them thoroughly.)

3. Cover and place in fridge until thoroughly chilled.

Mint Tea Punch

Lavina Hochstedler
Grand Blanc, MI

Makes 24 4-oz. servings

Prep. Time: 20 minutes
Steeping Time: 30 minutes
Chilling Time: 3–4 hours

4 cups boiling water
18 6" stems fresh mint leaf tea (spearmint works well)
½ cup sugar, *or more or less depending on your taste preference*
¼ cup lemon juice
3 cups pineapple juice
2 cups 7-Up

1. Bring water to boil in a good-sized saucepan.

2. Turn off heat and submerge tea leaves in hot water.

3. Allow to steep 30 minutes.

4. Remove tea leaves, squeezing them (but don't burn yourself) to extract the flavor.

5. Stir in sugar and lemon juice.

6. Pour into large pitcher or bowl and cool to room temperature.

7. Stir in pineapple juice. Cover and refrigerate until thoroughly chilled.

8. Just before serving, stir in 7-Up.

Tip: You can enhance the flavor by adding 1 more pint pineapple juice if you wish.

Old-Fashioned Lemonade

Marsha Sabus
Fallbrook, CA

Makes 12 servings

Prep. Time: 3 minutes
Cooking/Baking Time: 10–12 minutes
Chilling Time: 3 hours

1 ½ cups sugar
1 ½ cups water
1 Tbsp. grated lemon zest
1 ½ cups fresh lemon juice (8–9 lemons)
ice
thin slices lemon, *or* mint leaves, for garnish

1. In a small saucepan, stir together sugar, water, and lemon zest.

2. Bring to a boil, stirring constantly.

3. Boil 5 minutes, stirring often.

4. Remove pan from heat and let syrup cool.

5. When syrup is cool, stir in lemon juice.

6. Transfer to a glass jar or pitcher. Cover and refrigerate for up to 2 weeks.

7. When ready to serve, place 2 ice cubes in a tall glass. Add ¼ cup syrup and ¾ cup cold water. Stir well and garnish with lemon slice or mint.

Peachy Lemonade

Monica ByDeLey
Annville, PA

Makes 8 servings

Prep. Time: 3–5 minutes
Chilling Time: 3–4 hours

2 quarts lemonade
10-oz. can peach, *or*
apricot, nectar
1 cup frozen peach slices
fresh mint sprigs

1. In a 3-quart glass pitcher, combine lemonade and nectar.
2. Cover and chill thoroughly in refrigerator.
3. Before serving, stir lemonade mixture. Stir in frozen peach slices and mint.

Berry Cooler

Melanie Mohler
Ephrata, PA

Makes 8 servings

Prep. Time: 5–10 minutes

12-oz. can frozen juice
concentrate (your
choice of lime, lemon,
cranberry, orange, etc.)
48-oz. container chilled
seltzer water
fresh fruit, such as sliced
lemons, *or* limes, *or*
raspberries

1. Mix frozen juice concentrate and chilled seltzer water in a glass pitcher.
2. Top off with fresh fruit.
3. Serve immediately.

Party Punch

Hazel Lightcap Propst
Oxford, PA

Makes 28 8-oz. servings

Prep. Time: 10 minutes
Chilling Time: 4 hours or more

12-oz. container frozen
lemonade
12-oz. container frozen
orange juice
1 quart unsweetened
pineapple juice
1 pint cranberry juice
1 large bottle ginger ale

1. Prepare frozen juices according to directions on can in a large pitcher or bowl.
2. Stir in pineapple and cranberry juices.
3. Cover and chill.
4. Just before serving, blend in ginger ale.

Ginger Beer Fruit Punch

Barbara Sparks
Glen Burnie, MD

Makes 10–12 servings

Prep. Time: 10 minutes

2 cups cranberry juice
2 cups pineapple juice
2 cups grapefruit juice
sugar to taste
3 12-oz. bottles ginger beer,
or ginger ale

1. Mix the juices together in a 2-quart pitcher. If too tart, add sugar to taste.
2. Refrigerate until ready to serve.
3. At serving time, pour mixed juices into punch bowl over ice.
4. Add the ginger beer just as guests arrive.

Tip: Ginger beer is worth the search because of its zesty ginger bite. But if you can't find it, ginger ale is a very good substitute.

Without-Alcohol Wine

SuAnne Burkholder
Millersburg, OH

Makes 3+ quarts

Prep. Time: 10 minutes

1 ½ cups grape juice
   concentrate
1 cup orange juice
   concentrate
1 ½ cups water
¼ cup lemon juice
1 cup sugar
2-liter bottle ginger ale

1. Mix all ingredients
together in a large pitcher, jar,
or bowl, except ginger ale.
2. Just before serving, mix
in ginger ale.
3. Serve in individual
glasses over crushed ice.

Rhubarb Drink

Becky Frey
Lebanon, PA

Makes 4–6 servings

Prep. Time: 15–20 minutes
Cooking/Baking Time: 5 minutes
Chilling Time: 2–3 hours

3 cups uncooked rhubarb,
   diced
1¼ cups sugar
4 cups water
½ cup orange juice
juice of 1 lemon
1 cup ginger ale, *or* 7-Up
orange *or* lemon slices,
   optional

1. Place rhubarb, sugar,
and water in a saucepan.
2. Bring to boil and boil for
5 minutes.
3. Drain and strain rhu-
barb from syrup.
4. Pour into large pitcher.
Cover and refrigerate until
thoroughly chilled.
5. Add juices and ginger ale.
6. Serve in frosty glasses.
Garnish each with an orange
or lemon slice if you wish.

*Tip: Since rhubarb is more
readily available in spring and
early summer, you can cook
the first 3 ingredients and after
straining, can the liquid. It's all
ready to use anytime of year.
Just add juices and ginger ale
to serve.*

Raspberry Swizzle

Jennifer Archer
Kalona, IA

Makes 16 servings

Prep. Time: 10 minutes
Chilling Time: 15–20 minutes

2 tubs Crystal Light
   lemonade
3 quarts club soda, chilled
12-oz. container frozen
   limeade concentrate,
   thawed
1 quart raspberry sherbet
raspberries for garnish

1. Pour Crystal Light into
large punch bowl. Add soda
and limeade concentrate.
2. Stir until completely
dissolved.
3. Scoop sherbet into
punch 15–20 minutes before
serving.
4. Place a raspberry in
each glass of punch, or float
in punch bowl.

Creamsicle

Joyce L. Moser, Copenhagen, NY

Makes 15 servings

Prep. Time: 10–15 minutes

1 quart vanilla ice cream, softened
2 pints orange sherbet, softened
16-oz. bottle lemon-lime soda
1 quart milk
fresh orange slices, *optional*

1. Combine softened ice cream, sherbet, and soda in a large bowl or pitcher.
2. Gradually add milk and stir vigorously until mixture is smooth.
3. Serve in a punch bowl.
4. Garnish with orange slices if you wish.

Banana Nog

Esther J. Mast
Lancaster, PA

Makes 4 servings

Prep. Time: 10 minutes

4 ripe bananas, peeled
1 ½ cups skim milk
1 ½ cups plain non-fat yogurt
¼ tsp. rum extract
ground nutmeg for garnish

1. Add all ingredients except nutmeg to blender or food processor.
2. Puree until smooth.
3. Pour into 4 fancy serving glasses and top each with a pinch of nutmeg.

Berry Yummy Smoothy

Teddy Decker
Albuquerque, NM

Makes 2–3 servings

Prep. Time: 5 minutes

1 cup milk
1 very ripe banana, sliced
1 cup frozen mixed berries
¼ cup half-and-half, *or* ⅛ cup cream

1. Place all ingredients in blender.
2. Puree until smooth.

Strawberry Cream

Juanita Lyndaker
Croghan, NY

Makes 4 servings

Prep. Time: 5–6 minutes

2 cups stemmed strawberries, unsweetened frozen *or* fresh, cut-up if large

2–4 Tbsp. sugar, *optional*, and according to your taste preference
2 cups milk

1. Place strawberries in blender.
2. Add sugar if you wish, and milk.
3. Blend until smooth.

Variation: Instead of milk, use slightly softened vanilla ice cream or frozen yogurt.

Mango Lassi

Esther J. Mast
Lancaster, PA

Makes 1 serving

Prep. Time: 5 minutes

¼ cup yogurt, plain *or* vanilla
¼ cup skim milk
¼ cup mango puree
a few ice cubes, broken

1. Place all ingredients in blender.
2. Cover and blend just until well mixed.

Tip: Mango puree comes in a can and can usually be found in an Indian grocery store or in the international aisle of a traditional supermarket.

Fruit Smoothie

Jolyn Nolt, Lititz, PA

Makes 4 servings

Prep. Time: 5 minutes

¾ cup frozen unsweetened
   strawberries
¾ cup frozen blueberries
¼ cup sugar, *optional*
1 tsp. vanilla
milk to fill 4-cup blender
6 ice cubes (if fruit is fresh,
   not frozen)

1. Put fruit, sugar if you
wish, and vanilla into a 4-cup
blender.
2. Fill blender to 4-cup
mark with milk.
3. Blend until smooth.

*Variation: Add 6 broken-up
ice cubes to Step 1 if you use
fresh fruit instead of frozen.*

Very Berry Smoothie

Jenelle Miller, Marion, SD

Makes 2 servings

Prep. Time: 5 minutes

1 ½ cups frozen triple-
   berry mix (strawberries,
   blueberries, raspberries)
½ cup vanilla yogurt
⅓ cup raspberry, *or*
   cranberry, juice cocktail
⅓ cup milk

1. Place all ingredients in
blender.
2. Blend for 1 minute, and
then serve.

Orange Smoothie

Natalia Showalter, Mt. Solon, VA
Anna Musser, Manheim, PA

Makes 4–6 servings

Prep. Time: 10 minutes

2 cups milk
⅓ cup sugar
6-oz. can frozen orange
   juice concentrate
1–2 tsp. vanilla, according
   to your taste preference
12 ice cubes, broken up

1. Combine all ingredients
in blender. Blend until smooth.
2. Serve immediately.

*Variation: Replace half the
milk with plain or vanilla yogurt,
and increase sugar to ½–⅔ cup.*

Fruit Slush

Suellen Fletcher
Noblesville, IN

Makes 15 servings

Prep. Time: 20 minutes
*Cooking and Cooling Time: 30
   minutes*
*Freezing Time: 8 hours or
   overnight*
Thawing Time: 2–3 hours

1 cup water
1 cup sugar
1 large can crushed
   pineapple, undrained
3 ripe bananas
1 quart strawberries,
   stemmed, cleaned, and
   sliced
6-oz. can orange juice
   concentrate
1 concentrate can of water

1. In a saucepan heat 1 cup
water to boiling.
2. Stir in sugar to dissolve.
Set aside to cool.
3. In a good-sized bowl,
combine fruit.
4. Add orange juice concentrate, 6-oz. container water,
and sugar water to fruit.
5. Using an old-fashioned
potato smasher, crush fruit
and liquids together.
6. Cover bowl. Place
in freezer for 8 hours or
overnight.
7. Set out 2-3 hours before
serving to partially thaw.
8. Serve when mixture
looks like crystals.

Chocolate Smoothie

Jeannine Janzen
Elbing, KS

Makes 6–7 servings

Prep. Time: 5–10 minutes

2 ½ cups milk, *divided*
½ cup chocolate syrup
½ tsp. vanilla
1 quart chocolate ice cream, softened

1. In a blender, combine 1 cup milk, syrup, vanilla, and ice cream.
2. Cover and blend until smooth.
3. Add remaining milk. Blend.
4. Pour into cups and serve.

Chocolate Raspberry Frosty

Donna Treloar
Hartford City, IN

Makes 3 servings

Prep. Time: 3–4 minutes

1 pint chocolate frozen yogurt, softened
½ cup milk
½ cup fresh, *or* frozen (thawed), raspberries
2 Tbsp. raspberry syrup

1. Place all ingredients in a blender.
2. Cover and blend just until smooth.
3. Pour into cups and serve immediately.

Iced Coffee Treat

Meredith Miller, Dover, DE

Makes 6–8 servings

Prep. Time: 2 minutes

6 cups brewed coffee, still hot
½ cup sugar
1 cup cream
crushed ice

1. Dissolve sugar in hot coffee.
2. Stir in cold cream.
3. Serve in glasses filled with crushed ice.

Chocolate Almond Coffee

Sharon Wantland
Menomonee Fall, WI

Makes 4 servings

Prep. Time: 15 minutes

½ cup whipping cream
2 tsp. confectioners sugar
⅛ tsp. almond extract
4 scoops (1 scoop for each cup) chocolate ice cream
4 cups strong hot coffee

1. Beat the cream, confectioners sugar, and almond extract in a chilled bowl until stiff.
2. Put 1 scoop ice cream in each of 4 cups.
3. Pour coffee over ice cream.
4. Top with flavored whipped cream.
5. Serve immediately.

Capputeanos

Martha Ann Auker
Landisburg, PA

Makes 2 servings

Prep. Time: 2 minutes
Cooking Time: 2 minutes
Steeping Time: 5 minutes

2 cups milk
2 Tbsp. brown sugar
2 cinnamon apple-flavored
   tea bags
whipped cream for
   garnish, *optional*

1. In a small saucepan,
bring milk and sugar to
boiling point over high heat.
2. Remove from heat. Add
tea bags.
3. Cover and steep 5
minutes.
4. Remove tea bags. Serve
drink in mugs, garnished
with whipped cream if you
wish.

Apple Cinnamon Tea

Anita Troyer
Fairview, MI

Makes 4 servings

Prep. Time: 5 minutes
Cooking/Baking Time: 10–15
   minutes

2 medium-sized yellow
   delicious apples, peeled,
   cored, and sliced
5 cups water
2 Tbsp. orange juice
   concentrate
2 *or* 3 cinnamon sticks
¼ cup sugar

1. In a good-sized sauce-
pan, heat together apples,
water, orange juice concentrate, and cinnamon stick.
2. Simmer 10 minutes, or
until apples are soft. Stir to
blend ingredients well.
3. Stir in sugar until fully
dissolved.
4. Serve warm.

*Variation: Add a peppermint
tea bag to Steps 1 and 2.
Remove after simmering
mixture for 10 minutes.*

Hot Apple Cider

Andrea Cunningham
Arlington, KS

Makes 16 servings

Prep. Time: 5 minutes
Cooking/Baking Time: 1 hour

1 gallon apple cider
1 tsp. whole cloves
1 tsp. ground allspice
3 cinnamon sticks, broken
⅔ cup packed brown
   sugar, *optional*

1. Place apple cider in a
large saucepan.
2. Put spices in a coffee
filter or muslin tea bag. Tie
filter or bag at top. Place in
pan with cider.
3. Simmer for 45 minutes.
4. Taste. Add up to ⅔ cup
brown sugar if you wish. Stir
until dissolved.
5. Return to heat and
continue simmering another
15 minutes.
6. Serve warm.

A Tip —

   Don't be afraid to experiment and make changes in
recipes. If a recipe calls for an ingredient you don't care for,
either substitute something else, or leave it out.

Assumptions about Ingredients in *Fix-It and Enjoy-It 5-Ingredient Recipes*

flour = unbleached *or* white, and all-purpose

oatmeal or oats = dry, quick *or* rolled (old-fashioned), unless specified

pepper = black, finely ground

rice = regular, long-grain (not minute or instant unless specified)

salt = table salt

shortening = solid, not liquid

sugar = granulated sugar (not brown and not confectioners)

Three Hints

1. If you'd like to cook more at home—without being in a frenzy—go off by yourself with your cookbook some evening and make a week of menus. Then make a grocery list from that. Shop from your grocery list.

2. Thaw frozen food in a bowl in the fridge (not on the counter-top). If you forget to stick the food in the fridge, put it in a microwave-safe bowl and defrost it in the microwave just before you're ready to use it.

3. Let roasted meat, as well as pasta dishes with cheese, rest for 10–20 minutes before slicing or dishing. That will allow the juices to re-distribute themselves throughout the cooked food. You'll have juicier meat, and a better presentation of your pasta dish.

Substitute Ingredients— for when you're in a pinch

For one cup **buttermilk**—use 1 cup plain yogurt; or pour 1⅓ Tbsp. lemon juice or vinegar into a 1-cup measure. Fill the cup with milk. Stir and let stand for 5 minutes. Stir again before using.

For 1 oz. **unsweetened baking chocolate**— stir together 3 Tbsp. unsweetened cocoa powder and 1 Tbsp. butter, softened.

For 1 Tbsp. **cornstarch**—use 2 Tbsp. all-purpose flour; or 4 tsp. minute tapioca.

For 1 **garlic clove**—use ¼ tsp. garlic salt (reduce salt in recipe by ⅛ tsp.); or ⅛ tsp. garlic powder.

For 1 Tbsp. **fresh herbs**—use 1 tsp. dried herbs.

For 1/2 lb. **fresh mushrooms**—use 1 6-oz. can mushrooms, drained.

For 1 Tbsp. **prepared mustard**—use 1 tsp. dry or ground mustard.

For 1 **medium-sized fresh onion**—use 2 Tbsp. minced dried onion; or 2 tsp. onion salt (reduce salt in recipe by 1 tsp.); or 1 tsp. onion powder. Note: These substitutions will work for meat balls and meat loaf, but not for sautéing.

For 1 cup **sour milk**—use 1 cup plain yogurt; or pour 1 Tbsp. lemon juice or vinegar into a 1-cup measure. Fill with milk. Stir and then let stand for 5 minutes. Stir again before using.

For 2 Tbsp. **tapioca**—use 3 Tbsp. all-purpose flour.

For 1 cup canned **tomatoes**—use 1⅓ cups diced fresh tomatoes, cooked gently for 10 minutes.

For 1 Tbsp. **tomato paste**—use 1 Tbsp. ketchup.

For 1 Tbsp. **vinegar**—use 1 Tbsp. lemon juice.

For 1 cup **heavy cream**—add ⅓ cup melted butter to ¾ cup milk. Note: This will work for baking and cooking, but not for whipping.

For 1 cup **whipping cream**—chill thoroughly ⅔ cup evaporated milk, plus the bowl and beaters, then whip; or use 2 cups bought whipped topping.

For ½ cup **wine**—pour 2 Tbsp. wine vinegar into a ½-cup measure. Fill with broth (chicken, beef, or vegetable). Stir and then let stand for 5 minutes. Stir again before using.

Equivalent Measurements

dash = little less than ⅛ tsp.

3 teaspoons = 1 Tablespoon

2 Tablespoons = 1 oz.

4 Tablespoons = ¼ cup

5 Tablespoons plus 1 tsp. = ⅓ cup

8 Tablespoons = ½ cup

12 Tablespoons = ¾ cup

16 Tablespoons = 1 cup

1 cup = 8 ozs. liquid

2 cups = 1 pint

4 cups = 1 quart

4 quarts = 1 gallon

1 stick butter = ¼ lb.

1 stick butter = ½ cup

1 stick butter = 8 Tbsp.

Beans, 1 lb. dried = 2-2½ cups (depending upon the size of the beans)

Bell peppers, 1 large = 1 cup chopped

Cheese, hard (for example, cheddar, Swiss, Monterey Jack, mozzarella), 1 lb. grated = 4 cups

Cheese, cottage, 1 lb. = 2 cups

Chocolate chips, 6-oz. pkg. = 1 scant cup

Crackers (butter, saltines, snack), 20 single crackers = 1 cup crumbs

Herbs, 1 Tbsp. fresh = 1 tsp. dried

Lemon, 1 medium-sized = 2-3 Tbsp. juice

Lemon, 1 medium-sized = 2-3 tsp. grated rind

Mustard, 1 Tbsp. prepared = 1 tsp. dry or ground mustard

Oatmeal, 1 lb. dry = about 5 cups dry

Onion, 1 medium-sized = ½ cup chopped

Pasta

Macaronis, penne, and other small or tubular shapes, 1 lb. dry = 4 cups uncooked

Noodles, 1 lb. dry = 6 cups uncooked

Spaghetti, linguine, fettucine, 1 lb. dry = 4 cups uncooked

Potatoes, white, 1 lb. = 3 medium-sized potatoes = 2 cups mashed

Potatoes, sweet, 1 lb. = 3 medium-sized potatoes = 2 cups mashed

Rice, 1 lb. dry = 2 cups uncooked

Sugar, confectioners, 1 lb. = 3½ cups sifted

Whipping cream, 1 cup unwhipped = 2 cups whipped

Whipped topping, 8-oz. container = 3 cups

Yeast, dry, 1 envelope (¼ oz.) = 1 Tbsp.

Kitchen Tools and Equipment You May Have Overlooked

1 Make sure you have a little electric vegetable chopper, the size that will handle 1 cup of ingredients at a time.

2 Don't try to cook without a good paring knife that's sharp (and holds its edge) and fits in your hand.

3 Almost as important—a good chef's knife (we always called it a "butcher" knife) with a wide, sharp blade that's about 8 inches long, good for making strong cuts through meats.

4 You really ought to have a good serrated knife with a long blade, perfect for slicing bread.

5 Invest in at least one broad, flexible, heat-resistant spatula. And also a narrow one.

6 You ought to have a minimum of 2 wooden spoons, each with a 10-12 inch-long handle. They're perfect for stirring without scratching.

7 Get a washable cutting board. You'll still need it, even though you have an electric vegetable chopper (#1 above).

8 A medium-sized whisk takes care of persistent lumps in batters, gravies, and sauces when there aren't supposed to be any.

9 Get yourself a salad spinner.

Index

Fix-It and Enjoy-It 5-Ingredient Recipes

Fix-It and Enjoy-It 5-Ingredient Recipes

Index

About the Author

Phyllis Pellman Good is a *New York Times* bestselling author whose books have sold more than 9.5 million copies.

Good is the author of the first book in the *Fix-It and Enjoy-It* series, **Fix-It and Enjoy-It Cookbook: All-Purpose, Welcome-Home Recipes**, for stove-top and oven use. That flagship book, along with **Fix-It and Enjoy-It Diabetic Cookbook: Stove-Top and Oven Recipes—for Everyone**, are a "cousin" series to the phenomenally successful *Fix-It and Forget-It* cookbooks.

Good authored the national #1 bestselling cookbook **Fix-It and Forget-It Cookbook: Feasting with Your Slow Cooker** (with Dawn J. Ranck), which appeared on *The New York Times* bestseller list, as well as the bestseller lists of *USA Today, Publishers Weekly*, and *Book Sense*. And she is the author of **Fix-It and Forget-It Lightly: Healthy, Low-Fat Recipes for Your Slow Cooker**, which has also appeared on *The New York Times* bestseller list. In addition, Good authored **Fix-It and Forget-It 5-Ingredient Favorites: Comforting Slow-Cooker Recipes**; **Fix-It and Forget-It Recipes for Entertaining: Slow Cooker Favorites for All the Year Round** (with Ranck); and **Fix-It and Forget-It Diabetic Cookbook** (with the American Diabetes Association), also in the series.

Good's other cookbooks include **Favorite Recipes with Herbs**, **The Best of Amish Cooking**, and **The Central Market Cookbook**.

Phyllis Pellman Good is Senior Editor at Good Books. (Good Books has published hundreds of titles by more than 135 different authors.) She received her B.A. and M.A. in English from New York University. She and her husband, Merle, live in Lancaster, Pennsylvania. They are the parents of two young-adult daughters.

For a complete listing of books by Phyllis Pellman Good, as well as excerpts and reviews, visit www.Fix-ItandEnjoy-It.com, or www.GoodBooks.com.